The National Deal
The Fight for a Canadian Constitution

Robert Sheppard
Michael Valpy

 Fleet Books, Toronto

Dedication

For my parents, Barbara and Gavin

Robert Sheppard

For Leslie and my friends

Michael Valpy

A Fleet Book
Published by Fleet Publishers
A Division of International Thomson Limited
1410 Birchmount Road
Scarborough, Ontario, Canada M1P 2E7

Back jacket photograph: Robert Cooper

Canadian Cataloguing in Publication Data
Sheppard, Robert, 1952-
   The national deal
ISBN 0-7706-0019-0 (bound)
ISBN 0-7706-0057-3 (pbk.)
1. Canada - Constitutional history.   2. Canada - Politics and government - 1980 -*   I. Valpy, Michael, 1942 -   II. Title.
JL27.S53   342.71′029   C82-094843-8

Printed and bound in Canada

82 83 84 85 86 87 88 7 6 5 4 3 2 1

Contents

Preface

It is the ambition of almost every political reporter to write the sort of book that American journalist-historian Theodore H. White has been producing for decades — *The Making of the President, et sequens*, the inside story of a major political event. In Canada, there is rarely the sustained political drama on which to peg such a narrative. Election campaigns last only a few weeks, and a new and different crisis for each day's House of Commons question period is the menu of parliamentary politics. In the White genre, Peter C. Newman's *Renegade in Power*, the chronicle of the turbulent Diefenbaker years, and Jeffrey Simpson's *Discipline of Power*, the analysis of Joe Clark's brief interlude, stand out in a sea of political biographies and academic histories of the nation's progress.

Then the constitution story came along. It was the pure stuff of White — one of those uncommon events in Canadian political affairs (the building of the Pacific railway would be another) sufficiently prolonged in time and drama to offer a keyhole look at our political leaders engaged in a task much larger than themselves. White wrote: "History is chiefly gossip about great men as they behave under stress" — to which we would add: "and about ordinary men thrust into positions of great power and responsibility."

Our story spans eighteen long months — from the Quebec referendum on 20 May 1980 to the constitution bargain struck between the leaders of the federal government and nine of the ten provinces on 5 November 1981. Throughout this period, the Canadian people heard and read largely about an arid wrangle over abstract notions that few understood, fewer cared about and a great many came to be irritated by. The fault, we think, lies more in the mechanics of Canadian political journalism than in any aridity of the constitution events. It was not a juiceless wrangle at all; it was a great and absorbing human drama.

For those eighteen months, the constitution debate slowed the business of the nation to a sclerotic crawl. It dominated the agenda of every government from sea to sea. It mesmerized the press, touched every major institution in the country — the church, the courts, academia, the legal and business communities. It drew in Canada's ethnic communities, women's groups, aboriginal peoples, and inflamed — almost intolerably at times — the country's twin political crises of the 1970s and '80s: Quebec nationalism and western alienation. One political party, the NDP, was fractured by the issue, the wound still unmended. The Liberals were gravely crippled as a national representative force. Federal Conservatives were pitted against their powerful blood relatives in Ontario. Political friendships were destroyed; the dynamics of Parliament and federal-provincial relations were altered, perhaps permanently. You just cannot have a single event of this magnitude *without* there being great drama. Such is the tale we set out to tell: about the national political trauma that resulted in the revision of Canada's constitution — and the termination of Britain's embarrassing stewardship over our country's supreme legal covenant — after half a century of failed attempts.

When we embarked on the project in January 1982, we thought we knew the dimensions of our story. Both of us had reported on it from its genesis in the Quebec referendum campaign. Yet shortly after we began to pull together its component parts, we realized how badly we had underestimated both the amount of work that was going to be involved and the number of details that had been missed in the day-by-day accounts. The issue simply had been too complex, the passions of human interplay too intricate, too deep, for the techniques of history-in-a-hurry journalism to cope with. What began for us as a short endeavour took more time than we had ever imagined.

We came to the task with some notions already in place. Like many Ottawa political reporters, we harboured a covert admiration for Pierre Trudeau's daring unilateral ploy — the bold act of the strongman leader who thumbed his nose at his opponents (there were so many of them) and set off to revise Canada's constitution by himself.

But in writing this book, we have amended many of our initial perceptions — 'contextualized' them, if you will. There was, as usual, the best and the worst of the prime minister at work in this event: the derring-do, the nobility of purpose, sometimes the graceful humour, but as well the bullying, the wheedling, the adolescent pique and the icy cynicism. We also have acquired more respect for the philosophical and emotional genuineness of the opposing views, if not always for the personalities and tactics of those who espoused them.

No two people could be of entirely one mind about an issue as many faceted as this one. We are no exception. In particular, we have not agreed fully on two important elements: the actions of Margaret Thatcher's government in London, and the role of national Conservative Party leader

Joe Clark and his circle of advisers. Our differences concern interpretation rather than substance. One of us is more inclined to see the British government as the innocent, set-upon victim of Trudeau's machinations; the other is of a mind that the British were not above some political duplicity themselves. As for Clark, one of us feels he did the right things for the wrong reasons — that mainly his performance on the constitution was orchestrated by his greater concern with holding on to his job. The other prefers the view that Clark fought for a legitimate, deeply felt vision of the country and was misunderstood by the national press. For the most part, we compromised (the Canadian way?) after prolonged, late-night arguments.

We have left a lot of room for future academic grazing; there are so many issues to explore — legal, political, moral. What we have tried to present is a reporter's history. We have combined the anecdotes that have amused us with the inherent drama of the events themselves, with sketches of those most intimately involved, with the techniques of 'tick-tock' journalism.

What sustained our interest in the project was not only a fascination with uncovering more and more elements of the story, but also the realization that we had acquired a considerable amount of personal and political minutiae that otherwise might have escaped the historical record. We talked to people while their memories were still fresh. The private meetings, conversations and deliberations we have written about are reconstructed from nearly two hundred hours of taped interviews — most of them off-the-record — with the major participants in Ottawa, the provincial capitals and London. Those with whom we have spoken — the prime minister, the opposition party leaders, most of the premiers, constitution ministers, political aides, senior officials, senators and members of Parliament — have been, on the whole, flawlessly accommodating.

We offer the same bouquet to those of our colleagues whose files and memories we shamelessly rifled. One who deserves special thanks is John Gray, Ottawa bureau chief of the *Globe and Mail*, who gave up evenings and weekends to read and unmuddle our words as they came off the typewriter. We were blessed with luck in our editor, Jonathan Williams, who blended, as much as possible, two different writing styles and sat, awake, through uncounted tedious arguments over arcane constitutional points. And we thank Janet Hough and Kathryn Maloney of the *Globe*'s Ottawa office for their help with research and hours of typing.

One final word about our employers. *Globe and Mail* publisher A. Roy Megarry and editor-in-chief Richard J. Doyle participated in the constitution debate with an enthusiasm that some thought exceeded 'proper' journalistic deportment. We think, perhaps, that when Megarry thundered in speeches and Doyle thundered in editorials — frequently to the irritation of the federal government — they did so feeling the hand of history on their shoulders. Another publisher of the *Globe*, George Brown, had been very much a burr beneath the saddle of the government in his own constitutional time. It was Megarry who suggested we do this book ("It's been our story from the start," he said unabashedly). It was Doyle who let us arrange our schedules and often our travels in order to execute the task (and whose grumbles were only good-natured when the work never seemed to end).

> *I have come across men of letters who have written history*
> *without taking part in public affairs, and politicians who*
> *have concerned themselves with producing events without*
> *thinking about them. I have observed that the first are*
> *always inclined to find general causes, whereas the second,*
> *living in the midst of disconnected daily facts, are prone to*
> *imagine that everything is attributable to particular*
> *incidents, and that the wires they pull are the same as those*
> *that move the world. It is to be presumed that both are*
> *equally deceived.*

Alexis de Tocqueville, 1835
Democracy in America

Robert Sheppard
Michael Valpy
Ottawa, August 1982

1

The Canadian Way

bellum omnium contra omnes: the war of all against all

Thomas Hobbes, *Leviathan.*

Nation-builders at work. It is 7 September 1980, the night before the opening of the tenth round of negotiations to be held since 1927 on the reform of Canada's constitution. The prime minister, Pierre Elliott Trudeau, the ten provincial premiers and their respective constitution ministers are dining with his excellency the governor general, Edward R. Schreyer, a pleasant man with a consuming interest in peat moss. They are assembled in the elegant, ninth-floor dining room of the department of external affairs headquarters on Ottawa's Sussex Drive — a nice touch, bringing them together in a room redolent of the art of diplomacy, and in a building named after former prime minister Lester B. Pearson, contributor of "co-operative federalism" to the lexicon, if not excessively to the practice, of Canadian politics. Heaven knows what torments the gathering visits upon his departed soul.

The evening is designed as a working dinner. All ambience is conducive to a co-operative endeavour. It is intended that the eleven first ministers — as the leaders of the federal and provincial governments have come to style themselves — mellowed by good food, fine wine and the restraining presence of the head-of-state-in-residence, should work out the framework for their week-long conference that is to begin formally the following morning before the television cameras and a national public audience.

After fifty-three years of political effort, the prime objective has remained unchanged and unattained: to end the legal absurdity that requires Canada — a full-fledged nation — to trudge off to the former colonial power in Britain whenever it wants its constitution amended. No other autonomous state in the world has this problem. Few know it exists, other than Canadians.

The events of 7 September illustrate why more than half a century of failed attempts have preceded the evening at hand.

1

In the soft air of early autumn, the politicians mill on the terrace, smiling, chatting, drinking, with the Gatineau hills in fall splendour and the setting sun for a backdrop. Pierre Trudeau will recall later that on the terrace he was in good spirits ("The expanse of sky, the sun on the river . . .") Summoned to dinner, they pose quickly for a group photograph. René Lévesque is uncomfortable and nearly causes a scene when a functionary insists on removing the lighted cigarette and drink glass from his hands. The photographer manages only to snap off one fast shot before the group disperses. The first ministers sit down at the table and whatever *bonhomie* was among them on the terrace is sloughed like the scabbard of a sword. The prince and the barons, as they call each other from time to time (the metaphor of Runnymede is inescapable), are steel beneath velvet.

From the jellied consommé onwards, it is clear that any progress made during a summer of intensive groundwork preparations — by federal justice minister Jean Chrétien and his counterparts who carry the constitution brief for their respective provincial governments — has been swept off the gaming table. Discarded, too, is the rationale for urgent constitutional reform that had touched the nation in May: the promise of 'renewed federalism' made by the national government and the nine English premiers to Quebec during its referendum campaign on quasi-independence. There is no mood for consensus, no mood for pan-Canadian goodwill in external's dining room. Co-operative federalism is as dead as Pearson. Chrétien, recollecting the event more than a year later, rolled his eyes upwards, pain in his voice: "God, it was terrible." None of those present would dispute the verdict.

To begin with, it was a misbegotten idea to have the Crown's representative play host at a workshop of the most powerful and fractious politicians in the country, men who claim the supreme authority to change the fundamental law of the land. The governor general is a peter-pannish component of the Canadian body politic, surrogate of a constitutional monarchy whose sovereign lives more than three thousand miles away. Like the god of the ancient Hebrews whose name could not be spoken, the precise powers of Canada's governor general have been left unstated. Nobody has ever wanted to be specific about what he can *do*. The constitutional fiction of the office — the state's ultimate authority — works only if the position is untouched by politics and is respected absolutely by politicians. To that tough crowd, Schreyer hardly bore a vice-regal aura. Only three years before, he had been the socialist premier of Manitoba (the man who had defeated his government, Sterling Lyon, is sitting a few feet away); six years before that, he had committed Manitobans to the abortive 1971 Victoria charter of constitutional reform. Stripped of his titles and his home address at Government House, Schreyer is just another politician, an unelected one at that. He is not going to be a restraining presence for anyone.

Pierre Trudeau's summer-long threats to cut the Gordian knot himself
— to have the federal Parliament move unilaterally on constitutional
revision, failing the achievement of a negotiated agreement with the
provinces — are reaping a predictable response. The oatsy western
premiers, four strong winds, have blown into Ottawa with an audacious
taunt of their own: a proposal that one of their number (Lyon) should
co-chair the first ministers' conference with Trudeau, something never
before done. It is a red rag waved beneath the nose of a prime minister
who always has portrayed Canada as more than the sum of its parts.
("Who will speak for Canada?" Trudeau had asked rhetorically in 1978,
when the cacophony of provincial demands for more jurisdictional power
within the federation had reached a crescendo. In the prime minister's
mind, only the national government bestrode the nation, balanced all
regional views.)

British Columbia's William Bennett and Alberta's Peter Lougheed, both
with a marked dislike of Trudeau (and a certain uneasiness about each
other), float the co-chairmanship notion before the second course of
crabmeat créole is fully served. Bennett puts the argument: the summer
preparatory meetings were co-chaired (by Chrétien and Saskatchewan
attorney general Roy Romanow) why not the first ministers' conference?
The beguiling logic takes in no one. What the westerners are saying is
that the two levels of government are equal. ("Who speaks for Canada?
We all do," had been Lougheed's reply in 1978, as he reached for the
title of executive federalism's strongest proponent.)

The prime minister reacts instantly and provocatively: "You mean like
deux nations?" An obscure jibe for the uninitiated; the reference is to a
concept of special status for the province of Quebec within Confederation that had been embraced, disastrously, by former federal Conservative Party leader Robert Stanfield. The snide implication from the prime
minister is that the western premiers have been put up to the idea by the
separatist government of Quebec, that now he must deal with western
separatism as well as Quebec separatism. The mood in the room black-
ens palpably.

Some premiers suggest fighting the issue out in front of the television
cameras the following morning. Ontario premier William Davis, chewing
on his pipe, amiably tries to have the proposal shelved. The westerners,
picking up vocal support from some of their eastern colleagues, will not
budge. Newfoundland's strident-tongued Brian Peckford rages at the
prime minister's recalcitrance. Trudeau needles him, sneering at what
he calls Peckford's socialist alliance with Saskatchewan's Allan Blakeney,
leader of the country's only New Democratic Party government. Peckford,
a Conservative, snaps back with a comment about Trudeau's socialist
tendencies. The animosity between Trudeau, Bennett, Lougheed and
Blakeney, never far beneath the surface, shows itself in raised eyebrows
and sniffs of pointed disinterest whenever one of the four is speaking.

Eventually, the co-chairmanship proposal drifts away, but only because the first ministers find something new to fight about.

Trudeau wants to rework the agenda — an agenda to which Chrétien has already agreed (under duress, Trudeau feels). The federal government's most popular item, the constitutional entrenchment of a charter of rights, has been relegated to the bottom of the list. Some of the premiers have hinted publicly that they don't even want to discuss it at all until they reach an agreement with Trudeau on a redivision of powers between Ottawa and the provinces. Trudeau sees a gang-up. He wants an agenda that will go back and forth between issues that Ottawa likes and issues that the provinces like, giving both sides an equal chance to sell the rightness of their cause to the television audience. Once again, there is no movement, no hint of accommodation. Even Richard Hatfield of New Brunswick, an eventual ally of Ottawa, accuses Trudeau of intransigence.

Lougheed lets it be known that the Alberta delegation will be doing no more than going through the motions on constitutional reform until there is a new pricing agreement on oil and natural gas signed by his government and Trudeau's. Bennett lays down strict conditions for his consent to any new constitutional package: reform of the Senate and no federal excise tax on B.C. natural gas. Trudeau mutters about blackmail. Stubbing out cigarette after cigarette, Quebec's premier René Lévesque is enjoying the dinner hugely. "The princeling" — his new name for Trudeau — "is certainly in high dudgeon tonight," he keeps repeating in a mischievous stage whisper loud enough to be heard by the prime minister. Lévesque has more reasons than usual to be enjoying Trudeau's discomfort. Unknown to the others, back in his hotel room he has a copy of the federal government's top-secret negotiating strategy.

Enter the vice-regal presence. With his dinner party degenerating into name-calling and partisan jeers, the governor general gently tries to nudge the conversation back to a more courteous and constructive path. No one pays attention to him. Hatfield, the former drama student, tries to speed the meal to a close by theatrically signalling the waiters to bring in the coffee. They don't budge. Then Trudeau, sitting across the table from Schreyer, snaps crossly at him to "hurry up" and get coffee and dessert served so that he can go home. Nova Scotia's John Buchanan is visibly stunned at the prime minister's rudeness. Prince Edward Island's farmer-premier, Angus MacLean, turns to his seatmate, Ontario attorney general Roy McMurtry, and says hoarsely: "He can't talk to the head of state like that." McMurtry replies: "Well, he is. He's just reminding the head of state who the hell appointed him."

At this point, the waiters deliver the evening's *coup de farce*. Given the command to serve dessert, they bring in a cake for Blakeney's fifty-fifth birthday, cut it and begin taking around the portions. A small silence attends this activity, shattered by Trudeau's voice knifing through the room. "My God!" he says. "They're serving it according to precedence." Indeed they are. External's protocol-steeped attendants have taken the first slice of cake to the governor general. The second slice to the prime minister of Canada. Third and fourth slices to the premiers of Ontario and Quebec, the original partners of Confederation. Fifth and sixth slices to the premiers of the next-in provinces of Nova Scotia and New Brunswick. . . .

Trudeau, with the histrionic gesture of a man overwhelmed by ridiculousness, lays his head face down on the table like some forlorn Buddha. He remains like that for a long time, conversation around him fading into an edgy hush, all eyes turning towards him. Finally, the man at centre stage, he gets to his feet, both palms on the table. "Well, this is going to be a very interesting meeting," he says. And with that, his dessert untouched, he strides to the door. His Mountie bodyguard jumps up to go with him. A provincial minister sitting close by says he hears the prime minister of Canada say to his Royal Canadian Mounted Police escort: "Fuck off, and don't follow me home."

Back in their respective hotel suites, some of the participants call in their aides, one even telephones home to his wife, to say that the tenth conference on the reform of Canada's constitution is a failure. It had not even begun.

———————— ✦ ————————

Nation-builders at work. Because political science without biography is little more than taxidermy, the story of reforming Canada's constitution must begin with Pierre Trudeau and his indomitable will. A politician with less discipline, less singularity of purpose, could not have dragged the stone sled of the nation's constitutional business to the point he did.

Many others, including five prime ministers, had tried, and failed. It took Trudeau four tries and twelve and a half years, and he almost failed. To get what he got, he unleashed a never-before-seen demon of raw prime ministerial power — what someone called a *coup d'état* in slow motion — that took the combined forces of nearly every major institution in the country to tame into a legitimizing compromise. The provincial barons could not have done the taming alone, although they were bold to claim the credit. Sundered by regional jealousies, often overwhelmed by the national news media, unable to form a common front of positive purpose to fulfil public expectations, they merely came along at the end to snap shut the lock on the cage.

Over the eighteen-month period of his final assault on his objective — from 20 May 1980 to 5 November 1981 — Trudeau did not win all that he wanted, although paradoxically he won more than he set out to achieve.

He scored divisions in the country that only future generations will be able to repair. He perhaps destroyed for years to come the Liberal Party as a representative national force; but he had warned his party colleagues at the outset that that might likely be the case, that the battle would be bloody and the political costs high.

What drove him? He came to politics upon an honourable impulse — to bind his people, francophone Canadians, to the rest of the country, to make them feel at home from sea to sea. He came to establish a beach-head in English Canada for the notion that the French minority should have the fundamental right to use its language, to *live* in its language, in every part of Canada. "You have to give me language. It's my existence," he told Bill Bennett near the end as the two of them sat in the sunroom of the prime minister's residence at 24 Sussex Drive, talking about what each considered essential for a constitution deal. He won that on 5 November, after the premiers of English Canada were bullied and shamed into agreeing that language rights should become part of the supreme law of the land.

There were, in Trudeau's tactical approach to the constitution struggle, so many echoes of the frail Montreal boy who carefully marshalled his intellectual strengths to win in the classroom and taught himself self-defence to win in the schoolyard. Those who worked closely with him over the eighteen months marvelled at his stamina, as they saw, at the same time, that he was tiring physically. After the February 1980 election victory that pushed him back into the prime minister's job, he took to arriving later and later at his office in the morning, leaving earlier at the end of the day, accompanied by fewer of the black cases full of briefing books, not wanting to miss his nightly six o'clock swim. He was not yet a tatty-furred lion in winter, not yet the Old Chieftain of Sir John A. Macdonald in decline, but he needed to husband his resources for the constitution fight. And he did.

The constitution was the only brief Trudeau carried through that period, to the despair of those of his advisers and political colleagues who were working on other matters; indeed, to the despair of a country sinking deeper into economic malaise. Once certain of the rightness and necessity of what he was doing, however, Trudeau was unswervingly tenacious. Doubters, even the most influential ones such as Gordon Robertson, the former privy council clerk and bureaucratic Olympian of federal-provincial diplomacy, were pushed aside and ignored. The constitution struggle, for the prime minister and the team he gathered around him, had messianic purpose.

What did he want? Myth had it that he wanted to rewrite the entire Canadian constitution, from fish to Indians, monarchy to post office. "I might have as a professor done that . . . but certainly not as a politician," he said when it was over and done with. He wanted only the essentials, *his* essentials, the symbols that would give the country — like the tin-man of Oz — a heart: patriation (that uniquely Canadian word for the domiciling of its constitution), pan-Canadian language protections, a charter of rights and freedoms.

However, the constitution story needs more than one man — no mat-ter how wilful — to dunk a nation into trauma for eighteen paralyzing months. He initiated it, he exacerbated it, but he alone did not create the full psychosis. To see the bigger canvas, one has to look at the nature of constitutional nation-building itself, and at the other personalities and forces that were present.

———————— ❧ ————————

"It should be borne in mind that there is nothing more difficult to ar-range, more doubtful of success, and more dangerous to carry through than initiating changes in a state's constitution." The writer was Niccolò Machiavelli, and he was penning his warning to princes in 1513 in the world's most famous treatise on power politics. In 1980, those words (actually a paraphrase of Machiavelli's) hung framed on the office wall of Howard Leeson, Saskatchewan's deputy minister of intergovernmental affairs. Michael Kirby, head of Ottawa's federal-provincial relations of-fice, noticed them on a visit to Regina and jotted them down. They were later to appear in what to date is Canada's most fascinating treatise on power politics, the document on federal constitutional strategy known as the Kirby memorandum.

Constitutions are seldom written or revised in the leisure of peace-time. They are more inclined to be patched hurriedly together in the aftermath of war, dashed off by dictators desirous of legitimizing the coup that has installed them in the presidential palace, or imposed from afar, by exiting colonial powers. Constitutions are not really fit subjects for leisurely contemplation. The shaping of them is like no other political act; it goes to the root of a nation's self-image. Constitutions touch upon a nation's fundamental values and the deeply held, conflicting beliefs of its people. They put rules into words that must be lived with for as long as centuries. It is the essence of constitutions that, once agreed upon, they cannot be easily altered — creating great anxieties in the minds of the framers, who search and struggle for the right words that will protect their interests against all hypothetical encroachments. Constitutions in-vite argument: passionate, endless, enervating argument. Which is why the written Canadian constitution remained an act of the British Parlia-ment long after the country became independent. Canadian politicians could not agree on how to bring it home.

Canada thus accomplished the revision of its constitution against for-midable odds. That should tell Canadians something positive about themselves as a people. In addition, it was done in a prolonged, lively political drama, more raucous possibly than the country has ever seen. It had its meannesses and shabby little acts: the despicable undercutting of women's and native people's rights, in a charter designed to protect rights, will stick as a blot on the nation's history, a shameful mark of how Canada's most powerful politicians do business. Moreover, the revision of the constitution became law without the blessing of the provincial government of French Canada's homeland, Quebec; that too, is cause for disquiet. And finally, no woman was invited to play more than a minor role.

———————— ❦ ————————

Nation-builders at work. Eleven men, Canada's first ministers during the eighteen months of the constitution story, gave the country a primer on how not to negotiate anything. They were the ones who took it upon themselves to sit down and hammer out a deal. They did not trust each other; they did not very much like each other. As the months went by, some came to the point of not being able to talk to each other. Allan Blakeney codified the dynamics of the first ministers and the constitution in what he called the Five-Link Chain.

It began with Trudeau. He could not negotiate directly with any of the premiers opposed to him — the men who came to be known as the 'gang of eight'; he could bring himself to deal only with Ontario's Bill Davis, who alone of his two allies (the other being Hatfield) had access to the opposition. That was link one. Davis himself could not deal with most of his fellow premiers, particularly the powerful Lougheed who was a competitor for whatever national ambitions within the federal Conservative Party Davis may have harboured. Only with the clever, fastidious Blakeney did Davis feel he could talk freely, either directly or through their respective attorneys general, Ontario's Roy McMurtry and Saskatchewan's Roy Romanow, who were firm friends. That was link two. Blakeney and Lougheed were both westerners and, since they belonged to different political parties, their relationship lacked any element of competitive ambition. They could talk together. That was link three. Lougheed, because of his powerful personality (and his powerful oil royalties provincial bankroll, which was underwriting projects in several provinces to the tune of nearly two billion dollars), carried enormous influence with the remaining anglophone members of the gang of eight, particularly the flighty Peckford (link four), and he also had the best relationship with Lévesque (link five), whom he took to describing as "a strong provincialist" like himself, rather than a separatist.

Now and again, one of the links in the chain recognized absurdity in what was taking place. In November 1981, on the second day of the 'one last time' first ministers' conference (the threatening appellation was Trudeau's), the federal plotters and their allies were huddled in a fifth-floor room of the government conference centre while the gang of eight was sequestered on the other side of Rideau Street in the fairy-tale gothic Chateau Laurier.

Bill Davis had been called to a meeting with the gang of eight; late in the afternoon he returned to the federal strategy room to report that Lougheed would be coming across the street with a proposal.* Trudeau, in a rare lapse, let his guard down. Lougheed coming over? Thinking aloud, the prime minister wondered whether he should meet him. What could he want? Was it good tactics to meet him? Then he realized what he was doing: ridiculously agonizing over whether the prime minister of Canada should accede to a request to meet the premier of Alberta. He turned his dithering into a joke upon himself by parodying "The Love Song of J. Alfred Prufrock," T.S. Eliot's poem of aging and uncertainty. "Do I dare meet Mr. Lougheed?" he asked. "Shall I part my hair behind? Do I dare to eat a peach?"

Some first ministers were peacemakers and compromisers: their credibility and prestige suffered as a result. Not to be hard was to be seen as soft, appeasing, vacillating, and the two premiers most blackly tarred with this brush were Blakeney, the brainy prairie socialist, and Bill Bennett, the uncertain, unguided missile from British Columbia.

Both saw themselves, independently, as helpful brokers. Blakeney, whose wide-eyed visage and Pearsonian lisp gave him somewhat the

---

*Just before Davis arrived, Trudeau had been musing to the people in the room — they included the Ontario and New Brunswick teams — about his problems across the Atlantic. To bring the constitution legally back to Canada, there had to be an enactment of the British Parliament at Westminster (the alternative would be an embarrassing Rhodesia-style unilateral declaration of independence). The British had become infuriatingly reluctant to do the deed without substantial provincial consent, which Trudeau did not have. If he decided to demand compliance, he wondered, what pressures could he bring to bear on a balky Margaret Thatcher? Threaten to pull Canada out of the Commonwealth? Urge other Commonwealth members to expel Britain?

The queries were Trudeauesque: ask an outrageous question to stimulate the most creative cerebral response. But he also was serious and he had misjudged (a not uncommon failing of his) his audience. There are few starchier defenders of the monarchy and the British link to Canada than the Ontario and New Brunswick Tories, and Trudeau's remarks produced an uncomfortable silence — which Hatfield at last broke: "Tell you what, Pierre. I'll take care of Liz [the Queen] if you'll resign." There were chuckles all around; discussion moved on to other topics.

manner of a child at Disneyland, may have had the best understanding of the complex issues involved; but he scattered his bargaining chips too improvidently, and at the end was eclipsed by his attorney general, the television-handsome Romanow, as a card-player at the big game. Bennett, with a difficult job to do — he became both chairman of the gang of eight and spokesman on federal-provincial issues for all ten premiers — tried to be too clever in his brokering and wound up on the sidelines. Nova Scotia's John Buchanan flirted with peacemaking. A bland, amiable man with few ambitions and a perennially bored look, he soon found it easier to run with the pack.

At the very end, Bill Davis worked as a peacemaker. He had tired of first ministers' wrangling after the dismal conference of September 1980. He read the polls that showed how popular the charter of rights was in Ontario, cast his cards in with Trudeau, and in the spring of 1981 was handed back the majority government that his voters had taken away from him two elections before. In Ontario, it is easy to be pan-Canadian, and the swing-voters of his province still liked Pierre. At a pivotal point in the negotiations, Davis used the skills of his constitutional advisers and what remaining weight his once fat-cat province still carried in Confederation to try to reconcile the two camps.

It was perhaps Trudeau's misfortune that his allies — Davis and Hatfield — had so little real cachet with their fellow premiers, although for wildly different reasons. Davis, the smooth chairman of Queen's Park who had elevated bafflegab to an art form and made a virtue of the cautious pandering to the political middle — "Bland works," he once smugly assured the opposition in the Ontario legislature — was mistrusted by the premiers who held central Canada in contempt. Hatfield was not liked because he was, well, different. He was tall, big boned (unlike the rest of his fellow first ministers who were rather small men), lyrically articulate, and as likely to be found in a chic New York watering spot or exploring North African ruins as in his provincial capital of Fredericton. He was so many things that the Rotarian shopkeeper premiers of English Canada were not — a bachelor, incurably peripatetic, regarded by his colleagues as a bit of a flake. "There have been some awful things said about people here," Hatfield observed as the constitution accord was being signed. Pause. "Many of them by me about people who didn't agree with me." A sly joke.

In contrast, the remaining Conservative premiers were a clubby lot with a streak of iron-willed opportunism. Lougheed and Newfoundland's volatile Peckford would wait, lurking, in the pack until their instincts told them it was time to go for the jugular. Lougheed, often shy and uncomfortable in public with a tendency to grind his teeth under stress, was (like Trudeau) a very private man and (again like Trudeau) contemptuous of the national press. Manitoba's Lyon, the stubby, irascible,

Praetorian guardsman of a vanishing British Canada, was a fierce duellist with Trudeau, giving no quarter and asking none; he might have played a stronger role at the finish but an election campaign took him to other fields of conflict (and knocked him off). Prince Edward Island's Angus MacLean represented "Britannic decency" (as a Quebec functionary observed of him when MacLean came to Lévesque's aid during a tiff with Trudeau). Modest, unassuming — he was genuinely surprised when national reporters called on him for his constitutional views — he was also tired and eager to retire to his Belle River farm after thirty years in politics (six as a federal minister in the Diefenbaker government). MacLean perhaps represented a Canada — and a province — that was anachronistic; but if so, he did it with dignity.

Finally René Lévesque. He was the other spokesman for French Canada — the rumpled little man from the Gaspé, with the grand vision and the rubber-ball face that could change on an instant from cold scowl to charming insouciance, even when telling anglophone Canadians that he wanted to break up the country for the good of both partners. His duel with Trudeau was not for a fishing authority or a trade concession, but for a *pays*. As much a political folk-hero of Quebec as Trudeau, he was an immensely complex individual and incessant talker, whose idea of a weekend's relaxation was a Scrabble game, a science fiction novel and an escapist movie.

Nation-builders at work. The diverse personalities and backgrounds of the builders were mirrored in the visions of the country they came to espouse — often brilliantly, almost always with a depth of feeling — during the constitution debate.

How did they see Canada in 1980 and 1981? Trudeau, of course, had his vision: the renewal of the French-English partnership. He was also the academic, the intellectual student of Canadian federalism, who had seen the pendulum swing out too far (most of it under his stewardship in Ottawa) toward devolution of powers to the provinces, and now wished to rectify matters. This was time-honoured Canadian political action. Since its inception, the country has swung between periods of great centralization and periods of marked decentralization, depending upon economic conditions, technology and judicial decisions on the division of powers.

Lougheed, Blakeney and — running behind them — Peckford were premiers of provinces beginning to enjoy the idea of power shifting from central Canada to their regions, tracking the wealth of natural resources. They represented societies that had been too long under the thumb of central paternalism. They believed, quite passionately, that they could manage their societies themselves better than the far-off bureaucrats in Ottawa and the bankers in Toronto.

Bennett, the merchant, marched to his own drummer as much as did the people of that far-off beautiful corner of the country he governed. British Columbia, he repeatedly said, didn't want out of Confederation; it wanted in — it wanted more representation and influence in the central institutions of government: the Senate, the Supreme Court of Canada, the central bank, the regulatory agencies such as the National Energy Board, the Canadian Transport Commission, the Canadian Radio-television and Telecommunications Commission.

Finally, there was Quebec. There would not have been a constitutional crisis without Quebec. Quebec, as always, was at the core of Confederation's historic tension. Trudeau wanted his symbols enshrined in the constitution to fight Quebec nationalism. Lévesque was not going to give him those cards. Lévesque had his own vision: the two peoples of the northern half of the continent — French-speaking and English-speaking — linked but equal, each masters in their own house; Trudeau offered less than that, nothing better than a minority partnership forever in danger of being engulfed by the majority. To accept Trudeau's vision meant that Lévesque would have to forsake his own; it was politically impossible.

---------------- ❧ ----------------

The story has a beginning in Pierre Trudeau's will. It has an end in a twenty-four hour period on the eve of winter. From a Wednesday morning to a Thursday morning in the first week of November 1981, the path that has become *the* legendary journey of Canadian constitution folklore was blazed to a breakfast table, on to a kitchen pantry and back to a breakfast table. There were many, literally hundreds, of tributaries.

By twenty-five-past-eight in the morning on Thursday, 5 November 1981, as the last provincial premier laid down his eggy knife and fork in a private fourth-floor suite in the Chateau Laurier, the deed was done. The so-called gang of eight was in ruins. In those final hours, René Lévesque came face-to-face with the bruised egos and sweaty opportunism of Canadian *realpolitik*. His protection against Trudeau, the cosy, defensive alliance he had deliberately and somewhat cynically fashioned with his English colleagues, had evaporated. He had been outmanoeuvred by accident and political cunning, and had been crushed because of a fatal sense of false security: Lévesque had slept the night away while the others cobbled together a deal.

Within hours, Pierre Trudeau was to see the pristine beauty of his charter of rights deflowered by the tawdry exigencies of practical Canadian politics. The Canadian Way, the editorial writers dubbed it, seeking to ennoble the event. The Canadian Way — it became almost a chant among some of the peacemaker premiers, anxious for the middle road of compromise and tradeoffs. ("If I hear Bennett say that one more time, I think I'll throttle him," a weary Richard Hatfield groaned afterwards.) "The Canadian way" — Lévesque nearly spat the words out — is to leave Quebec alone when the crunch comes, the Quebec premier said that fateful morning in November.

The television cameras record Trudeau and the nine premiers of English Canada affixing their signatures to an accord on renewed federalism. They are exhausted men, politically and physically drained, their desire to fight sapped. Ted Johnson, Trudeau's executive assistant, sees his boss off from the conference centre in a black prime ministerial limousine and emits a rather contrived "Yahoo!" Few others are heard to cheer. Across the river in Quebec, reporters watch the little man from the Gaspé rubbing his eyes as he hurries across a windy tarmac at Gatineau airport for the flight home to his capital. Back to where it all began, and would begin again. . . .

———————— 🍁 ————————

Even when approaching it from the air in the late twentieth century, the first fortress city of North America is an impressive sight. The steep-walled architecture of the lower town and dock area casts the eyes upwards to the battlements and sturdy stone buildings of another era, from where the clean, wide boulevards stretch back to the concrete and glass structures of modern Quebec City. Further back still are the sleepy, well-kept bedroom communities of the civil servants, entrepreneurs and professionals — the emergent French elite. Here, in the modest suburb of Ste. Foy, in an even more modest bungalow, Claude Morin, the strategist of Quebec independence, ruminates on the past and future.

It is nearly two years since the spring 1980 referendum; nearly eighteen since he first became constitutional adviser to a series of Quebec governments. In a tiny book-lined study he built off the family rec room, with a thick padded door to block the noise from the television — only the cats are allowed to come down for the occasional visit — Morin shuts off the outside world and remembers. In his basement sanctuary, where the thousands of volumes threaten to topple on those sitting below, creating some trepidation in the visitor, there is only the calm, deliberate voice of someone who has watched the Quiet Revolution from its epicentre, and the repeated scratch of wooden matches to keep his faltering pipe alight.

Now the promises. Trudeau wasn't very specific, but you don't have to be very specific when you come and you say: 'We are going to change the federal system.' I remember the night he said that — even I was impressed, thinking, Oh, oh, maybe he's changed. Everyone understood that he would come with an attitude and

changes that would suit Quebec, maybe not completely,
but that would be relevant when compared with traditional federal positions. We didn't know what it would
be. We even criticized him at the time for being so imprecise and we challenged him to be more specific . . .

*Except for the bushy, swept-back sideburns, hinting at the equally bushy ego
below the surface, there is nothing outwardly ostentatious about Claude Morin.
He drives a battered old Buick long after his cabinet colleagues have opted for
shiny new limousines with televisions in the back seat. With disarming candour,
he explains how he plans to continue as propagandist for an independent Quebec.
One has constantly to keep recalling that it is he as much as anyone who is
responsible for the current state.*

All the provincial people made promises, too. This is a
very important element because you have no idea
[about] the influence this is going to have on the
future. The outcome of the November conference
contained everything, some kind of treason by the other
provinces, treachery and lies from the federal
government. English Canada against French Canada,
the rest of Canada against Quebec. It's part of our
history — that we've been cheated. That date,
November fifth, is going to be a very important and
dramatic date, historically speaking. That is something
that is not going to be erased . . .

*The people who became the Quiet Revolutionaries of the 1960s were originally
resolutely anti-nationalist, rebelling against the stagnant, Catholic conservatism of
the Duplessis regime. But the great reforms of that decade — secularizing and
modernizing the educational system, and laying the groundwork for a succession
of language laws that would lead to the assault on the English bastions of business in Montreal — slowly formed a new collective consciousness. They also
powered the state into the forefront of social change, eclipsing the church and
creating a fresh set of political myths for the newly emerging elite.*
    *As constitutional adviser to various Quebec governments from 1963 until
1971, Claude Morin was in the vanguard of many of these changes and helped
give the fledgling reform movement some of its intellectual muscle. More of a
strategist than an originator of political theories, Morin was a central force in
Quebec's reach for international status in the mid-1960s. (It was constitutional
expert Paul Gérin-Lajoie, then Quebec's minister of education and a long-time
academic friend of Pierre Trudeau, who put forward the notion that Quebec has
an international competence in its areas of jurisdiction.) Through his negotiations
with Ottawa, chiefly the parallel Quebec-Canada pension plan proposal in*

1963-64, Morin tried to fashion and popularize the idea of a fortress-province, in which the jurisdictions of the two levels of government are kept as airtight as possible, supported by exclusive provincial taxing powers. Overlapping programs would be negotiated away like peace treaties.

To him and others, such as then social affairs minister Claude Castonguay, can be ascribed the collapse of the Victoria constitutional conference in 1971, when the hapless Robert Bourassa caved in to the pressures of Trudeau and Marc Lalonde and then went home and yielded to the nationalists there, led largely by Morin and (independently) Claude Ryan, at that time the influential publisher of Le Devoir. *In 1976 Morin was elected to the National Assembly in the landslide victory of the Parti Québecois; and became dedicated to René Lévesque — "the greatest human being I have ever known" — and to his idea of sovereignty-association.*

The politician of Quebec made so much mileage with Riel and the conscription crisis. This is exactly the same. When the charter of rights is used against Bill 101, then people here will realize the daily influence on their lives, and the whole thing is going to start again. It's a political time bomb. . . .

2
The Promise to Quebec

20 May 1980

Referendum night in Quebec. At the Paul Sauvé Arena in Montreal's east end, the nationalists gather to take defeat but keep the faith. The little figure on the stage holding his hands, Canute-like, before him to halt the screaming cheers, is René Lévesque, looking much older than his fifty-seven years.

Only four-and-a-half years before he had stood on the same stage, surrounded by beaming colleagues, savouring a momentous victory. The mostly young crowd whooped, sang, blew whistles and air horns, and waved the blue-and-white Quebec flags wildly like revolutionary banners. It seemed then there could be no stopping the Parti Québecois; a mere eight years old, the party had vaulted into power, carrying the nationalist hopes of a generation.

But tonight — "We have to swallow it this time," Lévesque says — he is poignantly alone at centre stage. His second wife, Corinne Côté, twenty-one years his junior, stands discreetly back, her arms folded, hands clutching elbows, looking young and vulnerable. The only other person onstage is Lise Payette, the television talk-show host turned PQ cabinet minister, whose throwaway insult at the outset of the referendum campaign sparked a women's revolt.* Like the various faces of Eve, the two women stand back, but ready to comfort the man whose dream has been shattered by a society he had hoped to change. Tonight's crowd, though, calls for no ministrations. The cheering goes on and on, for an incredible eight, nine, ten minutes. There is to be no humiliation tonight,

---

*Payette labelled Claude Ryan's wife, Madeleine, an "Yvette", a Quebec storybook character known for her docility. The remark provoked a phenomenal protest movement. On referendum night she was supposed to be one of many cabinet ministers in attendance at Paul Sauvé, regardless of the outcome, but none of the others showed up.

despite the electorate's clear rejection of sovereignty-association. The final tally shows 59.6 per cent of Quebecers, including a majority of the French-speaking population, have marked their ballots for Canada. Yet René Lévesque, if he wants to, can take sustenance from having raised the level of Canadian consciousness to new heights, higher than any other Canadian this century, with the possible exception of John Diefenbaker in 1958 and Pierre Trudeau, with that once magic spark, a decade later.

Three times, his head cocked self-consciously, Lévesque tries to tamp down the crowd's emotional outpouring. He brushes away tears with his palms, acknowledging "this hurts more than any election defeat." But, he admits, "it is clear that the people of Quebec want to give the federal system another chance." In the heartrending speech that follows, Lévesque makes it plain who carries the responsibility for delivering that second chance — not Claude Ryan, the austere Quebec "pope" and official leader of the "No" forces, but Pierre Trudeau, the Quebec premier's long-time antagonist, whose entry into the referendum campaign he calls "scandalously immoral." Of Trudeau's campaign promise of constitutional renewal — a promise so vague as to defy definition, and yet so inspiring as to help swing the tide of battle — Lévesque now demands delivery. Feeding off the crowd's emotions, he does not analyse the defeat or really concede victory. Instead, in his own instinctively resilient manner, he ups the ante and turns the referendum loss into a new set of demands. He had asked for an improved bargaining hand to take to Ottawa but he did not get it at the referendum ballot box. So he takes the promise that denied him victory and insists that it be honoured. Fulfil the traditional claims of Quebec, he tells the Canadian prime minister.

Then shyly, and a bit off key, he begins the first verse of Quebec's unofficial anthem, chansonnier Gilles Vigneault's "Gens du pays," and the crowd roars back its affection. "À la prochaine" — until next time — Lévesque says at the end and leaves the stage, the anthem continuing into yet another chorus. Some reporters carry away the tiny fleur-de-lys flags on the press tables as souvenirs of a decisive moment in Canadian history.

———————— ✦ ————————

The debate for the hearts and minds of Quebecers, more than a century old but finding a sharper focus in the previous two decades, appeared to be reaching its climax in May 1980. The referendum campaign of the Parti Québecois government, part of its deliberate march to sovereignty, was impelling an already rapidly changing society into greater convulsions and tests of will. It was difficult for English Canada to appreciate the torment that the referendum choice brought to ordinary Quebecers — the constant debating that tore apart families and neighbours, and the pressure that came from the realization that the whole world was watching.

Canvassers covering the same street for different sides of the question discovered that people often tended to hide their true sentiments: there was immense sympathy for both visions and considerable fear as well. Parents in the English suburbs flew their children home from universities in other provinces, and even from the United States, so that every vote would count on the day. The elderly and infirm were pitiably mindful that their pensions and benefits come from Ottawa. Taxi drivers bemoaned the fact that the cost of gas might rise in an independent Quebec, jeopardizing an already difficult livelihood. A handful of prominent Anglos from old Quebec families were recruited to the "Yes" side, and in so doing, became ostracized by the rest of their community, even by members of their own families. Fathers and sons disagreed violently on the best way ahead. René Lévesque's brother voted against him; a sister of Monique Bégin, Trudeau's minister of health and welfare, and a nephew of Jean Chrétien voted for the independence option. Some found themselves almost physically unable to make the choice. A gardener, an emotional supporter of sovereignty-association, told an interviewer: "We were voting for our lives. I trembled as I marked my ballot." An astute Greek woman lamented: "One way or another, the immigrant loses." And a farmer's wife, wiping tears from her eyes after the vote, observed: "Maybe if it had been less democratic, we would have won."*

---------------- ❦ ----------------

When he waltzed back to power in February 1980, making him only the third Canadian prime minister to reclaim his job after an electoral defeat, Pierre Trudeau was definitely his own man. Cool and deliberate, vindicated by the voters and galvanized into action by the referendum challenge, he was, in journalist Richard Gwyn's phrase, "the happy warrior: cerebral and impassioned, serious and joyous, magical and political." The PQ had only recently published the referendum question, asking for "a mandate to negotiate" sovereignty-association. Ottawa's first secret poll

---

*The newspapers of the day abound with examples of the agony of the referendum decision but the best compilation is *Le confort et l'indifférence*, filmmaker Denys Arcand's remarkable documentary on the passions and humour of the referendum campaign, in which an actor, playing Niccolò Machiavelli, the scheming Renaissance statesman, is the master of ceremonies, and ordinary Quebecers and politicians play themselves.

afterwards showed the federal side down substantially for the first time in nearly two years.*

Panic seized the senior mandarins in the Langevin Block, where the prime minister's advisers ply their craft, and took hold of the upper reaches of the federal Liberal Party. Only Trudeau, calm and resolute, did not seem especially anxious. This was the battle he had been preparing a political lifetime for, the apotheosis of all that he represented. Finally, after years of skirmishing, there would be a direct confrontation, a choice — "a door has to open or be shut," he said. He was sure Quebecers would choose Canada.

Whether Trudeau was always this confident is open to debate. In the past he had flinched from directly challenging the Parti Québecois on a number of occasions — notably in 1977 when he refrained from using the (somewhat archaic) federal powers of disallowance on Lévesque's controversial language law, Bill 101, or even taking it on in the courts. (Ottawa appeared only as an intervener when private citizens brought suit.) Certainly he had not, until fairly recently, considered using constitutional change as the cure for the Quebec problem. In 1971 when he was told that Quebec premier Robert Bourassa had decided not to endorse the Victoria charter, Trudeau just shrugged. "What do you expect?" he asked. "The constitution is a can of worms." Privately enraged at all the wasted effort, he told his close advisers, "Fini les folies!" and the constitution issue was placed on the backburner for nearly five years.

Nevertheless, Trudeau could read the signs in Quebec as well as anyone. In the winter of 1975-76, the scandal-plagued Bourassa government was stumbling badly with the separatist PQ in the wings, waiting to pick up the pieces. Trudeau sent his cabinet secretary, Gordon Robertson, on a tour of provincial capitals to sound out the premiers on a modest series of reforms, mainly patriation and the amending formula nearly agreed to in Victoria. In March 1976 in Quebec City Trudeau sat down with Bourassa for a desultory private meeting. Bourassa told him he was reneging on an agreement to formally greet the Queen in Montreal on her arrival to open the summer Olympics and said he could not go along with constitutional reform in an election year. A furious Trudeau told

---

*Ottawa began taking detailed surveys of the Quebec situation in April 1979, a year before the referendum. Throughout most of that period, a majority of Quebecers rejected the sovereignty-association option, although the figures were quite close when respondents were asked if they would support a "mandate to negotiate." There were two important exceptions: in a poll taken in February 1980, when the federal election was still in progress and the referendum question was being debated in the Quebec National Assembly, 52 per cent favoured sovereignty-association, with 37 per cent against; in a poll three weeks before the 20 May vote, the federalist side fell behind with 35 per cent of support, compared with 38 per cent for sovereignty-association and 26 per cent undecided. For the exact wording of the referendum question, see the Glossary.

a scrum of reporters outside that he would proceed alone to patriate the constitution from Britain. It was the first indication of unilateral action, but, although it surfaced from time to time at news conferences, the threat always seemed rather empty.

The election of the PQ in November 1976, however, catapulted the question of constitutional reform back into prominence. Despite more than two years of squandered power in Ottawa, in which his Liberal government was beset by scandals, resignations, and broken promises, Trudeau's personal popularity soared in the wake of the PQ victory, and for a couple of months there appeared a real chance of a constitution breakthrough. It did not happen, largely because the prime minister's marriage was disintegrating in an embarrassing public spectacle, and because the premiers wanted considerably more items on the agenda, including greater powers for themselves. In January 1977, replying to Peter Lougheed, the chairman of the premiers that year, Trudeau said they were asking for "either too much or too little." If it couldn't be simple patriation, then Ottawa would want its own preferred topics on the agenda too. Back to the can of worms.

Despite this poor start, the federal government prepared for another major round of constitutional negotiations in the dying months of its mandate. With Marc Lalonde, his most trusted lieutenant, as minister of state for federal-provincial relations, Trudeau produced a policy paper called *A Time For Action.* This was accompanied by detailed draft legislation for constitutional reform, Bill C-60, which provided for considerable provincial collaboration in appointments to central institutions such as the Senate, the Supreme Court and regulatory agencies. Bill C-60 was "as much strategic as anything else," Trudeau admitted much later, designed to test the provinces' will for change. At the subsequent first ministers' conference in October 1978, the prime minister astonished many observers by offering to cede certain federal jurisdictions. "I've almost given away the store," he observed in exasperation at the closing press briefing. But there were no takers. Before the conference, at the premiers' annual August get-together, they had formed a grandly titled "common front" to insist that more of their items be promoted to the top of the agenda. When the eleven first ministers resumed meetings in February 1979, only weeks before the announcement of a federal election, there were even greater demands for capitulation.

During the final days of the 1979 election campaign, when Trudeau and all around him knew the end of the Liberal government was at hand, he began appealing more to history than to voters, returning to his constitutional passion. In long, rambling speeches in Montreal and Toronto, he laid out his plan to patriate the constitution, by regional or national referendum if necessary, if the premiers would not come to an agreement with Ottawa within two years. He still wanted a charter of rights but one that would be binding only at the federal level, allowing the provinces to opt in as they saw fit.

In the dying days of the 1980 winter campaign, less than a year later, with re-election victory almost assured, Trudeau tossed aside the arid scripts and returned to his constitutional dream. In Lévis and Toronto, he spoke movingly about his pan-Canadian vision. He did not come right out and say he was prepared to bash the provinces over the head to get his way, but in the subtle winds of domestic diplomacy, where every utterance is analysed for latent meaning by the practitioners, he did not have to. During the final hours of the contest, Trudeau demonstrated that he was on top of his own destiny by parodying W.B. Yeats's poem "The Second Coming":

> Things fall apart; the centre cannot hold;
> Mere anarchy is loosed upon the Tory party.

The message was clear, and it was directed more to the premiers than to the voters.

-------------------- ♣ --------------------

The born-again Liberal team that gussied up for the cameras at Government House on 3 March 1980, only eleven weeks before referendum day in Quebec, was a remarkable compilation, clearly designed with the forthcoming battle in mind. An unusually high number of the ministers (14 of 33) crowding into the formal photograph were French Canadian, holding such key posts as justice, energy, health and welfare, regional economic expansion, transport, and communications. The finance minister was a dour and remote Cape Bretoner but the two ministers of state were Quebecers. The key patronage posts — supply and services, postmaster general, and regional economic expansion — were all held by francophones. Fifteen of the ministers were new to the job, some rescued after years of obscurity on the backbenches. Four others were resurrected after political miscues that had either led to resignations or banishment from the charmed circle.* In short, it was a cabinet with strong French representation, greatly obligated to Pierre Trudeau.

Jean Chrétien, one of French Canada's most conspicuous achievers, was made justice minister and constitutional spear-carrier. He did not want the job, and the swearing-in ceremonies had to be held up for days

---

*André Ouellet was brought back to the cabinet not long after resigning in 1976 when he was convicted of contempt of court; Francis Fox resigned in January 1978 after admitting that he had forged another man's name on an abortion certificate; John Munro resigned in 1978 because he had called a judge on behalf of a constituent; Herbert Gray was brought back into cabinet after being demoted in 1974.

while he held out for reappointment to an economic portfolio. The first French Canadian minister of finance (1977-79), he looked on justice as the traditional dead-end for Quebec politicians, especially because of its built-in obsession with the constitution. Besides, there was another reason for his reticence, which he did not admit to until much later: "I was afraid of not succeeding . . . and I hate to fail."

But Trudeau prevailed — "Jean, it's been a bureaucratic problem so far. You will make it a political one." — and Chrétien fulfilled the dream of his dying father, whom he worshipped, and assumed the portfolio of Lapointe and St. Laurent. For Wellie Chrétien, "That was greatness!"

The self-styled "petit gars de Shawinigan" (although a robust six-footer), Chrétien would lose nearly twenty pounds during the referendum campaign, shouting himself hoarse in hundreds of small towns, his face twisted with fatigue. It was his third campaign in a year and the start of a long constitutional battle. Yet he brought to the fight the emotional patriotism that had been missing from the federalist side as well as a seemingly untiring talent for placating the haughty differences between Trudeau and Ryan.* He also cranked into gear the formidable election machine of the national Liberals, and spread around more than $3 million in federal advertising money wherever TV spots, billboards, and brochures could be put to use. It all came at a time when the Quebec Liberals were squabbling about their leadership role — trying desperately not to be upstaged by their federal cousins — and the PQ was appearing to claim the inside track.

The destiny of the new Liberal government in Ottawa was ground out in only a few short weeks following its re-election. The nine-month stint in the political wilderness had caused some soul-searching at the outer extremities of the party but did not impel the rank-and-file to try to impose new strategies. Allan MacEachen, who chaired the party's newly formed policy group, kept their recommendations under lock and key throughout the winter campaign. Rather, the government adopted a more interventionist approach, in keeping with the political philosophy of its leaders. Marc Lalonde recalled the sinking feeling he had after the Conservative win in May 1979, when he thought back over a decade of Trudeau government and was hard-pressed to name a significant achievement in many (particularly economic) portfolios: "It was quite clear in our minds that, if we came back, it would have to mean something," he told a magazine interviewer in 1981. "We got nickeled and

---

*Once, at the end of April when Trudeau was in Montreal for a speech to the city's Chamber of Commerce, the Liberals had a film crew ready in his hotel room for some promotional shots of him and Ryan which would be made into a television commercial. But, at the last minute Ryan decided not to go up to the room, apparently feeling that his services were better employed in the lobby, shaking hands.

dimed to death between '74 and '79, and we would not make the same mistake again."

Back in power, the Liberals were convinced Ottawa must reassert itself in a number of key fields — energy, regional economic development, fiscal transfers and constitutional reform — and these policies were struck in the weeks surrounding the Quebec referendum. According to Lalonde, there would be a new theory of national leadership: "You may convert just as many people by standing your own ground." The revived Trudeau Liberals embarked on a new age of confrontational politics — competitive rather than co-operative federalism, as one premier came to call it — and the buzzword in the corridors of power was "visibility," what Ottawa wanted and the provinces had. Tired of being seen as the mismanaged, debt-ridden government in uncaring central Canada (with many provinces able to balance their budgets and provide all sorts of nice things for their constituents, such as day care and dental insurance plans), this Liberal government planned to right the pendulum's swing of decentralization — all within the space of two years, the critical path — and claim the credit and the new revenues for itself.

Phase one was to be the constitution, followed closely by the national energy program and the cutback in transfer payments for social programs to the provinces. The constitution itself would not be the prime centralizing instrument; it was to be the symbol, the spearhead, of a more assertive federal presence.

In the spring of 1980, Trudeau was probably wielding more raw prime ministerial power than any of his predecessors. He had a majority government and was facing a dispirited opposition, consumed with its own leadership problems; his caucus and party were beholden to him for leading them out of the wilderness; and his declared intention to resign delivered him from the responsibility of constantly courting public opinion and made history his only judge. Moreover, his few promises in the winter campaign effectively gave him a free hand to pursue the national interest in his own fashion.

Meanwhile, in a well-conceived campaign, the Parti Québecois government unfolded its referendum plan in three stages. The cold plunge approach of declaring independence first and holding a referendum after to legitimize it, favoured by some cabinet hardliners, had been rejected for the soothing *étapisme* of Claude Morin. With all the linear, sequential logic of a chess game, Morin's constantly spinning mind mapped out a simple strategy. Move. Breathing space. Move. Breathing space. Check!

On 20 December, in the midst of the federal election campaign (and while Trudeau was still agonizing over whether he should return as Liberal leader), the PQ announced the referendum question: a soft, ambiguous request for a mandate to negotiate sovereignty-association.* It was a devastatingly sly manoeuvre to capture all those who were embittered about the federal system and yoke them with the hard-core supporters of independence, historically less than 20 per cent of Quebec's population.

After a cooling-off period, there was a three-week debate in the National Assembly, ostensibly on the rules of the campaign. Claude Ryan set upon the provincial government for organizing the campaign under two opposing umbrella groups. The Lévesque government used the debate to publicize its belief that a "Yes" vote meant pride over humiliation, equality rather than subordination in a federal system. All the PQ speeches in the debate were coordinated through the office of government house leader Claude Charron, and influential ministers were given specific times, to ensure the greatest media attention.

Lévesque opened the debate, arguing movingly that the sovereignty-association option (which he had first put forward in 1967) was the logical next step in the Quiet Revolution. Recalling the slogans of former Quebec premiers, like Jean Lesage's "maîtres chez nous," Daniel Johnson's "égalité ou indépendance," and even Robert Bourassa's "souveraineté-culturelle," Lévesque constructed an emotional march to destiny. To deny this, he maintained, "would reconsecrate Quebec's links to dependence, inequality and minority status with the rest of Canada." It was a commanding political performance, emotional but not histrionic, delivered with the controlled passion of someone who believes strongly in his cause. It was an appeal to the pride and destiny of Quebecers, the two founding peoples, not just one of ten but equals to equals.†

The Quebec government's campaign moved forward with apparently well-oiled ease and began to take on the mystique of a holy war. In mid-April, just days before the formal, five-week campaign officially began, the PQ inaugurated a shrewd ritual for conferring the faith. Lévesque flew about the province receiving petitions from small groups of people — lawyers, doctors, factory workers — as a testimony of their

---

*In her recent book, *Le pouvoir? Connais pas!*, former PQ minister Lise Payette recalls that the cabinet sat up all night trying to decide the wording of the referendum question; no one, not even Morin, seemed to know what it should be. She left around midnight, expecting that it would be decided another time, only to find it published the following day.

†The rest of the speakers from the government benches tended to follow this lead. The only sour notes were the implicit racism in the speech by cultural development minister Camille Laurin, who spoke of Quebec's subordination at the hands of "the Anglo-Saxon economic power," and others who distinguished between "authentic Québécois" (who would vote "Yes") and the rest. However, Liberals were not without blame, and in various rallies during the campaign some argued that a sovereign Quebec under René Lévesque would be authoritarian and racist.

adhesion to the "Yes" crusade. The premier ceremoniously accepted the testimonies and in return — passing along his benediction — presented the donors with a parchment commemorating the event. It had the impact of a religious ceremony, a public confirmation of a new order, building on peer group pressure. A public relations stroke of genius, it gave the PQ fresh momentum as they headed into the last lap.

———————— ❦ ————————

By contrast, the provincial Liberals appeared unprepared for the campaign and were losing ground in the opinion polls as referendum day approached. Federal government polling, begun only months before the Liberals lost power in 1979 and continued, with occasionally more expensive surveys, during the Tory regime, showed the provincial Liberals dropping steadily from a peak of 47 per cent popularity in December 1979 to a low of 34 in May 1980, three points behind the Parti Québecois. Taken as a whole, the polls reflected a Quebec essentially wary of sovereignty-association as a costly adventure and prone to play off its political leaders against one another. Support for Quebec Liberal leader Claude Ryan rose somewhat during the period Joe Clark was prime minister but dropped off again when Pierre Trudeau was returned to power.

The polls confirmed Conservative instincts that the referendum issue ranked beneath inflation and unemployment in the minds of Quebecers, but they gave no sign that Clark's new gambit of appeasement in federal-provincial relations was winning their hearts.* Indeed, the Tories' pragmatic approach to constitutional problems — surrendering jurisdiction over lotteries and offshore oil and gas, and making fisheries a joint concern — paled beside the impassioned rhetoric of a French Canadian homeland.

For the federal Liberals, however, these same polls had a different significance. They showed that economic fears weighed heavily on the minds of Quebecers and therefore buttressed the central strategy of the federal government to play up the high cost of separation. With their no-holds-barred attitude, the Trudeau Liberals prepared and distributed vast amounts of documentation showing the effect the federal government was having on the Quebec economy, particularly in bolstering the small, out-of-the-way textile towns which were experiencing immense difficulty competing against cheap imports. Throughout March, the first weeks of the Liberal return, the economic arguments against separation dominated the news media. Ministers rarely missed an opportunity to

---

*A detailed survey conducted for the Conservatives in December 1979 asked respondents how they would describe the attitude of the federal government under Mr. Clark towards the people of Quebec. A majority was not impressed: 33 per cent said somewhat unfavourable; 19 per cent said very unfavourable.

turn up in Quebec towns, no matter how small, to publicize the latest federal grant and to talk about medicare, old age pensions, and family allowances. It was the politics of fear, performed extravagantly, with the premiers of English Canada playing key supporting roles. Their sorties into Quebec had one essential purpose: to show the flag and to drum home the argument that an independent Quebec should expect no economic favours from the rest of Canada. Some of their speeches, Blakeney's and Davis's especially, had been loosely coordinated with Ottawa's campaign. None was welcomed by Claude Ryan, who had his own idea of how to conduct the referendum fight.

Elected leader of the Quebec Liberals in April 1978, Claude Ryan was like no other politician in the land. Coldly intellectual, even more so than Trudeau, and ascetic — he once told Trudeau that if he truly believed in the global ethic of sharing, he should give away all his worldly possessions — Ryan was actually feared in other political circles because of his stubborn independence. He was also a bit of a paradox, spending the first two years of his leadership touring the province, marshalling and purifying the Quebec Liberal Party, readying it as a government in waiting. But even though the referendum question had been known since mid-December, the "No" committee he chaired did not hold its first organizational meeting until 27 March, less than eight weeks from voting day.

Moreover, Ryan did not want anything to do with the federal side's politics of fear. In his view, the basic conservatism of Quebecers was healthy; it would lead them to make the right choice on their own without the hype and hoopla of modern-day politics to point the way. Consequently, his strategy was to stump the province, hamlet by hamlet, appearing on stage with local dignitaries, making his presence felt. It did not matter to him that his speeches would be given late at night after the television deadlines had passed (he would sternly rebuke the news media for not understanding the nature of his campaign style), it was enough to show the unruffled face, the dignified hawk-like presence, to assure the electorate that here was a man capable of assuming the reins of power once this forced period of trauma had passed.

Unfortunately for Ryan, even his supporters found fault when his pedantic performance did not catch the popular imagination. Commenting on the televised referendum debate in the provincial legislature, an angry Montreal *Gazette* called the Parti Québecois "the indisputable hands-down winner." The editorial writers of *Le Devoir*, Ryan's former newspaper, were more cutting: "The reputation for invincibility of the leader of the Quebec Liberal Party was shattered on the fast ice of the National Assembly."

In Ottawa there was growing consternation about Ryan's complacency and even greater worry over the long-term projections of the polls the

Liberals had inherited on returning to power. In March, on one of his first trips to Montreal to make peace with the provincial leader, Chrétien presented Ryan with an extensive $98,443 poll commissioned by the Tories the previous December, only to have it tossed back in his face. "I'm not blaming *you*, because it's a Conservative poll," Ryan said sternly, "but our party is close to the people and we don't believe in opinion polls." In Ottawa, where polling is next to cleanliness, they were exasperated. Ryan was rebuffing not only their support but their interpretation — economic fears — of the winning formula. It was the first of many occasions when the provincial leader would snub his federal counterparts, and led directly to a rancorous fight over representation on the "No" committee. In Ryan's view, the federal government should have exactly the same role on the committee as the by then decrepit Union Nationale party (whose former leader, Rodrigue Biron, had gone over to the PQ). Federal participation was "acceptable" Ryan told them, abstractedly consulting the ever-present black notebook he carried with him, but the Quebec Liberal Party was fully capable of handling this on its own.

While that fight was going on, nearly fulfilling the PQ's prophecy that all the squabbling groups would congregate under the "No" umbrella, the federal Liberals caught their first glimpse of Ryan's disorganization. In a conference room in Montreal's Bonaventure Hotel in late March, less than two months from voting day, Pierre Bibeau, Ryan's election chief, unfurled a twenty-foot chart and tacked it to the wall. In neat little boxes, the organizational flow structure of the "No" committee was set out. Ryan and the executive were at the top. Below them were the various sub-committees responsible for animating different groups in Quebec (youth, women, service clubs, ethnic associations) and for coordinating the campaign work (the telephone workers, pamphleteers, printers, and organizers of car pools). Bold lines showed the reporting mechanisms but the boxes themselves were faintly pencilled-in. As the insiders in the room crowded forward to study the chart more thoroughly, it suddenly dawned on them that there were no names on the chart! A plan had been devised but there were no people yet to make it work.

———————— ❧ ————————

In Ottawa, the panic took two forms. At the political level, the formidable Liberal machine geared up for an all-or-nothing rampage into Quebec politics. Not since the provincial election of 1939, when the federal Liberals swarmed into Quebec to defeat the anti-war policies of Maurice Duplessis and elect Adelard Godbout and his Liberals, had the party obtruded itself so boldly in the province's affairs. Chrétien and other senior Quebec ministers established a special committee of MPs to integrate federal intelligence-gathering throughout the province. It was a

remarkably enthusiastic and effective arrangement, generating a flood
of information on the minutiae of Quebec local politics and personalities. The committee met weekly and passed its views along to a special
cabinet committee of Quebec ministers that convened for two hours every
Tuesday morning to plan the federal government's referendum strategy.
This group then reported to Trudeau later that morning at the regular
meeting of the priorities and planning committee — effectively the inner
cabinet.

The committee of Quebec ministers was normally only a rather irregu-
lar patronage club but it took on new significance during the referendum
campaign and only rarely was there not full attendance. Indeed, Quebec
ministers were told not to travel out of the country or even out of the
province (except for Ottawa) unless they cleared it first with the prime
minister's office. They coordinated the advertising outlay, the timing of
ministerial pronouncements and the best parts of the province in which
to release communiqués. Towards the end of March, while the "No"
committee was just getting underway in Montreal, health minister
Monique Bégin discovered some year-old anti-drinking pamphlets with
exactly the same slogan — "Non merci" — as the federalist referendum
message. (It was not the slogan Ryan preferred.) The federal ministers
from Quebec immediately exploited this opportunity and the leaflets were
sent out as an insert in the April family allowance cheques, a not-so-
subtle reminder to recipients that Ottawa was their benefactor.

Chrétien personally sifted through every radio and television ad created for the referendum fight, as well as a number from various departments of state and Crown corporations, such as CN, that had been
pressed into service. Those that had a positive message about the country were quickly pushed to the top of the list, to fill space while the ad
companies worked up a harder line. The Canadian Unity Information
Office, Ottawa's propaganda arm, was instructed to step up its moni-
toring of Quebec events through weekly opinion surveys that began in
April, six weeks before the vote. *Some* of the federal plans were reported
to Ryan at the weekly meetings of the "No" committee executive. But
because of the acrimony between the two groups, more and more of
Ottawa's gambits were kept from him. The brochures, badges, and
promotional material that are the stuff of political campaigns were fed
directly to field organizers through the Liberal MPs' committee. "To this
day, I don't think Ryan realized where all his publicity came from," a
senior federal organizer said nearly two years later.

Once, when Chrétien didn't like Ryan's choice of campaign slogan —
"Mon Non est Québecois" — finding it too confusing, he had a batch of
buttons made up with a stronger message: "La Séparation. Non merci."
Furious at Chrétien's audacity in presuming to choose his slogan, Ryan
ordered the buttons removed when they turned up at a rally opening

the formal campaign in Chicoutimi in mid-April. A protracted argument ensued and it took several days for a compromise to be worked out: the simple "Non merci". By then Monique Bégin's inserts were already in the mail and full-size billboard ads with the same message had been found sitting around in her department's warehouse.* The committee of Quebec ministers gleefully adopted them and hurried out to purchase billboard space, pasting up as many of them as possible in the last weeks of the campaign.

———————— ❧ ————————

Meanwhile, in the blue-carpeted reaches of the Langevin Block, where even the wastepaper bins have locks, senior privy council officials were suffering their own torment. Convinced the federal side was about to lose the referendum, they were anxious that the prime minister not become too directly involved in the campaign, lest he give it greater credibility. They wanted Trudeau to stand aloof, preserving his authority for the next stage. An unflappable civil servant of the old school, de Montigny Marchand, was brought back from Paris to be the bureaucracy's eyes and ears on the cabinet's referendum committees. Just returned from a forced sabbatical at Harvard University, Michael Pitfield, the re-ensconced clerk of the privy council and long-time confidante of Trudeau, took charge of the gloom-and-doom strategies, which led to the occasional shouting match with more exuberant ministers like Chrétien, who felt the bureaucracy was dragging its feet at times.

Cautious and distant, Pitfield conceived a scheme to leapfrog the referendum outcome in the event Lévesque won. The federal government had introduced a referendum bill in 1978 but had allowed it to die on the order paper. In the spring of 1980, Pitfield began working on plans to revive this proposition so that Ottawa would retain the whip hand on national issues by being able to frame its own referendum question and target the area of the country — one province or nationally — where it wanted a referendum held. (The referendum notion was still pretty much a gleam in Pitfield's eye by 20 May but it became the nucleus of the so-called tie-breaking mechanism, which the prime minister inserted in the unilateral package at the last minute in October 1980 and which became the object of considerable provincial opposition.)

———————

*The ads, showing a wine glass being turned upside down, said "Non merci, ça c'est dit bien — No thank you, it's easy to say." They were the subject of a court challenge by the PQ, who said they contravened the spending guidelines for the campaign set out in provincial legislation. But the judge turned down the complaint on technical grounds.

The inserts in the family allowance cheques cost $80,000. They had the same image but a different slogan: "No thanks is an answer."

Buffeted by opposing currents, Trudeau carved out his own ground during the referendum campaign. He ignored the bureaucracy's advice to stay out of the debate, as well as that of some of the more emotional members of his cabinet (notably Monique Bégin and Pierre De Bané) who were urging him to enter the fray on an almost daily basis, to contribute his full prestige for Quebec. Mountainous accounts of public opinion and political intelligence were fed to his office to help in the writing of his speeches. But in the end, "so much of it was just Trudeau," an aide recalled.

So much of it was also purely tactical. Convinced that the PQ had shifted the meaning of the referendum away from the manifestation of popular will to a strategic exercise, the Liberals responded in kind. Jean Chrétien lost his voice shouting about "my Rockies" and poking fun at his own experiences in western Canada, but there were no specific promises made about how the federal system would be changed to accommodate the disaffected. Similarly, Trudeau did not mention his own constitutional goals during the referendum campaign. He lashed out at the separatists and their honour, and he tugged every Canadian symbol. But in all his public utterances during that period there is no reference to his long-cherished desire for an entrenched charter of rights or language guarantees to make French Canadians feel at home in the rest of Canada. He made four speeches, but it is impossible to say whether they turned the tide of battle, as Claude Morin would have us believe. More likely, they tended to reinforce Trudeau's image as the steadfast champion of French Canada, a Quebecer at the top of the heap, telling the people of that province they would be worse off if they abandoned Canada.

On 15 April, in the formal reply to the speech from the throne, Trudeau gave little comfort to those who saw renewed federalism entailing devolution of the central government's powers. The greatest enemy, he said, is "the enemy within." By that he meant

> when loyalties are no longer to the whole but there is a
> conflict in loyalties; when we seek protection of our wealth,
> our rights or our language not in the whole country but in a
> region or a province of that country . . . when there is a
> conflict of interest, not of laws which will be judged by the
> courts, the citizens must be convinced that there is a national
> government which will speak for the national interest and
> will ensure that it does prevail.

Turning to the referendum, Trudeau said it "is not the intention of the Government of Canada to go and wage the referendum battle," a flagrant misstatement given Ottawa's efforts behind the scenes, but that the government's response will be clear. Support for Lévesque's plan could lead only to a legal and political impasse. Sovereignty and association are inseparable concepts, the prime minister noted, quoting the Quebec government's white paper. But English Canada — himself and the other premiers — had made it clear that there was no interest in a common market arrangement with an independent Quebec. So there could be no association. If Mr. Lévesque wished to discuss pure sovereignty after 20 May, the prime minister would be forced to reply that the Quebec premier did not have the mandate for that alone. And anyway, Trudeau declared, sweeping his hands towards the 74 of 75 Quebec MPs on the government benches, Quebecers had only recently given him an overwhelming mandate "to exercise sovereignty for the entire country." End of debate.

It was a majestic performance, incisive, riveting (even for his opponents), demonstrating to everyone that Trudeau was back and in control. *He* was setting the agenda. On the talk shows and campaign trail in the days that followed, Lévesque was forced to argue how a "Yes" vote for sovereignty-association would not lead to stalemate. Trudeau's ninety-minute speech in the Commons, a little more than four weeks before referendum day, had thrown a wrench in the PQ's comfortable campaign.

Two weeks later, in an address to the Montreal Chamber of Commerce, he embellished these themes. Before a well-heeled audience, Trudeau attacked the ambiguity of the referendum question and taunted his opponents for lacking the courage of the early *indépendantistes*. "We know what you are asking for, Mr. Lévesque. But we do not know what you want."

Soon after that, 7 May, Trudeau jetted into Quebec City from Vancouver after a morning with the prime minister of Japan. He had passed up a trip to Belgrade for the funeral of Marshal Tito because "I felt the need to be among friends this evening." The Quebec event was a major rally for the "No" campaign and the municipal convention centre was jammed with supporters. Claude Ryan had given up his trek to the villages for a day to be on the same stage with Trudeau and a host of luminaries. Robert Bourassa was there. Jean Chrétien was present, with most of the federal cabinet, including defence minister Gilles Lamontagne, once the mayor of Quebec City. There was also a special guest: former Liberal premier Jean Lesage, the father of the Quiet Revolution, drawn back into the spotlight to refute the legacy Lévesque was claiming. Lesage did not speak for long and his voice was noticeably husky. The Florida tan and cheery wave could not disguise the fact that he had only months to live because of the cancer that was ravaging his throat.*

Trudeau had a simple message as he rhymed off a litany of influential

---

*Lesage had been sick for some time but it was confirmed only on the morning of the rally that he had incurable cancer and would have to start painful cobalt treatments. See the 1981 biography by Quebec journalist Richard Daignault.

French Canadians who had "defended" Quebec on the national stage. He was contriving to inject the "No" campaign with the same potent patriotic symbols that Lévesque had mostly appropriated for himself. For Trudeau, in this, his most partisan speech, the PQ were nothing more than "Yes-vote hucksters." Their vision represented the "ultimate cowardice: to have lacked courage, having led Quebecers to this historic turning point, to this moment when, as your friends say, 'We must finally stop talking about it, we must settle it, give an answer once and for all.' Well, they are not asking us to settle it once and for all. They are asking us to decide and vote on a question which puts our destiny in the hands of others."

On 16 May, four days before the vote, Pierre Trudeau, in his own fearless way, took his passion for Canada into the heart of the enemy's camp. At the Paul Sauvé Arena, where Lévesque had stood in November 1976, weeping with joy over the promise of a new Quebec, Canadian flags fluttered from the rafters and the capacity crowd was chanting Trudeau, Tru-deau and later, El-liott, El-liott, for the middle name Lévesque had gracelessly chosen to make a campaign issue. Earlier that day, lunching with Chrétien at 24 Sussex Drive, Trudeau had methodically gone over the opinion polls and the themes to be struck. Chrétien reported Lévesque's remark from the previous week that Trudeau was "naturally for the No" because his middle name was English.* Trudeau had not heard of it before. ("Boy, he was mad," Chrétien recalled.) After a few pensive moments, the prime minister turned to his justice minister and said, "This time we're going to do it." Chrétien came away feeling this was where it crystallized; this was when the decision was taken that constitutional change would be pushed through, unilaterally if necessary.†

That night, on the stage at Paul Sauvé, in an electrifying performance that reverberated throughout the province for days, Trudeau resumed his attack on Lévesque's scheme, once more challenging the ambivalence

---

*On 8 May, Lévesque told a heckler at a senior citizens' home in St. Leonard that Trudeau's position means "he has decided to follow the Anglo-Saxon part of his heritage." Growing increasingly sarcastic, he told the audience "Don't worry, the picture of Elizabeth on the dollar is not in danger of disappearing for some time yet."

†In an interview for this book, in May 1982, Trudeau said: "The time that Chrétien mentions is certainly a time that I thought we had to make our resolve clear — in other words, if we had to decide ourselves that we would proceed unilaterally if necessary [then] we would say *that* publicly, which was what I did a few days later . . . But I guess somewhere around the late '70s I began to leave the door open — at least in my mind — to the reality that we might never get agreement with the provinces, but it was worth trying one more time. It was during the referendum that I said to myself and to Chrétien, we just can't fail again this time."

of the referendum question and reiterating that a PQ victory would lead only to deadlock. Then, appearing to discard his written notes, he glared out at the audience and waited for a moment of calm:

> *I know that I can make a most solemn commitment that following a "No" vote we will immediately take action to renew the constitution and we will not stop until we have done that.*
>
> *And I make a solemn declaration to all Canadians in the other provinces: we, the Quebec MPs, are laying ourselves on the line, because we are telling Quebecers to vote "No" and telling you in the other provinces that we will not agree to your interpreting a "No" vote as an indication that everything is fine and can remain as it was before.*
>
> *We want change and we are willing to lay our seats in the House on the line to have change.*

There! That is it. That is the promise to Quebec in its entirety.

———————————— ❦ ————————————

It would be nice to say that, in this period of internal anguish, English Canada reached out its arms soothingly to Quebec and said all was well. But that would not be quite the case. One by one the various English premiers visiting the province laid waste the notion of any special economic association following a "Yes" vote. In all, five of them came with that message — William Bennett, Peter Lougheed, Allan Blakeney, William Davis and Richard Hatfield — disregarding for the moment the private club of leadership that normally keeps them out of each other's backyard. In April, Peter Lougheed made it clear that an independent Quebec would have to compete with international markets for Alberta oil. Adding insult to injury, he gave his speech in Toronto and then travelled to Montreal, bypassing Lévesque, his fellow premier, for an extraordinary private meeting with Claude Ryan, not only the leader of the opposition but a Liberal to boot.

Saskatchewan's Allan Blakeney, who has a fairly high standing in Quebec because of his image as an intellectual and honest broker, was the bluntest. An independent Quebec, in his view, should be expected to be treated as a separate country, like Australia, France, or Mexico.

William Davis, Quebec's neighbour and biggest trading partner, told the Montreal Board of Trade that Ontario would never negotiate any form of association with an independent Quebec. For the first time in his life, he even struggled through five paragraphs of egregious schoolboy French to do so. ("Even worse than John Diefenbaker's," one observer said.) But Davis's entrée typified the dilemma the shopkeeper premiers of English Canada had in reaching a French Canadian audience. He wanted to speak from the heart — and was indeed sincere and emotional in his sentiments — but had difficulty bridging the two solitudes. An English journalist from the West described Davis's speech as "quite moving." His Montreal counterpart merely noted that the premier of Canada's largest province could not speak French. Davis wanted to talk about constitutional reform but reporters persisted in questioning him about Penetanguishene, as well as his government's refusal to set up a French-language school board in the Ottawa area, as parents were requesting.*

During his visit, Davis gave interviews to Montreal's *La Presse* and Quebec's *Le Soleil*, which earned him front-page stories. But otherwise he was ignored by the Quebec media, provoking his staff to lodge a protest with Radio-Canada. In *Le Devoir*, editor-in-chief Michel Roy wrote a courteous but unenthusiastic editorial about Davis's contribution: "The intentions are generous. The concern to build a more equitable Canada comes through . . . But in all of this there is not the magic spark, the fluid which could still make a difference, the supplement of soul which the great hours of history sometimes bring about." On the verge of a momentous decision, Quebec was monumentally uninterested in tinkering with the present system. Or even with what English Canada was offering, assuming that even that could be defined.

Explicit in the statements of all the English premiers was that neither sovereignty-association nor the status quo were acceptable options. There had to be renewed federalism, some middle ground. But none of them were overly eager to be pinned down on what this idea of renewed federalism meant, especially for Quebec. They talked generally about greater provincial representation in central agencies and devolution from Ottawa of certain powers, particularly in the field of resources. But there was nothing about Quebec's role in Canada, the cultural duality, or any mechanism for protecting the French Fact. Blakeney dealt, somewhat abstractly, with the notion of special status for Quebec. But, in the main, the premiers kept to their own priorities. See, we have grievances too, they told Quebecers. You're the same as us. Except that in Saskatchewan and Ontario they don't have referenda on whether or not to leave Canada.

After the election of the Parti Québecois in 1976, renewed federalism became a growth industry with the intergovernmental set. The federal government published its white paper and draft constitutional bill in

---

*French language instruction in Ontario has always been a sensitive issue. Claude Ryan did not want Davis to visit Quebec during the referendum as long as the Penetanguishene issue was unresolved, a message that infuriated the Ontario premier when it was relayed to him by federal officials. However, before he travelled on to Montreal, Davis agreed to establish a separate French school in the town on Georgian Bay. The initial Ontario scheme had been to turn the matter over to a commission to study.

1978; four provinces, B.C., Alberta, Saskatchewan, and Ontario, put forward major documents as well.* The issue also interested a number of major organizations, such as the Canadian Bar Association, the Canada West Foundation, the C.D. Howe Institute and the Liberal Party of Quebec (the 1980 beige paper), all of which published major studies and recommendations. Finally, and in a quintessentially Canadian way, there was the Royal Commission Task Force on National Unity, headed by once and future Liberal minister Jean-Luc Pépin and former Ontario premier John Robarts, who in some respects began this final round with his Confederation of Tomorrow conference in 1967. The task force report in 1979 made the most sweeping recommendations of all the groups, including a form of special status for Quebec to recognize its distinct qualities. But it was promptly shelved by official Ottawa, and a peevish Trudeau shunted Pépin into the transport portfolio after the 1980 election, a job as far away from mainstream constitutional issues as possible.

In the final weeks of the campaign, particularly following the Trudeau-Ryan-Lesage rally in Quebec City, the referendum fight took on an ugly tone as the PQ fought desperately to salvage at least a majority of French-speaking voters. Angered by a Gallup poll at the end of April showing his side behind, Lévesque charged that the questions had been rigged to elicit a predictable response — but what could be expected "of an organization which is based in Toronto?" Two weeks later, in what may have been a thoughtless slip of the tongue, he drew a racial dividing line around the issue: "It is a question French Canada and French Canada alone must decide" — following that up a few days later with his cut at Trudeau's middle name.

As for the English premiers who visited Quebec, Lévesque told his audiences not to believe them; they would negotiate when the time came. In any case, he said, they are outsiders who are meddling in an internal Quebec matter. Premier Davis would find it strange if he, Lévesque, went to Ontario during that province's next provincial election and urged voters "to boot him out."

Few people can get under René Lévesque's skin as much as Pierre Trudeau. In his excellent biography, *René: A Canadian in Search of a Country*, Peter Desbarats describes the informal, late-night talks in Gérard Pelletier's Westmount home in the early 1960s when Lévesque was the rising star in Lesage's cabinet, and Trudeau was an astringent young law professor brought into the group for counterpoint. For hours Lévesque

---

*There were 137 federal-provincial conferences in 1978 alone, twelve of these on the constitution.

would ramble on about his plans and passions, becoming more and more caught up in the rhetoric of the Quiet Revolution, until Trudeau, his face until then an inscrutable mask, would bring him down to earth with a scornful jibe.

In this, the referendum debate gave history a chance to repeat itself. The day after Trudeau's speech in Montreal during the closing days of the campaign, Lévesque was at a luncheon gathering in a small shopping centre on the outskirts of Quebec City, about to make a few remarks to a group of local business people before continuing on the trail. He talked for more than an hour. His pent-up anger and frustration welled to the surface as he raged, more to himself than to those gathered in the banquet hall. Some sensed embarrassment, as if outsiders were witnessing a family fight to which they should not be privy.

But Lévesque was oblivious to everyone in the room. His hostility was focussed on Trudeau. He has lied to us before; he can't be trusted; remember wage and price controls. Each bitter memory sparked a new bout of oratory but they all came back to the same refrain: Trudeau lies; remember wage and price controls; Trudeau lies.

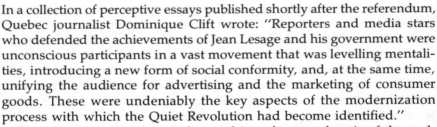

In a collection of perceptive essays published shortly after the referendum, Quebec journalist Dominique Clift wrote: "Reporters and media stars who defended the achievements of Jean Lesage and his government were unconscious participants in a vast movement that was levelling mentalities, introducing a new form of social conformity, and, at the same time, unifying the audience for advertising and the marketing of consumer goods. These were undeniably the key aspects of the modernization process with which the Quiet Revolution had become identified."

The referendum represented something of an apotheosis of these elements. Was it only chance that the main opponents in the debate were former journalists of long-standing? Lévesque had been a globe-trotting radio and television reporter in the late 1940s and 1950s, explaining the outside world to a changing, urbanizing society; Ryan, the puritanical editor of *Le Devoir* from the mid-1960s through the 1970s, the intellectual conscience of Quebec nationalism. Indeed, Pierre Trudeau, before he entered politics, was the founder and prime mover behind *Cité Libre*, a left-wing magazine for intellectuals in the 1950s and '60s that opposed the authoritarian nationalism embodied by Maurice Duplessis and the intellectual and moral bankruptcy of the Pearson Liberals.

In a way that was perhaps inevitable, the mythmakers of a generation came to embody their myths in the final struggle. What they said was perhaps not as important as what they represented. There was also a curious reversal of roles throughout the referendum campaign. Lévesque, who had been rooting around in Quebec politics since 1960, came to be seen as the high priest of nationalism, a role he had always fostered, but now he was rather above the grubby politics of it all, a leader whose indiscretions and slurs were instantly forgiven because he spoke from the heart. Ryan, on the other hand, the relative novice to active politics, was seen to be tremendously dependent on the political machine that he manoeuvred, in his own unique way, from riding to riding.

There was also a reversal of roles between Lévesque and Trudeau. The Quebec premier, the younger of the two by close to three years, was the father figure for the new generation, the pied piper whose message went out to the young and socially eager. Trudeau, older but fitter, had to cast off his earlier role as society's rebel, and run a campaign which, like those of Duplessis, appealed to the conservative elements in the Quebec psyche — to the old, the scared, and the infirm, who wanted the comfort of the status quo with only some modest betterment.

While a turning point, the referendum did not completely open or shut a door, as Trudeau thought it would. It was not an "endgame" but a continuation of the tensions that an urbanizing, self-confident Quebec had been evincing for decades. In many ways it represented the clash of myths from different generations — the old warriors who carried forward their battles and prejudices from the 1960s to a new period of rapidly evolving cultural and technological change. In the process it destroyed one of the most fundamental myths — that Quebec is a homogeneous bloc, a single collectivity, that knows how much of an opening it wants on the outside world.

The approximate 60-40 split on voting day reflected the deep cleavages in Quebec society. It was a clear victory for Canada but also a sweeping vote of discontent that would make negotiating a peaceful solution immensely difficult, especially if it were to be trapped by the perceptions of those warring for their respective visions.

About a week before the referendum vote, premier Lévesque was asked at a press conference whether he would negotiate 'renewed federalism' if he won the referendum and the sovereignty-association option were to be subsequently rebuffed by English Canada. After some circumlocutory rhetoric, the answer was given, almost shouted. "This is no renewed federalism. I don't see why I should speak of a hypothesis which doesn't exist. There isn't any."

3
The Roadshow and the Near Miss

The social and spiritual home of the Ontario Tories squats in an outwardly unprepossessing building on King Street East in Toronto. Named after the eighth child of Queen Victoria, the Albany Club is where Sir John A. Macdonald held court whenever he visited the Ontario capital. His bar tab is now respectfully framed in one of the salons.

It is a place to which all Conservative leaders or hopefuls eventually make a pilgrimage, either to be tested or to be rocked comfortably in the bosom of the Tory family. It was here that John Diefenbaker, in his seventy-second year, made his stand against those who schemed to unseat him as party leader in 1966. And it is here, in a private dining room, with the busts of party saints — Macdonald, Borden, and Meighen — standing guard along the dusty hallway, that Liberal justice minister Jean Chrétien sups the night after the Quebec referendum.

On a whirlwind tour of provincial capitals — all except Quebec City, where the Parti Québecois government is still licking its wounds — Chrétien is testing the will for constitutional change. Like Trudeau before him in 1967-68, and John Turner in the months leading up to Victoria in 1971, Chrétien is fulfilling a peculiarly Canadian odyssey: the lone prime ministerial emissary to the courts of the provincial barons. But inimitably, he is doing it in lickety-split time (three and four stops a day) and with his own definite ideas of what it is all worth.

Between morsels of roast beef soaking in juice, Chrétien tells the Ontario team, Bill Davis, Roy McMurtry, Tom Wells, the minister of intergovernmental affairs, and a cadre of select advisers, that constitutional reform is all well and good but one must not lose sight of the *real* objective of this exercise — to defeat the Parti Québecois and install a federalist party in Quebec.

———————— ❦ ————————

As objectives go, it was probably as good as any at that particular time. The previous night, in the aftermath of the federalist victory, Alberta premier Peter Lougheed pushed forward his own demands for a greater devolution of federal powers, particularly in the resource field: "We have aspirations here in western Canada too. . . ." Sterling Lyon of Manitoba warned Quebec not to "expect any favours" at the negotiating table, and Allan Blakeney and William Bennett reiterated their traditional demands for jurisdictional adjustments. Blakeney wanted more control over international trade so as to better regulate Saskatchewan's resource industries, particularly potash and heavy oil, both of which are largely exported from Canada. Bennett was preoccupied with reforming central institutions, such as the Senate, to give the far-off provinces a greater say in the decision-making process.

On Ottawa's Parliament Hill, where he just happened to be on business, Newfoundland's Brian Peckford was sweating profusely under the television lights and telling the country that the referendum results represented "a golden opportunity" to rewrite history. The first step, he said, should be to affirm the view that Ottawa is "the agent of the provinces . . . and not the other way around." It was an argument he embellished a short while later in a speech to the National Press Club, before eventually backing away when the editorial writers took after him, and some of his fellow premiers found it a touch too hyperbolic even for their plans.

On referendum night, Trudeau had made a touching plea for reconciliation and then retired backstage to shuffle his cards. The next day he set out his bargaining position in a thoughtful speech to the House of Commons. Except for federation itself and an entrenched charter of rights, including language guarantees, "everything else is negotiable." He was pressed by the opposition to be more explicit, but would not say whether the charter he envisaged would be binding on the provinces or simply on the federal government. Two days later in Quebec City, René Lévesque replied that the language issue was a matter on which he and the prime minister could not possibly agree. No Quebec government would consent to having its control over language and culture lessened by entrenched rights ultimately interpreted by judges in Ottawa.

Chrétien had not yet completed his tour of the provincial capitals but the battle lines were already drawn.

———————— ✦ ————————

Yet, despite the tough, predictable talk of Canadian constitution-making, there was an element to this latest round that had never been there before: the euphoria in official Ottawa at having taken on the most independent and best prepared of provincial governments and beaten it on its own turf. The referendum win, where Ottawa believed it had stepped in and rescued the situation from the foundering provincial Liberals, produced an enormous sense of self-confidence in the Trudeau government at the outset of its mandate. Whenever small groups of ministers or aides met, they patted themselves on the back for a job well done and planned even more aggressive strategies for the future. They were almost drunk with a new sense of power and accomplishment. It bolstered Marc Lalonde's assessment of "standing your own ground," and led him, at the start of difficult energy negotiations with Alberta a few days later, to open a new federal-provincial front: "We defeated those who wanted political sovereignty with economic association," he told the Canadian Manufacturers' Association. "We did not carry out this difficult battle to get economic sovereignty with political association." In the Langevin Block there was a determination among the constitutional planners to complete the job "before the snow flies."

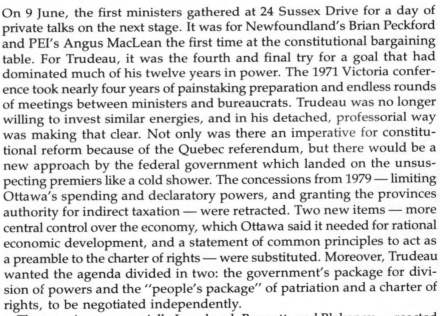

On 9 June, the first ministers gathered at 24 Sussex Drive for a day of private talks on the next stage. It was for Newfoundland's Brian Peckford and PEI's Angus MacLean the first time at the constitutional bargaining table. For Trudeau, it was the fourth and final try for a goal that had dominated much of his twelve years in power. The 1971 Victoria conference took nearly four years of painstaking preparation and endless rounds of meetings between ministers and bureaucrats. Trudeau was no longer willing to invest similar energies, and in his detached, professorial way was making that clear. Not only was there an imperative for constitutional reform because of the Quebec referendum, but there would be a new approach by the federal government which landed on the unsuspecting premiers like a cold shower. The concessions from 1979 — limiting Ottawa's spending and declaratory powers, and granting the provinces authority for indirect taxation — were retracted. Two new items — more central control over the economy, which Ottawa said it needed for rational economic development, and a statement of common principles to act as a preamble to the charter of rights — were substituted. Moreover, Trudeau wanted the agenda divided in two: the government's package for division of powers and the "people's package" of patriation and a charter of rights, to be negotiated independently.

The premiers — especially Lougheed, Bennett, and Blakeney — reacted sharply. They wanted the 1979 agenda back on the table and they objected to what they saw as the artificial divisions, especially to the notion that they were expected to barter improved resource rights for the augmented powers requested by Ottawa. A rather smug Trudeau kept repeating that it was now a different ballgame.

Other issues clouded the talks. Lougheed was hung up on the energy negotiations. Bennett wanted assurances that there would be no federal excise tax on natural gas in the next budget. Peckford demanded that fisheries, over which he wanted control, be added to the agenda, bringing the topics under discussion to twelve.* Lévesque and Trudeau entered into a prolonged and meandering exchange on the referendum, but Lévesque appeared to drift off at the end, one premier noted. He was hanging back in the discussion, "sort of half mumbling yes, half mumbling no," whenever his views were canvassed. "Lévesque was a political eunuch," another, a western premier, said privately months after the meeting. "It was up to the rest of us to take on Trudeau."

At the end of a day of sparring, the first ministers agreed to turn the agenda over to their constitutional ministers for a full-tilt set of summer-long meetings, and to reconvene in September for a formal conference before the television cameras. It was a sagging but conciliatory prime

---

*The twelve agenda items: *resource ownership and interprovincial trade* was the heading under which the provinces, particularly the western ones, hoped to aggrandize their resource powers, mainly by limiting federal involvement in these fields to emergencies and establishing their ability to control the price of resources across provincial boundaries (as the situation stands, provinces can set the price of a resource, say oil, only within their own borders, and need federal approval to sell it outside, which is why oil and gas prices are negotiated, usually over three-year contracts); *communications* represented a provincial attempt to gain control of licencing and regulating cable and radio stations that operated within provincial boundaries so as to (a) earn more revenues and (b) control their educational and cultural programming; *family law* was a generally agreed-upon devolution to the provinces of control over divorce and child custody laws, which foundered at the end when some provinces feared that an absence of national standards might lead to divorce havens; *offshore resources* was an attempt by the coastal provinces to be granted ownership of offshore mineral resources in the same way that Alberta, for example, owns the oil under its turf; *Senate reform* was the umbrella heading for discussing greater provincial involvement, mainly through appointments, in a variety of central institutions; *patriation and an amending formula* were the nub of the issue and the basis of the fifty-four-year-old roadblock because not everyone could agree on the best mechanism for changing the constitution in the future; *the charter of rights* had been a federal objective since 1967; *the Supreme Court* represented an attempt to entrench the high court in the constitution (it is currently only established by federal statute) and perhaps even enlarge it to give greater representation to Quebec; *equalization and regional disparities* meant entrenching at least the principle of distributing equalization payments to the poorer provinces and, if possible, devising a mechanism for doing so; *powers over the economy* was the new federal initiative (not realized) to break down provincial trade barriers and provide for a more free-flowing economic union; *the preamble and principles* were the prime minister's attempt to write down a series of common values to introduce the new constitution; and *fisheries* was an attempt to make a provincial or at least jointly shared jurisdiction of what is, under the British North America Act, completely federal because, as Trudeau liked to point out, "the fish move around!"

minister who explained the plan to the press that night. Less than a week later, he told Parliament that if there was no significant constitutional agreement by September, the federal government might have to act on its own to effect change. He described his policy as "deadlines but not belligerency," and it was more or less under this rubric that one of the more fascinating and bizarre exercises in Canadian political life was launched.

———————— ❧ ————————

Under intense media glare and rising public expectations, the constitutional roadshow of ministers, senior officials, and political aides took off like a shot off a shovel, playing in four cities — Montreal, Toronto, Vancouver, and Ottawa — for twenty-eight days during July and August, one of the rainiest summers on record. At times, in the crush of press, flacks, and media advisers, the troupe swelled to nearly three hundred people, more than most professional circuses and just as encumbered. One of the participants said it reminded him of "Nathan Detroit's floating crap game," except there was very little time for private merriment and the stakes were enormous — these men were dividing up a country!

In some ways, it was more like a T-group session for politicians and the press, or perhaps even a Moonie commune: long hours, largely (liquid) carbohydrate diets, and a series of adrenaline-pumping tasks for remote and uncaring masters. The process was extraordinarily confusing. Sometimes ministers met alone, sometimes with senior officials, sometimes in plenary session. Sub-committees were struck on all twelve agenda items, and, when each week was over, everyone dashed back to their respective capitals to take stock and plot the next round.

The co-chairmen — Jean Chrétien and Saskatchewan's Roy Romanow — were the yoked engines for the moveable meetings, their drive and bubbly personalities churning them forward. For hours in the private sessions they battered each other with their vastly different views of the country and then repeated the performance, in only slightly less severe language, for the television cameras at the end of the day. At night they often went out for a beer (Chrétien seldom drank more than one) and generally the arguments would start all over again. The intense, incessant debating "was probably the most intellectually stimulating period in my political life," Romanow recalled. But, except for the personal friendships and alliances that formed, the work itself was of almost no consequence. When the first ministers stepped back into the spotlight in September, the proceedings stopped dead; the fruits of the summer's labour were gathered into tidy piles and mulched.

Still, bringing the issues to the Canadian public was an important achievement, and the roadshow contained a fascinating mix of personalities and experience. Astonishingly, for a government that was gambling so heavily on constitutional reform, almost the entire front ranks of the federal team were new to the dossier. By the time he was appointed attorney general and justice minister Chrétien had spent half his twelve years in cabinet on the treasury benches, in economic ministries. John Roberts, his anglo counterpart for the summer, was a former foreign service officer and relatively junior minister, holding the untaxing environment portfolio.

Probably the most unusual addition to the federal team was its senior mandarin, Michael Kirby, a thirty-nine-year-old mathematician, who won brief prominence as the Machiavelli behind Ottawa's plans. Brash yet likeable, with all the breezy snap of racetrack tout, Kirby was the new troubleshooter, replacing the urbane Gordon Robertson, a bureaucrat's bureaucrat, as secretary to the cabinet for federal- provincial relations. A political fixer, who worked for then Nova Scotia premier Gerald Regan as well as Trudeau in the mid-1970s (he helped establish the wage and price control program in 1976), Kirby was (self-styled) "Trudeau's son-of-a-bitch," the new burr in the federal-provincial saddle, a seemingly tireless manager who, his wife said, had two speeds: flat out and dead stop. Under him, the constitutional section in the federal-provincial relations office doubled its staff, increased its polling and advertising budgets to an unprecedented degree, and adopted a markedly more assertive stance both within and without the public service.

Slightly more experienced were those who came on board during the last round of constitutional talks in 1978-79. Ontario's Tom Wells, fastidiously dressed and unfailingly polite ("one of the few politicians totally without guile," a counterpart from another province said), and Alberta's unflappable Dick Johnston, were the two most important of these arrivals. Manitoba's Gerald Mercier and Nova Scotia's Harry How, both attorneys general, played lesser roles.

The middle distance group, beginning in the 1976-77 period, comprised Romanow, Ontario's McMurtry, and B.C.'s then attorney general, Garde Gardom. Beyond those were the illustrious class of '71, those men who were at the grand Victoria conference when then B.C. premier W.A.C. Bennett (father of the present premier) led his fellow first ministers through the streets in a garish motorcade. Quebec's Metternich, Claude Morin (a civil servant in 1971), and New Brunswick's Richard Hatfield (his own intergovernmental affairs minister during the summer of 1980) were the only politicians of that vintage in the roadshow. But there were influential senior officials from that era also in the entourage: Alberta deputy minister Peter Meekison, Quebec's Robert Normand, B.C.'s Mel Smith and Ontario's Don Stevenson, each of whom played major parts in the unfolding drama.

Of the first ministers, only Trudeau, Davis, and Hatfield, the eventual allies, were veterans of 1971; Peckford and MacLean were new; Buchanan and Lyon had been present from 1978-79 (Lyon, as attorney general, had been in office for some of the run-up to Victoria, until June 1969 when the Schreyer government took over in Manitoba); and the others arrived for the second Trudeau round that fizzled out after a long exchange of letters following the election of the Parti Québecois in 1976.

❦

At the heart of the interpersonal relations emanating from the roadshow were "the lads," Romanow and McMurtry, little Roy and big Roy, as their friends and foes took to calling them, generally with affection. Their friendship went back to the mid-1970s, when they would rib each other about violence in sport and about who, as attorney general, was getting the most national publicity for prosecuting hockey goons (McMurtry in this case, because he instituted proceedings against some National Hockey League players). Both outgoing, flamboyant personalities, prolific talkers and "jocks", they soon discovered they had a lot in common besides politics and the law. Whatever one started, the other always had something to add. McMurtry found out Romanow was a jogger and racquet ball fanatic, so whenever the constitutional wrangles became too much to handle, they shot off for a quick match, or jogged down St. Urbain Street in east-end Montreal, around Vancouver's Stanley Park, or along the Rideau Canal in Ottawa. It was a small step from there to a few beers in the evenings, nearly always in some noisy hotel discothèque, where they'd sit in a corner taking in the sights and nattering about the constitution.

Except for the subject matter, they were much like any other pair of middle-aged businessmen, whiling away the hours away from home. Before long, other regulars joined them: Dick Johnston, a chartered accountant prior to entering the Alberta legislature; Tom Wells, advertising manager for the Canadian Medical Association before joining the Ontario cabinet; and Garde Gardom, a B.C. lawyer, who was part of the exodus of provincial Liberals to the ruling Social Credit party in 1975. Occasionally, others would tag along — Chrétien, Roberts, Hatfield, Newfoundland's Gerry Ottenheimer, and some of the senior officials Kirby, Meekison, Stevenson and Saskatchewan's Howard Leeson. As the summer progressed they became a fairly tight crew. ("Perhaps more than was good for us psychologically," one lamented later, thinking of the emotional letdown after September.) Even the Quebecers mixed in, although not a great deal. Morin's tastes are generally more intellectual — his only pastimes are fly-fishing and all-night poker games — and the Quebec delegation preferred to pass its evenings over long dinners in good restaurants. In any case, he and Chrétien were not comfortable in each other's company, as much for reasons of snobbery as political rivalry.

Genuine friendships grew out of that summer — Dick Johnston's daughter spent a few weeks with Tom Wells's family in Toronto and with the Chrétiens in Shawinigan learning French. (Johnston was reticent about discussing these trips because he didn't want it known in Alberta that he was fraternizing with the enemy in central Canada. After an oil deal between Ottawa and Alberta was eventually struck in September 1981, Lougheed admitted that it was a major political mistake to be photographed sipping champagne with Trudeau.) But the friendships were also based on a shrewd assessment that each connection would be useful eventually.

As co-chairmen, Chrétien and Romanow were thrown together, and given huge adjoining hotel suites en route. Initially they expected not to get along with each other because of their divergent backgrounds and political persuasions; in many respects, McMurtry was the glue that brought them closer. They made an unlikely trio. McMurtry, a big, sleepy-eyed Irish lawyer from Toronto, still plagued by college football injuries that put him flat on his back for weeks at a time, is a product of the Ontario Protestant Irish establishment, educated at private schools and infused with the social responsibilities of the privileged to do good. A keen landscape painter in his spare time and a bit of a prankster, he is also incurably irreverent and would privately refer to the provincial premiers as "the social climbers," whenever their ambitions seemed to outstrip his sense of fair play.

Romanow, the prairie-born son of Ukrainian immigrants, is highly competitive, hooked on baseball and intrigued by life in the fast lane. Friendly and effervescent, yet ultra-cautious about his public image, he ran unsuccessfully for the top job in the provincial NDP when he was barely out of his twenties. (Romanow's age is one of the best kept secrets in Saskatchewan. He will not divulge it. "Let's say I added a few years when I ran against Blakeney in 1970 and I may shave a few if I run again," he told one reporter with a wink.)

Then there is Chrétien, the second youngest of nineteen children of a Shawinigan machinist (only nine of whom lived past infancy), and a diehard Liberal since adolescence. At heart a small-town lawyer, steeped in the ways of rural Quebec politicians, whom he admires for their flair and joie de vivre, he is also a professional administrator (learning the craft at the hands of one of the great mandarins-turned-minister, Mitchell Sharp) who enjoys the good life in a fashionable Ottawa home.

Disparate backgrounds indeed. It sounds hokey but it was almost as if the three modern forces in Canadian society — the French Canadian, the WASP, and the Eastern European — somehow evolved their representative champions for this penultimate act of nation-shaping.

On the other hand, all three are lawyers in their mid-to-late forties, successful politicians and presumptive or wishful heirs apparent. Perhaps more important, they are all physical politicians who like to grab a person's arm when making a point and who find it impossible to be on the outside of any deal that is in the making.*

Romanow was enticed into the heady world of federal-provincial bargaining almost from day one as the roadshow opened in Montreal during the first week of July. Chrétien, sitting beside him at an Expos baseball game, not yet fully acquainted, casually remarked that this was how prime minister Lester Pearson developed the idea of a United Nations peacekeeping force on the Gaza Strip in 1957 — watching baseball. Barely allowing time for the comparison to sink in, Chrétien leaned forward conspiratorially to express his sympathies with Saskatchewan over a recent Supreme Court decision that limited the province's ability to regulate oil and gas production. He was a bit fuzzy on the details but he had instructed his officials to look into the matter and see if there might be a solution. The message was clear. Do you want to make a deal?

It wasn't quite the blatant proposition one gets in front of a Vancouver hotel, but it wasn't much more subtle either. In his own infectious, impatient way, Chrétien was letting the prairie boy know that if he wanted to play in the big leagues, here was his entrée. All summer, while the provinces had their backs up over Ottawa's new tough bargaining style, Chrétien was wheeling around the periphery, discussing Senate reform with B.C. and shared jurisdiction over fisheries with the Atlantic provinces, looking for a deal — a modest package with a little something for everyone that he could deliver to the first ministers in September. At the same time he was playing by the rules set down by Pierre Trudeau. At the start of the roadshow, Chrétien formally warned his provincial colleagues: "We would be failing in our responsibilities to the people we represent if we get involved in a process where the rights of citizens are traded off against powers of governments. Fundamental freedoms and the integrity of the constitution as a Canadian document expressing the aspirations of Canadian citizens must not be bartered against jurisdiction over fisheries or communications or anything else."

---

*McMurtry even left his hospital bed in 1971 to arrange the meeting between Bill Davis's supporters and the Allan Lawrence camp, following a bitter leadership contest. As Jonathan Manthorpe's *The Power and the Tories* makes clear, out of this affiliation grew the fabled Big Blue Machine.

Chrétien, when he was minister of finance, regularly used to try to bargain the weekly Bank of Canada rate. When Bank officials would come to him with their carefully prepared charts and graphs to explain why the rate had to rise half a point that week, he would reply, "Quarter of a point?"

At least that is what it said in his official statement. Backstage it was put in more earthy, Chrétienesque tones. There will be no fish for rights!

------------------- ❦ -------------------

On 2 July, in the cool confines of the legislature building overlooking the front lawn statue of Maurice Duplessis, which the Parti Québecois resurrected after years in storage, the Quebec cabinet met in special session to decide its strategy for the summer constitutional negotiations. In earlier, more soul-searching meetings after the referendum, the cabinet had decided to put off an immediate election until at least the fall. Now they were meeting, at Claude Morin's request, to approve his risky proposal of building a common front with the other provinces to block Ottawa's plans. Several of his colleagues were sceptical, citing Morin's own writings to show that a common provincial front that included Quebec was an impossible dream.

But Morin argued that the Quebec government must now be seen as one of the gang; it must swathe itself in a cocoon of respectability before daring to go back to the polls. The other aspect of his plan was a kind of Alphonse-Gaston ploy, by which Quebec would not put forward any new demands during this current round but would wait for Ottawa to go first and then evaluate things in the light of the province's "traditional" bargaining positions, already quite considerable (these filled a fifteen-page document tabled at the 1978 constitutional conference).

A vigorous debate ensued in which several ministers argued that Quebec should deliberately scuttle the patriation scheme in order to create an election issue for the fall, the issue being Trudeau's failure to carry out his campaign promises. But Morin pleaded, and was supported by Lévesque, that their government not only had to act in good faith, but must be seen as acting in good faith — even if this meant running the risk of a modest group of reforms going forward that might cool the public's ardour for more ambitious alternatives. "There was a big discussion in the party about whether I should take part in these discussions in such a way that they could succeed," Morin said later. "The answer I gave *personally* was yes."[*]

Morin's stratagem won the day, largely because it built on the position already adopted by the Quebec premier. Lévesque told his first press conference after the referendum: "I commit myself, not only to respect that majority will, but to invest all the good faith required in our participation in the negotiations which must once again come about." (In the weeks that followed, the PQ team laid out the theme that might have to

------

*Authors' italics, from a three-hour interview with Claude Morin in March 1982.

serve the party as an election platform: constitutional negotiations are upon us; we are tough bargainers; Claude Ryan is a patsy.) "I would say very simply," Lévesque went on, "that, for this period of constitutional effervescence which is supposed to begin, Quebec needs as never before, at the level of the provincial state, spokesmen who are at the same time inflexible on essentials and of total transparency."

As part of the "good faith strategy" the cabinet approved, Morin agreed to take along two other ministers (House leader Claude Charron and justice minister Marc-André Bédard) and to brief the press daily on the closed-door sessions. When the roadshow began the next week, Morin presented his federal-provincial colleagues with a mass of position papers on all the agenda items. They reaffirmed Quebec's long-standing view that the constitution should not be patriated unless it was the capping achievement on a new division of powers. The papers aligned themselves with other provincial positions on most of the issues but they held out strongly against entrenchment of language rights. "In fact, Quebec is inclined to believe that this debate might be only a pretext to modify Bill 101 so as to 'rebilingualize' Quebec and re-establish the free choice of language of instruction," Morin declared in an opening statement. The underlying sentiments were not far from the surface: "For us, Quebec is a distinct society that wishes to be recognized as such, that it is free to decide on its future . . ."

——————— ✤ ———————

The shopkeeper premiers who govern English Canada prefer not to be seen as grubby powermongers. Good administrators, yes. Powermongers, no. Whenever they discuss constitutional change and the jurisdiction over which they would like to exercise control, their arguments generally emphasize the efficiency of the new arrangements — *strong* provinces working hand-in-hand with a *strong* federal government. However, it did not take long for this façade to be chipped away when, towards the end of the first week of the roadshow in Montreal, the federal government introduced its plans for assuming greater regulation over the economy.

A forty-six page discussion paper, "Powers over the Economy: Securing the Canadian Economic Union in the Constitution," sparked off a ferocious debate that engrossed the ministers for most of the summer. Meticulously researched, the document identified in great detail the various barriers erected by the provinces to impede trade and labour. In a devastatingly understated way, it demonstrated that there is more freedom of movement for goods and manpower within the quarrelsome European Community than in Confederation; and it argued persuasively that provincial practices of preferential hiring and purchasing were costly and badly coordinated.*

Chrétien was especially proud of the document because it had been created by a largely francophone group of civil servants led by Gérard Veilleux, a rising star in the department of finance. (The idea for it all originated with retired civil servant Thomas Shoyama, one of the so-called Saskatchewan mafia who came to Ottawa in the 1940s and was deputy minister of finance under Chrétien; Shoyama, at Chrétien's request, submitted his views in a memo during the 1980 referendum campaign.) In 1978, at the last round of talks, Ottawa expressed its disquiet about the less than free circulation of goods, services, and workers within the country, but had no corrective proposals to put forward. In the summer of 1980 it was making up for lost time. The plan was to entrench mobility rights (the right to live and work in any part of Canada), revise section 121 of the British North America Act (a loose prohibition of tariff barriers between provinces) to make Canada a more fully-fledged common market, in which the courts would outlaw preferential practices except in emergencies, and to increase federal powers over trade and commerce.

Trudeau described the economic reforms as the most important element in the renewal scheme. (However, nearly all its elements were dropped when the federal cabinet moved unilaterally in the fall.) Ontario was also enthusiastic, seeing it as a way of recycling Alberta's petrodollars and creating broader markets for its own industry. Quebec, Newfoundland, and the western provinces, however, wanted no part of the scheme. Not only did they resent the implicit tradeoff for resource powers; they were aghast at the idea of bureaucrats on the Rideau assuming greater sway over regional economic development in their parts of the country.

By the roadshow's second week, in Toronto, the federal side was growing excited about the strains produced by its new strategy. For the first time in decades, the federal government was making significant demands of its own in constitutional bargaining and the tactic appeared to be forcing the provinces into "an uneasy search for common ground," a report to the prime minister during that period said. But the negotiations were becoming "more like a streetfight than diplomacy," a senior Ottawa official noted at the time; the participants were being pushed further and further into two camps (with the federal tactics helping Morin's goals) and the roadshow was looking bedraggled on a number of important issues. Senate reform, crucial for B.C.'s support, was put to one side

---

*Ottawa's case was helped immeasurably by newspaper headlines during the summer regarding the case of two Nova Scotian roughnecks who were denied jobs on a Newfoundland oil rig because of provincial regulations.

because no headway was being made; on the communications issue the two sides were philosophically at odds; jurisdiction over fisheries had divided the two most powerful Atlantic provinces, Nova Scotia and Newfoundland; and a near agreement on transferring control of family law to the provinces was hanging fire because of the righteous concerns of some provinces (primarily Manitoba) that their neighbours might create Nevada-style divorce havens, and the more pragmatic worries of New Brunswick and PEI that they might not be able to afford the new judges that would be required. On the two decisive issues that came to dominate the next stage — the charter of rights and the amending formula — there was very little movement or apparent interest.

The confidential report of the constitutional ministers to their political masters belied Ottawa's subsequent claim that the charter they imposed in the fall of 1980 had a provincial imprimatur. *Some* drafting was done on a charter by a sub-committee of officials led by the federal deputy minister of justice, Roger Tassé. But the ministers themselves were deeply divided on the principle of entrenchment and did not discuss the specific elements of the charter, except superficially. A poll taken in the final week of the roadshow found only four governments in favour of entrenchment: the central government, New Brunswick, Newfoundland, and Ontario, with the latter two expressing preference for an abbreviated charter that would be extremely limited in scope. All the other provinces were vigorously opposed.

More significantly, in a tentative draft put forward at the end of August, without prejudice to their basic position on entrenchment, the provinces emaciated the federal charter proposals. Legal rights were considerably reduced; all references to non-discrimination and mobility rights were deleted; a remedies provision for breach of rights was expunged, and an innocuous-sounding clause to preserve any rights that "may pertain to native peoples" was rooted out — all with the *unanimous* consent of the provinces. The provincial ministers also refused to make any recommendations on the controversial language rights section. In solemn bureaucratese, federal officials flagged these issues for the prime minister in their post-roadshow summation: "Finally, undoubtedly, the most significant issues remain the concept of entrenchment and the question of language rights."

The amending formula had a similar history. At Alberta's insistence, its preferred formula — which substituted for the rule of unanimity the right to opt out of any amendment which affected existing provincial powers — was put on the table during the week in Toronto and dominated the discussion there and in Vancouver. (Indeed, it came to be known as the Vancouver consensus, to disguise its origins. Lougheed calculated understatedly that any prescription that bore his stamp might not have great currency in Ottawa, or even at Queen's Park.) He had first put forward the formula during the last round in 1978 but there had been no takers. A year later, Newfoundland decided it liked the idea, and momentum for it slowly gathered during the summer of 1980, at least as everyone's favourite second choice. Ottawa's preference, the Victoria formula nearly agreed to in 1971, was a non-starter with the western provinces. British Columbia liked the regional concept of the Victoria formula but wanted it enlarged to include that province as the fifth region, along with Quebec, Ontario, Atlantic Canada, and the three other western provinces.

During the summer, Alberta's formula became the centre of provincial attention, chiefly because it was seen as the only serious alternative to the federal government's plan. But Ottawa and Quebec were curiously detached throughout much of this debate. Quebec officials were adamant that no decision should be taken until the question of the distribution of powers had been resolved. Their federal opposite numbers were enjoying the spectacle of the provinces fighting among themselves over the continuation of a veto for Ontario and Quebec. The only one who appeared disturbed by the ascendancy of the Alberta formula was Jean Chrétien, and for personal reasons. He did not want to go down in history as the man who was federal minister of justice when Quebec lost its constitutional veto.*

---------------------------------- ♦ ----------------------------------

Watching the roadshow unfold from the Olympian perch of his prime ministerial office, Trudeau was convinced that it would not succeed unless the premiers truly believed Ottawa was prepared to proceed without them if there was no agreement in September. So, throughout that wet summer, he took deliberate steps to stir the pot, achieving in the end much more than he had bargained for.

---

*It was only at the very end of the summer, as a consensus around the Alberta formula was jelling, that Quebec voiced its anxiety about financial compensation for those provinces that opted out of the future amendments. At the same time, Ottawa introduced the idea of a popular referendum on the American model, whereby three per cent of a provincial population could petition for a referendum on a constitutional change which the provincial government had rejected. Both notions were simply appended to the final confidential drafts for further discussion, apparently with only cursory interest shown by most of the participants.

During June and July, Trudeau and his external affairs minister, Mark MacGuigan, visited London, ostensibly on other business but primarily to talk about the constitution. Outside 10 Downing Street, Trudeau was coy about his private meeting with British prime minister Margaret Thatcher, an encounter which would return to haunt him when more of what transpired leaked out. MacGuigan, in contrast, was very direct about the necessity of provincial consent, after his discussions with Britain's foreign secretary, Lord Carrington. "I have no doubt that any government [in Britain] would prefer to have as much unanimity as possible [sic] but that is not a precondition." At the Liberal Party's national convention in Winnipeg on 4 July, Trudeau whipped the crowd into a fighting mood in support of his reform plans and attacked the premiers for the "distasteful" horse-trading of powers for rights that many of them seemed to be engaged in. And if any British MPs attempt to meddle in the affair? "Well, all I can say is they better not try!"

In July and September, Ottawa undertook three extensive opinion surveys (each costing more than $100,000) to determine the attitudes of Canadians to the constitutional muddle. Among other things, these showed the public overwhelmingly in favour of the main elements of Ottawa's "package" — patriation, an entrenched charter, language rights, and the free circulation of manpower — but on the whole preferring their governments to come to an amicable settlement of these matters.* The polls also asked, somewhat blandly, if Canadians would like to see the federal government keep the public better informed of its activities. The positive response set in motion the largest Canadian government advertising campaign in history.†

The first advertisements hit the airwaves in late July, just as the ministers and their retinue were assembling in Vancouver for the third week of talks. Over the sonorous tones of an announcer extolling the virtues of sharing and community, dramatic shots of geese in flight and flags snapping to attention mixed with sweeping panoramas of the Canadian landscape in a way designed to woo the public's patriotic impulses.

The provinces were outraged and demanded that the advertisements be withdrawn. Quebec cranked up its own modest campaign (less than $1 million at this point) to counter the federal propaganda. Bob Rae, the

---

*The September poll, taken after the failed first ministers' conference, showed about a third each of those canvassed blamed Trudeau, the premiers, and the climate of mistrust for the breakdown.

†When Parliament reconvened in October, the government tabled supplementary spending estimates requesting a nearly threefold increase, of almost $28 million, for the already flush advertising budgets of a number of departments. In 1980-81, the Canadian Unity Information Office had its publicity budget increased from roughly $10 million to nearly $26 million, the difference being more than the entire dominion of Canada spent in the first year of Confederation.

New Democrat's finance spokesman, quipped, "I'll never look at a Canadian goose again without thinking it's a Liberal in disguise." Certainly, the Liberals were stirring up things beyond expectations. But even the $6 million ad campaign paled beside the next federal shoe to drop — the apparently accidental leaking of a high-level memo from top mandarin Michael Pitfield to his boss, Pierre Trudeau.*

The Pitfield memo, which the prime minister's office downplayed as a routine planning document without official approval, surfaced on the day the ten premiers gathered for their August annual conference, that year in sunny Winnipeg. The memo suggested that Ottawa had already drafted a resolution to the British Parliament in advance of the federal-provincial conference and that it would be proceeding to amend the constitution unilaterally within days of the conference ending in failure, with the hope of wrapping up the whole matter by Christmas.

Nothing could have exacerbated the already severe mistrust between the two levels of government more than this explicit depiction of the federal government's attitude. Not only was Ottawa preparing to ram through changes to the fundamental law of the land without the approval of the other partners; it was preparing to do so in quick march fashion (its main worry seemed to be how to fit it around a budget debate in the fall parliamentary timetable). When the constitutional ministers gathered for four days of talks in Ottawa only days afterwards, their wrath was visceral. They demanded a guarantee that Ottawa would not act alone. A flustered Chrétien refused to give it, maintaining his sincerity in seeking a deal. No one believed him and the goodwill that had been built up over the summer began quickly to evaporate. Morin was openly sceptical but said Quebec would not pull out, in case that gave Ottawa the excuse to go it alone. "Sometimes we feel like a decoration. But it's better to be a decoration inside the room than outside the room," he told reporters. Ontario, the federal government's eventual ally, even circulated a legal opinion by its deputy attorney general, Allan Leal, that unilateral federal action would be against the law. There was talk of a sponsored referendum in the four western provinces to shore up their bargaining position on resource powers. Conservative leader Joe Clark, breaking his silence, floated the idea of a constituent assembly of MPs and MLAs (and a referendum if necessary) to write a new constitution.

The stress of the roadshow's final hours led to a tempestuous three-way debate on the issue which many felt underlay the whole proceedings — minority language rights. Nearly shouting, their faces contorted with rage, Chrétien, Morin, and McMurtry assailed each other's assumptions

---

*The reporter to whom the memorandum was leaked, Aileen McCabe, of the Ottawa *Citizen*, said later she did not feel it had been divulged deliberately. Her source was someone on the edge of the constitutional issue, who probably did not appreciate the full import of the memo.

and positions from their various solitudes. Chrétien and McMurtry charged that Quebec did not care a fig about the French outside its provincial boundaries. But Morin would have none of this holier-than-thou attitude from Ontario, which was still refusing to entrench the right to bilingual trials and legislature debates for its more than 600,000 francophones.

All summer these men had lurched uncomfortably towards a possible accommodation. Now they were poised either to consummate a deal or to retreat sullenly into opposite camps. It would be Trudeau's greatest challenge, his advisers told him. He had either to diplomatically gather the threads of a possible agreement or to demonstrate absolutely that such agreement was impossible. There could be no middle ground, no "near miss," in the jargon of the practitioners: "The [first ministers' conference] is now generally perceived, at least by the media and the public, to be the culminating point in the negotiating process," his advisers wrote in a lengthy memo at the end of August. "The challenge now lies with the federal government to try to bring out [sic] the agreement on a package which appears to be within reach [or], failing this, to show that disagreement leading to unilateral federal action is the result of an impossibly cumbersome process or of the intransigence of the provincial governments, and not the fault of the federal government."

✤

It was in the ninth-floor dining room at the Lester B. Pearson building of external affairs, on the eve of the first ministers' conference, that all the promise and hard work of the summer roadshow came awry. The private dinner, under the somewhat uncomfortable aegis of governor general Edward Schreyer, and from which Pierre Trudeau stormed out, perfectly exemplified the way Canada's political elite does its business, the incredible suspicion and mistrust, the war of all against all.

During the dinner, Morin and Lévesque circulated quietly, asking the other premiers where they intended to be later that night. Without letting on what it was, the pair said they had a very important paper they wanted to distribute; they made each premier promise not to let it out of his sight.

The document was a bombshell that changed the temper of the ensuing conference. Four days previously, Morin was handed a sixty-four page memo which he saw as "a gift from the gods" — the federal government's secret strategy paper for the conference, outlining its motives in opportunistic detail. At first Morin thought it was a ruse to trick Quebec into crying wolf. Discreetly, the PQ verified its authenticity and then for days Lévesque and Morin agonized over what to do. They decided they could not summon the press to publicize their find because it would then seem as if Quebec was out simply to scuttle the Ottawa conference. Yet, if the memo was distributed privately to the other premiers, it could help build a provincial common front and assert Quebec's leadership within it. At the end of the week, it could also be used to confront Trudeau in the final closed-door bargaining session.

As a precaution, the Quebec delegation rented a photocopier when they arrived in Ottawa and in the quiet of their hotel room produced ten copies, destroying the original leaked version. At eleven o'clock that Sunday night, copies were delivered by special messengers to each of the provincial premiers, setting the stage for yet another round in the intensifying war of nerves and mutual suspicion.

The Kirby memo, as it became known after its signatory, Michael Kirby, is a minor political science classic. Thorough, unflinching, and coldly pragmatic, it accurately analyzed the provincial positions on all the issues, pinpointed the questions on which manipulation might be possible and concluded with some advice drawn from an old master:

> *The probability of an agreement is not high. Unilateral action is therefore a distinct possibility.* In the event unilateral action becomes necessary, ministers should understand that the fight in Parliament and the country will be very, very rough. [*Kirby's emphasis*] *For as Machiavelli said: 'It should be borne in mind that there is nothing more difficult to arrange, more doubtful of success, and more dangerous to carry through than initiating changes in a state's constitution.'**

Written by a group of high-ranking bureaucrats just after the summer meetings, the top-secret memo, marked *Ministers' Eyes Only* on every page, was prepared for the priorities and planning committee of cabinet which met over the Labour Day weekend at Lake Louise in Alberta. It was divided into six sections:

I. The first assessed the mood of the talks and noted that the provinces appeared to be moving in two directions, some towards a deal, others back to earlier positions. From Ottawa's vantage, the role of Quebec remained ambiguous — "it has not on balance been an effective

---

*Kirby had jotted down the quote during the summer from a note Saskatchewan's deputy minister of intergovernmental affairs, Howard Leeson, had tacked to the wall of his Regina office. The actual quotation from *The Prince* says there is nothing more difficult than "to take the lead in the introduction of a new order of things."

defender of the interests of Quebec." Ontario was seeking to distance itself from Ottawa on some issues but was still a strong proponent of a charter of rights. The provinces were unanimous on the question of offshore resources and resented Ottawa's reluctance to accept the majority view. The federal challenge was to bring about agreement on a grouping of reforms with something for everyone, or else demonstrate that unilateral action was necessary because of an impossible process.

II. This section set out the federal strategy on each of the twelve agenda items. The most serious issues still outstanding were entrenchment of a charter of rights and acceptance of minority language guarantees. To soften the blow, Ottawa could offer a so-called override clause to allow legislatures to bypass certain rights in a charter, as well as grant delays of up to ten years to various provinces (particularly Ontario) to implement the language sections.

The memo suggested that Alberta would be isolated on part of the resource issue if a deal could be struck with Saskatchewan on jurisdiction over international trade; but it noted that acceptance of the Alberta amending formula would be seen as an important victory for the West and might allay some of the objections if Ottawa proceeded on its own. "It appears likely that one or more provinces would challenge the constitutionality of the federal government proceeding . . . without provincial consent." The key to any deal, it said, was for Ottawa to put the provinces on the defensive over the charter of rights and powers over the economy. The charter was clearly popular and "should be presented on television in the most favourable light possible"; premiers who opposed it should be cast as preferring to trust politicians "rather than impartial and non-partisan courts in the protection of the basic rights . . ."*

Because B.C. was demanding Senate reform (without which it would withold its agreement) and the other western provinces were agitating for greater resource control, "any agreement can only be on a very large number of items"; Quebec was a special case and needed, "if [it] was ready to sign anything," something on the Supreme Court, acceptable wording in the preamble, control over communications, and probably some interim solution on a proposed intergovernmental council, the first step to a remodelled Senate.

"A strategy aimed at demonstrating flexibility and goodwill should achieve such a deal. If it does not, it will at least create the conditions appropriate for unilateral action, for the federal government will have demonstrated that a failure can only be blamed on the provinces."

---

*During the televised conference, federal minister John Roberts made a gaffe while following this advice, asking rhetorically whether the people wouldn't rather trust the courts than the Trudeau government for the protection of their rights.

III. This set forth four possible courses of action for the autumn in the event that the conference failed. The memo noted that "the reform needs to be more than symbolic" to satisfy the promises to Quebec but, at the same time, given the expected opposition, should have something for all regions. The simplest course would be patriation and a charter binding only on the federal government, so that it would not affect provincial powers. A more difficult course would be to bind the provinces to the charter as well. The third alternative would include, besides, those items on which there was near agreement, such as family law, and transfer some powers to the provinces which were rejected only because they did not go far enough (i.e., certain aspects of communications and resources). The fourth "package" would add to this still further by taking for Ottawa those new powers it was seeking to regulate more carefully a central economy. Given the Liberals' lack of representation in the West, the memo's advice was that it would be much easier to withstand a provincial storm over the imposition of language rights in Quebec than tamper with the "regionally sensitive issue" of resources. It suggested that concessions to Saskatchewan (which would be vigorously pursued in the late fall), in order to break up a solid bloc of western provinces, would be a prerequisite for taking action on the third option.

IV. The timetable for unilateral action should be an early recall of Parliament and a swift (two-week) debate on the resolution before sending it off to Westminster, the officials recommended. There would be no room for public involvement; the objective was to free the Commons schedule for other matters, such as the budget and the energy program. Furthermore, "there would be a strong strategic advantage in having the joint resolution passed and the UK legislation enacted before a Canadian court had occasion to pronounce on the validity of the measure and the procedure employed to achieve it." A Supreme Court of Canada decision probably would take from one to two years (it actually took five months), so Ottawa's position should be that this is a political matter on which the courts have no business pronouncing. Remarkably prescient, the Kirby memo predicted that a court might very well decide that "the patriation process was in violation of established conventions and therefore in one sense was 'unconstitutional,' even though legally valid."

V. This section dealt with public perceptions and suggested that the prime minister make a major address on national television and radio to justify any unilateral move. It observed that the soft-sell approach of a "gentle" advertising campaign had proven to be effective and claimed that the only disadvantage was spending taxpayers' funds on such propaganda before Parliament pronounced. Two scripts were appended to the section: one dealt with a job applicant who was turned away because of provincial hiring laws; the other was a recreation of Donald Smith driving in the last spike of the first transcontinental railway. The camera cut to a giant Air Canada 747 racing down the runway towards the viewer while an announcer intoned: ". . . about the only thing in Canada that hasn't changed much is the constitution. Now's our chance to make it right. Make it work. Make it ours."

VI. The memo concluded that it would be politically easier to strike a deal on a relatively large cluster of issues, provided it included a charter of rights, than proceed unilaterally on a small one. Then it quoted Machiavelli's stern warning.

-------------------- 🍁 --------------------

If Canadians ever believed their political leaders shared a common spirit, the first ministers' conference in September 1980 destroyed that fiction. Rather than growing closer through four days under hot television lights, the premiers and prime minister used the platform to articulate, albeit at times admirably, widely differing views of Canada. Backstage it was no different, and the particular and intractable views of the participants led to inevitable failure.

The standard of debate was impressive. There were generous views on both sides — Trudeau's and Lougheed's, Blakeney's, and even Lyon's — provoking syndicated columnist Richard Gwyn to observe after a few days that Canadians were luckier than they thought: "If the two contenders for the world's most powerful office, Jimmy Carter and Ronald Reagan, had joined the horseshoe table in the Conference Centre to take part in yesterday's constitutional debate, they would have ranked, by any measure of verbal agility and of mental acuity, somewhere in the bottom third of the group."

But the opening speeches locked the players into set positions and denied them room to manoeuvre. It was clear to those in the know that Trudeau was following the Kirby script, keeping open both his options. For some, like New Brunswick's Richard Hatfield, this spelled certain disaster. Unlike the other first ministers, Hatfield had enormous emotional capital invested in the constitutional issue. Not only had he been around since Victoria in 1971 (where he recalls Liberal Senator Paul Martin coming to his hotel room in tears afterwards because Trudeau hadn't pressed the premiers hard enough for their commitment there), but he was the only one to be part of the roadshow that summer and he believed — he wanted to believe — that an accommodation was possible this time. Erratic and unpredictable — the *Globe and Mail* editorial board called him "a prancing buffoon" at one point when they disagreed with his constitutional warnings on the monarchy — Hatfield was often splendidly perceptive. And, as even the battle-hardened Quebecers noted, he was one of the few English politicians to understand that province intuitively.

On the Sunday night, after that horrible dinner with the governor general, Hatfield was having a drink in his hotel suite with a reporter when an officious Quebec bureaucrat delivered his copy of the Kirby memorandum. Annoyed at the build up Quebec had been giving this document, Hatfield casually took it into the bathroom with him; he did not read it but left it there to be found on a subsequent visit. It wasn't.

The next day, Bill Fox of the Toronto *Star*, one of a handful of journalists who followed the roadshow from city to city, asked Hatfield about "a document." There was no immediate reply, but later that night, after the opening speeches and some premiers' private gloating later about how well they had "put it to Trudeau," Hatfield called Fox and invited him over to his hotel. By then, one of Hatfield's senior advisers, Barry Toole, had already lent a copy to an old friend, CBC radio reporter Richard Inwood from Quebec City, who also had been inquiring about it. After he had called Fox, Hatfield also phoned Morin to tell him what he had done. Part of the story appeared the next day in Montreal's *La Presse*.*

On Tuesday, the resource issue was the centre of the public discussion but it was dramatically overshadowed by the publicizing of the Kirby memorandum that morning. By noon, the photocopying machines were overheating and the bulky document was being handed out in the far reaches of the conference centre like drugs in a schoolyard.

The revelation of its innermost strategy spooked the federal side and drew them back into a shell. They began to think there was a spy in their midst and the RCMP was called in to chase down the source of the leak.†
On the other side, it forced various provinces into already hardening positions. How could they be expected to negotiate in good faith, they protested, with a government that was so Machiavellian? Publicly they condemned the federal strategy; privately it was a different matter. Robert Normand, Quebec's deputy minister of intergovernmental affairs, later told Kirby that it was a "damn fine" piece of work ("maudit professionel"). For some, like Saskatchewan's Allan Blakeney, it sparked a

---

*Hatfield's motives are difficult to understand. Apparently fearing that the memo would be exposed at the end of the week anyway, he sought to minimize damage at the outset. He maintains to this day that he has never read the whole document and doesn't think much of bureaucratic memoranda in any case.

†It took nearly five months of investigation but the Mounties eventually got their man . . . sort of. The leak was traced to an executive assistant in the department of external affairs, who was confronted and had his security clearance rescinded. The man never admitted guilt and no charges were brought; his job downgraded, he left the civil service a few months later.

personal anguish. Unhappy at being depicted as the object of federal manipulation, he told some of his colleagues he wished he had never been shown the Kirby memo. For him, it appeared to add an extra layer of shabbiness to the whole affair.

All Wednesday was devoted unexpectedly to a debate on the charter of rights. It was, for the eleven first ministers, their finest hour. The political rhetoric fell away as they engaged in a sharp, committed intellectual debate over the value of an entrenched charter and the Canadian legal system. Seven of the eleven are lawyers (Bill Bennett ran the family hardware chain before he entered politics, Lévesque was a journalist, Peckford a high school teacher, and MacLean a farmer). Trudeau knew his subject well and the litany he recited of past wrongs that could be mitigated by a charter of rights was impressive. But Manitoba's Sterling Lyon was also well briefed on the issue and impressed many with a fine legal argument against entrenchment.

Oratorically, the first ministers fought to a draw but the numbers were not with Trudeau. He faced seven provinces opposing entrenchment in principle and three others with reservations about the proposed scheme. On the entrenchment of language rights, the participants were even more divided since the first ministers appeared intimidated by the prospect of political disfavour back home. "From time to time we did succeed to convince each other," Richard Hatfield observed at one point, "but we failed to convince ourselves that we could convince our constituents."

Thursday, the last public day of the talks, had a crammed agenda. It was the only time when tempers flared publicly: Lévesque charged that the prime minister was betraying his promise to Quebec for an overhaul of the federal state. Piddling symbolic gestures like patriation, and restrictive federal concessions, were not what won the referendum, Lévesque declared.

That night, Quebec quietly circulated a second fascinating document to the other provincial delegations. In response to continuing pressure to indicate their ultimate position on various items, and in anticipation of the private session the next day at 24 Sussex, the PQ government had prepared a discussion paper entitled "Proposal for a Common Stand of the Provinces." It was a remarkable and shrewd attempt to compromise on some minor points and to up the stakes dramatically on a host of other, more fundamental, matters.

———————— ✦ ————————

The first premise of the Quebec paper was that the individual items were not negotiable but had been put forward on a take-it-or-leave-it basis. The second premise was that this should be considered as the first stage only; another round of talks must be scheduled for three months time to discuss further devolution of federal powers in a variety of other fields. (These included curtailing Ottawa's spending power, declaratory powers and authority to act for "peace, order and good government," and devolving jurisdiction over culture, social affairs, urban and regional affairs, regional development, transportation policy, the administration of justice, and international affairs.) At that point, if *everything* was satisfactory, the federal Parliament could adopt its address to the Queen in early 1981, requesting a "suspensive patriation" that would take legal effect when the legislatures of all ten provinces approved. Trudeau could have his patriation and a (scaled-down) charter of rights, but the terms would be high. Quebec even tried to sneak in an only slightly watered-down version of its preferred preamble, to suggest a province's right to self-determination: "In accordance with the will of Canadians, it is the will of the provinces of Canada, in consort with the federal Government, to remain freely united in a federation, as a sovereign and independent country, under the Crown of Canada, with a constitution similar in principle to that which has been in effect in Canada."

The other items were equally audacious. On resources, Quebec proposed (to suit Lougheed) returning to the 1979 draft from which Ottawa had pulled back during the current round; on communications, it took the provincial draft rather than the federal one from the summer. Senate reform was postponed until the next round but Quebec proposed increasing the Supreme Court to eleven judges (five of them civil judges from Quebec, at least on constitutional matters) and that the chief justice alternate between an English and French appointment, to which the provinces must give their consent. The provinces would gain control of offshore resources, and Ottawa's demands for greater sway over the economy were reduced to urgings.

The charter of rights was clipped, so that only fundamental and democratic rights would be entrenched (with all existing laws deemed valid); and legal and non-discrimination rights would be subject to legislative overrides. Ottawa could entrench the official languages act if it wished, but minority language education guarantees were to be concluded only by multilateral reciprocity agreements among provinces. (Quebec consented to amend its controversial language law, Bill 101, to allow pupils into English-language schools if their parents were educated in English in other provinces — the so-called Canada clause — which Lévesque would refuse later.) For future amendments, Quebec agreed to the Alberta formula of opting-out on some matters (with unspecified provision for financial compensation) but wanted the Victoria formula, with the Quebec veto, to apply to others.

———————— ❧ ————————

The Quebec paper was shown to the premiers on the Thursday night and then discussed for an hour and a half at a breakfast meeting the next morning in Sterling Lyon's suite at the Chateau Laurier; from there it emerged with the grand title of the "Chateau consensus." However, it was a consensus only in the minds of some, and there was furious backpedalling by several delegations afterwards. Even Quebec the next day somewhat disowned the paper by characterizing it as merely a compilation of positions which, for each province, were not negotiable. In any case, the so-called breakfast consensus was given very short shrift by prime minister Trudeau when it was presented to him later in the living room at 24 Sussex Drive. "No deal. No deal. No deal. Maybe, but with modifications. No deal. Maybe . . ."

After that, there was very little left to say. "We never even got to any horse-trading," a senior federal adviser lamented the next day. The discussions fixed briefly on a more modest proposal: scaled-down resource powers for the provinces, in exchange for diminished powers over the economy for Ottawa, along with a more limited charter of rights, no entrenched language rights, and provincial ownership of offshore resources — but then became lost in an emotional debate between Lévesque and Trudeau on their respective visions of Confederation. The attempt to paste together a more moderate package fell apart because of Trudeau's refusal to consider anything other than full entrenchment of minority education rights or to give way on the offshore issue; plainly he did not wish to create another Alberta Heritage Fund with the coastal provinces.* This last point angered Bennett and Peckford and a brief shouting match ensued between them and Trudeau.

During the lunch hour, Lougheed ordered his car to be brought around without telling the others. He was ready to walk out then but didn't,

———

*It is now a well-known irony of Canadian political life that the idea for Alberta's burgeoning Heritage Fund came from Trudeau, who suggested that some resource revenues be hewed off from general provincial revenues because they were throwing a wrench into the computation of equalization payments, which are based on a federally administered formula that attempts to determine a provincial median. By demanding ownership of offshore resources, Peckford was also seeking to put these revenues outside the equalization scheme and instead, into the periodically negotiated price and taxation systems where there has been a history of federal-provincial competition for larger shares, especially since the mid-1970s.

staying until the adjournment at four. When the others left, Blakeney and Davis stayed behind to do "some missionary work," seeking an even smaller grouping involving family law, communications, and patriation with an amending formula. They also pressed Trudeau to make a constructive proposal on the offshore question. But the prime minister was not convinced that all the others would agree even to this, and demanded one of the federal items in return. The two premiers left to lobby their colleagues over the dinner hour, both believing there was little hope of success. (Davis's officials were given their instructions right away to start working on "the failure speech" for the next morning.)

Over dinner, Blakeney called Lougheed and Bennett; Davis, too, called Lougheed (twice), asked Hatfield to call Peckford, and sent two officials to Hull to deal with Quebec on the communications issue. There would be no deal. When the premiers returned to 24 Sussex at eight, Bennett, Lougheed, Lyon, Lévesque, and Peckford refused to change their positions on the federal agenda items unless the resource and language issues were resolved to their satisfaction.* The premiers eventually left 24 Sussex that night, Friday, 12 September, at nine-thirty. Astoundingly, they came to complete agreement on only one thing: no one was to tell the press what happened until they had made their public statements the next morning. With that constraint, Angus MacLean caused a flurry of excitement when he said cryptically: "I don't think Canadians will be too disappointed in what we have done." Lévesque was profusely apologetic when reporters surrounded his car at his Hull hotel: "If you only know how badly I feel as a former journalist who might go back to the business. I can tell you this . . . (pause) That the consensus is not to say anything until tomorrow morning." He was, he said, only allowed to talk about the weather; and, in his view, the weather was "clear."

✦

It was a tired and testy Trudeau who wound up the constitutional conference, admitting failure. His deadline was still to patriate the constitution by the summer. "But what I can do about [that] now is something I'll have to discuss with my colleagues." He brushed aside suggestions that Ottawa had planned the conference to fail, blaming instead the two irreconcilable visions of Canada — the view of some that Canada is an association of provinces, and his own that the country is "more than the sum of its parts."

---

*Blakeney tried a long shot over the dinner hour, sending an aide scurrying off to find him a copy of the National Energy Board Act. He hoped to convince Trudeau to amend it so as to have provincial representation, believing this might partly satisfy Peckford concerning Newfoundland's long-standing dispute with Quebec over that province's resale of cheap Labrador power to the US. Trudeau was only lukewarm, and Peckford found the idea small potatoes.

Lougheed and Blakeney shook their heads sadly at Trudeau's remarks. It was clear to them that he had not understood their offer of a new partnership. But the differences were brought home dramatically when Brian Peckford stated in his closing speech that the premiers' Chateau breakfast meeting "was one of the most significant hours I have spent since becoming premier of Newfoundland," and that he had come around to preferring René Lévesque's vision of Canada to Trudeau's. Peckford was speaking of the apparently reformed Lévesque, but there were sharp glances around the table at his remarks. Chrétien leaned forward and whispered in Trudeau's ear, "Have you got a bag? I want to vomit." Trudeau's eyes, too, flashed hatred. It looked for an instant as if he was going to reach across the room and shake the Newfoundland premier to his senses. Were there indeed two visions? Or was it the personalities of those who espoused them that had led to this deadend?

"People don't eat constitutions and, for the moment, they are not famished constitutionally," René Lévesque concluded, attempting to dismiss the prime minister's obsession with this issue. Anyway, he added candidly, "I am not the warmest federalist. I preached its replacement by another formula, which I must underline is still there, strongly supported by 40 per cent of the electorate, as a sort of insurance policy for the future."

4
Gentle Seduction:
The Cabinet Decides

"To go Cadillac." Trudeau said he liked the expression. "I will use it. I understand that this caucus wants us to go with the full package. To be Liberal" — he paused for just a moment to let the meaning sink in — "all the way down the line. Not temper our convictions with political expediency. If that is your will, I'm delighted to follow it."

17 September 1980. This was the essence of what the prime minister told his parliamentary caucus.

Sweat trickled down the faces of many in the West Block meeting room that day but not from anxiety. Liberal MPs, recalled to the capital for a special party caucus, four days after the premiers had left town, were determined to force a confrontation. They had returned in the middle of their summer vacation, still wearing the cotton golf shirts and casual attire of the barbecue circuit, and were in a fighting mood. Now they had found their banner — to go Cadillac.

When Trudeau embraced that cause at the end of a long day of emotional debate, they rose as one from the sticky, green vinyl chairs and applauded and applauded and applauded. It was the kind of ovation he received after leading them back to power in February, and, later, following the referendum victory in May. It seemed to go on and on.

Party caucuses are normally for private bitching, presenting an opportunity for the rank-and-file MPs to confront their parliamentary leadership. That muggy day in September, it was more like a war rally. The Quebec members in particular, buoyed by the referendum result and eager to establish a new, more generous set of language guarantees across the land, were passionate advocates of going it alone and entrenching a full charter of rights. Many argued that it would represent a return to true Liberal values; others, more pragmatically, saw it as a vehicle to undermine the Parti Québecois government. The support for unilateral action seemed widespread. Backbench MPs from Newfoundland, New Brunswick, Toronto, and northern Ontario spoke forcefully in favour. Veterans like Bryce Mackasey reminded his colleagues of the bitterness and division of the flag debate during Pearson's day but how it had all worked out in the end. Those members who had reservations wisely chose discretion.

Trudeau had warned the caucus of the consequences of unilateralism. "We might end up in four years time with a magnificent constitution but a defeated government," he had said at the outset. "How do you see your job here?"

"The way he said it, he wasn't trying to push us one way or the other," one MP explained later. "It was just the kind of view the man has."

Hazen Argue, the Liberal senator from Regina who (very briefly) at the beginning of the 1960s led the CCF, forerunner of the NDP, appeared to capture the mood of the gathering. A hulking prairie populist, who, when he talked, whirled his arms and hunched his shoulders like some giant shredder, Argue made an impassioned plea for going first class: don't stir up a hornet's nest for nothing. Quebec MPs nodded their heads in agreement. "Allons-y Cadillac," one chimed in — and the group had its rallying cry.

"The caucus is very bullish," Jacques Guilbault, the Montreal MP and national caucus chairman, told reporters as he came out of the closed-door meeting. "I think they're ready to go to war."

When the House of Commons is not in session, the federal cabinet holds its regular meetings in the Langevin Block just off Parliament Hill. It was here, in the fourth-floor cabinet room, around the old-fashioned walnut table on which the Borden government signed the conscription order during the Great War, that the new Liberal cabinet made an equally momentous decision in September 1980. The failure of the constitutional conference only days before had effectively called the government's bluff. Now it had to decide how large a constitutional package it dared impose on the provinces.

The flash point was the charter of rights. For nearly thirty hours in a two-and-a-half week period, the cabinet struggled with its collective conscience, becoming embroiled in an exercise that was highly personal and intellectually rigorous. From ten in the morning until late in the afternoon (once even into the evening), the cabinet debated the charter of rights clause-by-clause, drawing on the legal and political abilities of its members to fashion a new legislative code for the country and possibly a new platform for the Liberal Party of Canada. Senior officials waited patiently in the antechamber as the hours ticked by and requests mounted for more detailed information on this or that possible effect. Finally, it dawned on the astonished bureaucrats: for the first time in memory, perhaps in history, the elected ministers of the Crown (and a few senators) were themselves actually drafting an important piece of legislation. Inside the cabinet room, what began as a modest proposal swelled into a full-blown charter of rights; some ministers even competed with each other to incorporate various provisos. The debate was intense, full of emotion and therefore wearying. During their arguments, three ministers actually shed tears.

Throughout this collegial soul-searching, Pierre Trudeau stayed curiously aloof and Socratic, wearing the mask he usually reserved for more arcane matters of state, when he genuinely wanted a *government* consensus rather than one that bore his personal sanction. Keeping in check those ministers most closely involved with the issue (Jean Chrétien and John Roberts), Trudeau played devil's advocate on the composition of the charter of rights. Is it right for Canada? Will its disruption of the present legal system be harmful? How will they view it in the West? Relentlessly, perhaps caressingly, he drew out opinions from each of his ministers. He presented no arguments in support of an entrenched charter, leaving that for others, allowing the cabinet to create the momentum. "Don't do this for *me*," Trudeau repeatedly warned. "If you do it, do it because you believe it's right for the country." As the Kirby memorandum had warned, the political battle in the country would be "very, very rough." Although he didn't say it aloud, the prime minister did not want a repeat of 1978 when he girded himself for the same struggle only to discover that his cabinet were not alongside: then, with their four-year mandate coming to an end and the party sliding in the polls, that Liberal administration was not eager for a constitutional fight with the provinces as the prelude to a federal election.

In July, about the time the constitutional roadshow was setting out, Trudeau privately mused to a few close advisers that patriation and a charter of rights only applicable at the federal level would be "a very great victory indeed." But he did not pass on this view to his cabinet in September — at least not as his personal desire. Some would say later that the prime minister effectively seduced his colleagues during those few weeks, but it was an act in which the cabinet was a very willing victim.

Still cocky over May's referendum triumph, the cabinet saw itself as an enterprising new team attempting to reassert traditional Liberal values. There was a nucleus that argued for an image of quiet, good management but they were overwhelmed by those who, infatuated with the notion of making history, demanded initiative and achievement. Fuelling this zeal was the fact that the Liberals were still soaring in the opinion polls, in what appeared to be an extraordinarily long honeymoon. (By contrast, a year earlier over a similar period, the new Clark government had tumbled eight points in the monthly polls and were trailing the opposition Liberals by nineteen.) The Grits were searching for an issue to make their own and the charter of rights fitted the bill. All the polls showed that the charter was immensely popular throughout the country and, besides, it was regarded as being easier to sell politically than complicated energy deals or fiscal transfers, the two other matters on which the cabinet had decided to stake out its political turf.

Back in their ridings, ministers found it was easy to talk about the charter of rights at summer cook-outs and political rallies. The charter was in very high favour in Metro Toronto, particularly among the so-called ethnic communities which form the base of Liberal support in the city; private discussions with the Davis government revealed that they too saw the same political advantage in emphasizing the charter. Perhaps it could even be the Liberals' wedge into barren western Canada, some ministers argued; after all, the idea had been championed in Saskatchewan by both John Diefenbaker and Tommy Douglas in the 1940s and 1950s. The charter of rights was thought to be an invincible political tool, a modern-day Excalibur. As Chrétien often said later to his provincial opponents during the protracted negotiations: "You come out against the rights of Indians and women and the handicapped, and I'm going to cut you into little pieces."

At the start of the marathon cabinet meetings, Trudeau set down two imperatives. He would not use Westminster to transfer powers from the provincial sphere to the federal government ("There would be a revolution if we did that"); and he would not impose obligations on provincial legislatures. This ruled out enforcing official bilingualism on the courts and legislature of Ontario, as many in his party were demanding. But Trudeau's injunction was later broken when the resolution was being scrutinized by a joint parliamentary committee in the winter of 1980-81: increased language and non-discrimination rights for the disabled and native people — cutting directly into provincial legislation — were included to secure federal NDP and backbench Liberal support. The language guarantees, in particular, were sure to contradict Quebec's controversial language law, Bill 101.

Trudeau's cabinet style has traditionally been regarded as that of the sculptured consensus. As a variety of ex-ministers have testified, he was often influenced by the views of others, contrary to the public's image of him as authoritarian. "I've sat in cabinet and cabinet committees with four prime ministers — Mackenzie King, St Laurent, Pearson and Trudeau," former cabinet secretary Gordon Robertson once noted. "And of those four . . . I'd say that Trudeau probably was the most likely to be guided by consensus and the least likely to assert his own views." However, as George Radwanski made clear in his biography of Trudeau, the prime minister's cabinet style is "consensual, but . . ." Or, as Trudeau himself put it: "Yes, consensus-seeking — provided I'm sure that I can share the consensus."

Generally, there has been one exception to this rule. Constitutional reform, national unity, and bilingualism are subjects on which Trudeau exerted more personal control. If the cabinet agreement was not to his satisfaction, or all over the mark, he would say, "Well, I'll have to take this under advisement," and his colleagues knew that in the end he would make the decision himself. The question of national unity was his alone, as external affairs was Pearson's. And there were generally few brave enough to intrude.

This time, though, it was different. Although the prime minister still steered the debate, his superintendence was less obvious and his pleas for support more insistent. When the charter of rights arrived in cabinet, it came largely unencumbered with the background policy documents and preliminary committee work normally attached to important legislation. It was a fresh problem for a new cabinet beholden to Trudeau and well aware of his commitment to such a charter.

Ironically, Trudeau was a late convert to constitutional reform, even though he had always been a forceful proponent of an entrenched bill of rights. In the mid-1950s, as a youngish, left-leaning lawyer working for Quebec trade unions, he promulgated such a bill of rights, partly as a way of defying the excesses of the Duplessis regime. During that same period, while many French Canadian intellectuals were urging Ottawa to combat the oppressiveness in Quebec, Trudeau was, in his own words, "a fierce supporter of provincial autonomy." Indeed, his writings then and throughout the 1960s demonstrate an intellectual and practical aversion to constitutional reform. "The error, especially in terms of strategy, is glaring," he wrote in 1965. "Anyone who really wished a return to greater centralization [would] be only too glad — despite some feigned reluctance — to reopen constitutional negotiations. No doubt a few legal gestures would be made in the direction of Quebec's particular characteristics, but, in all probability, Quebec would receive less than it is gradually obtaining through the force of circumstances."

Like Eugene Forsey, with whom he was well acquainted at this time, Trudeau firmly believed in the creative muddle of existing structures. "Constitutional reforms are . . . a priority among others," he declared as a candidate for the Liberal leadership in 1968. "I said, and I remain convinced, that we would be wrong as Quebecers and French Canadians to invest all our energy in this sphere." The view was as much a part of his personal credo, to cast nothing in stone, as it was a warning to the nationalists in Quebec not to expect a radical restructuring for their benefit. By then, what appeared to be the penultimate round in the patriation conundrum was already underway. Hoping to capitalize on the enthusiasm of Expo '67 Ontario premier John Robarts convened his Confederation of Tomorrow conference in that same centennial year, opening his arms to his neighbour, Daniel Johnson, in an attempt to moderate the growing pains of the Quiet Revolution. Ottawa attended this conference only as an interested observer — the last federal-provincial conference on patriation had ended in disarray only two years before, when Lesage refused at the last minute to accept the Fulton-Favreau amending formula that had been nearly six years in the making.*

But the Robarts conference began a four-year chain of events that eventually led to Victoria in 1971. It was a far-seeing minister of justice, Pierre Trudeau, who set out Ottawa's objectives in the fall of 1967 in a speech to the Canadian Bar Association: "We have reached the conclusion that the basis most likely to find a wide degree of acceptance, and one that is in itself a matter calling for urgent attention, is a constitutional Bill of Rights." The bill he envisaged would be binding on both levels of government and would contain "all the familiar basic rights": freedom of belief, expression, and association, the right to a fair trial and legal procedures, and guarantees against discrimination based on race, religion, sex, and ethnic or national origin, as well as the right to learn and use either of the two official languages. "I can think of no better occasion for seeking to find a solution to the problem of developing a Canadian constitution in Canada — of finally 'patriating' our constitution — than when we have reached agreement on constitutional protection of the basic rights of the citizen." The agenda was his from the outset and it would stay that way, nearly intact, for fourteen years.

------------------- ❦ -------------------

Fifteen of the thirty-three-member Trudeau cabinet in September 1980 were lawyers but only a handful had any experience with constitutional law: Marc Lalonde and Jean Chrétien, who both held the justice portfolio during periods of constitutional reform; and Mark MacGuigan and Robert Kaplan, new ministers who had been languishing on the backbenches for many years. (Kaplan once won a gold medal in constitutional law in Bora Laskin's course at the University of Toronto; MacGuigan was dean of law at the University of Windsor before he entered politics).

Of the anglophone ministers, the latter two would take an active role in promoting the charter of rights per se, but others would be equally vigorous in speaking on behalf of various aspects of it. Gerald Regan,

---

*See Glossary.

Lloyd Axworthy, and James Fleming were all keen advocates of an entrenched charter. Axworthy and Fleming argued forcefully in cabinet for their respective interest groups — women and the multicultural community — but neither group was mentioned in the first public draft. Many of the Ontario ministers — Herb Gray, John Roberts, Jim Fleming, Bob Kaplan, Mark MacGuigan — were so avid about the charter that they nearly fell over each other to contribute to its composition. Roberts was eager to add the new economic powers Chrétien had introduced during the roadshow, but the cabinet thought this was going too far.

The only ones holding back were Jean-Jacques Blais, who feared an English backlash over the entrenchment of francophone rights, and Jean-Luc Pépin, who was prudently quiet during the cabinet debate, sensing a conflict of interest because of his recent co-chairmanship of the Task Force on Canadian Unity, which had advocated a form of special status for Quebec.

The only other cabinet ministers reticent about the charter were Charles Lapointe, minister of state for small businesses, who was worried about the adverse reaction in Quebec if the charter should undercut Bill 101, and Senator Ray Perrault from B.C., who expressed the view of Liberals on the west coast that Canadians don't like to see their two levels of government at loggerheads. No votes are taken at cabinet meetings but the informal tally in the prime minister's office during that September period was 29-4, an impressive show of support for the charter by any standard.

In some respects, the cabinet was psychologically prepared for a charter of rights by the time the issue came before it. Not only was there Trudeau's pledge, but the three main prongs of the new government's program — a national energy policy, rejigging fiscal transfers to the provinces and constitutional reform — were divided among the three senior ministers (Lalonde, MacEachen, and Chrétien), and there was a sense that if one went under, all might. ("In the federal government we fight on all fronts at the same time," Chrétien said that fall when he was asked whether the cabinet was planning any concessions on energy to secure a constitutional deal.) Moreover, the previous spring the government had been shamed into following the Tories' example and had introduced a freedom-of-information bill. So the intellectual barrier of devolving more power to the courts had already been crossed, even if the cabinet's commitment to freedom of information was less than ardent.

Throughout the summer of 1980, the cabinet was kept ignorant of the constitutional stratagems, mostly because ministers had their new portfolios to master but also because of the Trudeau government's paranoia over leaks. A cabinet minister who was not a member of the key priorities and planning committee said later that he could not recall when he was made aware that Ottawa might act unilaterally if there was no deal, but he remembered "feeling surprised at the end of the summer" when it became apparent that so many provinces were opposed.

Trudeau, of course, was kept abreast of the full strategy from the start. Every Friday during the summer negotiations, he received a lengthy memorandum on the week's progress, which he would study over the weekend. On Mondays, Chrétien and the two deputy ministers on the project (Tassé and Kirby) returned to Ottawa to answer the prime minister's often penetrating questions. Chrétien would come back most Thursdays to brief his colleagues at the regular cabinet meeting, but these appear to have been much less detailed in nature than the sessions with the prime minister and more concerned with the tradeoffs that might be necessary to secure a deal.

Ottawa's constitutional tactics were entrusted to a specially created group of eight civil servants and three outsiders, besides Trudeau and Chrétien. The outsiders were Pierre Genest, a senior partner in an influential Toronto law firm; Michel Robert, a well-connected Montreal lawyer who represented the cabinet before the McDonald Commission into the RCMP and who would later carry the constitutional case before the Supreme Court; and Ronald Watts, principal and vice-chancellor of Queen's University, a former member of the Pépin-Robarts task force. The officials were Michael Kirby, secretary to the cabinet for federal-provincial relations; Roger Tassé, deputy minister of justice; Nicholas Gwyn, a public servant in the federal-provincial relations office, who later was seconded to the Royal Commission on Newspapers; David Cameron, a bright young intellectual in the federal-provincial relations office; Barry Strayer, an associate deputy minister of justice with a long-standing academic interest in the entrenchment of rights; Frederick Gibson, another senior justice official, who worked with Kirby in setting up the wage and price control program in 1975 and who was later appointed interim head of the proposed new security and intelligence agency; Reeves Haggan, a well-seasoned bureaucrat who was eventually seconded from the solicitor general's department to the Canadian High Commission in London to field-marshal the negotiations there; and Edward Goldenberg, a Montreal lawyer, long-time aide to Chrétien, and second-generation constitutional adviser to federal governments (his father, Senator Carl Goldenberg, advised Trudeau at Victoria in 1971). At thirty-three, he was the youngest member of the group.

It was this cabal, acting on short notice, that created the document known as the Kirby memorandum in time for the early September meeting of the priorities and planning committee of cabinet at Lake Louise. Acting on his own initiative in mid-August, during a lull in the roadshow, Eddie Goldenberg drafted the first memo on the possibility of unilateral action. It was examined by the special group, set aside while negotiations continued, but then was resurrected a few weeks later for the Lake Louise agenda.

In the turn-of-the-century Rockies' railway hotel, however, the inner cabinet did not focus its attention on that aspect of the document. Instead, the debate ranged over what tradeoffs should be offered to the provinces, with the ministers exchanging anecdotes about the personalities of certain premiers. The long sections of the memo dealing with unilateral action and the post-September strategy were barely glanced at and took up no more than five or ten minutes of the cabinet committee's discussion. In the way of all politicians, they decided the best course was to put off for tomorrow what is not pressing today.

But the failure of the September first ministers' conference introduced a new dimension. Faced with the ardour of the parliamentary caucus after its 17 September meeting, the cabinet was thrust back into the decision-making chamber with new resolve. Some, like Roberts, Gray, and Axworthy, even expressed their personal support of a fully entrenched charter of rights before the cabinet meeting the next day.

The bureaucracy was also generally hawkish, there being what one minister called "a great community of interest" between the senior civil service and the cabinet. Top justice officials grew excited over the prospect of an entrenched charter, almost as if their careers had been building towards such an event. (Some, more closely involved in litigation, fought an unsuccessful rearguard action.) In the privy council office there was a considerable push toward the reassertion of central authority. Those participating in the summer negotiations were already aware that provincial opposition would be considerable. We might as well be hanged for a sheep as a lamb, they advised their political masters.

At the full cabinet session on 18 September, the decision was quickly taken to seek patriation, an amending formula and a charter of rights; the question of whether the charter would be binding on the provinces was left open. The two key issues at this point were mobility and minority education rights, part of the vision of Canada that saw freedom of movement and equality of opportunity for the two founding cultures. Almost without exception, the cabinet felt that minority language education rights must be entrenched in a new constitution, and the senior ministers, MacEachen, Lalonde, and Chrétien, who knew Trudeau the best, were vociferous spokesmen for this view.

After three hours, the cabinet adjourned until the following week. Drafts of the proposed charter were flown to Toronto, where provincial government lawyers pored over them and suggested a number of changes. Liberal MPs were sampling opinion in their ridings and reporting back to various ministers that a charter was still immensely popular. Nevertheless, the decision had still not been taken whether to impose it on the provinces or allow them the option of accepting certain central sections of the charter, as was proposed in the federal government's draft bill (C-60) in 1978. But by the time the cabinet reconvened, the momentum was overwhelming. Chrétien likened it to getting one's tie caught in the wringer. The decision to entrench language rights was the key; after that, everything fell into place. "The minute you take the first step of imposing anything, then you find yourself logically in the position of imposing it all," a senior official observed later. "And the 'all' got larger and larger."

Once the initial decision had been taken on the language issue, the problem became one of finding a way to explain to English Canada why the rights of French schoolchildren were more important than the rights of women and the aged. The political fear was of an anglophone backlash over the extension of French rights, and this provoked Toronto ministers to argue for references to other communities in Canada. The only two women in the cabinet, Monique Bégin and Judy Erola, demanded that non-discrimination on the basis of sex be spelled out explicitly in the charter, but they wanted an affirmative action guarantee to be included as well. Non-discrimination on the basis of age was at first agreed to dropped, agreed to again, dropped, and finally inserted at the last minute in the first published draft of the resolution. Chrétien was still trying to hold down the charter to approximately the levels discussed during the summer, but the cabinet was moving its reach well beyond the flaccid draft produced by provincial officials in late August. A compromise was momentarily struck on the so-called new rights of equality or non-discrimination. At first these were to apply only at the federal level, both because they would infringe the most on provincial jurisdictions but also because they would be a clear symbol of Ottawa's restraint. But already the rallying cry of Senator Hazen Argue, minister in charge of the Wheat Board, was catching hold around the cabinet table.

While Pierre Trudeau allowed himself to be wooed on the charter of rights, he was much more assertive about the matter of the amending formula. Most of the cabinet were not particularly interested in this aspect of constitutional reform, finding it too technical and preferring on the whole to leave it to the prime minister. In the weeks following the first ministers' conference, at the insistence of certain close advisers, Trudeau became convinced of the merits of including an entirely new element: a federally controlled referendum to be used as a tie-breaking mechanism. This idea was strongly supported by senior bureaucrats — Pitfield, Kirby, and (in a slightly more hesitant fashion) James Coutts, Trudeau's principal secretary at the time. It provoked a long, spirited debate in cabinet. Influential figures like Chrétien and Lalonde were against it, arguing that a referendum is a clumsy, divisive technique; having just come through the Quebec referendum in the spring, they did not wish to reopen old sores.

But Trudeau was keen on the notion, and despite significant opposition in cabinet, determined to make it part of the package. The tie-breaking referendum was a completely new force in Canadian constitutional reform. Trudeau became sold on it for a number of reasons: it symbolized the popular aspect of the package, by which the people of Canada would have the final say whenever their governments were deadlocked; it would affect future negotiations, in that the central government could threaten to use a referendum to outmanoeuvre a recalcitrant province; and (most important) it bequeathed to his successor the same trump card that he would use once and for all in the unilateral request to the British Parliament.*

In defending its unilateral initiative, Ottawa repeatedly argued that referenda were an acceptable part of constitutional change in other democracies, notably Australia and Switzerland, and were similar in intent in the USA, where two-thirds of the states have to ratify a constitutional amendment, some of which do so by a representative system of constituent assemblies. Moreover, the Trudeau government pointed out, the success rate for federally initiated referenda in Australia is not high and this example would surely temper the use of referenda in Canada.

The issue of a tie-breaking referendum, controlled solely by the central government, has never been debated in Canada. It was essentially a new idea that Trudeau unveiled in the fall of 1980. However, it had first seen the light in 1950, in Paul Gérin-Lajoie's seminal study, *Constitutional Amendment in Canada*, where the author threw it out casually as a possibility to consider. When he wrote the book, Gérin-Lajoie was a student at Oxford University; he would later be Quebec's minister of education during the Quiet Revolution. In 1950 Pierre Trudeau was a young lawyer, a friend of Gérin-Lajoie, and is cited in the book's acknowledgements as one of those who helped with the manuscript.

———————— 🍁 ————————

It was intended that the final cabinet meeting on the morning of 2 October was to be a short one to approve the printed resolution, which would be made public that night in a nationally televised address. The meeting

---

*There have been two referenda in Canadian history; more accurately, they were plebiscites, which only sound opinion and do not automatically bind a government to action as a referendum does. Both were divisive — in 1898 on prohibition, and in 1942 on conscription — and were largely tools of the executive to get around campaign promises they subsequently wanted to change. There were also two referenda in Newfoundland in 1948 on whether the island should join Confederation. The first was narrowly against, but left the issue unresolved because there was a third option on the ballot — remaining under a nominated commission — and none received an absolute majority. The second was narrowly for federation with Canada . . . and the rest is history.

went on for more than five hours. Trudeau's summation was "immensely fair," one minister recalled. He added up the strengths and shortcomings on both sides. If there was one theme, he noted, it was that of Hazen Argue: why not go first-class? It would be a tough fight. He expected his cabinet to shoulder their share of the burden but he, Trudeau, would lead it if that was what they wanted. There were nods around the table.

The decision of a few days previously was reversed; the non-discrimination rights were made binding on the provinces, subject to a three-year period of grace so legislation could be amended to correspond. The resolution was sent back to the government printer in Hull for the final changes. Trudeau had met privately the day before with Conservative leader Joe Clark and NDP leader Ed Broadbent, briefing them in varying degrees on the government's plans. Surmising correctly, he told his cabinet that Clark would oppose, but Broadbent might be brought onside. That night Trudeau unveiled his plans to the nation.

———————— ✦ ————————

The initial constitutional resolution — it would be amended five times before finally being made law by the British Parliament in the spring of 1982 — contained 59 clauses and an appendix annexing 29 other statutes to the basic law of the land. The charter of rights guaranteed specific freedoms, "subject only to such reasonable limits as are generally accepted in a free and democratic society with a parliamentary system of government," an attempt to walk a tight line between new powers for the judiciary and the supremacy of Parliament. Under five broad headings — fundamental freedoms, democratic rights, mobility rights, legal rights, and non-discrimination rights — the charter was set forth. The official languages act, applying to all institutions of Parliament and the government of Canada, would be entrenched, as would be the right to primary and secondary schooling in English and French on the basis of mother tongue, "where numbers warrant." A commitment to continuing equalization payments from rich to poor provinces would be entrenched, as well as a bland sop to the existing rights (whatever they were) of native peoples, the same clause that had been rejected by the provinces in August.*

For the amending formula, Trudeau proposed two more years of constitutional talks, during which the rule of unanimity would be retained. At that point, if there was no agreement, then his preferred formula (the Victoria one nearly agreed to in 1971, together with the tie-breaking mechanism) would go against that preferred by at least eight provinces

———————

*The initial charter said that it would not abrogate any rights "that may pertain to native peoples."

representing 80 per cent of the population (assuring an Ontario or Quebec veto) in a referendum — winner take all.

Trudeau's bold plan provoked a chain of reactions that no one quite predicted. "We were caught off guard," a senior federal adviser said later. "We knew it would be rough, but. . . ."

For the next thirteen months, the focus would shift away from the large horseshoe table in the government of Canada conference centre, the tournament site for executive federalism. Ironically, the new terrains of battle became the central institutions Trudeau wanted most to aggrandize — Parliament and the courts.

5

Trail-Driving the Dinosaurs (and other Tories)

The Liberals can flip-flop, the NDP can flip-flop, but if we flip-flop, it's with a capital F.

Richard Clippingdale, former senior policy adviser to
Conservative leader Joe Clark.

Dusk on Thursday, 2 October 1980. It is raining, and a lingering humidity makes the capital uncomfortable. In Parliament's South Block, the lights are ablaze in the sixth-floor suite of offices of the leader of the official opposition. When the House of Commons is not in session and the weather is warm, Joe Clark prefers to work here rather than in his Centre Block office on the Hill. South Block — the former Metropolitan Life Insurance Company headquarters on the corner of Wellington and Bank Streets — has better air-conditioning and the leader's entire staff within reach.

The time is seven-thirty. Clark has finished dinner with his two closest political confidantes, chief of staff William Neville and Senator Lowell Murray. The skittish, with whom the Conservative Party is abundantly supplied, would have been inclined to label it a political last supper for the Tory leader.

The week has been an unpleasant one for Joe Clark: on Sunday, a meeting with Quebec Conservatives, who had been squabbling publicly over who controls provincial party funds; on Monday, a tense get-together with Ontario's William Davis, a man with whom Clark has no rapport; on Wednesday, an audience with the prime minister, fraught with slippery portents; and, throughout the week, press commentary on a speech by Liberal pollster Martin Goldfarb, who had told New York advertising executives that the successful Liberal strategy in the federal election eight months earlier had been simply to play on the public's perception of Clark as inept.

Now, in ninety minutes' time, the prime minister is to unleash the dogs of furore across the land by announcing on national television his

78

intention unilaterally to patriate and amend the constitution. The moment Trudeau finishes, Clark must go before the cameras. But to say what? As usual, those who observe and report on federal politics will find a way to see Clark in a risible dilemma. He leads a party that has yet to find a position — or, more accurately, that has found too many positions — on constitutional reform. He is a general forever in danger of yelling "Charge!" and finding himself riding alone to meet the enemy. Alone, and fragged from behind.

Already this evening one flap has clapped and banged overhead like a summer stormcloud, before eventually blowing off in the wind. The word came up to the sixth floor of South Block that the NDP's Ed Broadbent was being allowed to go on the CBC network to say his piece immediately after Trudeau, and before Clark. That had been enough to melt the panelling in the opposition leader's boardroom, but the CBC assured the Tories that their man would follow right behind the prime minister.

Now a second flap is taking shape across Wellington Street, in committee room 307 of the West Block. Members of the Conservatives' constitution strategy group have gathered for an advance briefing on Trudeau's statement: federal-provincial relations critic Jake Epp, Senator Arthur Tremblay, senior policy adviser Richard Clippingdale and caucus staff members Ian Shugart and Kenneth Cruickshank, along with the party's House leader Walter Baker. Their briefing has been set for seven-thirty. Justice minister Chrétien and his senior assistant deputy minister, Fred Gibson, are to be on hand to answer technical questions. The Conservative group has a messenger standing by, waiting to rush the documents over to Clark, Neville, and Murray once Chrétien turns up with them.

The time moves towards eight o'clock. Gibson appears, Chrétien doesn't. No documents. There is an anxious call from a staff member in South Block: where are the documents? The Tories, with no paper in front of them, are playing Twenty Questions with Gibson. His answers are perfunctory. "Is there a charter of rights?" "Yes, there is a charter of rights." "Is such-and-such in the charter?" "Well. . . ." Eight-fifteen, eight-twenty. Chrétien appears, but without the documents. The cabinet, at the eleventh hour, has changed a key provision in the charter* and the documents have had to be reprinted. A few minutes later, they finally turn up. There is no time for a briefing. Epp and the others hurry through the rain to Clark's offices.

Is there worry at the top? Elsewhere in the Progressive Conservative Party of Canada on this damp, muggy evening, there is considerable anxiety. But not at the top. On the sixth floor of South Block, Murray

---

*The cabinet decided to make the equality rights section binding on the provinces, with a three-year grace period for them to make their laws conform.

and Neville have not been waiting for documents; they have been preparing Clark's television statement. The two have had no need of documents, since they have the party's strategy in hand. Whatever Trudeau proposes, Clark will oppose. Whatever the substance of Trudeau's proposals, Clark will try to avoid saying anything about them.

It takes Murray and Neville little time to finish writing the statement's first draft. Clark, as usual, begins rewriting it in his own words. When the group from the West Block rushes in, he is halfway through a response to something they have not yet given him the details of. The Conservatives, seemingly on a wing and a prayer and in their own distinctive way, are about to enter the constitution debate.

The role of the federal Tories in the constitution epic is one of the most dramatic scriptings in modern Canadian politics. By any recognizable yardstick, the party's unstable parliamentary caucus, during those eighteen months, should have ridden off in all directions, unhorsing Clark as leader in the process. The reform of the constitution, with its freight of fundamental values and philosophies, its indelible stamp of Trudeau on every paragraph, was a tool made by Satan to tear the Tories apart. The party's incompatible factions — regional and ideological, single-issue zealots and civil libertarians, blues and reds, dinosaurs and intellectuals — should not have survived it intact.

Yet they did, almost; not until the very end of the affair did the unity of the Conservative caucus peel at the edges. Rather, it was the more homogeneous, doctrinaire New Democrats who publicly and noisily fractured. The Tories, ironically, by staying together, by working effectively as a unit, conceivably handed Trudeau what victory he could claim. If they had not stalled passage — albeit, to some extent, because it was the only course they all could be certain to agree upon — of the government's resolution through Parliament until Trudeau had consented to refer it to the Supreme Court of Canada for a ruling, it is unlikely that he would have met subsequently with the premiers, "one last time," to try to reach an accord. And if he had not been able to go to Westminster with substantial provincial support, it is likely that not enough members of both Houses of Britain's Parliament would have held their noses — in Trudeau's phrase — to place upon the prime minister's package the legal blessing of Imperial sanction. The question is: what amazing glue kept the federal Conservatives together?

In part, it was luck and the mistakes of others — the Liberals, for one example; Ontario's Bill Davis, for another. To a considerable extent, it was the potent presence of Pierre Elliott Trudeau; few things unite the Conservatives as does the pathological dislike of many of the party's

MPs for the prime minister. But, in the main, it was the skilfulness of Joe Clark and the constitution group he gathered around him. Motive is important. Here was a classical case of the "invisible hand" in politics at work. Clark believed in the philosophical rightness of what he was doing, to be sure. But he also had a second reason, a more base one, for feverishly striving to make sure that what he and his caucus were doing met with success. He needed an issue that would sustain his leadership over a party increasingly disposed to dump him. Clark's second agenda was the tune written on the bass stave of the Tories' constitutional polyphony — it was seldom intrusive, but it was always there, always in the ear.

———— ✤ ————

The story begins with the election of 18 February 1980, when Clark's Conservatives, after 259 days of power, were shooed back into opposition. What remained of the parliamentary caucus was psychologically at risk. They were men and women who felt impotent, defrauded of office largely because of the clumsiness (real or perceived, it mattered not a whit in the feeling of it) of their own leaders and, of course, because of the perfidy of the Trudeau Liberals, who had stolen election victory with lies.

Those of us who saw the Conservatives around town in those bitter, late winter days were at times a little fearful for their state of mind. They were sullen, uncommunicative, unfocussed. More than a few of them were spending too much time at the National Press Club bar and too little time on the other side of Wellington Street in their Parliament Hill offices. Others were spending long periods in their ridings, brooding. Almost all were muttering against those within their ranks whom they held responsible for their misfortune — and no one was more muttered-against than Clark. He had two tasks as the days and weeks ticked off to the 14 April opening of the thirty-second Parliament. He had to hang on to his job, and he had to get his caucus back to work.

At first Clark had no sure sense if or when the constitution would rise as a dramatic issue, but there was a weight of probabilities: the Quebec referendum was soon to be held, and Trudeau was back in power — Trudeau with his concrete constitutional views and his Arthurian mission to safeguard the franchophone minority's cultural birthright in all of Canada. It required no gift of prophecy to suspect that the prime minister might reach for the hammer of constitutional reform to beat the separatists, and the provincial power-hoarders elsewhere.

Clark, as he himself acknowledges, is not a strong man on policy. Ideologically, he is a moving target, a political pragmatist; someone who reads people more keenly than he reads books. Journalists who have written about him over the years find it difficult to say what Joe Clark believes in. As he limped out of the February election defeat, Clark felt he knew too little about the constitution issue to grasp comfortably either its content or the political consequences of reform. He therefore made a decision: he and his party had to have an unequivocal position on the constitution.

> *The Conservative Party historically has been very leery of so-called national unity issues. There's a sense around that we lose on it all the time. I* [had] *grown increasingly worried about that wariness, because I think that elections are decided on that issue —* all the time.* *If we're disinclined to have a position on it, we're going to be beaten. Because the other guys do. That is the issue — when questions arise about the integrity of the country, that is the issue. And if we're afraid of bilingualism, if we're afraid of getting caught on something — as we have been, with cause — we put ourselves out of the game.*
>
> *All that became clear to me in '79, and clear to me in government. And I was determined that we were going to carry on* [after the 1980 election defeat] *and work out a respectable position on the constitution, and a different one from what I regard as the establishment Liberal position in Ottawa. I ran into that position. We had it in some of our public servants. It was not there particularly consciously, but it was there, and it affected what they were doing. Some had it consciously.*

There could be no Conservative position at all until Clark and his caucus had gained an education on what reform of the constitution was about. It had to be a position distinct from the Liberals' if for no other reason than that the Trudeauphobes within the Tory caucus would accept no other. Moreover, to achieve an identifiably non-Liberal position on the constitution meant acquiring a view of Quebec that was different from Trudeau's own.

Clark himself was already well on the way to holding such a view. His experience in government and as a political campaigner in French Canada had brought him to the belief that the francophone Ottawa establishment — those whom he saw inhabiting the upper reaches of the Liberal Party and the public service — looked upon Quebec in a different way from the majority of Quebecers. An avowedly anti-nationalist view, it held that

---

*Clark's stress, in an interview with the authors.

the brass ring of success for francophone Quebecers would be won by emulating what the Ottawa group itself had done — reaching outside the Quebec enclave to become leading actors on a greater Canadian stage.

Joe Clark believed that the majority Quebec view was not the product of a 'ghetto mentality.' Rather, it was shaped by cultural pride, having as its main objective the building of a strong society in French Canada's homeland — a thesis that joyously matched Clark's own rhetorical portrayal of Canada as a community of communities.

In setting down that phrase, "community of communities," we come to the nub of Clark's vision of the country, often puzzled over and derided, but little understood — probably because Clark explained it badly and may not have understood it himself; perhaps, as well, because most of the nation's leading political commentators come from central Canada or have attained their career goal of getting there.

No more lyrical description of the phrase exists than Jeffrey Simpson's, in his study of the Clark government:

> *Clark's oft-repeated phrase, "community of communities,"*
> *resonated with harmony and brotherhood. It was pleasing to*
> *the ear, soothing to the mind and even inspirational for the*
> *soul. As long as no one asked what the phrase meant, or how*
> *it should be applied, it stood the test of political rhetoric by*
> *offering no offence and inviting a wide range of*
> *interpretations.*

Simpson went on to say: "Although Clark used the phrase to laud the cultural diversity of Canada, he also applied it to the political realm of federal-provincial relations. It seemed to mean, in his vague definition, that the federal government had grown too powerful at the expense of the provincial governments." The expression must be examined, because if there was such a thing as a philosophical plinth on which the Conservatives' constitution policy was built, "community of communities" was it.

What Clark, going into power, may have thought about federalism, was not what he thought about it coming out of power. One of his first speeches in the 1979-80 election campaign — curiously, a speech never repeated — was a call on his home turf of Spruce Grove, Alberta, for more powers for the national government. Not by accident, one thinks, was the speech made in Peter Lougheed's realm, and what a distant cry it was from Clark's oratory of the election campaign of nine months before, when he had spoken sunnily of a national Conservative government reducing tensions between Ottawa and the provinces — seven of which already had Conservative administrations (Prince Edward Island having just acquired one shortly after Clark took office).

The truth is that nothing in prolonged opposition had prepared Clark and his caucus for the intractability and bloody-mindedness of the provincial governments on any and all issues touching their domains. When those issues arise in federal-provincial relations, as Simpson wrote, premiers turn colour-blind on party hues: "In fact, it is often easier for them to have a federal government of a different political stripe to blame at provincial election time."

By censuring Trudeau and the policies of the federal Liberal government for the demise of provincial Liberal governments, as Clark did in the 1979 campaign ("I have friends. Peter Lougheed is my friend. Bill Davis, Richard Hatfield, Sterling Lyon, Brian Peckford, John Buchanan are all my friends. Who are Pierre Trudeau's friends? Pierre Trudeau [this said with great scorn] has no friends!"), he was choosing to ignore one of the cyclical truths of Canadian politics.

The Conservatives formed the government in Ottawa for most of the nineteenth century. By the 1890s, every Conservative government in the provinces had been ousted. In 1911, powerful Conservative party machines in British Columbia, Manitoba, Ontario, and New Brunswick helped sweep Borden to power nationally. By 1919, nearly every provincial government in the country was Liberal. Canadians, in their crabbed, crofters' canniness, grow suspicious when their provincial governments are the same party as those holding power in Ottawa.

Perhaps Clark never meant "community of communities" to denote more than an affirmation of traditional Canadian pluralism, a pluralism more organic than the boundaries of provinces — Cabbagetown Toronto, Chinatown Vancouver, the Beauce, Cape Breton, Jewish Montreal, oilpatch Alberta, the Canadian Medical Association, the United Auto Workers, and the fact that Canadian journalists tend to know each other from coast to coast. Nonetheless, it is an entirely respectable, political view of the country. It is J.M.S. Careless's notion of the "limited identity" of Canadians. It is Northrop Frye's thoughts in his moving introduction to *The Bush Garden: Essays on the Canadian Imagination:*

> *It is not often realized that unity and identity are quite*
> *different things to be promoting, and that in Canada they are*
> *perhaps more different than anywhere else. Identity is local*
> *and regional, rooted in the imagination and in works of*
> *culture; unity is national in reference, international in*
> *perspective, and rooted in a political feeling. . . .*
> *What can there be in common between an imagination*
> *nurtured on the Prairies, where it is a centre of consciousness*
> *diffusing itself over a vast, flat expanse stretching to the*
> *remote horizon, and one nurtured in British Columbia,*
> *where it is in the midst of gigantic trees and mountains*

> *leaping into the sky all around it, and obliterating the*
> *horizon everywhere . . .?*
> *The tension between this political sense of unity and the*
> *imaginative sense of locality is the essence of whatever the*
> *word "Canadian" means. Once the tension is given up and*
> *the two elements of unity and identity are confused or*
> *assimilated to each other, we get the two endemic diseases of*
> *Canadian life. Assimilating identity to unity produces the*
> *empty gestures of cultural nationalism; assimilating unity to*
> *identity produces the kind of provincial isolation which is*
> *now called separatism.*

The stuff, not of canonical constitution-making, but of literature and soul; it is the nation's loss that Frye was not invited to rewrite the British North America Act.

The federal Tories themselves were hardly inspired canonically as they trudged back to work, on the benches opposite where they had sat a few long months before. As winter slid towards summer in Ottawa, and the constitution issue acquired body, the caucus had scant notion of how to apply anything it might have been thinking about constitutionally to what was going on.

------------ ✦ ------------

11 April. For the Tories, whatever the veils of mystery surrounding the government's intentions on the constitution, they were rent like sea-mist in a bright morning's sun on the day Jean Chrétien told reporters that "renewed federalism" could become the issue in the Quebec referendum campaign. Three days later, Parliament opened with a throne speech reference to constitutionally entrenched rights and language guarantees. The next day, 15 April, Lévesque announced the date of the referendum: 20 May. On 16 April, in a speech in Laval, Jeanne Sauvé, the speaker of the House of Commons, left no doubt that the federal Liberals would use constitutional reform to fight the Parti Québécois. Finally, four days before the referendum, Trudeau made his 'promise' to Quebec. The federal Conservatives were not even a distant blip on any of the major players' radar screens.

Joe Clark assembled a constitution expeditionary force of two political lieutenants, one master-sergeant, and a handful of bright, but very green, privates.

Jake Epp, MP for the southern Manitoba riding of Provencher, was platoon commander — the chief federal-provincial relations critic and chairman of the caucus committee on the constitution. He had not been first draft for the job; Perrin Beatty was. It is no slander against Beatty —

an intelligent, resourceful MP — to say that Clark's choice of him showed questionable judgment. Beatty would have been too young and too Ontario for the task of handling the national caucus on a matter as potentially rumpus-ridden as the constitution. To his credit, Beatty himself recognized his Ontario handicap. Epp was an inspired replacement.

Jake Epp is authentically what his brief biography in the *Canadian Parliamentary Guide* says he is: a high school teacher and former town councillor from Steinbach, the son of a Mennonite clergyman — betokening a small-town, unassuming, decent, thoroughly nice, teetotalling, deeply religious man. As Conservative minister of Indian and northern affairs, he had impressed Clark with his balance, administrative competence, and capacity to see things through — the last a valued quality in Clark's cabinet, many of whose members experienced heady confusion at having levers of power to pull. Epp was not closely identified with any caucus faction. As a Manitoban, he had a foot in each of anglophone Canada's two major solitudes, Ontario and the West. His leader's only anxiety about him was his depth of religiousness, but this concern evaporated once Clark realized that it was a standard by which Epp lived, not a shackle on his thinking.

Senator Arthur Tremblay was appointed intelligence officer; especially, he was the man who could reconnoitre for the Conservatives in the mysterious far country behind the Quebec lines. The previous summer of 1979, prime minister Clark had been forlornly beating the bushes for talented and respected Quebecers to become identified with his administration.* He wanted someone close to him who saw a Quebec that was not Trudeau's Quebec and who could act as a nexus between his government and Lévesque's Parti Québecois. A conversation with Bill Davis suggested Tremblay's name. The Ontario premier had come to know Tremblay in the 1960s when he was provincial education minister and Tremblay was Quebec's deputy education minister and a major architect of the Quiet Revolution. Davis had been impressed.

Tremblay had gone on to be Quebec's deputy minister of intergovernmental affairs between 1971 and 1977 before leaving public service, at age sixty, to teach at Université Laval. Clark offered him a senatorship — to the outrage of *bleu* wheelhorses who knew the rare patronage of a Conservative Quebec Senate seat should be used only as a prize for more carnal party service — and a mission: to seek out a "fresh face" for federalism. Tremblay accepted.

---

*The Clark Tories became embarrassed as the names of those who had turned down his overtures leaked out — notably Pierre Laurin, director of Université de Montréal's Ecole Hautes Etudes Commerciales and brother of Camille, and Justice Julien Chouinard of the Quebec Court of Appeal, later appointed by Clark to the Supreme Court of Canada (thus becoming one of the few items of evidence that the Clark government ever existed).

He was a peculiarly rewarding find for the Conservatives, belonging to the old-school elite of federal-provincial professionals, men such as Gordon Robertson, Claude Morin (whom Tremblay replaced in Quebec's intergovernmental affairs ministry when Morin left, eventually to run for the National Assembly), and British Columbia's Mel Smith. Tremblay was not one of the somewhat fishy Quebecers it was the party's occasional misfortune to attract. Neither was he a *vendu*, nor one of those French-Canadian elitists who held the Conservative Party in disdain. Arthur Julien Tremblay, B.A., M.A., M.Ed., drank beer, spoke English — impeccably after the third Carlsberg — with the kind of Charles Boyer accent Conservatives felt nice about hearing, and he talked of Quebec and the West as having the same problems with Trudeau. He was inclined to pedantry and was considered rather *passé* in PQ Quebec, but Tremblay was precisely the person Clark needed: someone who could intellectually reinforce his own intuitive feelings on the constitution. Clark called him "the informer of the unknowing."

The master-sergeant was Richard Clippingdale, a young Carleton University history professor and a biographer of Laurier, with the open face and manner of an appealing beagle and a nature that can be described as forgiving. Before the 1979 election, the party hierarchy (with Clark's knowledge) muscled him out of a well-deserved nomination in the Ottawa Centre riding in favour of economist Robert René de Cotret. Nonetheless, after a talk with Clark following the February election, Clippingdale accepted an offer to work in the leader's office as senior policy adviser with special responsibility for the constitution.

In the late spring, Epp set about reading everything he could on the constitution:

> The thing we had to face was, first, what was our view of the country — because we were getting tired of the argument that, "Well, you guys have no view. Trudeau's view you might disagree with but at least he's got a view, he's got a feeling of what the country's all about. You guys don't. You say it's a community of communities, it's an amalgam of shopping centres" — all those phrases flew around. Second, we had to blend caucus into a view of the country they could live with. Third, we had to react to the government. And, fourth, we couldn't be seen just to be carrying the baggage of the provinces.

Epp's first, second, and third points were essentially the same: the Conservatives needed a position that was not the government's. His fourth point alluded to the cross borne by his parliamentary colleagues, and he might have added a fifth: that, at least in the short term, the caucus had to set aside what it enjoyed most — the debate over their leader.

Epp's optimism was breathtaking: to chivvy the Conservative caucus into a harmonized view of the *country?* It had not been done before. His first step was to poke the caucus awake and see what happened. He called a first meeting of his federal-provincial relations committee and invited the caucus to attend. Few came, other than the designated core group,* and many of those who did made purple speeches damning Trudeau for what he was doing to the country ("stuff that Conservatives can recite at night like the rosary," said an MP who was there). Little was accomplished.

Step two was to organize a bigger meeting. Epp met Clark to discuss how to get the parliamentary party interested in the constitution. They agreed it was essential for the caucus to get the feel of the issue, to become comfortable with it, before the time came when the party would be required to take a public stand. The two men agreed that the more the caucus talked about the constitution, the better were its chances of arriving at Epp's Parsifalian blended view — one position that would satisfy all 102 of the party's MPs. Clark and Epp also wanted the caucus to feel that, in both of them and Tremblay, Conservative MPs had three people who were following the issue closely and could be relied upon for guidance.

Epp came up with the idea of a caucus retreat at O'Brien House. This rustic, stone-and-timbered mansion, owned by the federal government, stands on a conifered promontory above Meach Lake in the Gatineau hills north of Ottawa. One afternoon before opening prayers in the House of Commons, Joe Clark crossed the centre aisle to ask the prime minister if the Conservatives might borrow O'Brien House for a couple of days. Trudeau said yes.

The Meach Lake meeting at the end of July was critically important for the Tories. The discussion that went on there was as fascinating, in its context, as the debate that the New Democrats were to hold on the constitution a year later in Vancouver. Epp, Tremblay, and Clippingdale, all professional teachers, prepared for it as carefully as they might have organized an undergraduate course.

There was a thick, looseleaf-binder briefing book for each MP, setting down the known position of every government and interest group in the country on each of the twelve agenda items concurrently being haggled over at the summer roadshow by the federal-provincial constitution

---

*Epp had an excellent committee: former ministers David Crombie, John Fraser, Perrin Beatty, James McGrath and Senator Martial Asselin, former Manitoba premier (now Senator) Duff Roblin, and Senator Tremblay. Crombie, Fraser, McGrath, and to some degree, Beatty, were all red Tories.

ministers. Tremblay drew up an options paper, presenting a number of models, and combinations of models, on amending formulae, natural resource ownership clauses, minority language guarantees, rights' entrenchments, and so on. Outside experts were brought in, among them Queen's University political scientist Edwin Black and constitutional law scholar William Lederman. Former Halifax MP George Cooper, a lawyer working as a constitutional adviser to Nova Scotia's Conservative government, was invited, as were two leading members of the party in Quebec: Claude Dupras and Michel Doyon. Perhaps never before had so much careful and intelligent planning gone into a single caucus event.*

The agenda items and their multifarious implications were to be presented in as engaging a way as possible. Tremblay was to be introduced as a major figure at the meeting, a person of stature among Quebec's elite, now shaping the Tories' position on the constitution. There was to be no attempt by the organizers to reach decisions, to push the caucus into any set position; Epp felt that would be dangerously precipitous. He wanted the caucus to come to agreements step by step, leaving no one behind disgruntled and unsure, no one who later would bolt from the ranks. It was Epp's contention that opposition parties which take big public decisions before the time is right become big public targets, and are eventually deserted by their more faint-hearted adherents.

One final piece of business had to be dealt with before the Meach Lake conclave: Epp and Clippingdale had to go and spy on the roadshow. They hovered in hallways, foyers, hotel rooms, and bars (Epp drinking ginger ale), first in Montreal's Hotel Meridien complex, later in Toronto's Harbour Castle Hotel, doing their utmost to winkle out of provincial delegations what was going on in the closed sessions. Each night they phoned Clark with a progress report. It was an instructive experience for the two men, more for what they learned about the dynamic of constitution reform in Canada than for what they found out about what was happening.

They discovered that representatives of the federal and provincial executives considered the federal Tories to be non-players in the game. Epp and Clippingdale were frozen out on information: what they were told was generally accurate enough; they simply were not told much. Almost plaintively, Epp kept reminding the provincial delegations of the spectre of Trudeau unilateralism, admonishing them: "You are going to be the players until whatever the government is planning hits the House. If it is not in keeping with what you want, then we will become the players, and you will be crying for our help." Prophetic, but it didn't help him much.

---

*Epp later noted that he probably spent more on the constitution — an estimated $100,000 — than anyone on Parliament Hill except Chrétien, who controlled the Canadian Unity Information Office's advertising budget.

What they did learn of substance (supplemented by Tremblay's intelligence from his Quebec sources) led them to the conclusion late in July that the roadshow was unlikely to be successful. Epp told Clark in one report that it was turning into a cosy cadre of federal-provincial professionals who were not accomplishing much. Clippingdale, much later, used the metaphor of the British-Argentine dispute over the Falkland Islands. They were doing a lot of talking about a lot of things, he said, but sidestepping the central issue of sovereignty, merely going through the motions on the central questions of whether or not to agree on patriation with an amending formula, whether or not to agree on entrenching a charter of rights, whether or not to agree on language guarantees, leaving those decisions for the first ministers in the fall. As Epp, Clippingdale, and Tremblay made their final preparations for Meach Lake, they were just about convinced that Trudeau was going to opt for unilateral action.

───────────── 🍁 ─────────────

Early on the morning of 29 July, five days after Parliament recessed for the summer, forty-odd Conservative MPs and a few senators drove into the Gatineau hills. They gathered around the enormous dining table of the secluded old house and made ready to learn about the constitution. Epp, Tremblay, Clippingdale, and Clark were pleased with the size of the turnout.

The agenda called for an opening plenary discussion, at which Tremblay would present his options paper; then the group would split into three to talk about national institutions, division of powers, and rights and freedoms. Tremblay's options paper was so successful in stimulating discussion that the group decided unanimously to stay in plenary session. Besides, Epp had realized from the initial comments that differences within the caucus were so fundamental, and the level of knowledge so uneven, that sending them off to talk about specific issues would have been of little value. The Meach Lake Tories, *en masse*, were not yet ready to get past step one: patriation.

It was obvious throughout that the caucus felt nervous about the constitution question, fearing that, somehow, the government was going to outwit them — for instance, on the economic union proposals that Chrétien had presented to the roadshow. It is worth recording — at some length — who said what in the economic union debate. It shows both a many-minded caucus and a caucus with a number of members whose view of the country did not often stray from that of Trudeau.

Westerners went one way. Vancouver's John Fraser, the Tories' fisheries critic, made an impassioned defence of Bill Bennett's objection to Canadian Pacific of Montreal attempting to buy control of British Columbia's forest giant, MacMillan Bloedel. Fellow Vancouverite Pat Carney, an economist, worried about the economic disfranchisement of regions and sub-regions. Joe Clark asked rhetorically how far the federal government would go in its homogenizing assault on the country. It was part of the Canadian reality, he said, that provincial governments discriminated in favour of their own citizens; they were also more accountable to their voters than was Ottawa.

The Ontario members argued the opposite. Michael Wilson, former executive vice-president of a Bay Street investment house, said the government's economic proposals were right; Canada was in danger of balkanizing its own market. Kingston's Flora MacDonald spoke of the irony of Nova Scotia and Newfoundland having discriminatory legislation to protect jobs for their own residents when people from those provinces had populated large parts of Upper Canada. John Bosley, scion of an old Toronto family, wanted to know why there should be restrictions on his buying land in Prince Edward Island. John McDermid, whose constituency overlapped Bill Davis's provincial riding, said the party would have a difficult job opposing the economic union proposals in Ontario ("It's easy to be a Canadian, living in Ontario."). Perrin Beatty scolded provincial governments for their power-mongering: "If we're going to err on any issue, let's err on the side of Canada. Politically, it would be a mistake for us to go to bed with the provinces. Trudeau would like nothing better than some popular issue to take to the country in a referendum."

Still others took positions that belied regional stereotyping. Saskatchewan's Ray Hnatyshyn, the former energy minister who had been man-in-the-middle in the Alberta-Ottawa-Ontario oil price fight, argued that the Conservatives as a national party should not be seen to be saying ready-aye-ready to the provinces. Newfoundland's Jim McGrath thought Brian Peckford's discriminatory job legislation was in violation of the existing constitution, and he spoke of the 55,000 Newfoundlanders living in Toronto, and another 12,000 living in Fort McMurray, Alberta. Manitoba's Jack Murta agreed with him.

There was a pervasive feeling that the constitution debate had been reduced to a federal-provincial power struggle; and although the rules of the country were about to be changed, the federal opposition parties were being asked to rubber stamp whatever agreement was reached by the federal-provincial executives and submitted to Parliament. Later, John Fraser touched at the heart of what was bothering the Tories:

> *Here I was, a member of the privy council, a member of the opposition, an eight-year MP from British Columbia. And I was going to have visited upon me . . . a deal made by only the executives of the various provincial governments and the executive of one party in the House of Commons. No one else was going to get a look in.*

During the discussion on Quebec, Tremblay, by all accounts, put on an admirable performance as French Canada's Solon: instructing, displaying patience and equanimity. He presented Quebec in the context of western nationalism. He disarmed people, willingly conceding points about the intransigence of the Parti Québecois government.

One dramatic moment came on the second day at about five o'clock in the afternoon. A western MP suddenly pounded the dining room table and shouted: "What's Quebec ever done for us, for the country?" — the unmistakable implication being that "us" and the "country" were one and the same: English Canada. Tremblay had not spoken much that day, but he immediately waved his hand at Epp, chairing the discussion, who cut into the list of speakers and gave the senator the floor. "I don't intervene very often in these things," Tremblay said. "But I thought it might be appropriate to make the point that my people had been calling themselves Canadians for two or three hundred years before the rest of you borrowed the term." It was the right comment, in the right tone. Everyone laughed, including the table-thumper.*

———————— 🍁 ————————

Epp, Tremblay, and Clippingdale achieved their initial objective at Meach Lake: they had planted the seed of interest and seen it take root. They had demonstrated their own skills; no one could complain that the constitution issue was being stage-managed by Clark and his cronies. The three of them had been given a mandate to continue their work, even though it was an apprehensive mandate, full of prohibitions against Epp and Tremblay stating views publicly, especially those favouring what the Trudeau government was doing. Last, but not least, they had learned a lot about caucus feelings.

Begin with the disparate elements of the Tory caucus. There was what was known as the dinosaur wing, a group of political odds and ends branded by its Trudeauphobia. If Trudeau were to stand up and pledge support for something the Conservatives had just agreed to, this group would oppose it. Among its members (during the constitution debate, at least) could be counted Prairie MPs Dan McKenzie, Gordon Towers, Douglas Neil, Toronto's John Gamble, Nova Scotia's Lloyd Crouse, and the late member for Leeds, Tom Cossitt.

The caucus also had its single-issue zealots, people for whom such matters as abortion and property rights dominated all thought.

There was the serious right-wing — MPs such as Vancouver's Ron

---

*Joe Clark later said: "I'd been cajoling the caucus into a kind of grudging acceptance of Quebec, but Arthur started changing their minds."

Huntington and Nova Scotia's Elmer MacKay — who strongly objected to giving federally appointed judges power over legislatures to adjudicate rights. James McGrath initially supported this group on the charter but later changed his mind.

Finally, there was the group known as the progressive Ontarians, perhaps half the province's 37 Conservative MPs. They leaned towards Trudeau's proposals — particularly the entrenchment of a charter of rights — and found it painful to be opposed to things they considered not only intellectually attractive but politically sound. With them, for the most part, was the balance of the caucus's red wing.

All told, not a blendable bunch of people. They were not going to come together easily on unilateral action by the prime minister. They were not going to harmonize at all on the charter. On the other hand, Meach Lake had produced a consensus-in-progress on favouring patriation and had come up with something very close to a consensus on not wanting to be perceived (in the words of one senior party member) as being "owned by the provinces." It may not have looked like much. But, for the Tories, it was evidence that they could talk to each other and even have a measure of agreement on a national issue.

With Clark's earlier rhetoric on his provincial premier "friends" consigned to the ashcan of history, the Tory caucus view of provincial governments in the summer of 1980 was not flattering. At best, they were seen as friends of convenience; at worst, the provincial governments were regarded as a nuisance because the press and the public tended to see the federal Tories as their little buddies. As for the caucus view of individual provincial Conservative governments, it varied from province to province but occasionally bordered on the venomous.

Many in the caucus were still smarting over the buffeting Clark's government had taken from Lougheed and Davis on the oil- and gas-pricing negotiations. The relations between Davis's people and Clark and his entourage had been tart for several years; the Queen's Park view of them as amateurs rankled the Clark Tories. Western MPs resented being treated as country cousins by western governments, particularly Alberta's. Clark's office intensely disliked Peckford and talked about New Brunswick's Richard Hatfield as King Flake. Friends, indeed. As for Quebec, despite all his efforts, Clark led a caucus which had little understanding of French Canada and which in many ways felt antagonistic towards it.

And, of course there was the bass continuo of Clark's leadership, unrelentingly weaving its melancholy counterpoint. Through July and August, his hold on his job deteriorated from uncertain to precarious. The party's national director, Paul Curley, sent him a memorandum telling him he was dead in the water, with more than 60 per cent of the party membership opposed to his staying on. The party's hierarchy was arguing over when (not if) to hold a leadership review vote. Against that backdrop, Epp, Tremblay, and Clippingdale organized a third meeting, set for late August in Toronto's Royal York Hotel.

They wanted to convene in Toronto for three reasons: to show the party flag for the first time since February in the city where they had lost the last election; to show a federal Conservative alternative to constitution reform in the region most supportive of Trudeau's intentions; and to provide a handy location for the large number of southern Ontario MPs. Howsoever, the Royal York was where the Conservatives made their major mistake of the whole constitution epic.

Epp's caucus committee had earlier discussed the idea of a constituent assembly and had liked it. The notion was that reform of the constitution would be taken out of the hands of the federal and provincial executives and given over to an assembly of government and opposition politicians from Ottawa and the provinces. If necessary, the assembly's eventual proposal would be put to the people by referendum.

The constituent assembly idea would satisfy complaints made at Meach Lake that the federal opposition parties were not being allowed to participate in the rewriting of the nation's rules. It had links with tradition: among the fathers of confederation, who worked on the British North America Act from 1864 to 1867, were opposition politicians. A constituent assembly would not be as contentious a forum as a federal-provincial executive conference and thus stood a better chance of forging an accord on the redistribution of powers. It was an answer to the almost certain prospect — as things appeared in late August — of unilateral action (something upon which Tremblay was leery of having the caucus focus its, or the public's attention: "If we spend all our time discussing unilateral action, that will give a cast of legitimacy to it. Basically it should be thought of as unthinkable"). It would satisfy the public's desire to see the two levels of government stop fighting and get on to matters the public considered more important, especially the state of the economy. Proposing its creation offered the Conservatives a stance on the constitution that easily would be recognized as different from the positions of the provincial governments and the Trudeau Liberals.

On each one of those points, Epp and his constitution group had made the correct analysis. But they took the wrong action. The MPs attending the Royal York meeting discussed the idea in closed session. Late in the afternoon, they opened the doors, called in the press, and Clark gave a speech in which he proposed the constituent assembly and the possibility of a referendum to ratify its work. Speech and proposal were an instant dud.

One of Lowell Murray's maxims is that you can never tell how an issue will cut until you bring it out in the open. The assembly proposal underestimated the public's keenness to get rid of the constitution. For months and months, they had been hearing their federal and provincial governments bicker about it. Now they were hearing Clark say: "Whoa. Back up. Undo it all. Let's start afresh."

The constituent assembly was an idea whose time had passed. The message signalled was, "Here's Joe . . . late again." It was a large blunder, proof of Epp's warning that opposition parties which take big decisions provide big targets for others to shoot at. Clark's speech — calling for more participation by the federal Parliament, exactly what his caucus members had been saying they wanted — underscored Tremblay's fears: it was interpreted by the press to mean that Clark was favouring some kind of federal unilateral action. The only good thing politically about the constituent assembly idea was that it allowed Clark to say *something* about the constitution. Otherwise, the day at the Royal York had not been good.

❦

September. For every yin there is a yang. The failure of the first ministers' conference in the second week of the month liberated the federal Tories from several problems. In one swoop, many of the matters on which they did not have a position were either taken off the game board or could be moved now to one side. The departure of the premiers from Ottawa, grousing, and the signals emanating from every cranny of the capital that Trudeau was going to go it alone, at last gave the Tories their issue: process.

Process is Canadian constitutional shorthand for the way things get done. Process lies at the bottom of Trudeau the Wood King's mystic riddle: "Who speaks for Canada?" and the delphic Lougheed's grim reply: "We all do." If you propound a model of Canada as a federal state of balanced, more or less mutually exclusive jurisdictions divided between the provincial and national governments — where one side cannot change the rules of the federation without the agreement of the other — then you make an argument on process. If you believe that the national government is the only government representing all Canadians, and therefore has the political legitimacy to act alone, to break an impasse, to change the rules in the absence of a rule-changing framework in law, then you make another argument on process. Joe Clark, leader of the federal Conservatives, the party of the outer regions (in spirit if not always in geography), took process argument number one. It was such a natural route to take.

It should be understood that throughout the spring, during the summer roadshow, and throughout the Meach Lake and Royal York meetings — setting Clark's speech and the constituency assembly proposal aside —

the party's leadership had said next to nothing publicly about the consti-tution. That was the wish of caucus. Epp's comment to reporters after Meach Lake, for example, was a model of circumspection. Talking about the constitution, he said, was a long, slow process. Period. Now, with unilateralism, the federal opposition parties were to become players. The forum was no longer to be the federal-provincial conference; it was to be Parliament. Clark was upon the moment when he would have to take a position. He could no longer wait for his caucus to "blend". The task was to pick the position that had the greatest hope for harmony.

Clark had to oppose Trudeau; otherwise he would lose his dinosaurs, lose his party in the West and lose his job. He could not oppose the substance of an entrenched charter of rights; that would cost him the progressive Ontarians and probably his job. He could not support the substance of the charter; that would lose him the support of everyone except the progressive Ontarians and the rest of the caucus red Tories — as well as cost him his job. The safest group to deny gratification to was the progressive left wing; they were the most susceptible to reasoned argument. The safest issues to take a stand on were process and the amending formula; both, happily, could be made to fit Clark's "commu-nity of communities"concept. There really was not a great deal of head-scratching on the sixth floor of South Block about what to do.

"Community of communities" was to be brought to the defence and preservation of Canadians' "limited identity" and — bass continuo — to Joe Clark's job as leader. The warcry was to be that Pierre Trudeau must be stopped from forcing Canadians into his straitjacketed vision of the country.

The line was clear on process: even the Ontarians could be brought to oppose unilateralism. The Victoria amending formula — Trudeau's fa-vourite, with its individual vetoes for Ontario and Quebec — had not even been discussed seriously at the roadshow, and was anathema out-side central Canada. The Vancouver consensus amending formula — with its opt-out "checkerboard" provisions, and its requirement that a constitutional amendment needed the approval of the national Parlia-ment and at least two-thirds of provincial legislatures representing at least 50 per cent of the population (meaning that Ontario and Quebec would veto if they opposed an amendment together, but not necessarily if one acted alone)* — had the most support in the Tory caucus.† The Vancouver consensus wasn't tidy, but neither is Canada. The Tories' constitution group were a little woolly on the formula's provision for

---

*See Glossary.

†The Kirby memorandum suggested that the federal government also could have lived with it. But some of Clark's advisers, notably Lowell Murray, urged the Tories to be cautious in endorsing it.

financial compensation for those provinces opting out of an amendment, but were content to let time bring clarification.*

——————— ❧ ———————

On 30 September, Clark had just begun a speaking tour in northern Ontario. The prime minister's office telephoned and asked if he could meet Trudeau the next day.

Neither Ed Broadbent nor Clark likes the prime minister. Broadbent and Trudeau have a certain intellectual rapport; Clark and Trudeau don't even have that. They have minimal contact. Not once had Trudeau invited Clark to 24 Sussex Drive; not once had he invited Clark to his office or to dinner to discuss the state of the nation.

One previous encounter still rankled in the opposition leader's mind. In 1978, Trudeau had asked Clark to come down to his office (their Centre Block offices are on the third and fourth floors respectively, in the south-west corner of the building) to talk about the leak of secret documents to Conservative MP Tom Cossitt. The prime minister wanted Clark to invite Cossitt to Clark's office where he would be confronted by the solicitor-general and the commissioner of the Royal Canadian Mounted Police. Clark had refused, and had been suspicious of prime ministerial invitations ever since.

Clark descended the steps to Trudeau's office on the afternoon of 1 October, convinced the prime minister was going to try to manipulate him in some underhanded way. The meeting was brief — no more than twenty minutes. Trudeau began by asking for confidentiality. Clark replied that he would discuss whatever the prime minister said to him with his constitution advisory group. Trudeau then proceeded to outline his broad intentions on the constitution.

There would be unilateral action to break the federal-provincial deadlock and make good on the promise to Quebec. Trudeau did not give details; rather, he spoke of a number of actions the government might take (this was not entirely dissembling on the prime minister's part; the cabinet was still making up its mind on what should be done). Clark asked how Trudeau thought his action would be received in the West. Trudeau replied that someone else was going to have to worry about the West, not him. Clark asked if Trudeau was sure of his legal ground on unilateralism. The prime minister replied that in strict law there was no problem. He said there was constitutional jurisprudence on the activities

---

*The Conservatives almost underestimated the importance to Quebec of financial compensation. Although they proposed it as an amendment to the resolution — it was not in the government's initial package — they did so desultorily. Not until the final debate in Parliament did the Tories, wishing to be champions of Quebec, turn financial compensation into a steamy issue.

of the former colony of Southern Rhodesia that ran counter to what the Canadian government was intending to do, but he implied that the reference was too exotic — and, indeed, there was hardly a parallel — to be taken seriously. Trudeau asked for Clark's support; the opposition leader gave no commitment.

That night — the eve of Trudeau's broadcast on national television — Clark threw a party at Stornoway, the opposition leader's official residence, for Conservative MPs and their spouses returning to the capital for the beginning of the next parliamentary session. Epp and Clippingdale were there. Clark took them aside and told them about his talk with the prime minister, emphasizing Trudeau's comment on the West.

The following afternoon, the team all gathered in the South Block boardroom; Neville, Murray, Clark, press secretary Jock Osler, Epp, Tremblay, Clippingdale, and House leader Walter Baker. Clark again recounted his exchange with Trudeau. The boardroom group went over where the caucus stood, and what position Clark could take that would best mirror where the caucus stood. There was little debate, little disagreement, few worries.* The meeting ended in the early evening. Clark, Murray, and Neville went off for dinner, a last matey breaking of bread before going over the top of the trenches.

———————— ♣ ————————

Thursday night, 2 October. The prime minister's statement before the television cameras was lyrical, beguiling, compelling. There was to be action on the constitution, taken alone by the federal government. There was to be a charter of rights and freedoms, enshrining in the country's supreme law the noblest values Canadians wanted for their nation. There was going to be no more intransigence tolerated from the provincial governments. Trudeau would not bargain "freedom against fish, fundamental rights against oil, the independence of our country against long-distance telephone rates."

Shortly before the prime minister's address, Joe Clark completed his own statement. The constitution team and House leader Baker heard what he was going to say. There were no disagreements. They watched Trudeau speak on television. Clippingdale telephoned Hugh Segal, Bill Davis's chief political aide, to tell him the position Clark would take. Clark took the elevator to the lobby of South Block. He walked the few hundred feet east on Wellington Street to the National Press Building, entered the theatre and took a seat on the dais with the washed-out blue backdrop and the Canadian flag behind one shoulder. He put on his unctuous, public frown and began.

———————————————

*Almost the sole concern was how the press, the provincial governments and Quebec opposition leader Claude Ryan would react.

Unilateralism, he said, was divisive. It was damaging to the country, a betrayal of those Canadians who had believed Trudeau's promise of renewed federalism — especially those Canadians who had voted against Lévesque's sovereignty-association. The referendum mechanism Trudeau was proposing "lets Ottawa write the provinces out of the constitution." The amending formula that Trudeau wanted (the Victoria one) was regionally discriminatory.

Then, tough words: "There are times when a government proposes to act against the essential interests of the nation. At such a time, the role of the opposition leader is not to submit to the government but to fight for the larger interests of Canada. The Trudeau government has a majority in Parliament. It will not be stopped unless the people of Canada can be aroused to the abuse — to the potential damage to our country — that the government now proposes. . . . My colleagues and I accept our responsibility to the longer term interest and stability of Canada. We will lead the fight in Parliament. . . ."

It was a deliberately harsh attack. Bass notes and treble notes on the Tory staves sounded together. Joe Clark would be as tough as Pierre Trudeau; he would be a champion of his own vision of the country.

The charter of rights had not even been mentioned. A reporter asked if Clark thought the stand he was taking would be popular. The opposition leader replied: "The majority of Canadians may not be with me yet," but added that as more and more Canadians saw the threat to Confederation that the prime minister had posed, they would come over to the Conservatives' position.

———————— ✦ ————————

On Friday morning, 3 October, and for a number of days thereafter, the mildest word to describe the Conservative caucus was nervous. Nervousness is intrinsic to the opposition politician's mentality; his job is to oppose, but so often he cannot be sure if what he is opposing is wrong. Trudeau had sounded good. The charter of rights, as every poll showed, was politically attractive. Television is not kind to Clark. There was a widespread feeling within the caucus that he had overdone it, been too bombastic, that his statement had been clumsy, and (less forgiveable) that he had not explained his position well. A number of Ontario MPs, in particular, were genuinely surprised at the acerbity of his words.

It is interesting to speculate on where this nervousness in the caucus would have led if Bill Davis on that Friday had not dropped a bomb at Queen's Park. The federal Conservatives knew the Ontario government was going to support Trudeau's resolution, but they were not prepared for what Davis had to say. There had been no hint from Segal, in his conversation with Clippingdale, about what was coming. What Davis did was to call on federal MPs and senators to reach beyond "narrow partisanship" and back Trudeau's national objectives — a statement instantly interpreted by the federal Tories as a slap at Clark's leadership. Driving the message home, seemingly, one of Davis's aides sniffed to a *Globe and Mail* reporter: "We had genuinely hoped Clark's response would be more moderate, containing some opposition and some support."

If Joe Clark had disturbed Queen's Park by what he said, it was as nothing compared to what Bill Davis's statement did to Clark and the federal caucus. Most leading Ontario MPs instantly went to ground and could not be found by the press. Enough of the province's members made their way into public print, however, to leave no doubt as to the agony the premier's words had caused.

St. Catharines' MP Joseph Reid equivocally equivocated: "I might be riding the fence at this moment." Paul Dick, an eastern Ontario member, did not mince words: "I'm going to wait until caucus [meets] and see if it can convince me to follow my leader." Asked by a reporter, somewhat naively, what would happen if Clark insisted on unqualified support, Dick snorted: "Tough!" William Kempling, from Burlington, said people in his Dundas hometown had thought Clark's TV statement "seemed kind of hard-nosed". An unnamed Ontario MP was quoted as saying: "It's not a [federal] leadership test because of what Bill Davis has said. It's Joe who has drawn the wagons into a circle for a battle. No one else has."

The most surprising comment came from Walter Baker, who had been one of those in the sixth-floor boardroom, privy to what tack Clark was going to take. Baker acknowledged that he and his leader were not entirely of one mind on the issue, carefully adding that he was "convinced that differences between us are not profound." Walter Baker was very nervous.

But the Davis bomb was just that, an explosive mistake, and one so recognized within a short period by Davis's own advisers, who quietly put out the story that the implied challenge to Clark had been unintentional, and that Davis had not read the statement carefully enough in advance. Its initial effect had been to spook the Ontario Tories; its longer-term effect was to push many of them closer to Clark's position. They did not like opposing the Trudeau resolution or Davis, but they liked even less being embarrassed by what they saw as the Ontario premier's public attack on their caucus and their leader.

Clark, Epp, Neville, and Murray were like firefighters rushing from blaze to blaze in those first weeks after the TV statements. Press comment was mainly against Clark. The twitchy Ontarians needed handholding. Federal cabinet ministers were going out across the land to make speeches, give interviews, talk to editorial boards. The Conservatives mobilized. Leading Conservative MPs, Epp in the vanguard, set out on the same public-opinion-moulding campaign. The uncertain members of the caucus had to be persuaded. They were reminded that the leader now had staked out a position, and that a flip-flop — a word to conjure recollections of the Clark's government's notorious policy reversals — would look appalling.

Clark's caucus supporters marshalled an array of sparkling arguments to win over their doubting colleagues. No Canadian political party with a sense of history could accept one government acting unilaterally to change the rules of the federation, especially without Quebec's approval. The constitution issue presented an opportunity for political realignment between Quebec and the West, both of which held the same grievances against the central government. The Progressive Conservative Party could be both the architect and the beneficiary of that realignment.

Some of the provincial governments were slow to respond. In the case of Brian Peckford, the Conservative cause was not being helped by what Clark's people considered the Newfoundland premier's stupid and immoderate statements. Nova Scotia worried Clark's senior advisers. George Cooper, advising premier Buchanan on the constitution, was trying to find out what there was in the Trudeau resolution that the Nova Scotia government could live with; Buchanan himself was being reluctant to take a stand.

But probably Clark's advisers were most worried about Claude Ryan. They felt the Quebec Liberal leader should have been speaking out conspicuously for Quebec's federalist nationalists; instead, they saw him agonizing privately and dissembling publicly. One night, Lowell Murray drove across the Ottawa River to the Gatineau valley community of Kirk's Ferry to spend an evening at the home of political scientist John Trent. Trent was one of the principal authors of the beige paper, the Quebec Liberal Party's blueprint for constitutional revision.

Murray wanted to know what was going on with Ryan. Trent explained some of the political difficulties with the provincial caucus in Quebec City, but he failed to allay Murray's brooding. For Murray, personally, it was the command of history that the Conservative Party — having mortally wounded French Canada with the execution of Louis Riel and hurt it with a hundred smaller cuts since then — should resist unilateral constitutional change if the governing and opposition parties of Quebec opposed it.* Clearly the Party Québecois government was hostile. But an alliance with the Quebec separatists — *alone* — was hardly sustainable in the Conservative caucus. Before the caucus would let any of the party's leaders talk about the Tories being on the side of Quebec, Ryan and his Liberals would have to declare their opposition. Ironically, the federal

---

*Obeying that command, Murray voted against the final resolution. Ryan, by then, was adamantly opposed.

Tories, so concerned about being seen as mouthpieces for the provinces, were trying eagerly to coax provincial people to be spokesmen for Clark.

Gradually the days of worry slipped away. The parliamentary party began scoring points in the Commons debate and winning procedural battles as the constitutional resolution moved into the committee stage. Conservative MPs also were seeing public opinion inch its way toward them on the process issue: unilateralism was becoming unpopular. Playing the treble notes of the Tory initiative, Epp demonstrated his talent for consensus-building. He called together his constitution committee almost every day, welcoming any member of caucus who could attend (and many did). He made sure that it was known widely that strategies would not be embarked upon until they had first been run through the committee. That was of major importance in the uneasy October ambience; there could be no suspicions within caucus that Clark and his inner circle were stage-managing the constitution issue.

The longer the Conservatives could avoid arguing substance, the longer they could avoid the danger of falling out with one another. If a caucus vote had been taken at any point in October or during most of November, a majority would have opted to have the party boycott the parliamentary committee that was to study the resolution — the *Trudeau* resolution — clause by clause, or at the least resist dismissing the charter.

Epp won a narrow mandate to take part, a mandate quickly strengthened by the skilful performance of his committee members and by the ham-handedness of the Liberals and their defeat on the issues of strictured deadlines and televised committee hearings. Epp himself was impressively deft. When Senator Jack Austin, the Liberals' strategy chief on the parliamentary committee, sat down with his Conservative and NDP counterparts to arrange for the appearance of witnesses, he was amazed that Epp agreed to hear first from nationally known individuals and groups who would speak in support of an entrenched charter. Austin saw Epp falling for the Liberals' scheme to sell the charter so thoroughly to the public that objections to process would be dismissed. But Epp regarded it as an opportunity to sway the minds of Tory MPs opposed to the charter, so that the remaining threats to caucus unity would be swept away.

Later, he, Tremblay, and Clippingdale came up with another device to "blend" the caucus on the charter — what Epp called "our Achilles heel". The device was called "rerouting". It allowed Epp to tell the parliamentary constitution committee on 20 January that it was "the popular will that we have a charter of rights and freedoms for the Canadian people embedded in the constitution" — a position many miles distant from the majority view of caucus two months earlier that the party should boycott discussion of it.

Rerouting meant Parliament would vote in favour of the charter but not include it in the resolution sent to Westminster. The resolution would ask only for patriation of the BNA Act with an amending formula. Once the BNA Act had been patriated, Parliament would recommend the charter to the provinces as the first constitutional amendment, with no provision for provincial opting out if the amendment achieved support from the required number of provinces.* The Liberals called it intellectual dishonesty: either the Conservatives were for the charter or they were not. But the Grits did not have the untethered bulls in their caucus that the Tories had in theirs.†

Meanwhile, the process issue allowed Clark to take a firm stand in clear opposition to Trudeau, and helped him unite his caucus. Clark — with Tremblay as cerebral mentor and Epp as dextrous puck-handler — felt at ease with the issue, probably more comfortable with the constitution than he had felt on any other major policy matter. Still, there were clouds. . . .

———————— ❦ ————————

Murphy's Law — what can go wrong, will — tends to govern relations between the Ontario Conservatives of Bill Davis and the national Conservatives of Joe Clark. The bonds between the two groups are complex and intense. There are all the connections of close siblinghood: a familiarity that is at once affectionate and nasty. The Ontario Tories are the most federally minded of provincial Conservatives, as Ontarians are the most federally-minded of Canadians ("It's easy to be a Canadian, living in Ontario"). The national party's base of support for programs and money is in Ontario. Ontario Conservatives have seldom refused to dispense patronage to federal Tories whom the national party wanted looked after (but who couldn't look after themselves). The essential Conservative organization in the province is the same for both parties. What this propinquity means is that, when ill-will breaks out between them, it does so usually with the double-mean enmity of a house divided.

Let us return to the summer roadshow, and Epp and Clippingdale on their mission to gather intelligence. The Ontario delegation was friendly, polite, willing to meet with them. But Epp and Clippingdale got the impression that their Ontario cousins were being less than frank with them, refusing to acknowledge them as players in the game. They felt

———————

*Under the Vancouver consensus formula.

†But that didn't mean the Tories were free entirely of disingenuousness. Under "rerouting" via the Vancouver amending formula, the charter would be voted on by each provincial legislature, all of them likely to be dominated by majority governments. That opened the door again for the provincial executives to barter rights against fish, oil, and long-distance telephone rates. The Conservatives argued that provincial executives would not be able to withstand the pressure of their publics for a charter of rights. Maybe yes, maybe no. See Lowell Murray's maxim.

the Davis delegation would just as soon tell them to shoo-fly. At one point, Epp asked Tom Wells about official bilingualism — the extension of section 133 of the BNA Act to give the French language legal status in Ontario's legislature and courts. The federal Liberals want to see section 133 applied to Ontario. Should the Ontario and federal Conservatives have a common position, Epp wondered. Wells said the prime minister would never impose section 133 on Ontario; he said Queen's Park and Ottawa have an "agreement". Shoo-fly.

Move forward a few weeks to 10 September and the first ministers' conference in Ottawa. Davis is there, of course. He heads a minority government but in the next few months would be calling an election. This speech at the conference's morning session left the slight impression that Ontario might accept section 133 in the interests of national unity. It took nearly two hours for every premier to have his say (Davis, by precedence, had spoken first). In that time, an edition of the *Toronto Star* had appeared with the headline: "PM plans French status for Ontario."

Wells came up to Epp, sitting in the observers' section of the government conference centre, and asked agitatedly if Epp had heard of the *Toronto Star* story. Telephone calls were going back and forth between the Ontario delegation in Ottawa and the Ontario Conservative Party in Toronto. When the last premier finished speaking, Davis requested permission to clarify a point in his speech; he said he did not intend to leave any impression that Ontario would accept section 133. What of the "agreement" between Queen's Park and Ottawa? The *Toronto Star* story is no doubt wrong, but the political success of the Ontario Conservative Party over the years is attributable to being prepared against surprises and upon maximizing resources.

Epp, Clippingdale, and Tremblay were invited to dinner to talk about reconciling differences. The federal Tories, who were shoo-flied in the summer, might be needed in the winter in a parliamentary debate on a unilateral resolution that imposes 133 on Ontario.

They met that night in Ottawa's best-known eating place of political intrigue, the Canadian Grill in the basement of the Chateau Laurier. Wells and Hugh Segal were there for the Ontario side. By coincidence, it happened to be the night of a federal byelection in Hamilton West, a long-time Conservative seat made vacant when Lincoln Alexander was rewarded by the Ontario government with the chairmanship of the provincial Workmen's Compensation Board.

The dinner was a serious, intense affair. The Ottawa Tories wanted to make Queen's Park understand the feeling of the country beyond Ontario. Tremblay, in his orderly, logical way, laid out the issue. He came to the heart of Ontario's concern: whether Trudeau would impose official bilingualism. "You have become as selfish as the rest of us," Tremblay said, speaking as a Quebecer. "That is okay. But don't ever say that you are speaking for Canada when, in fact, you are speaking only for Ontario." It was a pregnantly thoughtful moment — jarringly interrupted by the arrival from the next table of Eddie Goldenberg, Chrétien's assistant. He had bounded over like a puppy to talk about the first returns in the byelection.

The group waited for him to finish talking and go away. Tremblay picked up his theme. Ontario, he said, had now become a province *comme les autres*, grasping for whatever it could get, fearful of losing its traditional power in Confederation. Wham! Back came Goldenberg with more by-election news. Not good, not good, he blurted; the Conservatives are in trouble. The table waited for him to go away. Again they tried to recapture the mood, ease back into their discussion — Wham! Goldenberg returned once more.

Finally, they signalled the maitre d' and asked if they could have a private room. The group was shown to a small room behind the Canadian Grill's stage. It took time for them all to settle in, to pick up the mood of the discussion once more . . . Wham! Goldenberg found them, and reported that the Conservatives had lost the seat to the Liberals. The federal people could have shot him. Murphy's Law.

Not much came of the dinner, either.

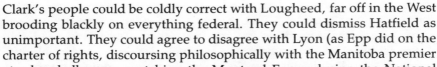

Clark's people could be coldly correct with Lougheed, far off in the West brooding blackly on everything federal. They could dismiss Hatfield as unimportant. They could agree to disagree with Lyon (as Epp did on the charter of rights, discoursing philosophically with the Manitoba premier at a baseball game, watching the Montreal Expos during the National League playoffs). They could try to forget that Peckford existed, and even be a little pushy with Buchanan and MacLean. They could do none of those things with the people at Queen's Park. The ties were too close.

The relationship between Queen's Park and Clark's office began to sour soon after he won the national party leadership in 1976. The original reasons for the coolness have blurred, but essentially they were rooted in mutual mistrust. Clark wanted Davis's Big Blue Machine kept at arm's length from the federal party; he resented what he considered a kind of aunty-ish condescension from Queen's Park. Clark and his circle suspected a certain number of Davis's people of badmouthing Clark to the premier (in particular, the Clark group had doubts about Davis's deputy minister in the premier's office, Ed Stewart, suspecting him of being a closet Liberal).

Moreover, Clark's people were still disgruntled over Queen's Park's behaviour in the oil- and gas-pricing dispute. In turn, Queen's Park had thought Clark's henchmen were amateurish in office, and lacked appreciation of the political niceties — for example, Lowell Murray's decision to direct a government advertising contract to a firm that had contributed a modest $5,000 to the federal party, rather than awarding it to the Big Blue Machine's own Camp Associates. Moreover, there is a distance between Davis and Clark that they have never been able to overcome. They do not communicate well with each other; they do not have the same style; they cannot put their feet up together. Neville and Segal developed a standing joke about their leaders. Each time after Davis and Clark had met, Davis would go to Segal and Clark would go to Neville, and they'd ask the same question: what the hell was that all about? Neville and Segal would get together, agree on what the meeting was about and report back to their chiefs.

On the constitution, there was no doubt that Davis accurately assessed the general Ontario feeling, which was that the national government was fine, the charter of rights was a good thing, and let's stop all the talk and fighting and get on to something important. That political acumen, however, elicited charges of cynicism from the federal Tories, accusations that Davis was doing no more than reading the bottom line of his polls in advance of an election campaign and pandering to the swing voters of Toronto and other cities — the same swing voters who had defeated Clark's Conservatives in 1980.

There also was a more generous Ottawa Tory view of Davis, one that accepted his constitution position as respectable but yet flawed by an imperfect understanding of what was happening elsewhere in the country. In fact, the Queen's Park people — in particular Segal — accepted a process argument on the constitution antithetical to Clark's: federal-provincial negotiating had become pathological; the two orders of government were indulging in an increasingly tawdry power scrap; the integrity of some of the provincial premiers was questionable; Ontario's attempts at conciliation and statecraft (Davis had made some overtures in September) had gone for naught; the only way out of all the negativism at the bargaining table was unilateral patriation. Moreover, Hugh Segal, the product of Jewish Montreal and the major intellectual influence on the premier on the matter of the constitution, was a genuine believer in strong central government (as incidentally, were McMurtry and Wells).

The federal Conservatives might have been more accepting of the Queen's Park position if Davis's people had not become so irritatingly aggressive about it. First, there was the premier's statement the day after the television announcements. It sorely aggravated anti-Davis feelings among western MPs (Ron Huntington of Vancouver, for example, delivered a stinging attack on Davis in caucus) and generally made life uncomfortable for Ontario members. Western MPs were opposing

Trudeau on the constitution and that, in the West, was being on the side of the angels. Ontario MPs were not only opposing "their" premier; they were resisting a constitutional proposal that was politically attractive to most of their constituents. They didn't need Davis making things worse for them.

There were other annoyances. Bill Neville became incensed one night, watching Wells and Roy Romanow on CBC's *The Watson Report*. Wells, in Neville's view, was parroting the straight Michael Kirby line. Neville called Segal the next day and angrily complained.

Segal himself infuriated the federal caucus, particularly Western MPs. He was accused of being the main author of Queen's Park's constitution policies, of being the puppet-master of Wells, of being in bed with Kirby, of working hand-in-glove with Ottawa Liberals at the federal Conservatives' expense. When the federal Conservatives read the Kirby memorandum, they got in a twist over a passage that singled out Queen's Park (and who else but Segal) as warning the federal government that a unilateral package would not stand up against concerted political opposition; thus the Liberals would be advised to run fast with it to Westminster. Treachery.

Segal further appalled the federal Tories by arranging for Darwin Kealey, Ontario's assistant secretary to the cabinet for policy, to be seconded briefly to Kirby's federal-provincial relations office. It was an established program to transfer provincial public servants into the federal mandarinate temporarily to foster greater understanding between Ottawa and the provinces. But the federal Tories did not consider Kealey an ordinary public servant. He was a very political public servant — a member of the Big Blue Machine who had run twice as a candidate for the provincial party.

The Queen's Park position on section 133 provoked charges of hypocrisy from the federal caucus. Here was Davis calling on all Canadians to welcome a constitutional charter of rights, the same Davis who had consistently rejected constitutional language rights for Ontario's 600,000 francophones. The federal caucus was ruptured briefly on the issue when David Crombie and John Fraser spoke out in the parliamentary committee in favour of extending section 133 to Ontario, and Senator Asselin offered to move an amendment imposing section 133 on Ontario if the Liberals would support it.*

Ill-will between the two Conservative parties reached the point where it threatened self-interest. Late in 1980, national party director Paul Curley

---

*The Liberals did not take the senator up on his offer. The Conservatives, grudgingly, later found a way to avoid the issue on principle: the same principle of process they had adopted for the whole constitution, i.e., that the basic structure of federalism should not be weakened by the arbitrary acts of one legislative level.

and Ontario federal caucus chairman Michael Wilson flew to Toronto for a meeting in Davis's office. Attending for Ontario were the premier, the ubiquitous Segal, Eddie Goodman, Camp Associates' Norman Atkins, and Patrick Kinsella, Curley's counterpart in the Ontario party.

Davis let it be understood that he would be calling an election soon and that he did not want any bumpiness in his relations with the federal Conservatives; indeed, he hoped for their enthusiastic support. It was further made clear that the Ontario Conservatives would not be campaigning directly on the constitution; indeed, they would stay clear of the subject, and it was assumed that the federal Conservatives would not be highlighting their constitutional differences with Queen's Park. Finally, it was understood that Davis would be giving Clark the strongest support he could muster in the upcoming federal leadership review vote.

These "understandings" were somewhat less than a *quid pro quo*. It would have been unthinkable for the federal party not to support the provincial party in an election (many of the Ontario campaign workers were both federal and provincial party members). Moreover, it would not have made sense for Davis to do anything else but publicly support Clark's continued leadership (and by the time the meeting was held in Davis's office, the premier had already spoken out in support of Clark). Whatever the premier's political ambitions on the national stage, he was not ready to act on them, and they would not have been served by the federal party at that point decking itself out with a new leader. Rather, the purpose of the meeting was to minimize the risk of unpleasant surprises, and to maximize resources — hallmarks of the Big Blue Machine's efficiency.

A second noteworthy meeting was a dinner at Stornoway in January. Queen's Park's Kinsella, Atkins, and Segal, and Ontario party president David McFadden, sat down with Clark and his inner circle. It was just before Davis called his election. The "understandings" reached at Stornoway were similar to the "understandings" reached in Davis's office, with the additional detail (some recall) that Davis would send a letter supporting Clark to every delegate who would be voting in the February leadership review, and would make a special effort to get Ontario delegates into Ottawa where the vote would be held. Constitutions are constitutions. Politics are politics.

----------- ❦ -----------

There were few unsatisfactory endings for Joe Clark's Conservatives and the constitution. The parliamentary committee debate on section 133 was over and done with before Davis called his election. There was little mention of the constitution in the Ontario election campaign. Clark campaigned for Davis. Davis carried out his promises of support for

Clark. Clark was able to make much use of his own performance on the constitution to convince delegates of his worthiness. Material distributed to delegates by the party executive said that now was not the time — in constitution mid-debate — to change leaders; Trudeau would use it against the party, and it was the federal parliamentary party that was frustrating Trudeau's constitutional plans. Clark's purplish public utterances — his bass motif — detracted somewhat from the nobility of the Conservatives' cause. But that increasingly had become his style.

The parliamentary party, in its battle for a less regionally discriminatory amending formula, succeeded in creating public understanding of and public support for a complex issue, no easy feat. Finally, the Tories' filibuster in the Commons in March and April of 1981 — a piece of parliamentary pyrotechnics — derailed the government's constitutional fast freight to Westminster and rerouted the resolution into the Supreme Court. The eight-day procedural trickery blew apart the government's timetable. It ended on 8 April after an astonishing bargaining session between Trudeau, Clark, and Broadbent on the floor of the House of Commons. After the decision of the Newfoundland court of appeal, the prime minister, acknowledging that the Tories had brought all government business to a halt, agreed to suspend debate on the resolution until after the Supreme Court of Canada had ruled on its legality and constitutionality. It was the *de facto* end of unilateralism. The Tories had won on process.

Only one incident marred their victory — the April accord of the gang of eight. The federal Conservatives felt that they had struggled titanically to make room for the provincial governments, only to have the eight come to Ottawa and make what Clark's people considered an asinine offer: patriation, with not even a mention of the charter of rights, and an amending formula the federal government could not possibly accept. "Our whole strategy had been to create some kind of window for federal-provincial consensus," a senior party member said. "And then these guys arrive in town and lay down that. The April accord was an embarrassment to us."

Clark met Lougheed in Ottawa; he came out of the meeting and, turning to an aide, said: "Are we living in the same world as they are?"

In November, when the caucus finally got to pronounce on a resolution agreed to by the federal government and nine of ten provincial governments, only seventeen of the 102 members voted against it. And at the end, Robert Stanfield, the national party's former leader, asked a group of Conservatives whenever before had the party had a single position on the constitution. The people around him smiled, and shook their heads in happy amazement.

6
Grit in the Pure Left

. . . for how we live is so far removed from how we ought to live, that he who abandons what is done for what ought to be done, will rather bring about his own ruin than his preservation.

Niccolò Machiavelli, *The Prince.*

November in Vancouver. The shankend of the year, 1980, is upbeat for west coast New Democrats. Michael Harcourt, a bald, gangly, thirty-eight-year-old lawyer, municipal councillor, and sometime provincial NDP candidate, has been elected mayor, whipping the political right on both the working-class east side and the well-to-do west side of the city. Ed Broadbent, former professor of political science at Toronto's York University, and federal leader of the NDP since 1975, has flown out from Ottawa for a victory celebration.

Even in the rainy winter months, this most playful of Canada's metropolises lures eastern visitors into a civilized abandon. Following the victory party, Broadbent has gone off for dinner at Nibbles, a trendyish uptown restaurant owned by fellow New Democrat Laurier La Pierre, television interviewer and flamboyant Québecois transplant. With Broadbent are his new executive assistant, Norman Simon (a former trade union official, who landed on Parliament Hill just as the constitution bomb dropped), west coast party organizer Sharon Vance, and the diminutive, boyish MP for Vancouver-Kingsway, Ian Waddell.

During the meal, Waddell and Broadbent tangle in hot debate over the federal party's position on the constitution. Their voices rise like smoke to heaven; their language grows blue. Simon, embarrassed, tries to shush them, but both are having too good a time to be shushed (not for nothing is Broadbent called Rent-a-Rant by the production crew of CBC's "As it Happens").

Waddell is an acolyte of British Columbia Supreme Court Justice Thomas Berger — he was one of the lawyers on Berger's Royal Commission into the effect the proposed Mackenzie valley pipeline would have on the lives of northern native peoples. Waddell warns his leader that he will break party ranks and oppose the Liberals' plan to patriate and amend the constitution unilaterally, unless Broadbent gets Trudeau to accept an amendment to the charter that will recognize historic aboriginal rights. Broadbent, who faces a badly divided parliamentary caucus less than two months after he has committed his party to the support of Trudeau's resolution, retorts that Waddell should make up his mind what he is: a politician or a single-issue zealot.

The politician, Broadbent argues, has an obligation to the whole community he serves. Is Waddell saying he will reject a constitutionally entrenched charter of legal rights, of democratic rights, of equality rights, simply because he cannot win satisfactory wording on aboriginal rights? If that is Waddell's position, Broadbent says, then he should quit politics and pick up again as a lawyer, defending the causes he supports. As a politician, he has a responsibility to serve the broader public, a duty that transcends his personal values and objectives. By now, Broadbent can dispense this particular thesis with his mind on automatic pilot. It is the argument he has used time and again with his caucus since some of its members, especially those from the West, grew mutinous over his constitutional pact with Trudeau.

The Nibbles debate rolls on after the plates have been cleared, interrupted only by solicitous enquiries about the desirability of further post-prandial *pousse-cafés*, and, at one stage, by Waddell dispatching the waiter, whom he once defended on a marijuana charge, to fetch Broadbent a cigar. At last, emotions released and intellectual muscles oxygenated and stretched, the party gets up to leave. Customers at surrounding tables break into applause. *Very* Vancouver.

Those members of the NDP who are students of socialist history live in horror of factionalism on the left, regarding it as the debilitating disease of their end of the political spectrum. It is a pathology far more melancholy than, say, the chaos that regularly afflicts the federal Conservatives, whose problem, in essence, is merely that they have become the mainstream party of perpetual opposition in Canada. Tories fight with the almost happy macho mindlessness of boys in a schoolyard, but dissidence on the left is religious in its intensity — in the commitment and viciousness of its divided camps. Such is what struck the NDP on the constitution issue.

The federal caucus ruptured publicly after months of trenchant, and enervating, internal dispute. By February, 1981, the three prairie provincial parties, led by the country's one NDP government at the time — Saskatchewan's — had parted ways with the federal leadership after a rude and bitter falling out. The full federal party later would split apart at its July convention, nearly four in ten delegates voting against what Broadbent had done. The personal abuse exchanged by party members on opposite sides of the issue rose to shameful levels. Friendships were broken, collegial bonds severed. At times, the party tore at itself with a meanness it would have considered too uncivilized to use on Tories or Grits.

If one goes in search of the spark that set off the conflagration, it is not necessary to look much beyond Ed Broadbent and his principal advisers. On the night of 2 October 1980, Broadbent followed Trudeau and Clark on national television and offered his party's general support for the federal government's resolution. He did it with the best will in the world. Alone of the three national party leaders, the NDP leader took his position on the constitution with no secondary agenda tucked in his back pocket.

Broadbent was a popular public figure who had no need to demonstrate his leadership capabilities. He believed he led a party that could — in all its branches save Quebec's — come to grips with, and uphold, the resolution's substance. He was embarked upon no burning mission. He was trying neither to encase his footprints in the nation's history, nor to prove that he could bloody the nose of every provincial premier on the block.

But Broadbent lacked the radar — built into Joe Clark's brain — that should have warned him that all his colleagues were not going to salute when he said salute. He lacked it because, unlike Clark, he had had no need to develop it. In the assessment of one senior federal party member, the grave tactical error Broadbent and his advisers made was to agonize over whether unilateral action was philosophically correct; they paid insufficient attention to "endgaming" — to the political effect of Trudeau acting unilaterally. Joe Clark, the professional politician and wily survivor, could never move without first checking upon his western nationalists, without first scanning the range, course, and speed of his Trudeauphobes. Ed Broadbent, the academic political theorist from Oshawa, could accept neither western political alienation nor Trudeauphobia as sufficient intellectual barriers against doing what he believed was right for the country and correct by his party's standards.

The federal NDP leader genuinely liked the pith of the Trudeau package, seeing it as something fundamentally matching his party's historic policy. Broadbent believed that first ministers' conferences were utterly useless as a negotiating mechanism for revising the constitution. He believed that one-time-only act of unilateralism — something that finally would give the country a framework in law for future constitutional change — was the only way out of the political stalemate. More: he believed that his caucus was behind him, and that the provincial parties, except Quebec's, were all either with him or travelling in the same direction. Broadbent was not wrong; he just wasn't right.

As leader of what had become an overwhelmingly western parliamentary party (27 of 32 MPs), Broadbent underestimated the depth of prairie political alienation from the central government, an estrangement personified by a powerful dislike of the prime minister. While he expected conflict between the federal and provincial levels of government, he anticipated nothing of the magnitude that was produced, nor did he imagine that the issue would scotch the snake of the country's political institutions for as long as it did. Furthermore, the NDP leader did not anticipate the difficulties that would be created by an unusually young, inexperienced, and idealistic federal caucus. And lastly, Broadbent did not foresee that the Liberals would be so politically insensitive in dealing with the resolution — first refusing to open the parliamentary committee hearings to radio and television coverage and then insisting on unreasonable deadlines for them that would have prohibited dozens of groups from appearing or preparing briefs.

Broadbent struck the spark that fired his party's discord. But whether he could have steered some clever Clark-like path on "substance" until his party harmonized on "process" (the NDP wound up with the mirror-image problem of the Conservatives) is a moot point.

New Democrats, as members of a national party of federal and provincial branches, were divided on both the substance and process of constitutional reform. In truth, the party's image (to non-New Democrats) of doctrinaire homogeneity is often more superficial than it appears. The party is a *mélange* of -isms: trendy, European-style democratic socialism, Marxism, trade union conservatism, roseate academic utopianism, pan-Canadianism, populism, regional nationalism — divisions that constitutional conflict inevitably would widen.

The politician of Machiavelli's cast — it was Niccolò's argument Broadbent was making with his caucus — indeed has a special "morality". It is different from that of the Christian or liberal democrat who projects his personal morality onto the state, and different from that of Plato, who said the just state reflects the just man. Machiavelli's politician is accountable to the entire *polis*, with its myriad competing value systems. Of course, Machiavelli's politician did not live in a multicultural, three-party, two-language federal state of ten provinces, two territories, and three major aboriginal groups. We can only imagine what he might have done with Trudeau's resolution.

———————— ❦ ————————

Six days in the life of John Edward Broadbent   Although the constitutional preparation carried out within the federal NDP during the summer of 1980 was extensive, it was considered nowhere near as crucial for the party as was the work undertaken by Jake Epp and Arthur Tremblay for the Conservatives. No one foresaw the importance of debating the issue first in caucus before presenting a policy to the public. Patriation had been the policy of the NDP and its predecessor, the Co-operative Commonwealth Federation, since 1932; a constitutionally entrenched bill of rights had been party policy since 1944. For the most part, the party had given up trying to shape a Quebec policy (although after the 1980 election Broadbent made Saskatchewan MP Lorne Nystrom his constitutional critic largely because he spoke French).* At any rate, most of the preparatory work carried out by party committees and staff dealt with the division of powers, a matter which, with one major exception — resource ownership and control — became irrelevant once unilateral action on Trudeau's "people's package" was positioned on the skids.

On the afternoon of Wednesday, 1 October, Broadbent talked to Trudeau in the prime minister's Centre Block office for an hour, about three times longer than the Trudeau-Clark conversation. The prime minister explained in some detail the resolution and statement he intended to present the next night. Broadbent said the charter of rights was weaker than his caucus would like. Trudeau agreed that it was deficient, and gave Broadbent firm assurances that he would accept amendments to improve it, if the NDP leader could mobilize support for it within his party.

Broadbent also told the prime minister that the package should contain unqualified affirmation of provincial ownership of natural resources and strengthened powers over resource management (he was specifically pushing the interest of the NDP government in Saskatchewan, which had been denied power by the Supreme Court of Canada to impose indirect taxation on its natural resources and to exercise jurisdiction over interprovincial trade). Trudeau said he would consider the matter.

Ed Broadbent came away feeling enthusiastic about all he had heard and immediately got together with Nystrom, NDP House leader Stanley Knowles, and his senior staff members — Norm Simon, party secretary Robin Sears, caucus research director Marc Eliesen, and press secretary Peter O'Malley. He told them he believed that Trudeau wanted to be flexible, wanted to do his best to fashion a consensus. Broadbent personally felt that nothing in Trudeau's proposals was at variance with the several prognostications that the caucus had considered and had accepted in the abstract, and that had been discussed with party members across the country. There had been, in fact, a specific discussion in caucus on unilateral action.

---

*The NDP is the most unilingual (anglophone) of the three federal parliamentary parties. During the constitution debate, three members of the caucus could work in French: Nystrom, Burnaby MP Svend Robinson, and Toronto MP Robert Rae (who later would become leader of the Ontario NDP). Broadbent's French was once described by a francophone journalist as "a language other than English".

The NDP leader said he was convinced he could get a good amendment on resource ownership and control. He thought the proposed amending mechanism was sensible. Nystrom had met Chrétien that same day and had been told by the justice minister that Claude Ryan would certainly oppose the resolution. Nystrom asked Broadbent his opinion on this. The leader replied that he thought Ryan's objection would be only *pro forma*; his own view was that the issue would lead to some sharp, emotional debate across the land but that it would be over and done with in two to three months. He recommended that the party support Trudeau's package in principle — drawing specific attention to the absence of a guarantee of provincial resource control and to the deficiencies of the charter — and subsequently push hard for amendments. There is a difference of recollection on the group's reaction to Broadbent's proposal. One account says the leader was cautioned against committing the party to anything; the other account says he was not.

Normally, before making a major statement on party policy, Broadbent would have consulted his caucus. In this case, some of the parliamentary members had not yet returned to Ottawa for the new session that was to begin on 6 October. But, much more to the point, Broadbent did not feel that consultation was necessary. In his opinion, everything Trudeau intended to do fell within the perimeters of what the caucus had discussed and accepted. Consequently, he hardly gave a thought to his colleagues on the Hill; his concern was with the response of the provincial parties, and he set about telephoning each leader.

His impression from these conversations was that he would be supported by the four parties in Atlantic Canada, by Michael Cassidy in Ontario, by Alberta's Grant Notley, and by British Columbia's David Barrett. Broadbent learnt that he would not be supported by the quasi *indépendantiste* party in Quebec, but then he had not expected to be. He would get qualified backing from Manitoba's Howard Pawley, but the cautious Blakeney was undecided. The call to Blakeney was, of course, the most important one of all.

The Saskatchewan government had a special character in the skein of Canadian politics. It was the country's only NDP administration; moreover, Blakeney's brains and Romanow's co-chairmanship of the summer roadshow, combined with his television good looks, attracted more national attention to Saskatchewan's government than the province's size and clout within Confederation might otherwise merit. As regards the relationship between Ottawa and Blakeney over the constitution, there are two schools of thought. One is that the Trudeau government and the Michael Kirby bureaucracy considered it of great tactical importance to have a western province bolstering the resolution. The second is that, from the beginning, the Liberals' strategy (shaped by Trudeau's Alberta-born principal secretary, James Coutts) was to see the NDP, the Liberals' real political opponents in the West, split over the constitution on the divided-they-fall thesis. Broadbent is a student of socialist history (G.D.H. Cole's six-volume *A History of Socialist Thought* used to be in his office); Broadbent unquestionably wanted Blakeney's support.

The federal leader hoped that satisfactory amendments on resources would wipe away Blakeney's hesitancy, and he told him that he probably could get other changes, too. Curiously though, Broadbent did not tell Blakeney about the referendum provision, either because he forgot or did not know.* Blakeney got off the telephone and immediately called a meeting of the available members of his cabinet. One of the decisions taken was that Romanow should be dispatched to Ottawa to talk things over with the federal leader.

The next day, Broadbent went on television, telling the nation that "my party and I" accepted unilateral action. He said they also approved of the proposed amending provisions and entrenchment of rights. Then he talked about the proposal's "shortcomings", one of which he wanted to stress:

> *I searched in vain for a sign that the government's view of justice went beyond the important realm of individual rights. The prime minister has been aware for months, indeed years, that Canadians, particularly those outside of Central Canada, have wanted the assurance that their provincial governments own and control their resources. Without exception, there were thousands of people in every province who thought resource control was the most pressing constitutional issue. When these Canadians, therefore, look at tonight's proposals, they will feel cheated. . . .*

Much of the preliminary press commentary about the package was favourable; Broadbent was generally commended, and Clark's Conservatives were said to be on the wrong side of the fence. The press also quoted Lorne Nystrom as saying that he was "shocked and surprised" by the package, that it fell far short of meeting the legitimate complaints of western Canada. The difference in tone between Nystrom's and Broadbent's statements was noticed.

At some point before Sunday, 5 October, Broadbent and Trudeau met again. This time, the prime minister made the first of his concessions to the federal NDP — the one that would bring the party into formal alliance with his government. Trudeau agreed unconditionally — that is, without simultaneously adding the economic union powers to his resolution — to accept amendments specifying provincial ownership of resources, provincial authority to impose indirect taxes on them, and

---

*Broadbent later could not recall where Trudeau had told him about it in the conversation. The issue became a sore point with the Saskatchewan NDP.

concurrent provincial jurisdiction (with federal paramountcy*) over interprovincial trade. These were three of the four amendments Broadbent had asked for — the fourth, concurrent provincial jurisdiction over international trade, Trudeau had rejected; the agreement represented a major shift by the prime minister. Until that point he had insisted on linking the economic union powers to any constitutional powers given to the provinces on resource control.

Trudeau offered to announce the changes in a press statement. Broadbent said he preferred publicly to demand them and have Trudeau publicly accede to the request.† They agreed to make public an exchange of letters in a few days' time. Broadbent also extracted a promise from Trudeau not to take the matter to cabinet until just before the announcement, so as to avoid leaks.

On the Sunday, in Ottawa, Broadbent held his first meeting with Romanow. He told him what he had won from Trudeau and formally asked for support from the Saskatchewan government. Romanow was wary, admitting early in their conversation that there were political risks in his administration yoking itself too precipitately to the federal Liberals. Time was needed, Romanow said, to "condition our people". There were problems with French language rights in the West, and he was worried about the possibility of Trudeau doublecrossing them on the resources amendment (Broadbent said *that* was why he had asked for an early public commitment from the prime minister).

While admitting that his premier would like to support the package, Romanow emphasized that Blakeney wanted to see everything — particularly the resources amendment — in black-and-white; he also would have to talk to his cabinet and caucus, and assess the mood of the public.

The two men — whose relationship is watchfully correct rather than warmly chummy‡ — then went over the resolution, clause by clause. Romanow was uneasy about many of the legal rights sections; he wanted to know exactly what Broadbent and his caucus were intending to ask for on aboriginal rights; he did not like the wording of the equalization clause; he very much didn't like the referendum proviso that Trudeau might use, as Romanow correctly surmised, to end-run provincial opposition to an amendment.

At the end of the meeting, Broadbent asked what sort of presentation Romanow would make to the Saskatchewan cabinet. "Good news, bad news," Romanow replied. The good was that the resolution — with the

---

*See Glossary.

†For obvious reasons — or, as Broadbent told Romanow at their first meeting, for "strategic" reasons. It would make clear that the federal NDP, by giving the resolution its general support, could get Trudeau to make improvements.

‡It cooled markedly over the next year.

resource amendments — would have something in it for everyone and would throw a bodycheck at the alliance of the five most intractable provincial governments: British Columbia, Alberta, Manitoba, Quebec, and Newfoundland. The bad was that unilateralism was an assault on Canada's federal nature, and that support of the resolution would put the NDP into the arms of the Liberals in western Canada. On balance, Romanow guessed that his government would accept it. But he warned Broadbent of a danger: that they could be giving the Saskatchewan provincial Conservatives a ticket to power. A prescient man.

On Monday, 6 October, Broadbent met his caucus. To his surprise, he found that a considerable number of them had strong reservations about the package and were critical of him for having gone so far, so soon, in his television statement. Several MPs privately thought their leader's television address had been a media tactic, urged on him by press secretary O'Malley — a bow to the public opinion polls, rather than a careful consideration of the resolution's substance. Those who believed passionately in a strong charter of rights dismissed as inadequate the one put forward by the Liberals. A number of the prairie MPs liked neither unilateralism nor being in bed with Liberals.

Abstract caucus discussions were one thing; Lowell Murray's axiom — You can never tell how an issue will cut until you bring it out in the open — was something else. It had taken just six days for the constitution issue to wedge a fencepost into the party.*

Six months in the life of John Edward Broadbent   From early October onwards, the politics of the constitution became steadily more intolerable for the federal NDP leader — in his caucus, and in his transactions with the prairie provincial parties (all three of which eventually opposed him). The issue became, Joe Btfsplk-like, his personal black cloud, leavened only by the sparkling support of David Barrett and the British Columbia party.

Barrett, one of nature's large-scale political characters, had glanced at the constitution resolution, decided it matched what J.S. Woodsworth had talked about fifty years earlier and, perhaps alone among the country's political leaders, did not give it another thought. "The constitution on a scale of ten was never more than one and a half to me. The whole

---

*Fencepost imagery, vis-à-vis the NDP, surfaced on at least one other occasion. A federal cabinet minister, reflecting on Ottawa's failure to convince the Saskatchewan government to support its resolution, commented grumpily: "Blakeney will die with a fencepost up his ass."

debate was a gross waste of time," he told a visitor to his office a few weeks after the Queen had travelled to Ottawa for the proclamation ceremony. His personal thoughts aside, Barrett's support of the Trudeau resolution was decisive for Broadbent. Without it — without any western NDP chieftain backing him, and particularly without the support of the powerful B.C. provincial party — Broadbent would have been under painful pressure to reconsider his alliance with Trudeau, leading to a loss of face that would have been tremendously damaging to his leadership. Dave Barrett had no qualms about the constitution resolution. He just thought it was irrelevant, and he wanted it to go away.

So did Broadbent, desperately. The issue dominated his caucus in early October 1980, and did not cease to dominate it until fifteen months later. The compact over the resources amendment brought no peace. The party's MPs fought over everything: the Senate veto; the referendum provision; official bilingualism for Ontario (publicly promised by the caucus as an NDP amendment, later reneged on under pressure from the election-bound Ontario NDP); legal rights; women's rights; unilateralism; in-bed-with-Trudeauism.

Svend Robinson, the party's twenty-eight-year-old justice critic, voted against the resolution on first reading in the Commons because he considered the charter of rights so badly flawed. Other members — among them Ian Waddell, Jim Fulton, and Jim Manly from British Columbia, Cyril Keeper from Manitoba, and Peter Ittinuar from the Northwest Territories — repeatedly warned Broadbent that they would oppose the charter if it was not amended to recognize aboriginal rights, something Chrétien had said the government would not accept. Nystrom grew more strident in his opposition to unilateralism and was joined by fellow Saskatchewan MPs Simon de Jong, Douglas Anguish, and Stan Hovdebo. A fifth Saskatchewan MP, Roman Catholic priest Bob Ogle, told Broadbent that, although he thought his leader was dead wrong on the issue, he would support him, but only because "You're the Pope and I'm the priest." British Columbia MPs Pauline Jewett and Margaret Mitchell argued that the caucus should not sanction a charter that did not recognize the equality of men and women.

The political strains led inevitably to a deterioration in personal relationships. Broadbent came to believe that most of the opposition that was hung on the hatrack of unilateralism was really political nervousness at being in the same camp as Trudeau; he was intolerant of such dogma. His arguments with Nystrom became more bitter. Svend Robinson had offended him by voting in principle against the resolution. Broadbent responded by deciding to keep him off the parliamentary constitution committee, despite the young lawyer's expertise in civil rights, but he was persuaded by others in the party to change his mind. Nystrom and

Robinson, the party's two permanent members on the committee, were accused by some of their older colleagues of arrogance and condescension. One exchange is reported to have begun: "Look, punk, I've been in politics longer than you've been alive."

Robin Sears, the federal party secretary, was called up to the Hill from party headquarters to help cool caucus tensions. A skilled, highly intelligent political practitioner, Sears was also Broadbent's chief contact man and bargainer with Coutts, Kirby, and others on the government side. But some members of the caucus saw him as Broadbent's enforcer. Nystrom and Robinson both mistrusted him and did not like having him around the committee hearings, so Sears discreetly stayed away, reading the transcipts instead. Western MPs, in particular, were suspicious of Sears; they tended to see him as a central party apparatchik.* One described him as "weird — an academic dandy, another O'Malley; it was Sears and O'Malley advising Broadbent."†

The atmosphere was even more poisonous at the staff level, either because they felt freer than their principals to kick each other, or because they thought that by getting into the fray they could win brownie points from the MPs for whom they worked. Sears was obliged to draw up a code of conduct for them, applauding the suggestion of one staff member, who proposed putting up pictures of the Conservative and NDP caucuses side-by-side, with the sign "Bad Guys" under the Tories and "Good Guys" under the New Democrats, so everyone would keep in mind who were friends and who were enemies. On one occasion, Sears angrily reprimanded an MP's administrative assistant, who haughtily had taken it upon himself to start telling other MPs what would and would not be considered as suggestions for amending the charter of rights.

Broadbent laid the blame for many of his problems on the fact that he led a parliamentary party in large part composed of boy — and girl — scouts, a troop of burning idealists, defenders of causes. Twenty-four of the thirty-two MPs had been elected for the first time in either the 1979 or 1980 elections (plus Robert Rae, who won his seat in a 1978 byelection, and Pauline Jewett, re-elected in 1979 after being out of the House since 1965). Fifteen of them were under forty. For most of the younger and newer MPs — but as well for a few of the older and experienced ones — the constitution was an issue that unleashed their hopes and passions for a better Canada. It was not a topic for brokerage politics; they would

---

*Despite his west coast roots. He is the grandson of one of the party's great elders, long-time Vancouver Island MP Colin Cameron, and the son of Vancouver journalist (later Toronto-ized) Val Sears.

†Several of the younger caucus members resented the press secretary's influence with Broadbent. They considered O'Malley to be skilled at his job, but far too guided by the need to grab media time, regardless of what he advised Broadbent to say or do to get it.

be damned if they were going to put "how we live" ahead of "how we ought to live". The NDP caucus had little time for Machiavelli's politician.

Towards the end of the year, positions hardened in caucus, reaching a dangerous point for Broadbent. He had by this time acknowledged to his parliamentary colleagues — wryly quoting one of Tommy Douglas's lines: "I don't need your support when I'm right, I need it when I'm wrong" — that he should have consulted them before committing the party, if for no other reason than to remind them of what they all had discussed in the abstract. Now they were in trouble. One straw poll had produced a 16-16 split; only one person would have to shift his or her vote for Broadbent to be in a minority. Something had to be done.

Next to the anti-unilateralists and the Trudeauphobes (Broadbent wasn't sure there was a dividing line between them) those in favour of strong aboriginal rights formed the largest caucus opposition bloc to the leader. Chrétien had been adamant that aboriginal rights could not go into the charter. Doubting that he could get the government to change its mind,* Broadbent nonetheless went to Trudeau and asked him to insert a clause recognizing aboriginal rights.

The request turned into a rigorous debate. Trudeau opened Socratically by asking Broadbent to tell him what an aboriginal right was. Broadbent's rejoinder was to ask Trudeau, rhetorically, to define what was meant by religious freedom in the seventeenth and eighteenth centuries when many abstract rights first were written down. They weren't defined, Broadbent said; there was simply a sense that they existed, that they went with a notion of freedom which consisted of the state allowing a broader range of tolerance. But it was not something that had been spelled out.

Trudeau suggested the courts could give away the city of Vancouver if some Indian group made a successful case in law for the recognition of aboriginal rights to the British Columbia lower mainland. Broadbent replied: "You're the trained lawyer; I'm not. I'm a political theorist. But judges don't make decisions on that basis; they won't give away the city of Vancouver. Freedom is an evolving notion. It doesn't come from absurd judgments."

Broadbent left the meeting feeling he had made the better argument. But he was irritated because Trudeau never concedes a point — a reason for Broadbent's personal antipathy to the prime minister: he has come to believe that Trudeau likes to argue more than he likes to get the truth,

---

*Broadbent and Ian Waddell already had held meetings, in Broadbent's office, with Michael Kirby, deputy justice minister Roger Tassé, assistant deputy minister Barry Strayer, and (occasionally) Chrétien to talk about an aboriginal rights amendment. The justice department officials repeatedly made the same argument: that aboriginal rights could not be defined; therefore, they could not be protected in the constitution.

which Broadbent, the political philosopher, considers an intellectual weakness. He regards Trudeau as a lawyer's intellectual, who likes best to win a point and therefore sees truth as an adduction, a moving target, rather than something that is absolute.

──────────── ❦ ────────────

Early in the 1981 new year, the native rights issue, still unresolved, led indirectly to one of the most absurd incidents of the constitution epic. Annually, the governor general gives a skating party, to which the cabinet, MPs, members of the diplomatic corps and whatever else passes for the *haut monde* in Ottawa are invited. Ian Waddell attended with a friend, Nancy Allen, an assistant to NDP MP Terry Sargeant.

Waddell had just returned from Vancouver, where he had had a long talk with his mentor, Thomas Berger. The MP was depressed by the constitution debate and by the charter of rights that now was taking shape before the special parliamentary committee. Berger, on the other hand, had been enthusiastic, praising the charter's symmetry: first, the base — a recognition of the nation's two founding peoples, French and English, with their important language rights; then, on top of that, like the next layer of a cake, recognition of the country's immigrants and the multicultural nature of Canadian society; and then, above that, recognition of rights for disadvantaged groups. What was missing was what Waddell considered most important: the bottom-most layer of the cake — recognition of the rights of Canada's original people.

With these thoughts on his mind, he turned up with his companion and his skates at Rideau Hall, took a few turns on the governor general's rink, and then went into the residence for a buffet dinner. Waddell, Nancy Allen, Vancouver Island MP Jim Manly, and his wife, Eva, took seats together at a table, and Waddell went off to get drinks.

As he was returning from the bar, he and Trudeau passed each other. "There's the fighter for the Indians," said Trudeau, ski-sweatered, as he walked by. Waddell decided not to let the opportunity slip. He put down his drinks and buttonholed the prime minister, launching into Berger's symmetry argument, praising the charter but pointing out that rights for the true founding peoples were missing. Trudeau used the same question that he had put to Broadbent: How do you define aboriginal rights? "Look," said Waddell, "that's the justice department's argument. Do you want to be on their side, or do you want to be on the side of Laskin, Spence, Hall, and Berger — on the side of what some of the really good minds in the country are thinking?"* Waddell returned to his table.

An Englishman had taken a chair next to the Vancouver MP. He said

───────────

*The reference was to the three Supreme Court of Canada judges who had given the minority ruling in favour of the Nishga aboriginal rights claim in the 1973 *Calder* case — and to Berger, who had been the lawyer for the Nishgas.

hello to Waddell, without at first introducing himself. They began talking about the constitution. Waddell, presenting the party line, told him it wasn't a bad constitution package, especially now that the NDP had secured the resources amendment. The Englishman replied that the resources amendment was useless. Waddell shrugged and said: "Well, at any rate, it's going to get through the British Parliament." "How do you know that?" asked the Englishman. "Because I'm told by my leader, Mr. Broadbent," Waddell replied. "He's been talking to Mr. Foot" (British Labour Party leader Michael Foot). "Well, I'm telling you, don't be too sure," said the Englishman. "And I'm the British high commissioner." Waddell's plummy-voiced seatmate was Sir John Ford, amateur puppeteer, verse writer and, as he said, Britain's high commissioner to Canada.

A chain of events was rapidly forged. Waddell, astonished, and of a mind that Sir John might be meddling improperly in domestic Canadian politics, first asked — Waddell being Waddell — the governor general what he should do about it. Schreyer shrugged and told him it was no big matter. Waddell then told Bob Rae, who told a friend of his in the department of external affairs, who told external affairs minister Mark MacGuigan, who called Waddell the next morning to ask him more specifically about the incident, speaking darkly about it being the tip of the iceberg of Sir John's activities. Because MacGuigan had called him, Waddell then told Ed Broadbent who, against the advice of Waddell and Stanley Knowles, raised the matter at Question Period in the House and later called a press conference. Waddell, looking wretchedly embarrassed — which he was — stood beside his leader like a son beside his father, while Broadbent complained to reporters about Sir John's interference.

Sir John, a man who had experienced thornier diplomatic patches than this,* instantly called his own news conference in the theatre of the National Press Building. Striking a pose of the unflappable raj facing lesser breeds — he sat tilted far back in his chair, fingers laced behind his head — Sir John amiably dismissed the fuss. He said that he merely was revealing some British perceptions of what was going on, something perfectly proper for a diplomat to do. He succeeded in making the affair look as idiotic as it was.

———————— ❧ ————————

Two days later, Chrétien surprised everyone, disregarding the advice of the justice department, by announcing he would accept an amendment on aboriginal rights. The wording was worked out by justice department lawyers on the one side, and, on the other, mainly by Donald Rosenbloom, a young Vancouver lawyer and former associate of Berger's, by

———
*He was one of Britain's negotiators before it entered the European Community. For a fuller account of the British constitutional connection, see Chapter 10.

representatives of the main native groups, and by one other legal adviser to the NDP, whom no one in the parliamentary party will name.

The amendment helped Broadbent in caucus, giving him, at last, a
comfortable majority — a majority which grew, as more of the pro-charter
people in the caucus became happy (Margaret Mitchell and Pauline Jewett
on women's rights, for example) with improving amendments. That left
just the anti-unilateralists and Broadbent's other dolorous road through
the constitution — the one that led to the prairie parties.

The leadership of the federal NDP has contended that the country
could have been spared six months of torment, and yet have been given
a stronger charter of rights, if the Saskatchewan government had got off
the fence in the winter of 1980-81 and supported the federal resolution.
They argued then and now that Saskatchewan, by joining Ottawa,
Ontario, and New Brunswick, could have swayed the more flexible
provincial governments of Nova Scotia, Prince Edward Island, and British
Columbia — or, at the very least, created a different dynamic (it would
have been Ottawa and three provinces, with governments representing
all three national parties, against the rest) that might have led to an
earlier resolution of the conflict.

The Saskatchewan side has maintained that Broadbent showed his
cards too soon. If he had been less peremptory in backing the Liberal
resolution — if he had paid more heed to the West's antagonism toward
Trudeau and central Canada — he might have been able to drive a harder
bargain. Moreover, he might have been able to give the Saskatchewan
government the time it felt it needed (as Romanow put it in his first
meeting with Broadbent) to "condition our people" into accepting
Trudeau's proposal.

There are truths in both arguments. It does not follow, though, that
each side could have accepted the other's advice. On the one hand,
Broadbent's caucus was determined to accept and improve the charter of
rights, even though Blakeney did not like entrenching rights that would
be subject to judicial rule. Besides, as Broadbent pointed out to Blakeney's
people, once the resolution came before Parliament, the federal NDP
could not stay mute; it had to make a decision. On the other hand, it is
questionable whether, given the Saskatchewan public's enmity towards
Trudeau and the central government (an aversion encouraged by forceful Conservative premiers on either side of Saskatchewan), they would
even have been "conditioned" into accepting a Trudeau resolution.

It was an exceedingly difficult issue from the beginning, made worse
by the politicians acting as politicians. For instance, in the weeks immediately after Trudeau's announcement, the Saskatchewan government
made it clear that it was interested in a good natural resources amendment. But two things annoyed the chaps in Regina: one, that Broadbent
and his advisers seemed determined to negotiate the amendment's

wording on Saskatchewan's behalf; two, they felt the federal NDP lacked the constitutional expertise to negotiate well. Romanow, who had hurried to Ottawa after the television statements, was quickly grumbling to his cabinet colleagues that he was spending half his day in Broadbent's office talking about the resources amendment and then going along the corridors of Centre Block to talk about the same thing with Chrétien — first correcting what the justice minister said he had been told by Broadbent that the Saskatchewan government wanted.

The Blakeney government's account is that, with Broadbent in the middle as a kind of interpreter, the negotiations got too fuzzy and frustrating, and so finally Saskatchewan just let them peter out. The federal NDP version is that the Saskatchewan government kept finding new things that it was not happy with about the whole constitution resolution — basically because it did not have the political will to make a decision on it. Relations cooled between the federal and Saskatchewan parties at about the same rate as the fighting and yelling was amplifying in the federal caucus.

Thus Broadbent was a man beset on all sides. What angered him were the reports from Regina — reports quoting Chrétien — that the Liberals cleverly had emasculated him by locking him into an alliance so quickly. And what infuriated him were the statements from members of the Saskatchewan government that the dispute had become an issue of centralism versus decentralism. Broadbent was willing to acknowledge an argument of unilateralism versus negotiated settlement, but the centralism-decentralism theme he considered guff. The Trudeau resolution, with its resource amendment, he regarded as both a protection of provincial powers (because there would now be a legal framework to prohibit unilateral federal action from happening again) and a devolution of powers to the provinces. Furthermore, he prided himself on being an intellectual socialist, committed to dismantling the centralized monolithic state. The notion that he was some centralizer from Ontario, who did not understand the regions, was in his view monumentally unfair.

There were other goads. Grant Notley, the head of the Alberta NDP and its sole member in the provincial legislature, had initially defended the resources amendment, and Broadbent had understood from him that he would rally behind the resolution. In the end, he didn't. Howard Pawley of Manitoba was more negative than positive throughout the winter. Blakeney proposed a meeting of Broadbent and the four western provincial party leaders (plus Romanow) in Calgary on 18 January to see if differences could be reconciled. Barrett said he wasn't interested in being there; he didn't intend to change his mind and he was certain that the others would not change theirs — how could they, and not look politically foolish? He advised Broadbent not to go, telling him it would be a waste of time.

Broadbent went but, because of some Ottawa commitments, he was late and kept the others waiting. This led to a row between his assistants and Blakeney's people, who implied that Broadbent had been late deliberately. While their staffs fought, the party leaders were cordially correct — and Barrett was right: no one's mind was changed. Blakeney then continued on west for a winter vacation in Hawaii, ensconcing himself as the central prop of the Hawaii Affair.

———————————— ❧ ————————————

What lends credence to the suspicion that the Liberals were interested more in splitting the NDP than in wooing Saskatchewan's heart is that for a long three months — from mid-October to mid-January — Ottawa's interest in negotiating with Saskatchewan was desultory. When the talks between the two governments drifted into silence, no heavy breathing telephone calls from the national capital encouraged Saskatchewan to come back to the couch and sit down. And when Blakeney had appeared before the parliamentary committee on 19 December to present the changes his government wanted in the resolution, there had been no response from Ottawa. An informal pipeline had been kept open between the two governments — the pipe, interestingly, was a pair of the country's most seasoned political pros: one-time privy council clerk Gordon Robertson and former Liberal minister-of-everything Jack Pickersgill — but it did not seem to do much.

Then, on 14 January 1981, Romanow got a telephone call from Chrétien. What was Saskatchewan's bottom line? Romanow repeated the main points of Blakeney's 19 December submission: some provincial jurisdiction over international trade in natural resources, and either provincial capability to block the federal government's power to use a referendum in the amending formula, or provincial power to trigger a referendum. Chrétien said the federal government would yield on neither point. Romanow offered a compromise: certain administrative powers on international trade, abandonment of the referendum, and Ottawa's promise that there would be no further surprise amendments to the resolution. Chrétien said he would phone back. Six days later, on 20 January, energy minister Marc Lalonde* rang Romanow. They agreed that officials from the two governments would meet immediately in Toronto, to be joined by Lalonde and Romanow later.

What had rekindled the federal government's ardour? The evidence pointed to two things: a hardening of public opinion against unilateral action by Ottawa, and a growing twitchiness in the federal government

---

*Chrétien had become ill, with exhaustion, and was in hospital for a short time.

over what British parliamentarians might do to a unilateral resolution opposed by six of the ten provincal governments.

When Lalonde called him, Romanow was already in the Toronto area, staying at the Four Seasons Hotel and making speeches: one at McMaster University in Hamilton, the second to be given on Saturday, 24 January, to the Toronto Ukrainian Professional Businessmen at the Royal York Hotel. Michael Kirby turned up at Romanow's hotel, with justice officials Roger Tassé and Fred Gibson in tow. Howard Leeson, Saskatchewan deputy minister of intergovernmental affairs, flew in from Regina. Their first meeting went nowhere.

On the next night, Thursday, there was progress. The federal negotiatiors were interested in talking about a provincial blocking mechanism on the referendum. They were willing to consider some provincial jurisdiction over international trade — regulation of the rate of production, but not regulation of prices. Lalonde flew in from Edmonton on Friday morning to join the talks. The others moved to an airport hotel to meet him.

Just as Lalonde joined the talks, the parliamentary committee in Ottawa was about to accept a property rights amendment, introduced by the Conservatives and supported by the solicitor general, Robert Kaplan. As a condition for the Toronto talks continuing, Romanow insisted that this amendment — which would conflict with Saskatchewan's land ownership restrictions — be withdrawn. Lalonde agreed, but his aides could not reach Kaplan in time to call him off; the Saskatchewan delegation reached Nystrom, however, and asked him to filibuster the passage of the amendment until the Liberals could sort out their signals.*

Romanow also wanted to talk about the Senate, a major concern of Blakeney's: there must be no full Senate veto. Kirby and Lalonde said that something would have to be done for the senators because of a serious Senate revolt brewing over the thinning of their veto to a mere suspensive check on the Commons. The government was afraid of seeing its resolution stopped in the Upper House. Lalonde and Kirby did not make clear what doing "something" for the senators meant, but Romanow assumed it meant that some sort of guarantee of tenure would be offered to existing Senate members, followed by major reform of the institution. However, nothing was put down on paper.

It was now Friday evening. Many things had been written down on paper. The two sides were talking about a full proposal being agreed to by their respective governments. Romanow was not over optimistic about the outcome, but when he called Blakeney in Hawaii to tell him about it, the premier urged his attorney general to do everything he could to

---

*Chrétien, back on the job the following Monday, withdrew the amendment, thereby putting one more burr into the Conservative saddle.

reach a deal. Then Blakeney said he wanted to see for himself what had been put on paper. He asked Romanow and Leeson to come to Hawaii.

Lalonde flew on to Montreal that night. The paperwork was completed Saturday morning. It was agreed that the Saskatchewan government would have a deadline of late Monday to decide on accepting any package. Kirby and Gibson returned to Ottawa.

Romanow was reluctant to travel all the way to Hawaii since he didn't feel positive about the federal offer. Leeson, too, was suspicious of the negotiations, worried that there might be more changes once Saskatchewan became locked into an alliance. Immediately after his speech to the Ukrainian businessmen on Saturday night, Romanow got on the telephone and started canvassing members of the Saskatchewan cabinet. He explained the details on the package and asked for their opinion; nearly all were willing to leave it to the premier to decide.

Meanwhile, in Ottawa on Saturday afternoon, Gibson was called by Kirby and told to fly to Hawaii, too. First, however, he was to go out to the prime minister's country residence at Harrington Lake in the Gatineau hills to talk to Trudeau and Chrétien. There, Trudeau gave him a letter for Blakeney, setting down the federal government's offer. Gibson left Ottawa on Sunday morning on what should have been a short connecting flight to Toronto; but because of bad weather, his plane was rerouted to North Bay. He spent hours in that airport before hopping on another flight heading west. The weather also had stalled Romanow and Leeson in Toronto; they went by road to a New York state airport and picked up a Honolulu-bound flight — looking an odd pair among the holiday-goers, in their fur hats, boots and leather coats — arriving within an hour of Gibson, who had been in transit for twenty-two hours. It was late Sunday, 25 January. Romanow and Leeson checked into their rooms on the seventeenth floor of the Ilikai Hotel. Gibson was one floor below — federal-provincial symbolism, 4,800 miles from Ottawa. Blakeney was to fly in from an out-island in the morning and meet them in Romanow's room.

The agreed-upon format was that Blakeney and Trudeau would exchange letters setting down what each side was prepared to give. If the deal fell through, all letters and documentation — draft paragraphs for amendments, and so on — were to be returned. Gibson and the Saskatchewan trio began the Monday meeting by going over every piece of paper. The federal side presented a small change: rights for the physically handicapped were to be inserted in the charter. The Saskatchewan people did not object to rights for the physically handicapped; but the change itself made them nervous.

One of the conditions on which there had been concurrence in Toronto was that no more amendments could be accepted after the consummation of their deal — with the understanding, of course, that the federal government was unable to tie the hands of Parliament (a caveat that Leeson and Romanow feared Ottawa might use as a ruse to sneak something by them, such is the paranoia of federal-provincial relations). The no-more-changes agreement was discarded as politically unworkable, but the Saskatchewan team was left with the impression that the federal government was gradually losing control of its own resolution. Chrétien, having returned to work, was negotiating with the senators, and could not make a deal, and he was negotiating with Saskatchewan about the Senate and could not make a deal — there was still nothing on paper about the Senate — and suddenly up pops rights for the physically handicapped.

During the day Blakeney asked about the Senate. Leeson and Romanow explained their interpretation of the Kirby-Lalonde statement about doing "something" for the senators — which they assumed meant some grandfather sop for the incumbents, followed by fundamental reform of the Upper House. Blakeney appeared satisfied with that (Romanow himself was beginning to feel more optimistic that a deal could be reached.) The Saskatchewan side then wrote out what it called a "draft acceptance" of the Trudeau letter, which Blakeney initialled but did not sign. It contained some minor adjustments to the language of Trudeau's letter and a proposal from Saskatchewan that no closure be imposed on the debate when the resolution returned to the House; there was to be "fair debate" — a little kiss-and-makeup-gift for Broadbent and the federal NDP caucus. The "draft acceptance" was given to Gibson.

There then occurred a bizarre twist of history. It was five in the afternoon, Hawaii time, ten at night in Ottawa. Blakeney and Romanow were standing on the balcony of Romanow's room, hanging over the rail, watching a tennis game seventeen floors below. They could just glimpse a corner of the ocean. Gibson had gone back to his room. Blakeney was waiting to speak to Trudeau. The feeling in the Saskatchewan people's minds was that a deal was within reach. Fate then inserted a fickle finger in the form of a flat tire on Trudeau's limousine as the prime minister was being driven from Montreal to Ottawa.* The delay it caused was enough to snarl the prime minister's busy schedule, and it was decided in Ottawa to put off the call to Blakeney until the next day.

So, instead of talking to the prime minister that Monday afternoon, Blakeney got to thinking on the balcony of Romanow's hotel room, and he said to his colleague: "Roy, run by me one more time what Kirby said we're going to do with the Senate." Romanow repeated Kirby's statement about having to do "something" for the senators. Blakeney said: "We have nothing in writing on this. Are you sure it's not doing something

---

*Not an uncommon occurrence. Because of its armour-plating, the limousine weighs 8,500 pounds, making it hard on tires.

for the *Senate*, as opposed to the senators" — which is a neat distinction? The Senate as an *institution*?

Romanow said he would call Kirby immediately and ask him. Blakeney followed his attorney general into the room and sat on the bed. Kirby came on the line. He started to repeat what he had said in Toronto about the government having a major uprising in the Senate. As Romanow listened to him, and didn't hear a specific answer to his question — was the government giving a sop to the Senate or to the senators? — he began to doubt his interpretation of what Kirby had said in Toronto.

Romanow hung up the telephone at the end of the conversation and said to the premier: "Well, I think you asked a very good question because now I'm uncertain." Blakeney replied that the thing to do was to have Gibson come in on Tuesday morning and bring with him all the proposed amendments that the government intended to make to the charter. The next morning, 27 January, the premier found what he was looking for. The wording of the amendment on the Senate was to continue a full veto for the *Senate*, not the incumbent senators.

Gibson was prepared for this moment; he had received his instructions at Harrington Lake. When — or if — the time came to discuss the Senate veto, he was to say: "We would very much *like* Saskatchewan onside, but we *need* the Senate."

Blakeney went out alone for a walk. He walked out on the hotel dock and stayed there for nearly an hour, thinking. Gibson went back to his room. When Blakeney returned, he said, "I don't think we can go for this." Romanow and Leeson agreed. The federal side could not be trusted. Blakeney then talked to Trudeau and took a plane at midday back to his out-island. For want of a workable prime ministerial limousine — perhaps — a federal-provincial agreement fell through.

All the speculation about whether the deal fell through because somehow Blakeney and Trudeau misinterpreted each other on the telephone is just that: empty speculation. There was no misinterpretation. The deal was off before Blakeney got on the telephone. As for Trudeau's final cryptic comment that has stirred so much comment, the most accurate version seems to be these words, said archly in response to Blakeney's remonstration: "You fight your senators, and I'll fight mine" — which, given that Allan Blakeney had no senators, appears to mean that the prime minister was letting him know who was carrying the burden. "If the Senate is the only thing between us, we'll fight the senators together," Trudeau added, but Blakeney would not accept the fight.

Gibson, Leeson, and Romanow went out on the town, and spent the night and some hours of the morning arguing about what went wrong. Later, Romanow received a gift from Gibson, a wry novel called *Zinger and Me*, written by political scientist Jack MacLeod of the University of

Toronto. The novel suggests that Saskatchewan socialists are really conservatives — Gibson's thesis too. There was a warm inscription to Romanow, recalling The Hawaii Affair.

The relationship between Trudeau and Blakeney was perhaps the coldest among the first ministers. There are theories why: of the eleven, Trudeau and Blakeney are the most intellectually gifted, something that has touched them both with *hubris*, neither has ever bested the other in debate, which rankles them both. What was chilly before Honolulu — Trudeau had told his aides repeatedly in advance that Blakeney would never make a deal — was now icy.

Romanow and Leeson got back to Regina to be told that the story making the rounds in Ottawa was that Blakeney had reneged on a signed agreement — an apparent reference to the premier's cautiously initialled, but cannily not signed, "draft acceptance" which the meticulous Gibson had reported to Ottawa. The federal NDP caucus, hearing conflicting stories from the Liberals and from Regina, was baffled about what had happened. Broadbent invited Romanow to Ottawa to explain Saskatchewan's side of things.

It was not an easy pair of meetings Romanow attended on 2 February — first with Broadbent and his senior staff; second with the federal caucus. They were rather more of an inquisition than an affable gathering of socialists to discuss perfidious Grits. The meeting with Broadbent and his advisers was especially touchy on the subject of the Senate. There were suggestions (most directly from Broadbent and Marc Eliesen) that the Senate was a manufactured issue — that the provinces had agreed two years before that there would be no change to the Senate, and the federal amendment was essentially maintaining the status quo. Romanow replied that it wasn't the Senate issue specifically that had scuttled the deal but rather the tone of the negotiations, the untrustworthiness of the federal side.

Word leaked out in Ottawa of what Romanow had said to the federal caucus — that there would be no deal between the federal and Saskatchewan governments. Two weeks later, on 18 February, Nystrom, and his Saskatchewan colleagues Anguish, Hovdebo, and de Jong, broke publicly with the rest of the federal caucus to oppose the resolution because of its unilateral imperative, the Senate veto and the referendum proviso. Saskatchewan's NDP government officially opposed it one day later. (There was no serious attempt, after that, to overcome the differences between the NDP federal and prairie leaderships. Pawley and Notley followed suit behind Blakeney. Federal party members from the prairies who stayed loyal to Broadbent's position — particularly Regina MP Les Benjamin — were subjected to abuse and public humiliation (Benjamin's wife fled in tears from one political meeting in Regina where her

husband was insulted). Benjamin, a folksy trade unionist, simply had
decided that Trudeau's action on the constitution was closer than Blakeney's to both his own view and to the traditions of the party. Partly
because he said publicly what he believed in, but also because his federal constituency overlapped Blakeney's provincial constituency (and,
therefore, many of the same people belonged to both riding organizations) he became the target for what he himself called political knee-
capping.

The best that could be said about the Ottawa meeting on 8 March
between Blakeney, Broadbent, and their senior staffs was that (in Norm
Simon's words) it was quieter than Calgary. Blakeney accused the federal NDP of circulating the story that he had been offered everything in
Honolulu but had said no because he couldn't sell a Trudeau resolution
at home. Robin Sears countered by charging that Leeson had been putting
out false information about the federal NDP. Bill Knight, Blakeney's
principal secretary, complained that Pauline Jewett had come out to
Regina and said intemperate things about Blakeney. The federal group
grumbled that they had not been invited to send any of their top people
to a Saskatchewan party council meeting to explain their side of the
issue.

The following day, Blakeney met the executive of the Canadian Labour
Congress. The strongest message he received from Dennis McDermott
was that the CLC president wished the constitution issue would go away
so that the politicians could talk about unemployment, inflation and
patriation — as he put it — of the economy. Blakeney mused (for the only
known time) that perhaps he had made a mistake in sitting on the fence
for so long, that perhaps he would have been wiser to oppose the
resolution back in October.

There was little respite for Broadbent through April, May, and June.
The issue which he had been convinced would vanish by Christmas had
not even abated by the early summer. Blakeney, to Broadbent's horror,
became one of the gang of eight (something that Romanow had vowed
repeatedly — as recently as his last meeting with the federal caucus in
February — would never happen). The Newfoundland Supreme Court
astonished Broadbent by ruling against the legality of the federal resolution. He was speaking in London, Ontario, when the decision came
down, and Trudeau phoned him there. Jokingly, Broadbent said: "I know
why you're calling." Trudeau didn't laugh. They agreed that there was
now probably no alternative to referring the whole resolution to the
Supreme Court of Canada for a ruling. "If we lose there," said Trudeau,
"we'll go down the tubes together."

On 2 May, Broadbent went before a special meeting of the NDP federal council to defend his position, to explain — six months to the day

after he had gone on national television — his honest, guileless stand, why he had done what he did. It is unlikely he changed any minds. It had been a terrible six months for him.

✦

Broadbent's two roads of dolour on the constitution came together on 4 July in the War Memorial Gymnasium at the University of British Columbia. In the almost sub-tropical lushness of a Vancouver summer, the national New Democratic Party gathered for its biennial convention. The highlight, one of the stellar moments in the party's history, was the constitution debate.

All the party's giants spoke, with the soaring evangelical oratory of which only firebrand socialists and full gospel pastors are capable. Tommy Douglas, Blakeney, Broadbent, Barrett, Nystrom, Notley, Bob White of the United Auto Workers, Fonse Faour of the Newfoundland party, Alexa McDonough of the Nova Scotia party, Stanley Knowles — each one addressed the convention. There was a magnificent tableau surrounding the speaking of Knowles, something that would become etched in the memories of those who saw it.

Nystrom spoke before him, forcefully and attractively — but one became conscious, as Nystrom went on, of a stirring in the crowd, a gathering expectancy. Knowles had appeared at a microphone on the other side of the gymnasium floor. Out of a sea of garish sports shirts and beefy, red, trade union faces, the pale wraith-like, almost translucent visage of Stanley Knowles, in his sombre grey suit, loomed out of the crowd. It was Doom. It was Doom, waiting for Nystrom to finish speaking. When it was at last the turn of the veteran MP for Winnipeg North Centre, wave after wave of cheers rolled up to him. "You're cutting into my allotted time," he snapped into the microphone. And they hushed, instantly.

With humour, wit and the experience of half a century of pulpit* and hustings oratory, Knowles told the convention it would be unthinkable for a socialist, progressive movement to obstruct the prime minister's constitutional revisions. Patriation and a charter of rights were things the party had fought for, he said, for over fifty years. The premiers had no moral authority to halt progress. He talked about Manitoba premier Sterling Lyon's objection to the idea of an entrenched charter of rights. "Sterling Lyon doesn't speak for all the people of Manitoba," he said, slyly — because what he also was saying was that Allan Blakeney didn't speak for all the people of Saskatchewan. When convention chairman

---

*Stanley Knowles is a United Church clergyman.

Robin Sears waved his hand at him to signal that his time was up, Knowles pleaded failing eyesight. When Sears said, "Will you please conclude, Stanley?," Knowles pleaded deafness.

He tossed aside as a false issue Blakeney's objection to the Senate veto: "The resolution doesn't give it one more bit of power than it has now." Again and again he defended the charter as an instrument that "advances the things that we stand for." When he finished, the cheers were deafening.

The speaker who followed him, former Ontario MP John Rodriguez, committed the major gaffe of the convention. He actually criticized Knowles — over what he had said about the Senate — and was booed, the only time this happened during the entire debate. Nystrom, who had organized the speakers' list for those opposed to Broadbent's position, muttered that he wished he had not let Rodriguez speak.

The most humourous moment came when Dave Barrett attempted to get the debate cut off before Romanow could speak — a small morsel of revenge for Romanow having come out to British Columbia to speak publicly against Broadbent's, and Barrett's, stand. The move was stopped.

Broadbent carried the day with 63 per cent of delegate support. It was a slap. If the opposing vote had been much larger, it would have been an attack on Broadbent's leadership, and he would have put his job on the line and made it a leadership issue.

The summer passed. The Supreme Court of Canada decision came down: legal, not constitutional. Denis Healey, the British Labour Party's deputy leader, phoned Broadbent and said he could no longer guarantee Labour parliamentary support for the resolution when it got to Westminster. Privately, Broadbent described the ruling as a "stupid goddamned decision". Publicly, Broadbent the political theorist, exercised the Politician's morality, the morality that serves all the competing values of the *polis*. In a public statement, he urged the prime minister and the premiers to go back to the bargaining table of a first ministers' conference — and hammer out an agreement. It was not how Broadbent once thought things "ought to be done"; it was how they now were.

7
The Candy-Coloured Charter

Providence never intended to make the management of public affairs a mystery, to be comprehended only by a few persons of sublime genius, of which there are seldom three born in an age.

Jonathan Swift, *Gulliver's Travels.*

In the fall of 1980, in a chandeliered ballroom in Parliament's West Block, the Liberal government lost control of its constitutional strategy. The centrepiece — the candy-coloured charter of rights and freedoms that was to be the prize in Trudeau's reform package — was wrenched from the cool hands of the government planners, and taken over by ordinary Canadians and parliamentary backbenchers. The supposedly first-class charter, the subject of so much agonizing debate in cabinet during September, was given a rude dousing the next month when it was held up for public scrutiny and comment at a special joint Senate-Commons committee. Canadians wanted a charter of rights; that was clear. But they wanted a much better one than was being offered.

"Thanks but no thanks," said the Canadian Civil Liberties Association (CCLA), urging the government back to the drafting table. A step in the right direction but "seriously flawed" was the verdict of Gordon Fairweather, Canada's urbane human rights commissioner. The proposed rights for women would leave them worse off than before, the Canadian Advisory Council on the Status of Women argued in a well-documented brief submitted to the parliamentary committee that had been charged with studying the resolution clause-by-clause.

The image of Canada as a fair and tolerant country was shattered by the great number of Canadians who appeared before the committee to express their discontent with the meagre charter and argue for stronger constitutional protections. Those politicians who had boasted so glibly of Canada as a just, discrimination-free society were quickly disabused of the notion. The widespread public response to the charter's composition amazed government and opposition politicians alike. The advice the public tendered was both discerning and down-to-earth, from a raft of weighty legalisms to the proposal from a Charlottetown man for what he called "the lobster-trap" solution — a national referendum to settle the constitution dispute. "This," he argued, "would give platinum personality prime minister Trudeau a golden opportunity to use his silver tongue to explain [his] gems of political philosophy." Obviously, the public was going to insist on the government going first-class.

———————— ❦ ————————

It was an unusual setting to recast a charter of rights — a huge, outdated ballroom above the main parliamentary cafeteria. Once the scene of other historic federal-provincial confrontations, long abandoned for the more sumptuous conference centre, the makeshift conference table in the centre of the room seemed out of place with the brocade wallpaper, twenty-foot mirrors and cut-glass chandeliers from another era. It was here in 1968 that Lester Pearson began the first of a series of first ministers' conferences, which led up to Victoria three years later. The television cameras then captured a tough, self-controlled minister of justice, Pierre Trudeau, taking on an equally tough Quebec premier, Daniel Johnson; Trudeau was immediately catapulted into the front ranks of those capable of succeeding Pearson. It was in this same room in December 1979 that the then opposition Liberals, spirits bolstered by liquid cheer at their annual Christmas party, gave otherwise retiring leader Pierre Trudeau a chainsaw "to cut down the Tories" in the ensuing budget debate.

Then, in the fall and winter of 1980-81, the salon became the site for another extraordinary political convocation, the special joint committee on the constitution. The twenty-five MPs and senators who made up the core of the committee — the unsung Fathers of Re-Confederation* —

_____

*The committee members were an unusual lot. Many fitted the historical image of their constitutional forebears — dour Scots, loquacious Irishmen, shrewd French-Canadian tacticians — and there was a preponderance of lawyers and Roman Catholics, explaining why the abortion issue became so central at times. Yet the committee also included a Mennonite school teacher from southern Manitoba, a Saskatchewan farm boy of Danish extraction, an electrician and carpenter from PEI, two Jewish lawyers, three former mayors, and a Vancouver civil rights lawyer, born in Japan. The youngest member, Liberal MP Jean Lapierre, a hardworking street-smart lawyer from Quebec's Eastern Townships, was only twenty-four.

Most of the committee stuck it out to the end (a rare parliamentary feat) but others rotated or appeared only when they had special interests to defend. By the close, nearly 120 MPs and 50 senators — almost half the political life on the Hill — had sat around the constitutional table. The core members for the Liberals were: Senator Harry Hays and MP Serge Joyal, the two co-chairmen; Senators Jack Austin, Maurice Lamontagne, Carl Goldenberg, William Petten and John Connolly; and MPs Bryce Mackasey, Ronald Irwin, Eymard Corbin, George were petitioned by 914 individuals and 294 groups, stating what they wanted done with their constitution. The first parliamentary committee to have all its hearings televised sat a total of 267 hours on 56 days. Their detailed, clause-by-clause consideration of the charter lasted for more than ninety hours.

More often than not, the hearings went on late into the night, the debates careening wildly between shrill partisan rhetoric and sincere collegiality, sometimes with the mood changing eerily on the spur of the moment when the government conceded a hard-fought-for point.

But much of the wheeling and dealing took place in the corridors and cloakrooms outside, where officials huddled to discuss drafting changes, and politicians negotiated feverishly with lobbyists. It was here that Jean Chrétien jollied along groups of francophones from Manitoba, Saskatchewan and Ontario, or sipped coffee quietly with handicapped persons in wheelchairs. Once, more animatedly, he stood toe-to-toe with Sol Sanderson, the no-nonsense head of the Federation of Saskatchewan Indians, each man jabbing a finger vigorously at the other's chest.

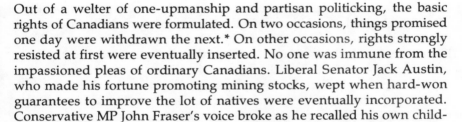

Out of a welter of one-upmanship and partisan politicking, the basic rights of Canadians were formulated. On two occasions, things promised one day were withdrawn the next.* On other occasions, rights strongly resisted at first were eventually inserted. No one was immune from the impassioned pleas of ordinary Canadians. Liberal Senator Jack Austin, who made his fortune promoting mining stocks, wept when hard-won guarantees to improve the lot of natives were eventually incorporated. Conservative MP John Fraser's voice broke as he recalled his own childhood in Yokohama, Japan, and recounted how later, in Vancouver, he had watched his Japanese Canadian friends being taken away and interned during World War II.

The constitutional fight brought an entire school of soreheads and axe-grinders to the fore. A group from British Columbia wished to have the right to digest hallucinogenic mushrooms enshrined in the constitution. Two University of Toronto professors wanted rights for trees, to protect against unrestricted foresting. A Vancouver lawyer sought to limit the Canadian prime minister's term to a maximum of five years. And there

---

Henderson, Coline Campbell, Jean Lapierre and Robert Bockstael. For the Conservatives: Senators Arthur Tremblay, Duff Roblin and Martial Asselin; and MPs Jake Epp, David Crombie, James McGrath, Perrin Beatty and John Fraser. The two regular New Democratic Party members of the committee were Svend Robinson and Lorne Nystrom.

*Property rights and an amending mechanism for aboriginal rights.

was a plethora of single-issue interest groups on the American model, opposing higher taxes, nuclear proliferation, abortion, gun control, and the ban on capital punishment, some of which found their champions on the Commons benches.

But, in marked contrast, there was the serene dignity of the Nishgas, the small west coast band whose persistence led to a landmark court decision in 1973, opening the door to the acceptance of the concept of aboriginal rights by governments. Their presence added a certain poignancy to the deliberations, as did the bright spirited arguments from blind law student David Lepofsky on rights for the handicapped.

The three parties fell over each other to put forward 123 amendments to the Liberal cabinet's supposedly first-class charter; more than half of these were accepted by the time the committee reported in mid-February. At that point, very few federal politicians seriously denied the merits of entrenched rights; they fought madly over which ones, but in only a few short months, the concept of an entrenched charter had become a motherhood issue.

From the word go, the special committee was a fiercely partisan forum. When the Liberals used closure in the Commons to move the debate to the committee stage, a handful of Tories, led by Robert Wenman and the late Tom Cossitt, charged up to the Speaker's chair angrily demanding their right to be heard. The closure vote had been delayed until two in the morning while Tory backbenchers yelled across the floor that the Liberals were using the techniques of Nazi Germany. Joe Clark and Liberal Ronald Irwin, Chrétien's parliamentary secretary, engaged in a private shouting match by the opposition leader's desk while the deputy Speaker tried in vain to restore order; Calgary's Harvie Andre, a close friend of Clark, chased Irwin across the floor of the Commons, threatening him with his fists. Extra security guards were called in to patrol the members' lobbies. Afterwards, under the television lamps in the outer corridors, the Tories sent up a frenetic chant of "Joe! Joe! Joe!" to show support for their leader.

This frenzied factionalism was carried over to the opening meeting of the special committee on 6 November, where there was the first of many procedural wrangles over televising the proceedings (Liberal senators complained that the harsh lights hurt their eyes) and a disconcerting (for the Liberals) backscene kerfuffle over the chairmanship. The first choices, Senator Maurice Lamontagne and MP Bryce Mackasey, were scuppered at the last moment, when Lamontagne, an acknowledged constitutional expert, became testy about Trudeau's methods and refused to share a television screen with Mackasey, his old rival from the Pearson cabinet.

(In one of the more callous incidents in this extended wrangle, Mackasey was telephoned at his mother's funeral only days before the committee was to start its work and was told by Chrétien that he was being dumped because Lamontagne had pulled out. He groused for several weeks, even voting against the party on two occasions, before developing into one of their more effective performers on the committee.)

To replace these two, the Liberals turned in desperation to the reliable, if somewhat old-fashioned, Senator Harry Hays, and their most talented pariah, Serge Joyal. It was hard to imagine two more widely divergent characters than Joyal, the dapper, almost delicate, Montreal MP in his mid-thirties, with decidedly cosmopolitan tastes, and Hays, the crusty, wise-cracking, seventy-one-year-old Alberta rancher and cattle auction-eer, who was saved from repeated attacks of foot-in-mouth disease by his co-chairman's deft use of the gavel. Once, after a particularly detailed critique of the charter by a prominent women's group, Hays thanked "the girls" for their contribution and then mused about what would happen if all their points were taken: "No one would be home to look after the babies."*

In Liberal Ottawa, where conformity and party discipline are prized above all, Serge Joyal's elevation to the co-chairmanship was an impor-tant signal to other potential mavericks that there could be life after Elba.†Former Liberal cabinet minister Warren Allmand doggedly attended the committee hearings as an unwanted spare, waiting for a chance to speak on two issues he considered crucial: native rights and language protection for the English minority in Quebec. Chiropractor Jean-Robert Gauthier, Liberal member for an Ottawa riding, became the voice of the franco-Ontarian community and argued strenuously for the extension of official bilingualism to the courts and legislature of Ontario. Louis Duclos, a little known backbencher outside his Quebec City bailiwick, made waves on the front pages of English Canadian newspapers for denouncing the

---

*Hays, a good-humoured, grandfatherly type, who often entertained Joyal with back-of-the-hand comments during particularly ponderous speeches to the committee, was the Liberal's pre-eminent bagman in Alberta and a wealthy cattle rancher until his death in 1982.

†The party's most celebrated black sheep (he also has a rather esoteric interest in the history of antique costumes), Joyal became a hero in Quebec in 1976 when he, Pierre De Bané, Louis Duclos and Jean Marchand broke publicly with the Trudeau government in support of the Gens de l'air, a group of Quebec pilots and air-traffic controllers embroiled in a bitter dispute over the language of the skyways. Joyal was the most prominent of the four rebels because he became the breakaway union's lawyer against the federal government, a post he held until he became a cabinet minister in December 1981.

In the early days of the Gens de l'air crisis, Marc Lalonde led the fight in caucus to have Joyal expelled; and in a vintage prime ministerial rage, Trudeau dressed down Joyal one night like a wayward son, throwing books and papers around his office for emphasis.

unilateral imposition of the Trudeau plan, particularly in the field of language rights. Allmand, Duclos and Gauthier all voted against the resolution on final reading and represented a pervasive sense of discontent within the normally happy Liberal family. The issue was nearly always the same — language rights — although two Ontario Liberals (Stanley Hudecki and Garnet Bloomfield) voted against the final accord because they believed the charter was unclear on abortion.

Among the Liberal committee members, chosen essentially for their loyalty and regional balance, there were some like Eymard Corbin, the steel-edged Acadian backbencher, and Jean Lapierre, who were also ready at times to rock the boat over language rights. "This is torturing me," Lapierre admitted at one point. "It isn't just a political decision . . . it is larger than that."

For their part, the Conservatives turned out their best political performers for the committee fight; six of their eight regulars had been ministers in the Clark government. But they could not always see eye to eye on tactics and concocted much of their daily strategy on the run, occasionally after virulent disagreements behind the scenes. The party had one objective — to delay Trudeau's constitutional juggernaut until the provinces could stop it, either through the courts or by way of a counter-offer. But, at the same time, they did not want to be on the wrong side of history, and so became swept up in an impulsive drive to create more rights. For some, like Jake Epp, the party's main constitutional spokesman, this was fine. He was gambling that a popular charter of rights might lead to a *rapprochement* between Ottawa and the provinces; he threw himself into charter-building to stave off the post-election doldrums that afflicted so many of his parliamentary colleagues. Yet there were others, led largely by Newfoundland's James McGrath, who actively wanted the committee to fail in order to underline the wrongheadedness of the government's approach. McGrath was also, initially at least, philosophically opposed to an entrenched charter.

The internal dilemma peaked on 20 January, when the federal Tories, after considerable soul-searching, threw their support behind a strengthened charter of rights — but only if the Liberals would agree to leave its implementation to the provinces. Epp declared grandly that the party's stance reflected "the popular will that we have a charter of rights and freedoms for the Canadian people embedded in the constitution," a policy the Liberal government had been following since 1968. But the Tory proposal was based on the then highly improbable assumption that many of the provinces would reverse their long-standing positions and ratify an entrenched charter at a new federal-provincial conference. As for the apparent contradiction, Manitoba's Senator Duff Roblin said that faced with the "clash of two great principles," the party felt the jurisdiction of one level of government could not be violated by the other. (The January position of the Tories also would have left the charter subject to the opting-out procedure in the amending formula preferred by the dissident provinces, so that basic rights might have been applied unequally across the country; they changed that in April 1981 so that, once accepted by seven provinces and Ottawa, these rights would apply throughout Canada.)

During the committee stage, trying to straddle the fence, the Tories put forward twenty-two amendments to strengthen the charter (seven were accepted) while still decrying its imposition on the reluctant provinces. But if there was inconsistency here, it was nothing compared to the confusion within the ranks of the NDP. Support for 'Trudeau's charter' was undermining the party's electoral base in the West and had led to embarrassing schisms between the national and prairie provincial parties. Wracked by internal dissension, the federal caucus split essentially along East-West lines. Its main constitutional spokesman, Saskatchewan MP Lorne Nystrom, actively promoted the charter throughout the committee stage, yet agonized over the propriety of the process. When the Blakeney government decided against it, he did as well, in a dramatic split with federal leader Ed Broadbent in February 1981.

Nystrom's seatmate on the committee, Svend Robinson, voted against the charter on first reading because it lacked sufficient guarantees, and then played a vigorous role putting forward the bulk of the NDP's forty-three proposed amendments, many of which were accepted.

Within weeks of the charter's unveiling in October 1980, both Trudeau and Chrétien were apologising for its inadequacies. The rights package was a compromise, they said, based on the summer's federal-provincial discussions. The weak areas — the limitation clauses, the short list of equality rights, and the inadequate guarantee for native peoples — they blamed on the provinces. But in fact, as confidential drafts from the summer show, the charter in the initial resolution was founded almost totally on the federal government's preferred draft, which turned out to be not as first-class as some in the cabinet had claimed. The provinces wanted one even more skeletal.

Pierre Trudeau, who had spent much of his political life urging Canadians to live within their means and lower their expectations, was now deliberately fanning the flames, exhorting Canadians to reach for excellence. The public was taking him at his word and demanding, through their representatives, a say in the articulation of their common rights.

As it had during the referendum period and the roadshow negotiations, the Trudeau government adopted a bifurcated strategy in the fall of 1980, unwilling or unable to put all its eggs in one basket. It tempered the pursuit of excellence by contriving to fashion a bill of rights that would not offend the provinces too much, yet one that would win the broad support of the electorate.

Ottawa's equivocation was evident throughout the fall when the government first toughened and then backed away from a series of deadlines, unable to make up its mind whether to ram the resolution through swiftly, or develop a pace that might allow some provinces to lend their support. (At this time, both Saskatchewan and Nova Scotia were looking for a 'political solution' and did not immediately join the other six provincial governments in challenging Ottawa through the courts.)

But the most illuminating example of the indecision at the top was the debate over whether or not to televise the proceedings of the special parliamentary committee, as the opposition were demanding. The debate went on for days in Parliament, with the Conservatives slowing down the business of the House with procedural points to make their case. Still the cabinet held out. Liberal strategists were afraid of the scrutiny the television cameras would provide. In their view, television would expose the proceedings to grandstanding and the charter to a host of irrational attacks that would be difficult to rebut in these circumstances. They weren't above using television to advance their message, but only when they could control the medium absolutely as an advertiser. It was only after the Liberals caved in to the pressures and allowed the cameras in, that they admitted they had misread the situation totally.

"We became aware rather quickly that Canadians were watching," Senator Austin, the Liberals' quiet-spoken committee leader and former principal secretary to Trudeau, said afterwards:

> *The television eye raised the stature of the whole proceedings. I would go out of the committee and people would say "We saw you on television," or "We saw the committee," or "The Japanese presentation was moving," or "The presentation by the women's action committee was just excellent; I never appreciated their point of view before."*
>
> *All of us began to feel that with the country watching, truly watching, at a level that was serious and intimate, we had to be better than we ever had been before in bringing forth our own view of things. Well, to be better means to think more deeply, to be more careful, to be more analytical. Of course you had to present things with emotional charges but they had to hang together. So TV turned out to be the best discipline.*

Despite its hegemony over the field of constitutional change, the Liberals did not know exactly who their constituency was. So, progressively, as the pressures mounted for a better charter *and* for more provincial consensus, the government began to let slip its initial objectives, lurching from one short-term strategy to another in classical crisis-management fashion. Throughout that fall, the overwhelming interest in the charter of rights, encouraged by the televised proceedings, took on its own momentum; Trudeau's principles and limited goals were compromised in the crush of personal relationships and interest-group pressures. Strong cabinet representation to include property rights led to a quiet arrangement whereby it was decided that they would be put in if an opposition party proposed them; this way the Liberals could claim it was not just them who were imposing on the provinces. In December, Trudeau could not bring himself to overrule two of his most influential ministers, MacEachen and Lalonde, who were arguing for an extension of the committee mandate because they were seeking the goodwill of Parliament for economic and energy legislation that would be as contentious as the constitution. In January, the prime minister bowed to repeated lobbying by Broadbent and others to augment native rights, an issue over which the federal NDP was threatening to withdraw its support for the entire package.

Between October 1980 and November 1981, the charter of rights was sent back to the government printer five times for major revisions. In January 1981 it was extensively rewritten by Chrétien while it was still before the parliamentary committee; several new sections on native, legal and language rights were added, as well as a new "remedies clause". This last is a mechanism that allows the courts to cope with violations of rights as they see fit, ordering compensation or remedial action — a seemingly innocuous but considerable aggrandizement of judicial powers.

On 13 February, when the committee's report was tabled in Parliament, it contained an historic new addition to the native rights clause, acknowledging and affirming aboriginal and treaty claims and titles and, for the first time, recognizing the Métis as an indigenous people with fundamental, though undefined, claims. Two months later, on 23 April, following an extraordinary debate on the floor of the Commons on the merits (sacrilegious and others) of entrenching a reference to the supreme being, the Liberals agreed to a preamble setting out the supremacy of God and a special clause affirming the equality of the sexes. Both these were part of the negotiated truce which ended the Tories' unprecedented blockade of Commons business and their successful effort to submit the full resolution to the Supreme Court of Canada.

In the spring of 1981, the charter's guarantees went far beyond anything envisioned by Diefenbaker in the 1950s or Trudeau at Victoria (the prime minister referred glowingly to the new bill as a model for the rest of the world) but it was subsequently gelded in a shabby breach of faith with those groups that had been given an unexpected opening to fight for its improvement. The native peoples, women and the handicapped were a significant contributory stream in the development of the constitutional proposals but they were muscled out in the end.

On 5 November, as part of the accord reached with the nine English premiers, a legislative override was introduced to allow governments the final say over court decisions. Three weeks later, after extensive lobbying of provincial capitals, the native and women's rights clauses, which had been allowed to fall to the floor in the late-night cut and paste session that produced the final deal, were partially reinstated, and the charter was sent off to Britain for final legal sanction.

✤

The *non obstante* override — the escape hatch introduced at the eleventh hour to reassert parliamentary supremacy — is a peculiarly, perhaps embarrassingly, Canadian device. It does not appear in the bill of rights of any other country, but is a feature of John Diefenbaker's 1960 bill of rights (which is not entrenched), as well as those of Alberta (the one with the widest powers of exemption), Saskatchewan, Quebec and Ontario.* The override applies to fundamental legal and equality rights in the charter and must be reaffirmed every five years if it is used. It satisfies those provinces which opposed an entrenched charter on principle, and makes life a little easier for legislators to give more direction to the courts in controversial areas (abortion, for instance) without requiring laborious constitutional amendments to change court decisions.

But the override bothered many Liberals for political reasons; they had invested heavily in a 'pure' charter of rights and were now hearing from various groups who felt cheated. At the end, however, there was hardly anyone left to champion those who were looking to the courts for better treatment. The protagonists, exhausted by the long ordeal, were basking nevertheless in the new-found compromise. Only Svend Robinson, the NDP's stubborn young justice critic, voted against the package *specifically* because of the override provision.

On the day the accord was signed, a weary Trudeau told one of his ministers who asked why the prime minister had agreed to an override

---

*Latin for "notwithstanding", the *non obstante* clause does exactly what its name implies. It allows a legislature by resolution, debated and voted upon, to pass laws, notwithstanding the fact that they violate certain provisions of the charter. The clause was advanced during the roadshow by Ontario and Alberta. Roy McMurtry liked to describe it as an important safety valve, politically difficult to use, and Chrétien dubbed it the "McMurtry clause" because he had occasional difficulty pronouncing *non obstante*. The override in the Diefenbaker bill was used only once, in 1970, during imposition of the War Measures Act, when the Trudeau government suspended *habeas corpus*.

on the charter: "Look, we're both lawyers. We know a signed deal is better than a fight."

Human rights, by and large, have not been badly served in Canada, although during the last fifty years there have been some remarkable violations. As particular examples of infringements, Trudeau was fond of pointing to the deportation and internment of Canadians of Japanese ancestry in British Columbia during World War II (although Japanese-Americans were also put in camps at that time, despite the USA's long-standing bill of rights), as well as to the Draconian press laws passed by the Alberta government of William Aberhart in the 1930s; and the padlock laws discriminating against alleged Communists and Jehovah's Witnesses, introduced by the Duplessis regime. The latter two were overruled by the Supreme Court of Canada, on constitutional grounds. Trudeau seldom mentioned his own imposition of the War Measures Act in 1970 — when hundreds of Québecois were arrested in the middle of the night and detained for long periods without access to a lawyer — although this is possibly the most vivid example of where a fully entrenched charter would have an immediate effect, assuming it provides the unequivocal right to due process of law. In Canada, this is now only a theoretical possibility: the proclaimed charter has the override provision, so that legal rights can be suspended temporarily.

Those who argued against an entrenched charter said it would only benefit lawyers and would create unnecessary litigation, most probably by the better organized and wealthier lobby groups, who could afford expensive court battles. The strongest argument against entrenching rights was that it would grant more power to the federally appointed non-elected judiciary to deal with what are essentially political problems. As Douglas Schmeiser, a former dean of constitutional law at the University of Saskatchewan, put it: "It is a worrying prospect that five old men, a bare majority on the Supreme Court, could rule on the great social and political issues of the nation contrary to and regardless of the wishes of the populace." It was precisely this point that Saskatchewan's Allan Blakeney addressed when he appeared before the special parliamentary committee in December. As well, he wanted the term "fundamental justice" excised from the charter because it was too close to a guarantee of "substantive due process," the basis on which US courts struck down state and federal legislation attempting to limit certain corporate excesses during Roosevelt's New Deal.* It was a concept, until then alien to Canadian jurisprudence, that allowed a court to interject its own view of appropriate public policy, rather than being mere arbiters

---

*The clause which offended Blakeney is still intact but now subject to the override. It reads: "Everyone has the right to life, liberty and security of the person and the right not to be deprived thereof, except in accordance with the principles of fundamental justice."

and interpreters of legislation. For Saskatchewan's democratic socialist government, which prided itself on its innovative economic and social policies, this developed into a matter of very great concern.

———————— ❦ ————————

In Canada, the far-reaching new powers being given the judiciary will probably surface first in the field of minority language education. Should provincial governments refuse to act reasonably in providing such services (as was the case historically with Manitoba), then the top court would effectively decide educational policy by ruling on such key phrases as "where numbers warrant".* An entrenched charter opens up myriad matters where the courts could have great discretionary power. Are discriminatory work laws or affirmative-action programs constitutional? Does abortion violate the pursuit of life and liberty? Does film censorship inhibit freedom of expression? Even though the legislative override is designed to bypass adverse decisions in these fields, it would still pit politicians against judges in a socially disturbing way.

The charter is supposed to apply only to governments and not to the private sector. But the drafters ignored the warning of McGill University law professor Maxwell Cohen that the court-applied remedies section should be expressly limited to the public sphere. As a result, nobody, not even federal justice officials, knows how broadly the courts might apply the basic rights to private transactions. As recently as 1980, Madame Justice Bertha Wilson, then of the Ontario Supreme Court of Appeal, said in a creative ruling that the rights envisioned in the Ontario Human Rights Code embodied society's values and, therefore, could be used for a civil suit rather than a mere grievance to a human rights commissioner. The top court overruled her but a new generation of more adventurous judges might adopt an entirely new approach.† Before the ink was dry on the November 1981 accord (and before the British Parliament had passed the charter into law), a seminar of corporate lawyers in Toronto was told that, with a little judicial luck and some imaginative arguments, a host of federal regulatory laws might be overturned because of the charter of rights. Peter Hogg, a respected Toronto law professor, noted on another occasion that Ottawa's vaunted national energy program could be an early victim because it discriminates between Canadian and foreign-owned oil companies. Non-discrimination rights, however, do not take effect until April 1985.

———————— ❦ ————————

*See Glossary.

†Judge Wilson was appointed to the Supreme Court of Canada in March 1982, replacing Ronald Martland, who retired in February on his seventy-fifth birthday.

Constitutional bills of rights are essentially a post-war phenomenon. In 1948, Winston Churchill, in support of the movement for European unity, argued that "in the centre of our movement stands the idea of a Charter of Human Rights, guarded by freedom and sustained by law." A few years later, British constitutional lawyers helped to prepare the European Convention on Human Rights, an indication of slowly evolving attitudes towards entrenched rights in a land where the supremacy of Parliament is continually being upheld.*

In Canada, the first parliamentary motions supporting the concept were proposed in 1945 by members of the CCF party and John Diefenbaker, an eminent trial lawyer who had entered the House of Commons in 1940. In 1947, a joint committee of the Senate and Commons studied the prospect of adopting a bill of rights for Canada but, after canvassing provincial attorneys general and deans of law schools, concluded that "the power of the Dominion Parliament to enact a comprehensive Bill of Rights is disputed." A few years later, a Senate committee reported that an entrenched charter would require a constitutional amendment but that, as an interim measure, the federal Parliament should adopt one for its own legislative jurisdiction. This is exactly what the Diefenbaker government did in August 1960, after nearly two years of debate. But the Diefenbaker bill of rights is only a federal law and it fared poorly over the next decade, as a series of conflicting judicial opinions held that it is mainly an interpretative statute that does not override other express legislation. After some forceful decisions at first, the court began retreating from the concept that the bill of rights superseded Parliament's will.

In 1967, Pearson and his justice minister, Pierre Trudeau, published Ottawa's new proposals for a fully entrenched charter of rights. A decade later the Canadian Bar Association, in a book-length publication called *Towards a New Canada*, lent its influential voice to the cause. It was during the 1970s, too, that bills of rights made their greatest strides at the provincial level; seven were enacted and the other three strengthened. Ontario had been first off the mark in 1962 with a modern bill, followed by Nova Scotia in 1969. (Saskatchewan had a human rights act dating back to 1947, when Tommy Douglas was premier, but it was largely unused, since it left enforcement to the courts. Ontario was the first jurisdiction to proclaim anti-discrimination laws for race and religion, in 1944.)

In Quebec during the mid-1960s, when law professor Pierre Trudeau made his jump to federal politics, a provincial rights charter was very much part of the intellectual climate. It was a main issue during the 1966 provincial election, in which power was wrested from the Lesage Liber-

---

*A good part of the debate on Britain joining the European Community centred on whether the sovereignty of Westminster would be circumscribed.

als and returned to the Union Nationale under the revitalized leadership of Daniel Johnson, whose new slogan "l'Égalité ou indépendance" characterized a more strident constitutional approach. The Quebec Charter of Human Rights and Freedoms — almost exactly the title of the Ottawa proposal — is the most far-reaching of the provincial rights codes and clearly the one on which the federal version is modelled. Enacted by Robert Bourassa's Liberal government only a few months before its defeat in 1976 (human rights are not necessarily successful electoral tickets), it was added to and improved upon by the Parti Québecois when it assumed power.

However, the provincial dislike of Trudeau's proposed charter went beyond who was the best provider of basic rights, the federal or provincial government. For decades there has been a legal-academic spat in Canada over which jurisdiction *is* actually responsible for the basic civil rights, and the seminal Supreme Court decisions on this matter do not give a complete answer. The British North America Act says civil rights are a provincial concern, but courts have sometimes ruled that basic rights, such as freedom of expression, have a national dimension. The list of what the provinces didn't like about an entrenched charter was quite long: the sweeping new powers being given to the courts; the hint of American jurisprudence infecting the language of the legal rights section; the prospect of expensive and time-consuming redrafting of provincial legislation to comply with the new code; and the direct recourse to the courts by wronged individuals, bypassing the human rights commissions that all provinces now have in place.

Strengthened provincial rights regimes are probably still the best way to handle most civil rights grievances, experts tend to agree. But there are weaknesses to provincial codes. Only three (Alberta, Saskatchewan and PEI) apply retroactively to all legislation, as the new charter does. Two of these, Alberta and Saskatchewan, have override clauses for new legislation, and Alberta gives its cabinet enormous regulatory powers to exempt certain individuals or the government from application of its charter. Their human rights commissioners are also appointed at pleasure (unlike tenured judges) and so could be removed at whim, and there is a basic sameness to the provincial bills, which all have been designed essentially to prohibit discrimination in housing, the ownership of property, advertising and employment. Furthermore, while provincial commissioners hand down many creative judgments, these are not always well publicized, so the deterrence factor is weak. There are often huge backlogs in provincial commissions, and the rights differ from province to province. For example, only Saskatchewan's code guarantees the rights to conscience, religion and freedom of the press. Four provinces guarantee freedom of expression, and Newfoundland and PEI forbid discrimination on the basis of political belief. Only Quebec prohibits discrimination

on the basis of sexual orientation, and all provinces except Alberta outlaw discrimination on the basis of marital status. The age category in
which discrimination is prohibited differs across the country, so a forty-
year-old seeking a job in New Brunswick is on a different footing from
his counterpart in Nova Scotia. And only half the provinces expressly
provide for non-discrimination against handicapped people.

It was this attempt to construct a common set of values that, more
than anything else, characterized Trudeau's obsession with a charter of
rights. In the 1950s, when he was a proponent of entrenched rights, it
was because he saw them as a legal tool for the individual to fight the
powers of governments. But nearly thirty years later, a charter of rights
had taken on a different hue. If not the capstone, it was at least to be the
buttressing arch of nation-building, directing attention to the central institutions (ultimately the Supreme Court of Canada), a national instrument that would cut across regional loyalties, as the CPR did for Sir John
A. Macdonald a century before.

But there was still a caution to the charter of rights that belied Trudeau's
boldness in pushing it through.

The opening section, or limitation clause, was originally the most
widely criticized — by more than a score of influential groups, such as
the Canadian Bar Association, the Canadian Human Rights Commission,
the Canadian Advisory Council on the Status of Women, the Canadian
Jewish Congress, the United Church of Canada and the Canadian National Institute for the Blind.* Not only did it contain weasel words to try
to make the charter more palatable to the provinces but it lacked pizzazz.
Maxwell Cohen, the erudite law professor and longtime acquaintance of
Trudeau, said a charter of rights "should sound a trumpet, should be a
Jericho . . . stating a national system of values for a long time to come.
It should not be a simple detailed catechism of behaviour." Tough-minded
women lawyers were more blunt. They labelled the limitation words "the
Mack truck clause" because it provided a loophole big enough for that
kind of vehicle to drive through. Every group suggested dropping the
reference to "parliamentary system of government," and some would
have had the rights put beyond the reach of legislatures, even in emergencies. The new phrase, "demonstrably justified," while common in
French jurisprudence, has little usage in English law. It was the brain-
child of Roger Tassé, the quiet-spoken deputy minister of justice. The
phrase reflects the concern expressed by Dr. Wilson Head, president of

---

*It now reads: "The Canadian Charter of Rights and Freedoms guarantees the
rights and freedoms set out in it subject only to such reasonable limits prescribed
by law as can be demonstrably justified in a free and democratic society."

It used to say: ". . . such reasonable limits as are generally accepted in a free
and democratic society with a parliamentary system of government."

the National Black Coalition of Canada, among others, that the burden of proof to limit rights must rest on governments.

The legislative override was introduced in November, to satisfy those provinces which would subscribe to a charter only if their legislatures could have the final say on policy matters. There was a mixed reaction to it from the various interest groups. Walter Tarnopolsky, the immediate past president of the CCLA and one of Canada's foremost experts on civil rights, gave qualified approval to the new safety valve. But the issue divided civil libertarians. Some applauded the accord for giving the charter much-needed legitimacy; others found the watering-down intolerable.

❖

The second section of the charter deals with fundamental freedoms, such as freedom of conscience, religion, thought and freedom of the press. Only minor changes were made here; on the recommendation of the Canadian Bar Association, they were intended to make the charter compatible with the International Convenant on Civil and Political Rights, to which Canada is a signatory. In leaving it basically untouched, Ottawa ignored the worries of police chiefs and Crown attorneys that freedom of conscience is a vague concept and that might make it difficult to enforce drug and morals offences. (It is a defence the west coast mushroom eaters might try.) Ottawa also disregarded the fear of the Canadian Jewish Congress that freedom of expression might countenance hate literature (this problem was addressed later by the *non obstante* override, which could be used to uphold legislation in the event of a court challenge). In November, the fundamental freedoms section created a last tug-of-war between Ottawa and the provinces, when Alberta held out for it to be made subject to the override. Acceptance of that was the basis for an implicit deal, making the override subject to a five-year "sunset provision," at which point legislatures must justify its continued use.

To the section dealing with democratic rights, only minor changes were made. This sets out the right to vote and also declares that no Parliament or legislature may sit longer than five years, except in an emergency, when its life can be sustained by a two-thirds vote of the assembly's members. The drafters rejected a recommendation to remove the contentious phrase "real or apprehended" to define emergencies — a holdover from the War Measures Act. This section, together with mobility and language rights, were the only ones to escape application of the legislative override.

The mobility rights section, one of the most controversial throughout the long constitutional battle, was not changed at all during the parliamentary revisions, except at the last, when the "Peckford wiggle" was added to appease the Newfoundland premier. This revision would allow provincial governments to maintain discriminatory hiring and purchasing practices if their rate of employment was below the national average — a *sine qua non* for Newfoundland, which wanted to ensure its workers first crack on the lucrative offshore oil rigs. Although this section was one of the cornerstones of Ottawa's plan to regain greater central control of the economy, and consistently popular in a nation that is constantly "going down the road," the Trudeau government unexpectedly refused to augment it, despite the pleas of a variety of influential groups. The Canadian Bar Association, the Canadian Jewish Congress and the Canadian Chamber of Commerce, among others, urged unsuccessfully that the right to travel, take up residence and pursue a livelihood anywhere in Canada, be extended from citizens to any landed immigrant, refugee, or permanent resident.

These same groups and others also urged the inclusion of the right to own property, first rejected by the federal government out of deference to the provinces, but accepted a month later when it was put forward by the Conservatives. Part of the Liberals' plan to trap the Tories into supporting a key component of the charter, it recoiled when it was discovered that the trap had a double door. Solicitor general Robert Kaplan, pinch-hitting for an ailing Jean Chrétien in late January, followed the script to the letter, as it had been set out in a cabinet minute, and accepted the Conservative amendment on property rights. The Tories knew that the amendment would not sit well with some Conservative provincial governments like PEI, but they did not expect the federal Liberals to accept their proposal and reasoned that the mischief it would cause between the Liberals and the NDP (who were defending Blakeney's interests) was worth the risk. Unknown to those around the committee table, energy minister Marc Lalonde was then engaged in secret discussions with the Saskatchewan government in a Toronto hotel room, trying to win its constitutional support by offering a better resource arrangement. A prerequisite of the deal was that Ottawa withdraw the property amendment, putting the Liberals in the embarrassing position of granting certain rights one day and retracting them the next. The whole episode underscored the intensely partisan framework on which the charter of rights was built.

———————— ✦ ————————

In the shaping of the new charter, the government's most far-reaching amendments were to the section on legal rights, often disregarding the misgivings of its main ally, Ontario. Roy McMurtry's legal officers had pored over the drafts of the first effort, even to the point of inserting their own preferred language. But in January, when Chrétien divulged the extensive rewrite, McMurtry was in London lobbying the Brits, oblivious of the changes. (It was partially this slight that caused him to suggest that Ottawa should frame its own reference on the constitutionality of the scheme for the Supreme Court — advice that ran counter to the official line in Ottawa and at Queen's Park, that there was nothing wrong with the process and that the courts should not even be involved.)

Writing criminal laws is a federal responsibility. But, in the Canadian system, the provinces are accountable for the administration of justice, and procedural rules in an entrenched charter could undermine provincial laws. Despite stiff opposition, Chrétien adamantly kept the opening reference to "fundamental justice." He did, however, bend to pressure from the Canadian Bar Association and various civil liberties groups to drop the qualifying phrases that might have been used to support certain questionable police practices.* Drafters essentially followed the version suggested by professors Cohen and Irwin Cotler of the McGill law faculty, so that the new protections are more akin to the US model. This puts the onus on the courts to decide what constitutes a reasonable search and seizure or an arbitrary detention. As a result of the many representations, individuals would gain more rights after their arrest by the police, including, for the first time, to be informed of their right to retain and instruct counsel "without delay," a clause bitterly objected to by police organizations. However, the cabinet rejected proposals to introduce the right to remain silent on arrest and the right to legal aid. But the committee stage allowed it to correct a remarkable omission from the first draft — the right of an accused person not to be compelled to testify against himself or herself — by borrowing a phrase from the Diefenbaker bill of rights.† The Tories also forced the government to guarantee deaf people the right to an interpreter in court trials.

The most fascinating legal debate at this stage was whether there should be a provision governing the admissibility of evidence. Various legal experts, including Professor Tarnapolsky of the CCLA, argued with great passion that the initial provision effectively would entrench a 1970 Supreme Court decision, which opened the door to the use of so-called

---

*Excised were the qualifiers that subjected legal rights to procedures already "established by law," a phrase civil libertarians argued could justify questionable methods stemming from superiors' orders, such as those detailed by the McDonald Commission into RCMP wrongdoing.

†The new section 11(c) says: "Any person charged with an offence has the right not to be compelled to be a witness in proceedings against that person in respect of the offence."

tainted evidence obtained by other than strictly ethical means.* On the other side, police groups, Crown attorneys, and certain lawyers and retired judges maintained just as intensely that, without such a provision, Canada would move closer to "the poison fruit doctrine" espoused in the USA, where illegally obtained evidence can invalidate a guilty verdict and has occasionally done so, often in spectacular circumstances. Both sides wanted to leave it to the courts to determine case by case, but they could not agree on how this could best be done. Chrétien eventually dropped the controversial clause but, responding to other pressures, consented to a back-door solution and introduced a broad new remedies section, which empowers the courts to deal with rights violations as they see fit.

Adopting a Conservative amendment on the exclusion of evidence, "where it would bring the administration of justice into disrepute" — this had been a long-standing recommendation of the Law Reform Commission of Canada — Chrétien did not succeed in stifling the controversy. Curiously, the opposition to the move was led by Roderick McLeod, a high-ranking justice official in the department of the Ontario attorney general. McLeod wrote a series of long articles, one of which appeared on the op-ed page of *The Globe and Mail*, condemning the new charter for introducing the worst aspects of American justice. However, it was not immediately clear whether he was carrying on this campaign with the approval of his boss, Roy McMurtry, whose government was not only supporting the process but actively campaigning in favour of the charter of rights in a spring election. That little mystery was cleared up right after the Ontario Tories were returned to power with a landslide majority. McMurtry wrote to a number of federal MPs (including many Tories who were angry about the double standard), urging them to digest McLeod's articles and accordingly amend the federal resolution before it was sent off to Westminster. Some of these MPs raised the issue in debate, but there were no amendments put forward. Nobody was interested in being Ontario's lackey.

✦

---

*In the case of *Wray*, police used some rather rough tactics to force a murder confession and to learn the whereabouts of the murder weapon. The trial judge and the Ontario court of appeal rejected the confession as involuntary and unfair and for bringing the administration of justice into disrepute. The Supreme Court overruled them, however, saying: "There is no judicial discretion permitting the exclusion of relevant evidence, in this case highly relevant evidence: the revelation of the murder weapon — on the ground of unfairness to the accused." The original clause in the charter that aroused such debate said simply that no provision of the charter "affects the laws respecting the admissibility of evidence in any proceedings or the authority of Parliament or a legislature to make laws in relation thereto."

The most politically popular section of the charter was that entrenching the so-called new rights of equality or non-discrimination. Revised by the parliamentary committee, it contained one of the few ringing declarations in an otherwise prosaic code:

> *Every individual is equal before and under the law and has*
> *the right to equal protection and equal benefit of the law*
> *without discrimination and, in particular, without*
> *discrimination based on race, national or ethnic origin,*
> *colour, religion, sex, age or mental or physical disability.*

In essence, the revisions reflected the anxieties of women's groups and legal authorities. "Every individual," a phrase that has a legal history, replaced the blander "everyone," and the syntax made it clear that the guarantees apply both to the substance and to the administration of the law. Despite intense lobbying, Chrétien refused to expand the references to include sexual orientation, marital status, or political beliefs. But he maintained that the guarantee is open-ended, so that the courts can still order remedies for discriminatory behaviour that is not explicitly mentioned. The only addition to the list was the specific reference to the mentally and physically disabled, whose cause both the Tories and NDP took up in earnest. The handicapped also had influential champions in the Liberal caucus, including Dr. Peter Lang and David Smith, a Toronto MP who headed a special task force on handicapped rights, and cabinet ministers from Toronto and Winnipeg, where the main lobby groups were located.

But while equality rights became a motherhood matter in the committee, the two language rights sections were wrenching apart the federal parties. The official section effectively entrenched the Official Languages Act as it applied to all federal institutions, putting it out of reach of unilateral amendments by future Parliaments. Trudeau's bold 1969 venture, making the English and French languages official throughout Canada at the federal level, is now chiselled in stone, requiring the constitutional approval of Quebec (or any other province) before it can be changed. The new charter also binds the government of New Brunswick, at its own request, to institutional bilingualism in that province, along the lines already constitutionally mandated for Quebec and Manitoba. The proposed language requirements for New Brunswick are even more stringent than those for the federal government: for example, they require bilingual services at *all* provincial government offices rather than just at head offices. This effectively sets up four distinct categories of constitutionally entrenched bilingualism, with progressively less onerous requirements for New Brunswick, the federal government, Quebec and Manitoba. But the cutting issue throughout the parliamentary committee's meetings, and indeed during the constitutional battle, was whether official bilingualism should be required for the courts and legislature of Ontario, where the largest francophone population outside Quebec resides.

The "section 133 debate," as it became known, split the national parties. At one point, nearly twenty Quebec Liberals threatened to revolt if official bilingualism were not imposed on Ontario. But the prime minister held a private lunch in December for the Liberal committee members, which helped somewhat to cool the rebellion. The New Democrats promised to present an amendment forcing Ontario to comply, but they backed off at the last minute after some arm-twisting from the Ontario provincial party, which was fighting an election. Several Conservative MPs, including David Crombie, a former mayor of Toronto, spoke movingly in favour of section 133: "We can no longer afford in this country a symbol that says if you are French in Ontario you have a lower colour than if you are English in Quebec." But, with one dramatic exception, the Tories would not break the party line of refusing to impose anything on the provinces. The exception was Senator Martial Asselin, an ardent French-Canadian federalist, who offered during the committee to introduce an amendment himself if the Liberals would support it. Nobody did.

Throughout it all, the Davis government remained strangely intransigent on the issue, convinced its position was being misunderstood. In 1867, when Ontario was stridently Orange, the matter was not even academic. Section 133 was incorporated in the British North America Act as much to ensure the survival of the French language in Quebec as to recognize the bilingual reality (more appropriately, the two solitudes) of that province. By the time of the Victoria Conference more than a hundred years later, Ontario was prepared to enshrine some institutional bilingualism, for the legislature, though not for the courts. But ten years and two minority governments later, it was backtracking even on this, although it was willing to provide French services where it felt numbers warranted.

During the negotiations leading up to the September conference, the Ontario government occasionally leaned towards acceptance of official bilingualism, but the poor negotiating climate, and a Toronto newspaper headline predicting that Trudeau would impose it, spooked the Big Blue Machine into retreat. Many believe there was a deal between Trudeau and Davis over this issue. There was. But it was more implicit than anything else: Ottawa would not impose institutional bilingualism on Ontario in exchange for that province's support of the rest of the constitutional package. Trudeau asked Davis directly on only one occasion to accept section 133 — in October 1981, following the Supreme Court of Canada's decision questioning the propriety of the federal initiative. At this point, Trudeau was under immense pressure from his Quebec supporters to make the project more palatable, and official bilingualism in Ontario would be a major symbolic gesture. But Davis was also being pressed by his bedrock supporters, who did not like being politically in league with Trudeau anyway, and particularly now that the Supreme Court was casting doubts on the appropriateness of the resolution. Even with its new majority, Ontario would go no further.

During this period Chrétien was also, on his own, trying to influence his Ontario counterparts to accept Section 133. He called McMurtry and Wells repeatedly and even went so far as to enlist the aid of a Shawinigan constituent, the grandmother of Hugh Segal's wife, Donna. But none of his efforts were successful. The Ontario Tories were borrowing the *étapisme* approach of the Parti Québecois — trying to implement bilingual conditions without fanfare, so as not to alienate the "hoary-Tory" vote in their political heartland. At the same time, they needed a solid issue to convince party militants that they were not totally aligned with Trudeau and were willing to deny him a fundamental component of his national vision. Sadly, this had to be it. The Lévesque administration mocked Ontario for not guaranteeing such services, but it would not horse-trade to bring this about, preferring an obstinate Ontario as the model on which to base changes in Quebec society and hang the separatist option.

Agreeing to institutional bilingualism would be little more than a symbolic step for Ontario, which already provided most of these services anyway. Most major pieces of legislation are now routinely translated, French is occasionally spoken in the legislature at Queen's Park, criminal trials are bilingual, and civil cases can be held in French in certain designated districts. The province's record is probably better than New Brunswick's, which has a greater proportion of French-speaking citizens and which passed an official bilingualism act in 1969 (it was not proclaimed until 1977). But Ontario still missed that "supplement of soul" (as a Quebec journalist said) because its policies were timid and parochial at a time when great statesmanship was required. Its opportunity to be the great conciliator between Quebec and the rest of Canada — the John Robarts dream — was not exploited. It allowed its citizens to continue in the comfortable belief that English is good enough for anybody. French is only the language of French-Canadians; it can be doled out in small measures by politicians as a sort of gift, but it is not a fundamental right.

Even more deplorable was the fact that the Davis Tories were willing to fan the anti-French sentiment to win an election. In November 1980, while the 133 issue was before the special parliamentary committee, internal Tory polls showed that Davis's support was slipping because he was backing Trudeau's constitutional scheme. In a by-election in Ottawa-Carleton, the testing ground for the provincial election four months later, Davis strategists decided to show that the premier was still "holding the line on some things," even if he appeared weak on the constitution. A Conservative brochure distributed in the riding accused provincial Liberal leader Stuart Smith of approving of "official bilingualism" while Davis was forcing Ottawa "to back away from a blanket bilingual policy in favour of Ontario's existing policy of providing French language services where numbers warrant." So much for the promise to Quebec.

❦

But while the fight over official bilingualism shook up the politics of English Canada, the entrenchment of minority language education rights struck at the heart of Quebec's language policies. Although it was part of the Victoria agreement, several provinces (particularly in the West) were now backing away from entrenched educational rights, and Lévesque was proposing a new plan. In 1978, the premiers unveiled a reciprocity scheme that would bypass Ottawa and ensure that their language rights were determined through multilateral provincial arrangements. But the scheme was so much rhetoric, and nothing ensued. In September the federal cabinet decided to bind the provinces to minority education provisions based on mother tongue, a clumsy mechanism that might require politically volatile language tests in recalcitrant provinces, particularly Quebec, where there had been riots over similar tests during the early 1970s in the Montreal suburb of St. Leonard. The cabinet decided against pure freedom of choice because the concept provoked fighting sentiments in Quebec, something like rep. by pop. in another era. Trudeau would not agree to a two-tiered or special status solution, so the 'mother tongue test' was agreed upon, because it was the only way assimilated francophones outside Quebec could be guaranteed their child's education in French. Although Ottawa argued, even in court, that it was only reflecting the principles enunciated by the premiers in 1978, the entrenched provisions directly contradicted the intent and letter of Quebec's controversial language law, Bill 101.

In January 1981, during the parliamentary committee stage, and as a result of intense lobbying within the federal Liberal caucus, the cabinet added the so-called "Canada clause" to the charter, hoping to make it more saleable in Quebec. This clause guarantees instruction to the children of Canadian citizens who had primary schooling in one of the two official languages anywhere in Canada, such as an Ontario business executive moving to Montreal or a Quebec Cree whose mother tongue is neither English nor French. The Canada clause was almost part of Bill 101 but was taken out at the last minute as a sop to placate the nationalists. It was supported by Claude Ryan and the Quebec Liberals, and opinion polls showed Quebecers largely in agreement with it. On several occasions (for instance, the September 1980 first ministers' conference), René

Lévesque said he regretted not including such a clause in his language law, but the conditions in Quebec were not yet right, and stern measures were needed to preserve the French culture. However, whether he could ever afford to alienate his nationalist constituency by such a move was debatable.

In November, after the accord had been struck, Trudeau imposed just the Canada clause section on Quebec. The mother tongue provisions are still in the charter but only come into force in Quebec once it agrees. Trudeau went out of his way to explain that this was not special status because the same provision was offered to the other provinces who, at that point, did not take it up.

The language issue was probably the most explosive throughout the parliamentary committee hearings, and the Liberals used their majority position backstage in the steering committee to restrict the appearance of nationalist Quebec groups. Of the individuals who did speak on this issue, such as Maxwell Yalden, the federal government's official languages commissioner, and representatives of the Canadian Jewish Congress and francophone groups outside Quebec, the message was to broaden rather than confine language rights; Yalden and the Canadian Bar Association urged complete freedom of choice. The issue was also splitting the Liberal caucus and dominating its weekly meetings. Montreal MPs argued strongly for the Canada clause, which would benefit Quebec's other cultural groups. New Brunswick and Ontario members and ministers petitioned vehemently in favour of greater protections for their constituents. At their insistence, the section dealing with "where numbers warrant" was slightly rewritten, so that designated bilingual districts would be avoided. This was not enough for Liberal backbencher Jean-Robert Gauthier, who angrily voted against the resolution and boycotted the patriation ceremonies. (However, he declared his twenty-two-year-old son, Pierre, a "young achiever," to go in his stead, so he could meet the Queen when she came to Ottawa in April 1982.)

The language provisions were not blunted by the legislative override. The binding ingredient for Trudeau's vision of the country — to enable the two founding language groups to feel at home in any region — they are also the new charter's cutting edge. Its legitimacy and ability to act as a cohesive intrument will likely be forged in the language challenges brought by Quebec. Ironically, where enactment of the Official Languages Act in 1969 spurred a backlash in English Canada over bilingual cornflakes packages and the like, the tinder box this time will no doubt be Quebec — a measure either of how much Canada has advanced as a nation or, more likely, how much the two main language groups are still out of step.

_____ ❦ _____

In his report to the Commons in February 1981 on the work of the special parliamentary committee, co-chairman Serge Joyal argued that the contribution of ordinary parliamentarians should now become a formal part of the constitutional amendment process. This is not likely to happen. The special committee had been the cradle of Canada's new charter of rights, but its handiwork was merely endured by those in power and ignored when it suited their purposes. After the final deal had been struck, the National Film Board, in conjuction with the Canadian Broadcasting Corporation, produced a documentary film on the constitution crisis and completely overlooked the work of the committee.

On 16 April 1982, on the eve of the official proclamation by the Queen, Chrétien hosted a gala dinner in the Parliament buildings for all those who had participated in the process. It was a loud, boisterous, off-the-record meal with considerable wine, toasts and witty political speeches by the participants about each other's roles. The members of the committee were invited. But they might as well not have been. There were no toasts to their contributions, no good-natured jokes at their expense. They were forgotten men.

8
So Long as the Rivers Flow

I myself am an old man, and as long as I have lived, my people have been telling me stories . . . and they did not tell me that I was only to live here on this land for a short time. We have heard that some white men — it must have been in Ottawa — this white man said that [the Nishgas] must be dreaming when they say they own the land upon which they live. It is not a dream. We are certain that this land belongs to us.

Gideon Minesque, spokesman for the Nishgas, 1915.

Snapshots of deception.

Click! The ballroom of Ottawa's Skyline Hotel, 29 April 1980. The date is significant — it is just three weeks before the Quebec referendum. Prime minister Pierre Trudeau has come to speak to one thousand status Indian chiefs and elders attending something called the first (it is not clear if there ever was a second) National Conference of Chiefs on the Constitution.

Trudeau's speech is lush with rhetoric and references to Indian myth (there are enough allusions to geese to foreshadow the Canadian Unity Information Office's commercials). With beguiling humility, the prime minister appeals to the chiefs to "treat this country better than it has treated you in the past." He speaks optimistically of native people's involvement in the negotiations for reform of the constitution that are certain to follow on the heels of the referendum.

Then he makes his pitch. Addressing the chiefs and elders from Quebec, he urges them to vote No in the referendum, "to make sure that your goose is not cooked." A Yes vote, he says, will bring to a standstill the process of renewed federalism, "in which you and your people have so much at stake". Energy minister Marc Lalonde comes to the conference the next day and promises the Indians that they will be allowed to sit at the constitutional bargaining table to discuss issues that concern them. The Quebec federalists need every vote.

───────── ❧ ─────────

160

Click! Some time in the hours before 2 October 1980 and the unveiling of the prime minister's resolution on unilateral constitutional reform. Edward McWhinney, constitutional law scholar at Simon Fraser University and legal adviser to the Alberta Indian Association, asks justice officials in Ottawa if there is any reference to aboriginal peoples in Trudeau's resolution. He is told no.

By one account, McWhinney argues there has to be something for them, at least a gesture. At the last moment, he gets Senator Ray Perrault of Vancouver to urge Trudeau to include a new section 24 in the charter of rights.* It reads: "The guarantee in this charter of certain rights and freedoms shall not be construed as denying the existence of any other rights or freedoms . . . that pertain to the native peoples of Canada." McWhinney writes later that the clause carried almost no weight in law; it merely says that there are whatever rights there are, without saying what they are.

———————— ♣ ————————

Click! Room 200 of Parliament's West Block: the splendour of chandelier and rich brocade, the aura of importance given by television lights and men in dark suits. Tuesday, 6 January 1981. Elder Lina Nottaway, a gaily coloured bandana around her hair, a red handkerchief being knotted and unknotted in her hands, sits nervously in a witness chair before the special parliamentary committee on the constitution. She is of the Algonkians of north-western Quebec. Alone of the ten native groups appearing before the committee, her people have not travelled to Ottawa with a lawyer. In the dead of winter, they have come by themselves to ask members of Parliament to rewrite a constitution that recognizes their claims of ownership to the lands of which their forebears were the first human inhabitants and which they still occupy.

Lina Nottaway speaks to the committee in Algonkian, her words translated by another band member. She tells of the animals in the forest, of canoeing down the wild rivers, and of how God gave the land to her people. Solomon Wawatie, who accompanied her, says: "All we want is respect for our way of life. You have your people and we have our people and we can reach agreement on the life of our children and the future of our land."

The prime minister has said aboriginal rights cannot be recognized in a constitution until they are defined. The constitution must be brought home first. Then aboriginal rights can be discussed.

———————— ♣ ————————

*The same clause that had appeared in the federal government's confidential summer draft of the charter.

Click! The same room 200 on 30 January. Nothing spurs the soul to action so much as a lover's menaced jilt. The threat of the federal NDP caucus to withdraw its support of the constitution resolution, unless it is amended to include a clause recognizing the existence of aboriginal and treaty rights, has pushed the government into a change of heart. Trudeau and his justice minister, Jean Chrétien, abandon their argument that aboriginal rights cannot be written into a constitution until they first have been defined, in the process overriding the views of their own officials.

With the TV cameras recording every poignant moment, and several observers and members of the parliamentary committee in tears, Chrétien introduces his aboriginal rights amendment. First, he turns to the presidents of the three national native people's organizations who are sitting in the observers' seats behind him — Del Riley of the National Indian Brotherhood, Eric Tagoona of the Inuit Tapirisat of Canada, Harry Daniels of the Native Council of Canada — and says to the committee co-chairmen: "May I invite the three leaders to come and sit right here, to join me?" He gestures to chairs beside him, usually occupied by senior civil servants. When the native leaders are seated, Chrétien laughs and says: "Now they are my advisers."

The ceremony is played out like the official opening of a shopping plaza in a small town. Chrétien gives Peter Ittinuar, the Inuit New Democrat MP from the Northwest Territories, the honour of reading the natives rights amendment in English. Next, the justice minister gives former Indian and northern affairs minister Warren Allmand, a tireless champion of native rights, the honour of reading the amendment in French.

Jake Epp makes a pretty speech. "I say it quite openly, Mr. Chairman, it is a difficult role very often to convey to other Canadians that if justice is to be done in the country, it must . . . be done first to Canada's aboriginal people."* Epp is a Mennonite; his ancestors came to Canada to escape injustice. His Liberal counterpart on the committee, Senator Jack Austin, is a Jew; he and his people know not only injustice but genocide. Austin's voice breaks with emotion as he calls the amendment an "incredible accomplishment of Canada. . . . I think it proves just how strong, how practical, how pragmatic, but particularly how just and equitable Canadians can be and are." Chrétien says over and over again that night how pleased he is.

(Two weeks later, in a speech in the Commons, Indian and northern affairs minister John Munro asserts that the rights of native people will

---

*On 20 January, Epp, the Indian affairs minister in Clark's Conservative government, had agreed with Chrétien in committee discussion that native rights was too fuzzy a concept to be entrenched in the constitution without further definition.

never again be abused if they are entrenched in the constitution. Failure to entrench them, he says, "would be an intolerable disappointment for native people, in fact, [for] all Canadians. . . . Regardless of the outcome of future discussions on the constitution, I believe that as a result of the proposed charter and its provisions, no one in Canada, no government or individual, will again be able to put aside or disregard the rights of Canada's original peoples.")

The heart of the amendment is virginally simple in its wording: "The aboriginal and treaty rights of the aboriginal peoples of Canada are hereby recognized and affirmed. In this act, 'aboriginal peoples of Canada' include the Indian, Inuit and Métis peoples of Canada."

Click! Again room 200, Monday, 1 February. Just two days after Jean Chrétien's grand ceremony, he tries to take the bones out of the amendment. He does this by introducing a second amendment that would permit Ottawa and any province — without participation of the native peoples — to reach a bilateral agreement that would nullify the protections of the aboriginal rights clause.

It is, of course, the provincial governments that are most opposed — and opposed strongly — to the recognition of aboriginal rights. Under the constitution, property rights are a provincial jurisdiction. Thus, most court actions on aboriginal rights would be against the provinces (except in the northern territories) rather than Ottawa.

After a furore of corridor arguments, Chrétien decides not to proceed with his second amendment.*

Click! The government conference centre, downtown Ottawa. Thursday, 5 November 1981. A yellow mimeographed sheet of paper spells out the five principles of the constitutional accord reached between prime min-

---

*Chrétien's position on native rights requires further explanation. One of his less understood reasons for opposing entrenchment was his concern that "carving them into stone" could harm certain bands who might wish to reopen unfair and archaic treaties but who would be told no by the courts, that a deal is a deal.

On the second amendment he tried to introduce, Chrétien thought the bilateral agreements might be a way of arriving at beneficial deals between Ottawa and a particular province on native rights that other provinces (fearing the precedent) might block if the deals were subject to the general amending formula. The native groups argued that the bilateral agreements amendment might be acceptable, but only if the aboriginal peoples concerned had a seat at the negotiating table and a veto.

ister Trudeau and the nine anglophone Premiers. The press has only minutes to read it before the historic first ministers' conference is adjourned and the scrums and news conferences begin. Harry Daniels, the normally flamboyant Métis leader, is sitting in the press section of the conference room, reading the accord. "Well, it's gone," he says quietly to a reporter beside him. "I knew it would be." Gone?

In secret bartering, the federal government has agreed to the removal of the aboriginal rights section in exchange for its charter of rights being accepted by seven more premiers. Only two or three journalists at the time bother to ask why it has been taken out. "The native people didn't like it themselves," Bill Bennett tells one of them, a line used by Trudeau at his press conference several days later.

John Munro — who told the Commons it would be "an intolerable disappointment . . . [for] all Canadians" if aboriginal rights were not entrenched — tells reporters now that it is the provinces' fault that they have been removed (as if his government had not been a party to the deal). Senator Jack Austin, subsequently appointed by Trudeau to be minister of state responsible for native land claims, says: "I grieve for what was done." But he also says he would have done the same thing as Trudeau if he were prime minister.

───────── ✦ ─────────

Click! Bella Coola. Saturday, 7 November. The Nuxalk, a small band living on British Columbia's north coast, takes back the ceremonial blessing bestowed on prime minister Trudeau eleven years before. Click! Click! Click!

───────── ✦ ─────────

It is not a large part of the constitutional story, the account of what happened to aboriginal rights. There are some snapshots not yet shown — in the end, for instance, a weakened version of Jean Chrétien's clause was put into the resolution. However, it is one of the most important parts.

Here were federal parliamentarians, led by Pierre Trudeau, engaged in constructing a charter of rights and freedoms that would symbolize the noblest Canada that could be. Yet to achieve this goal, Trudeau and his cabinet — and other politicians on both sides of the House of Commons' central aisle — were prepared to sacrifice recognition of the rights of Canada's original peoples. Of all the paradoxes that surfaced in the constitution jumble, this one was the most intolerable.

Judge Thomas Berger of the British Columbia Supreme Court came close to getting himself removed from the bench for his outspoken criticism of the removal of aboriginal rights. He was counsel for the Nishga Indians in their famous 1973 Calder case, argued before the Supreme Court of Canada. In his book on human rights and dissent in Canada, Berger wrote that "aboriginal rights are the axis upon which our relations with the native peoples revolve. To recognize aboriginal rights is to understand the truth of our history, while, for the native peoples, such recognition is the means by which they may achieve a distinct and contemporary place in Canadian life."

Aboriginal rights, it is argued, are the recognition that, before Europeans came to Canada, the land was inhabited by complex societies with a European-style notion of proprietary interest in the land they occupied. In some cases that interest had been extinguished by treaties (which, *quod erat demonstrandum*, was evidence of the recognition of aboriginal title); in many cases — particularly in British Columbia — it had not.

The position taken by various Canadian governments on aboriginal rights has been whimsical for more than a century, inviting no confidence from native peoples. Ottawa accepted the notion of aboriginal land claims in the mid-1870s, during part of the early 1900s and since 1973. Otherwise it did not. In 1927, for example, the Indian Act was amended to make it an offence to raise or provide money for any Indian band to pursue a land claim. The penalty was a maximum $200 fine or two months' imprisonment. In 1969, Trudeau delivered the government's edict on native rights: "Our answer is no. We can't recognize aboriginal rights because no society can be built on historical might-have-beens." As for the provincial governments, most consistently have been opposed, although in varying degrees of rhetoric, depending on the mood of the times and the political stripe of the governing parties.

What advanced the cause by a major step was the 1973 ruling of the Supreme Court of Canada in the Nishga land claims case. Six of the seven judges acknowledged the existence of the concept of aboriginal rights — saying, in other words, that the aboriginal societies discovered by the European explorers did have a claim on the lands they occupied similar to the European notion of ownership. Three judges said the Nishga claim to their land on the north coast of British Columbia still existed; three said it did not — leaving a tied court. The seventh judge gave no opinion on the substance of the claim, instead dismissing it on a technicality.

Until the ruling in the Nishga case, the farthest the courts had gone before was to recognize that native peoples had what is known in law as a "usufructuary interest" in the land they occupied — meaning they used it and occupied it as squatters but could not lay claim of title to it. As a result of the Nishga decision — and because there was a minority Liberal government dependent upon the NDP, which favoured aboriginal rights — Ottawa changed its policy and said it would negotiate land claims.

The next stage, then, was entrenchment. With recognition of aboriginal rights placed in the constitution, native groups would no longer have to argue that those rights, in the abstract, existed; they would be able to move on to the next step and argue whether they had aboriginal title to a particular piece of land. Thus, the Chrétien amendment was a major advance, even if the rights weren't defined.

That last statement, however, is by and large a white man's notion. It presumes a monolithic view of the issue by Canada's aboriginal peoples, which most certainly was not the case. Canada's 1.3 million aboriginal peoples comprise about forty-five different groups, speaking twelve different languages (apart from English and French). There is no reason to expect that they should embrace a single constitutional goal any more readily than should the francophone premier of Quebec and the anglophone premiers of the other nine provinces, or for that matter than should the nine anglophone premiers themselves.

The twenty-five thousand Inuit, who had the advantage of always having dealt with a single government — Ottawa's — were the most unified and best organized on the constitution. The one million Métis and non-status Indians,* grouped under the umbrella organization of the Native Council of Canada (NCC), were the next best organized. That was because — in seeming paradox — they had almost no standing in law. But that gave them the most to gain and the least to lose. The three hundred thousand status and treaty Indians, represented by the National Indian Brotherhood (NIB), with all their tortured history of legal and administrative battles with Ottawa and the provinces, were the most divided on what they wanted.

Add to this diversity of peoples three other factors. The native peoples are justifiably suspicious when dealing with white Canadians. They belong to societies where many acts of collective life are different from the same acts in white Canadian life. Furthermore, they have hired a lot of lawyers over the years who have given them conflicting, and sometimes bad, constitutional advice.

———————— ❦ ————————

They missed deadlines. There is, as an example, one unhappy account of the chiefs of Ontario's sixty-seven thousand status Indians scrambling throughout the summer of 1980 to arrive at a consensus on aboriginal

---

*Treaty and status Indians are those whose rights and privileges are written down in treaty and federal administrative law under the Indian Act — hence their rights are referred to as "defined". Métis and non-status Indians do not have defined rights, but have some undefined rights — for example, the general commitment in the Manitoba Act (now part of the constitution) to provide the Métis settlers with their own hayfields.

rights before the first ministers' conference that September. They failed. The only common request they could take to Ontario's Bill Davis was that he press his fellow first ministers to allow native peoples to sit at the constitution bargaining table. Davis said no.

They tried grand gestures. In October 1980, the NIB opened an office in London and began lobbying British MPs to block passage of Trudeau's resolution until it contained satisfactory aboriginal rights. That same month, the NCC went before the Bertrand Russell Peace Foundation — an international tribunal on human rights in Amsterdam — to try to get the Canadian government declared guilty of 'ethnocide'; they succeeded, but it made very small news at home.

In November, the most bombastic group, the Union of British Columbia Indian Chiefs, chartered a train — the Constitution Express — to bring several hundred Indians across the country to Ottawa. The chiefs said that if they got no satisfaction from the federal government, they would travel on to New York to petition the United Nations general assembly either to declare Canada's Indians to be a separate nation or to pronounce the United Kingdom government responsible for their welfare (it was the British government that had signed the treaties before Canada's existence as a sovereign nation). Later, as the issue dragged on, delegation after delegation of western Indians crossed the Atlantic in full feather head-dress to traipse through London and continental Europe's capitals attempting to rouse opposition to the Canadian government.

Many of them were bad politicians — understandably so in a number of cases. In the late fall of 1980, for example, the NIB refused to be grouped together in a common front with the NCC. They were afraid that, by so doing, Ottawa would make the argument that status Indian rights — defined by law and treaty — should be downgraded to the same level as the Métis non-defined rights. It was an argument not without logic, given the federal government's past duplicity, but it still allowed Trudeau and Chrétien to sidestep the aboriginal rights issue by saying they were dealing with a divided house.

The native groups were, from time to time, bullheadedly extremist. A number of the Indian chiefs — most notably those from British Columbia — refused to appear before the parliamentary committee to make their case. They argued that nothing the committee agreed to would have any binding effect on the government. Chief Wayne Christian of the Spallumcheen band of the Shuswap Indians announced when he got off the Constitution Express: "We're not here to listen; we're here to demand." Other chiefs said they would only talk to "heads of government" — meaning they were a separate nation in themselves. Only at considerable risk to his own job did the temperate, low-key Del Riley, president of the NIB, decide after two weeks of agonizing deliberation, to appear before the committee.

What rights did the native peoples want? Everything from assurances that land claims would be met, to pledges of native self-government within their own domains, to special protection against encroachment of modern North American life on the territories they inhabited.

It was the Inuit who caused a change in political attitude, who convinced at least the moderate elements in the leaderships of the other groups to take a more subtle approach to the federal government. While the Indians and, to a lesser degree, the Métis were making loud noises at press conferences, representatives of the Inuit Tapirisat were turning up day after day at the parliamentary committee hearings, sitting in the observers' section and watching. They had their own MP, Peter Ittinuar, to feed them a kind of insider's diet of information about what was going on. The Inuit came to the conclusion that the committee was not a toothless body but a forum where change to the government's resolution could be effected.

Their Ottawa representatives talked to the Ottawa representatives of the Council of Yukon Indians which, in turn, in January sent word to its legal counsel — Vancouver lawyers Donald Rosenbloom and Jim Aldridge — that there was hope for some movement. Rosenbloom found a business reason to come to the capital, where he could sit in on the committee's hearings and talk to members of the NDP caucus. It is a tribute to the caucus — which applied the political pressure on the government: aboriginal rights or no more NDP support — and the leaders of the three national native groups and Rosenbloom that a fragile consensus was worked out. Negotiating in Ed Broadbent's office, Rosenbloom and the native leaders worked out a wording that was finally accepted by Chrétien.

The rights that the justice minister agreed to put into the charter were in three parts. The Indians, Inuit and (for the first time in any official federal document) the Métis would be recognized as the aboriginal peoples of Canada. The existence of aboriginal and treaty rights were "recognized and affirmed" — meaning, that, by dint of their being entrenched in the constitution, they could not be abrogated by any statute passed by a federal or provincial legislature. A third provision said that nothing in the charter could limit native people's rights — meaning that the charter's requirements that all laws in Canada be applied equally to all citizens could not be used, for example, to block special native hunting rights.*

---

*They would, of course, be subject to the charter's general limitations clause, which says that all rights must be subject to what is "reasonable" in a "free and democratic society," and to the sexual equality clause, which overrides every other right in the charter. This means that sections of the Indian Act discriminating against rights and privileges of Indian women would have to be expunged.

The government's acceptance of those rights was as much a triumph for native politics as it was for Canadian justice. Unfortunately, neither triumph was permanent. The common front fell apart within days. Western Indian chiefs accused Riley of selling out his people and clamoured for his resignation. By 16 April, the NIB formally reversed itself and opposed the rights amendment. Five days later, Harry Daniels called Canada a racist state and said the amendment was not enough: there had to be specific wording affirming that aboriginal rights took precedence over federal and provincial laws, and guarantees that violations of aboriginal rights would be heard by the courts.

The National Indian Brotherhood fervently launched itself on its London strategy, putting itself in league with the devils — the gang of eight provincial governments who were most opposed to the inclusion of aboriginal rights in the constitution. According to more than one estimate, the Indians spent over half a million dollars to lobby the British government, backbench MPs and members of the House of Lords — most of it band money, some of it (sadly) the proceeds of sales of historic artifacts.

Against the advice of some of their more experienced legal counsel, provincial Indian associations in British Columbia and Alberta went into the British courts to seek a declaration that the British parliament still had legal obligations to the Indians of Canada as a result of treaties signed with the imperial crown before Canada existed.

In the minds of some lawyers who had worked with the Indians, they got bad advice from Canadian lawyers and from British ones, too — in particular from Conservative MP Sir Bernard Braine, noted defender of obscure causes and claims of unheard-of peoples on remote archipelagos.* It is British constitutional practice that a decision by the executive relating to foreign affairs is binding on the courts. Thus, once the Foreign and Commonwealth Office decided that Canada was a fully independent nation (despite its constitutional anomaly), the courts' hands were tied vis-à-vis the Indians. The decision meant that all obligations the British parliament once had to the Indians passed to the Canadian government in 1931 on the enactment of the Statute of Westminster.

Lord Denning, the master of the rolls, gave a graceful ruling, declaring Britain's responsibilities were over, but saying that historic guarantees to the aboriginal peoples "should be honoured by the crown in respect to [the Canadian government] so long as the sun rises and the rivers flow". But it was elegant verbiage, no more; Lord Denning's *obiter* did not extend across the sea.

---

*A London newspaper noted that, in taking up the case of the Indians, Sir Bernard was applying himself to his largest land mass.

Both the NIB and the NCC had rejoiced when the Supreme Court of Canada delivered its September ruling that the federal government's resolution was unconstitutional because it lacked substantial provincial support. The Inuit Tapirisat did not. It had maintained its support for both unilateral action on the resolution and the aboriginal rights amendment. Inuit leaders suspected that if the federal government had to return to the bargaining table with the provinces, the most likely casualty would be native rights. They were, of course, correct.

No explanation that is completely satisfying has ever been given for dropping the rights clause in the accord. Accounts from provincial delegations vary: some say it was given up almost by accident, or by a kind of osmotic, unspoken agreement; others stick to the line that it was discarded because the native peoples themselves did not accept it. On the federal side, there are reports that the prime minister was surprised to see it missing when the proposals drawn up by the provinces were placed before him — but that he shrugged and accepted it. No one from any delegation, federal or provincial, says the issue was debated at any length in the private sessions.

To its shame, the federal NDP caucus took two weeks before saying it would vote against the resolution unless recognition of aboriginal rights was restored. Ed Broadbent and his senior advisers were angry with the Indians and Métis for having reneged on the amendment which the New Democrats had worked so hard to win. But in one of Canada's most worthwhile collective acts, public opinion compelled the first ministers to restore the full force of women's equality rights (which also had been scrapped in the accord) and a watered-down version of aboriginal rights.

The diluted version, accepted by the federal and provincial governments in late November (and proposed by the Alberta government), said that *existing* aboriginal and treaty rights would be recognized. Chrétien quickly argued that the addition of the word "existing" did not change the meaning of the original clause. There were many who disagreed with him.

Civil and native rights lawyers pointed to the principle in law of statutory interpretation, which says that every word in a statute has meaning and must be considered by the courts. Thus judges would be required to say: "The word 'existing' is there because the legislators wanted it there. Therefore they intended it to mean something." Outside the federal justice department and the offices of the provincial premiers, the prevailing legal view was that the aboriginal rights clause, weakened by the word "existing", would only protect rights already determined in law (i.e., in various treaties and protections set down in the Indian Act); the constitution had been pulled back from affirming the abstract notion of aboriginal rights.

———————— ❦ ————————

The constitution story added one more dark chapter to the relationship between Canada's original peoples and the country's white governments. The Indians and Métis were in part the authors of their own misfortune. If they had been as politically astute as the Inuit — if they had recognized the value of the wording they had achieved and had supported Trudeau's resolution — they would have made it powerfully difficult for the prime minister to abandon them in the final bartering that went on in November. Native rights lawyers such as the NDP's Ian Waddell have argued that the only thing radical about the whole charter of rights was its aboriginal rights clause.

But the mis-steps of the native politicians do not cancel the shabbiness of the white politicians. The Indians and Métis were opposed to the clause that was in the constitution because they wanted more; Trudeau and the premiers used that as an excuse to give them less. That final snapshot shows the nation-builders with a face of shame.

------------------- ❦ -------------------

A nation-builder at work. The House of Commons, the afternoon of 23 March 1981, and the occasion for a full-dress speech on a matter of public policy by the prime minister of Canada. Pierre Trudeau was in magnificent form. For six months he had let the constitutional debate swirl around him; now he was answering his critics. Pouring scorn on those who would delay the project, or stop it entirely, Trudeau told a full chamber that there was no time like the present for action and "no longer room for either the cowards or the uncommitted." Acknowledging right away that his reform scheme had scored divisions in the country and among the premiers, he set forth a fairly simple defence: "Lest the forces of self-interest tear us apart, we must now define the common thread which holds us together. If this realization of our identity involves hard choices, whoever said that the coming of maturity was easy?"

For nearly two-and-a-half hours — more than three times the normal length of parliamentary speeches — Trudeau stood on the Commons floor, animated, jabbing his finger at his opponents, occasionally pleading with them. It was not quite Sir John A. Macdonald ("These hands are clean") defending his honour in November 1873 in the face of the Pacific railway scandal. But it had that same resonance of history, an almost desperate once-in-a-lifetime performance. Liberal MPs who packed the government benches egged him on throughout and exploded in a standing ovation at the end, joined by about two dozen spectators in the standing-room-only visitors' gallery. Even The Globe and Mail *editorial board, no friend of Trudeau, gave him grudging approbation: "It was an eloquent plea to the jury."*

Since October, the constitutional wrangle had dominated the nation's business. Parliament had become the forum for a wide-ranging and bitter debate, in which the constitution served as the theoretical wedge for all kinds of discontent:

abortion, metric conversion, capital punishment, rail policy — the list seemed never-ending. Joe Clark spoke six times in the debate, for nearly an hour on each occasion, denouncing the way the initiative was being carried out by the government. Trudeau kept his peace, waiting for the end in order to sum up, as he does in cabinet. And now, it appeared, the end was near. The Quebec election was three weeks away, two more provincial courts were ready to pass judgment on the process, and the dissident premiers had planned a meeting in Ottawa to devise an alternative plan. The Liberals wanted the debate over with before all these events took place and so had invoked a form of closure, expecting to finish it off within days. With the vote on time allocation pending that evening, Trudeau rose to defend what he called "a crucial step in nation-building."

By turns pensive, sarcastic and elliptical, but always dramatically compelling, Trudeau attacked the provinces as rapacious and narrowly self-interested, and the Conservative opposition as a party that had squandered its faith in the future. Even Claude Ryan did not escape having his nose tweaked when Trudeau observed that the Quebec Liberal leader had come around to endorsing an entrenched charter of rights only after a papal encyclical a few years before.

The provinces, the prime minister said, had "lost their virginity" in 1966 when Quebec premier Daniel Johnson linked patriation to increased provincial powers, and they had been making even greater demands ever since. As for the Tories: "I say with regret that, though the Conservative Party played an eminent role in the creation of Confederation, they have long since abandoned that spirit of decisiveness." Staring fixedly across the floor at Clark, Trudeau asked rhetorically what would be the victory cry of those attempting to derail the constitutional revision because of its divisiveness: "Praise God, we have defeated the charter of rights and freedoms?"

The prime minister did not advance any new arguments in favour of his constitutional plan, and it was the first speech in which he did not rely on the two competing visions of Canada to make his case. Instead, he enumerated the political arguments that had been used to attack his policy on the constitution. Then he lit into them one by one, reasoning that his resolution did not violate Canadian legal or political traditions, nor give the federal government more power at the expense of the provinces:

> In sloughing off the last vestiges of colonialism, in entrenching those values Canadians hold in common, we are merely setting the stage for a contest about the kind of Canada we will have in the future . . . Will we be highly centralizing? Will we be a loose confederation of shopping centres, as some wag said about Los Angeles? Will we be something in between? I don't know.

As for the rule of unanimity, that is a notion Trudeau derided as "wrong in theory and in practice . . . Is there one single town council, school board, labour union or corporation which could operate if the unanimity rule were to apply to all basic questions?"

The prime minister concluded by doing something he rarely does: he pleaded for support, albeit somewhat jeeringly — *"It is easy to keep one's hands clean when one has no hands."* He asked those opposed to him to consider whether the rights of Canadians would be better protected if the constitutional resolution was defeated. *"Would aboriginal rights be more entrenched? Would women be more equal? . . . Would God be more present in our laws?"* Then, quoting French poet Charles Péguy, the prime minister urged on the committed in a peculiarly Trudeauesque way: *"Everything begins in mysticism and ends in politics. What really matters is that mysticism not be devoured by the politics to which it gave birth."*

It was not quite a knockout punch — if only because his opponents were then gathering momentum and were able to dodge the blow. (The Tories deflected the import of what he had said by upbraiding a prime minister who had spoken for well over two hours, but who had then tried to restrict others to twenty-minute speeches; and by undertaking a mammoth filibuster in the Commons days later to resist closure.) But it was certainly the kind of haymaker an aging heavy-weight would throw for his last try at the champion's crown.

Four days later an unusual and revealing thing happened at the prime minister's press conference: the questions ran out a good five minutes before the session was to end, probably the first time in his thirteen years as head of Canada's government that Trudeau's willingness to answer had exhausted the reporters' desire to question him. The subject — the constitution — had everything to do with it. *"I guess we all see the inevitable,"* Trudeau shrugged. *"What's the point of hitting your head on the wall?"*

9
The Short, Nasty Life of the Gang of Eight

April is the cruellest month, breeding
Lilacs out of the dead land, mixing
Memory and desire, stirring
Dull roots with spring rain.

T.S. Eliot, *The Waste Land* I, The Burial of the Dead

Spring does not always bring the same efflorescent quality to Ottawa as it does to other world capitals. Large patches of hard, brown grass and dirty snow often dominate the lawn on Parliament Hill well into April, while last year's litter, corroded by road salt, blows about in the cool winds. It is here on 17 April 1982 that Canada's renewed constitution is proclaimed amid a pelting rainstorm. It was here, nearly a year to the day earlier, that Trudeau's adversaries enjoyed their greatest, though ephemeral, triumph.

❦

The public signing of a counter accord on 16 April 1981 by eight provincial premiers is the most audacious manoeuvre of the so-called gang of eight, the defensive alliance brought into being by Trudeau's unilateral action. With all the trappings of provisional government, the premiers arrive in the nation's capital and secrete themselves away for talks that continue until two in the morning in the sumptuous VIP section of the Chateau Laurier Hotel known as the Gold Key rooms. Group Chairman Sterling Lyon has brought a suitcase of liquor from Manitoba to help defray some of the costs. In another room down the hall, their ministers and officials lie low, while the press is kept at bay at the end of a long corridor, behind a locked and guarded door. The elaborate signing ceremony the next day takes place in the conference centre, and the premiers insist on full security, protocol, personal staffing and communications systems for an event that is all over in three hours. Its purpose is pure and simple: "The one area where we have shown some weakness — that we were not able to agree amongst ourselves — had been repudiated today," Peter Lougheed tells reporters. Over and over again.

The brave common front papers over a number of cracks but, nonetheless, it is an historic event. For the first time, a Quebec premier agrees to patriation of the constitution and an amending formula without either a new division of powers or an explicit veto for that province. Lévesque's critics will charge that he has traded his provincial birthright for a mess of pottage — a cosy compact with the "English" provinces to defeat his arch rival, Pierre Trudeau. The charge is a telling one.

The bonhomie of the formal accord masks an extraordinary night and several weeks of strain and brinkmanship that nearly tear apart the alliance. At the last minute, René Lévesque wants out. He is only brought to the throe of a momentous political decision because of the personal loyalties that he has formed with the other seven premiers over the previous six months, and the common front tactic of which he was the principal architect. Having used the group of eight to regain some political respectability and snatch a provincial election from the overconfident Quebec Liberals, he is trapped by the commitments that have been given on his behalf and the events that have been set in motion. The months leading up to April 1981 were an agonizing political period for Lévesque, in which he had to face the same electorate that had rejected his referendum option only a year before. But now, arriving in Ottawa on 15 April, two days after a decisive election victory, which caught some of the eight by surprise (they were half-preparing to push ahead without Lévesque) the Québec premier is buoyant and cocky. All his instincts warn him off the provincial accord. He does not believe Trudeau can accept what he and the seven other premiers are proposing, but he does not want to go down in history as the premier who signed away his province's traditional veto. It is Quebec's birthright, he tells his fellow premiers repeatedly that long night. The decision is eating at him.

For the other premiers in Sterling Lyon's suite, the preliminary kibitzing over Lévesque's electoral success soon gives way to a sense of alarm and betrayal. The conference centre has been booked for eleven the next morning but the eight may not have a deal after all. Bennett, Blakeney and Buchanan are particularly upset. They have lobbied strenuously over the last few months for changes to the Alberta amending formula that would blunt the opting out aspect and so make the offer more palatable to Ottawa. They thought they had secured agreement on these revisions during a telephone conference call the previous week, before the Quebec election. Lévesque had said he approved of the changes generally, with only one or two minor matters to be worked out. His fellow premiers

had no idea this included removing something they viewed as essential
— the requirement of a two-thirds vote in a legislature for opting out to
take effect — and they grow increasingly resentful about the late-hour
haggling.

Lévesque does not come right out and say he will not sign the document. But he wants the signing ceremony put off, stalling for time and
pleading that he must discuss the ramifications of it all with his new
cabinet. Bennett and Blakeney sustain the pressure: a newly elected
premier with a majority government doesn't need cabinet approval for
anything, they taunt him; he is his own boss. Quebec politics are different, Lévesque replies, telling the westerners they do not comprehend
the subtleties of administering that province. Lévesque is especially sharp
with Blakeney. He blames Saskatchewan for leaking parts of the agreement and breaking the understanding that all would be kept quiet during the Quebec campaign. After failing to negotiate a private deal with
Trudeau and only then joining the group of eight, Saskatchewan is in no
position to be dictating terms, Lévesque sneers.

After hours of argument, the others back off: the two-thirds requirement is dropped. The accord is sent out for redrafting. But the English
premiers want Lévesque to scratch *their* backs, too, by signing blank
copy pages for a cross-country newspaper advertisement, setting out
the accord; the premier's solemn signatures are clustered beneath a large
Canadian flag. Lévesque grumbles at this but Bennett, whose idea it
was, is determined to wear him down. Finally, exasperated, Lévesque
snatches the pen, scrawls his signature and, scooping up the sheaf of
papers, bashes Bennett over the head with it in a way one premier later
describes as "somewhat playfully." "There," Lévesque says, "I've signed
your damn ad." The meeting adjourns.

----------- ❦ -----------

The April gathering of the gang of the eight made it nakedly clear that a
deep political chasm separated them from the other three governments
in Canada. It created two intractable camps, both believing that political
might makes right. In one group were Liberal prime minister Pierre
Trudeau and two Conservative premiers; opposing them were eight governments, representing four parties at different points on the political
spectrum. It was not ideology that held either side together. It may have
been contrasting views of the country, even though the group of eight
sheltered an avowed separatist. Too frequently, the motives were personal and tinged with spite.

Despite their formal request for Trudeau to talk to them around the
bargaining table in a spirit of compromise, none of the premiers took up

The Globe and Mail, Toronto

Constitutional nightmare.
The Globe and Mail, Toronto

*Reprinted with permission
— the Toronto Star Syndicate*

In April 1981, a month before his court heard the constitutional case, Chief Justice Bora Laskin met the leaders of the three parliamentary parties and Senate speaker Jean Marchand at a prayer breakfast on Parliament Hill. Left to right: Ed Broadbent, Joe Clark, Bora Laskin, Jean Marchand and Pierre Trudeau. *Canapress Photo*

Prime Minister Pierre Trudeau brings down the gavel to open the "one
last time" constitutional conference in Ottawa, 2 November 1981.
Robert Cooper

The backroom boys: (left to right) Michael Pitfield, clerk of the privy
council; Michael Kirby, secretary to the cabinet for federal-provincial
relations; and Hugh Segal, federal-provincial adviser to the Ontario
government. *Robert Cooper*

The gang of eight breakfast together, 3 November 1981. Clockwise from left: Brian Peckford of Newfoundland, Allan Blakeney of Saskatchewan, Angus MacLean of Prince Edward Island, John Buchanan of Nova Scotia, René Lévesque of Quebec, Peter Lougheed of Alberta, William Bennett of British Columbia and Sterling Lyon of Manitoba (back to camera). *Canapress Photo*

Left to right: Peter Lougheed, William Bennett and Allan Blakeney share a light moment, 3 November 1981. *Robert Cooper*

Brian Peckford (right) pursues a point with Peter Lougheed (centre) as
the Wednesday, 4 November 1981 meeting adjourns for lunch.
Angus MacLean and government officials are in the background.
Robert Cooper

Ships that pass in the night: the premiers of central Canada, René
Lévesque and William Davis in the private negotiating session,
4 November 1981. *Robert Cooper*

Peter Lougheed and René Lévesque during a break on
4 November 1981. Who stands accused? *Robert Cooper*

While the bargaining goes on in another room, senior federal justice officials, led by Barry Strayer, prepare the various draft proposals. Left to right: Mary Dawson, Gerard Bertrand, Barry Strayer and Fred Jordan. *Robert Cooper*

Half the gang of eight at coffee break during a private session. Left to right: Angus MacLean, Peter Lougheed, Brian Peckford and William Bennett. *Robert Cooper*

Keeping the channels open on the second last day: Tom Wells, Ontario
minister of intergovernmental affairs; William Davis; and
Roy McMurtry, Ontario attorney general, with Allan Blakeney.
Federal adviser Michael Kirby and John Buchanan are in the rear.
Robert Cooper

On Thursday, 5 November 1981, at 9:30 A.M., Trudeau awaits the
premiers and their final offer, worked out overnight. *Robert Cooper*

Tense corridor discussion on the morning of the final deal, Thursday, 5 November. Left to right: Michael Pitfield, Jean Chrétien, Pierre Trudeau and William Davis. *Robert Cooper*

Signing the constitutional accord: Michael Pitfield, Pierre Trudeau, Michael Kirby and New Brunswick's Richard Hatfield; Hugh Segal and deputy minister of justice Roger Tassé are in the rear. *Robert Cooper*

While the ten other governments sign the constitutional accord,
René Lévesque, the former journalist, slips away to be by himself
with the morning paper. *Robert Cooper*

The political lieutenants: Jean Chrétien, Roy Romanow and
Roy McMurtry after the pact has been signed. Next to Chrétien is
his long-time aide, Eddie Goldenberg. *Robert Cooper*

The deal has been struck, and the federal team marches down to the
television cameras at 12:30 P.M., 5 November 1981. Left to right:
Jean Chrétien; Michael Pitfield; Pierre Trudeau; James Peterson,
Liberal MP, Willowdale; Michael Kirby; and Roger Tassé.
Robert Cooper

Thumbs up for the television cameras in the conference centre, waiting
for the congratulatory speeches to begin on 5 November 1981.
Robert Cooper

The Quebec camp during the closing statements, the "hymn to unity."
Left to right: René Lévesque, minister of justice Marc-André Bédard
and constitutional adviser Claude Morin. *Robert Cooper*

Reprinted with permission — the Toronto Star Syndicate

Registrar-general André Ouellet was the final person to sign the
constitutional proclamation on Parliament Hill, 17 April 1982.
Watching near the table on the left are Gerald Regan, Jean Chrétien
and Pierre Trudeau; Michael Pitfield and Michael Kirby flank
Queen Elizabeth. *Canapress Photo*

Reprinted with permission — the Toronto Star Syndicate

the prime minister's rather casual offer to meet him while they were in Ottawa. Indeed, the contents of the accord were transmitted to Trudeau by messenger; no-one deigned to walk the few hundred yards down Wellington Street to Parliament Hill. The whole affair smacked of medieval armies encamped on opposite sides of a meadow, despatching heralds with ornate challenges.

Trudeau, to be fair, was not particularly accommodating either. Only days before, in a puckish mood, the prime minister told reporters that he didn't feel he would be very welcome at the premiers' gathering. "I don't think I'll stand outside . . . twirling my cap and waiting to be invited in."

The April accord was clearly a banner of battle, the right's ultimate position. Despite the soothing talk of compromise, there was no flexibility in the common front. But there was not much on the other side either. Chrétien's gruff dismissal of the offer within an hour of its being made only consolidated the opposition ranks and rekindled their rancour. At the same time the federal allies were not totally united. While the eight premiers strutted before the television cameras in Ottawa, Richard Hatfield was in Fredericton, grappling with his caucus. The New Brunswick Tories did not like being the only Conservative government in Atlantic Canada supporting Liberal Ottawa and they were pushing their leader to find a *rapprochement* with the dissident premiers. During the morning of 16 April, the day the accord was signed, Hatfield phoned Sterling Lyon in Ottawa to say he would consider adding his signature if equalization and language rights could be included. Lyon promised to call back after he had talked about Hatfield's offer with the other seven, but he never did.

Meanwhile, the New Brunswick premier called Trudeau to explain what he had done. The prime minister was aghast. "My God, Richard, what if they accept!" But they didn't. It was Allan Blakeney, the last aboard, who returned Hatfield's call, as much out of politeness as anything else. There had been some discussion about the proposal, he said, but most of his fellow premiers had left town without coming to an agreement. Miffed at being treated so cavalierly, Hatfield easily won over his caucus and told a press conference that he would not relinquish his support of the federal charter of rights for some vague promise of accommodation later. The Supreme Court of Canada was set to hear the constitution case in two weeks time and the battle lines would stay drawn until it brought down its decision five-and-a-half months later.

———————— ✦ ————————

The defensive alliance that would eventually metamorphose into the gang of eight formally began on 14 October 1980, twelve days after Trudeau announced his unilateral initiative. At Toronto's Harbour Castle Hotel, in a suite of rooms overlooking Lake Ontario, nine premiers met for breakfast, "rallying around the chairman," Sterling Lyon, one of them said later.

Because of a mix-up, which he took as a slight, Richard Hatfield was not told of the breakfast meeting and so did not show up until two hours later for the mid-morning gathering. The New Brunswick premier had left the failed first ministers' conference the previous month, condemning the prospect of unilateral action and urging another meeting around the constitutional table. He had reiterated his distaste for Ottawa's course of action after a session with his caucus in Campobello, in the wake of Trudeau's announcement.

Now he was having second thoughts; the attitude of his fellow premiers and his own pricked pride were prodding him in a contrary direction. Unlike the other premiers, who had been huddling with their top strategists and, in some cases, consulting opinion polls, Hatfield had a unique way of sniffing the political winds. He spent the two days before this meeting by himself, in Montreal, walking around without any political hangers-on, calling friends and relatives across the country ("people whose opinions I respect for a variety of reasons") about what he should do on the constitution. It would be — as it was with so many of the others, if for different reasons — a highly personal decision, impenetrable to the observer and, as John Kennedy once wrote, "mysterious even to those who may be most intimately involved."

At the breakfast meeting in Lyon's suite, the premiers were fracturing into three blocs. For one of the few times in his political career, the prudent Bill Davis was carving out a position without any provincial allies. Normally an extremely canny political operator, who tests all the winds before sailing forth, he went immediately on record as supporting the Trudeau plan, even to the point of urging federal Tories to break with Joe Clark on the issue. Nothing the others could say, including their pleas for party unity, would change his mind. The western premiers generally viewed Davis's position as crassly political, an attempt to cash in on the popularity of a charter of rights in this, an election year in Ontario. But the Big Blue Machine's polls showed that support for Trudeau was a dubious, although not unmanageable proposition, and there were many in the Ontario cabinet, even among Davis's chief advisers, inveighing against this unholy alliance.

However, it was the premier's decision to make, and he, personally, was fed up with the interminable bickering and with his fellow premiers using the patriation debate as a bargaining counter for more powers. Of course, it was easy being a Canadian from the porch in Brampton or on the dock by the summer cottage on Georgian Bay. Ontario was going through troubled times (by 1980 it was technically a have-not province) but it still had sufficient political clout at the centre by virtue of the ninety-five MPs it sent to Ottawa. The decision to support Trudeau was therefore partly comfortable, partly heroic. As John Robarts's education minister in the 1960s, Davis had become convinced that entrenching minority language rights, at least in the field of education, was a critical and sensible step in nation-building. He had proposed in 1979, at the tail end of the last constitutional round, that Ottawa at least should patriate "without the hindrance of the provinces." Trudeau's plan went much further than Davis would have liked but deep down he felt it was "essentially right", and he could stomach the rest, especially if it all could be accomplished quickly and without too much turmoil.

In the middle group that day were Saskatchewan's Allan Blakeney and Nova Scotia's John Buchanan, both pragmatic Maritimers (Blakeney had been transplanted) who preferred a political solution and wanted to get back to the bargaining table. Blakeney, who was ideologically closer to Ottawa Liberals than many around the table — "a bit of a federast," as someone put it — was convinced Trudeau would not proceed alone and was merely looking for a new opening to convene another federal-provincial conference. In September he had fought Trudeau on the need for having what Blakeney termed "a double majority" for constitutional change, pluralities in Parliament and among the provinces. But he was not a simple province-firster, like many of his confrères, and had a genuinely pan-Canada outlook on many issues. In the mid-1970s Blakeney had even proposed a national energy fund, in which the resource provinces would recycle some of their windfall profits — an idea that was anathema to Peter Lougheed, who turned it down flat when Joe Clark suggested it during private negotiations in 1979. Furthermore, Blakeney saw minority language rights as part of "the Confederation bargain". He was prepared to accept them for his province, although only if other premiers did the same.

Buchanan was not as optimistic about Trudeau's intentions but he was much less of a constitutional philosopher than Blakeney, and more inclined to make a deal. If a door was left open, he wanted to peep in to see where it would lead. Moreover, he and Peckford were jostling over who would be the pre-eminent spokesman for Atlantic Canada in the gang of eight. They disagreed sharply about the two key issues for the Atlantic provinces — fisheries and offshore resource development — and Buchanan was far more interested in carving out his own distinct position on these questions (for local political consumption), particularly if it meant that Nova Scotia might get a head start on the development boom by being less intransigent. Buchanan told his fellow premiers that while he would personally like to support them in court action, he must first seek the approval of his cabinet. He stayed for the group (of seven) photograph at the end of the day — Blakeney, Davis and Hatfield had already gone their own ways — but then called Lyon a week later to say he would not be joining the others for the time being.*

The remaining six premiers were determined to beat Trudeau in the courts and so establish their legal as well as political right to be regarded as his equal. For Peter Lougheed, that was a principle that had been steadily developing since he took power in September 1971, determined to have a different constitutional outlook from his predecessor, Harry Strom. He came shortly to repudiate the Victoria charter, which Strom had signed only months before. In 1966, as the youngish leader of the Conservative opposition in Alberta, Lougheed had called for "a halt to the growing regionalism in this country [and] a return to a strong central government . . . Our peculiar combination of parliamentary system within a federal state requires statesmanship by the premiers in resisting provincial political gains to the detriment of national strength."

A decade later, he had become the chief spokesman for greater provincial rights. On the election of the Parti Québecois in 1976, Lougheed said he empathized with their desire to be masters in their own house. On Quebec referendum night, he observed that his government's constitutional position was "probably the strongest document for provincial rights of any provincial government in Canada . . . we will approach the table as we always have with the view that Canada will be stronger if the provinces are stronger."

At the core of the dissident group were three elements, sometimes fusing into one: the iron personalities of Lougheed and Lyon; the scheming of Claude Morin for a common front, a panacea not always fully shared by Lévesque; and the intense personal dislike many in the group felt for Pierre Trudeau. During the ensuing months, whenever spirits sagged, Trudeau's name was all it took to get the bile secreting. In October 1980, probably the only two of the dissenting premiers who were not animated by spite were PEI's Angus MacLean, who joined as much from a deep-seated conservatism and a desire to be part of the pack as anything else,

---

*By the time Hatfield, the latecomer, was told of the divergent viewpoints of his fellow premiers that October morning, he had already made up his mind. He told his nine colleagues that he would be supporting the federal initiative, providing he could secure a couple of relatively modest changes: the entrenchment of official languages for New Brunswick, and different wording on the equalization formula already in the resolution to represent the will of the majority of the provinces. His announcement provoked little comment.

The following day, seated across from each other on the brushed-suede couches in Trudeau's parliamentary office, the prime minister patiently heard Hatfield out and then readily acceded to his demands. Welcoming his new ally, Trudeau said: "All I can tell you is that I admire the elegance of your position."

and Lougheed, impelled, it appeared, more by the contest than by any personal grudge. Intensely competitive, a streak he attributes to his mother, Lougheed compensated for his short stature to succeed (briefly) as a professional football player with the Edmonton Eskimos. While there was no love lost between him and Trudeau, colleagues of both have observed a curious respect, despite, or perhaps because of, their many tangles. "They're both tough, mean sons of bitches," a Trudeau man said. "But they came to admire each other for that. One thing Trudeau remembers is that Lougheed's never lied to us. He's always played it straight."

There are some who see in Peter Lougheed the young boy who crept into his grandfather's Calgary mansion during the Depression, while it was boarded up and ready to be auctioned off for a fraction of its worth, vowing to restore the family to its former status.* But while Lougheed was patrician-born, his outlook appears to be more akin to that of Alberta's new *arriviste* class, the rough and tumble entrepreneurs, who were determined to hold on to their hard-won fortunes in the face of outside raiders.†

Lougheed's constitutional stance did not fully mature until late 1978 largely as a result of the resource battles he had been having with Ontario and the federal government. In late 1972, convinced that Alberta gas was being undersold, he created a two-tier system — one price for Alberta and another for the rest of the country. Bill Davis was furious — Ontario consumers would be bearing the brunt of these new charges — and was forced to fly to Edmonton to discuss the proposal with Lougheed personally, because the Alberta premier would not meet face to face with an emissary, only with a fellow first minister. The symbolism of the Davis visit tickled Lougheed immensely and he made sure the point was noted: "The East is used to us westerners coming to them on bended knees. Now we hold the high cards in terms of energy and we plan to use

---

*Lougheed's grandfather, Sir James Lougheed, was born near Brampton, Ontario in 1854 but moved west after his law degree, making his fortune in land speculation around the turn of the century. He was a Calgary law partner of R. B. Bennett, later Conservative prime minister. In 1889, Sir James was nominated to the Senate by Sir John A. Macdonald. Already a wealthy man, Lougheed's family owned a twenty-six room mansion in Calgary, which they called "Beaulieu," occasionally entertaining visiting British royalty there. However, as Allan Hustak points out in his biography, *Peter Lougheed*, the family wealth had dissipated by the end of the Depression, and "Beaulieu" and all its fine furnishings were sold for paltry sums.

†To find the premier's dimly lit office in the Alberta legislature, one has to wend one's way through a maze of guardians and outer offices to the very rear corner of the building, symbolic of the almost bunker mentality that at times seems to grip the Alberta government.

them." Davis's second visit, in the spring of 1973, was even more elaborately staged: as the Ontario premier's chartered jet touched down, so too did a green-and-gold helicopter carrying Lougheed from the opposite direction. Like heads of warring nations choosing neutral ground to discuss a peace treaty, the two leaders held their talks in the airport's VIP lounge.

The resource battle with central Canada increased in intensity following the 1973 Middle East war and the subsequent dramatic rise in the price of OPEC oil. Lougheed not only demanded market value for his oil, but he was fighting federal attempts to siphon off some of the windfall profits in order to compensate for imported oil in the East. The first salvo was John Turner's 1974 budget which, among other things, declared that provincial royalty costs were no longer deductible from federal income tax. Oil companies made a show of sending their rigs south to more hospitable corporate climes (they eventually returned) and Lougheed, resonant with anger, told the television cameras that "the whole concept of taxing the resources of the province is going to destroy Confederation as we know it. It violates the whole spirit of Confederation." Journalist Christina Newman portrayed him then as a man "whose soul seems as clenched as his jaw line."

At first blush this determination to make the East pay more for western resources should not have stood Lougheed in good stead with René Lévesque, whose Montreal refineries are heavily dependent on foreign crude and federal subsidies. But the two men found their visions of Canada contained considerable common ground — particularly their perceptions of the two orders of governments as co-equals; "small c confederation," one observer put it. Although Lougheed was to the manor born (like Trudeau), he was also very much a self-made man (like Lévesque). Each of them admired the other's stubborn streak, and seemed to look on their relationship as a kind of learning experience.* Within the angry eight, the Albertan was Lévesque's touchstone, the colleague in whom he had the most trust. Together, they formed the hard centre of the gang of eight, exerting a kind of gravitational pull on those who occasionally considered other tacks. Their lieutenants, Dick Johnston and Claude Morin, each played the tough cop at the ministerial level.

Lévesque's distrust of Trudeau was deep-seated; some close observers say they have detected in him a certain inferiority complex in Trudeau's presence, the college drop-out who spent much of his university years playing bridge in the cafeteria. Publicly the two men profess that their

---

*In his biography of Lougheed, Hustak writes that the Alberta premier flinched from contesting the national Conservative leadership in the spring of 1976 because he did not understand Quebec and did not want to be the prime minister who might preside over the break-up of the country if the separatists were elected there, as they were in November of that year.

differences are solely ideological; privately Lévesque resents Trudeau's intellectual veneer, and Trudeau is jealous of Lévesque's reputation as the more able political communicator.

During the September conference, both Bennett and Peckford knocked heads with Trudeau over resource issues and were resentful of his scornful jest that they were trading fish for rights. In their interchanges, Bennett and Trudeau had a way of "looking right past each other," one premier observed; "they never seem to connect."

The overall bearing of the dissenters, however, was perhaps best characterized by its chairman, Sterling Lyon. Uncompromising and harsh-tongued, both in public and private, he had been fighting Trudeau's desire for an entrenched charter of rights since they were both fellow attorneys general in the late 1960s. "We beat him then and we can do it again," the Manitoba premier repeatedly told his comrades. Lyon's contention was that Trudeau did not understand Canada; the prime minister was "a mid-Atlantic person with a mind-set somewhere east of Iceland." For Lyon, the task was simple: to force Trudeau "to swallow twelve years of fetishes." ("I've looked up the word in a dictionary," he told a reporter later. "And it's absolutely the right one!")

——————— ♣ ———————

Within a week of the Harbour Castle meeting, attorneys general and officials from the six most strongly opposed provinces congregated in Winnipeg to plot their courtroom strategy. They made it known that provincial references would be made to the courts of Manitoba, Newfoundland and Quebec, to test the constitutionality of the proposals.* The next day, 24 October, the Liberal government moved closure in Parliament to hurry the debate into the committee stage.

Throughout the fall and winter, while the charter of rights was being studied by the special parliamentary committee, the dissident provinces huddled together in a defensive posture, concentrating on their legal challenges and publicity campaigns. Quebec, as usual, was the most skilful at bringing the cause to the public's attention. A series of billboard and television advertisements were produced, showing a federal

---

*These three particular courts were chosen because they represented a founding province (Quebec), one carved out of a territory by federal legislation (Manitoba), and a former dominion (Newfoundland) which had joined Confederation of its own volition. In the main, a sub-committee of three decided upon the court tactics and drafted the questions: Kerr Twaddle, the Scottish-born lawyer retained by the Lyon government; Melvin Smith, B.C.'s deputy minister of intergovernmental affairs; and Yves Pratte, a retired justice of the Supreme Court of Canada and former chairman of Air Canada, who became Quebec's chief constitutional counsel for the next twelve months.

fist crushing the Quebec flag and the reproof: "Minute, Ottawa!" The Lévesque government also distributed a television commercial which presented a parish priest criticizing the Trudeau proposals; this enraged the federal cabinet (Chrétien most of all), which ironically was embroiled just then in a controversy over whether there should be a mention of God in the constitutional preamble. In early December, the PQ demonstrated that it was not a spent force politically by holding a major rally at the Montreal Forum; René Lévesque addressed a crowd of 14,000, the largest political meeting in the province since the referendum campaign.

Meanwhile, by late December, the opinion polls were making it clear that a majority of Canadians in all regions disapproved of the way Trudeau was proceeding with the reform plan; the same polls gave the federal Tories a boost, indicating that the party was shrewd not to commit itself on the substance of the reform. Public opinion still overwhelmingly supported the elements of the resolution — an entrenched charter, greater mobility rights, and minority language guarantees — and would continue to do so. But the spectacle of warring governments grated on Canadians. The greatest condemnation was expressed on the Prairies and in British Columbia, where the anti-Trudeau sentiment bordered on uncontrollable rage, and the constitutional issue became the lightning rod for all sorts of western discontent with Ottawa.

Trudeau had never had much success in western Canada; he couldn't seem to visit the place without insulting it. "Why should I sell the Canadian farmers' wheat?" he rhetorically asked prairie wheatgrowers in 1969. A decade later, he passed up a Liberal policy convention in Vancouver, complaining of a bad cold, only to be photographed before the west coast meeting was over, boogieing at a New York discotheque. After the 1968 election the Liberals held twenty-eight seats in western Canada (including four in Alberta); after the 1980 election they had only two, neither west of metropolitan Winnipeg. Provincial Liberal parties in the West were decrepit versions of their former selves.

Pierre Trudeau appeared never to understand the western psyche and behaved, as Richard Gwyn has pointed out, "time and again as a Brahmin among the untouchables."

Yet although western discontent was deep-seated, the blame cannot all be laid at Trudeau's doorstep. There were tremendous fundamental differences within the region: Saskatchewan, the only province where the two founding peoples are both minorities; Alberta, where resource issues are as sensitive as language in Quebec and political moderates are in a minority; British Columbia, where the political strife is infused with wackiness and an extra dollop of hard-nosed British trade unionism. As Peter Lougheed was fond of warning: "We have aspirations here in western Canada and we trust that he [Trudeau] will look at the results of

February 18th [the 1980 federal election], and not May 20th [the Quebec referendum], when he is considering the situation with regard to western Canada."

Trudeau did not heed that advice; he had a different interpretation of those dates. On 28 October, a federal budget was brought down with an ambitious national energy program as its centrepiece. Westerners saw it (correctly) as a raid on their burgeoning resource revenues; two nights later, Lougheed took to the airwaves with an emotional Churchillian appeal. He told Ottawa that unless it changed its plans, he would turn down the oil taps in three successive stages; he told his fellow Albertans that, although they may have to fight on the beaches and the tar sands, they must never give up. The day before, striving to make peace, Trudeau only stirred the pot further by saying to a group of Regina Liberals that westerners were overreacting to his government's policies and were sounding a bit hysterical.

———————— ❦ ————————

The energy battle, which would not be settled until September 1981 (about three weeks before the Supreme Court's momentous constitution decision) brought Lougheed into the contest with an even firmer resolve; he began to take more interest in the machinations of the group of six. The new banker of Confederation, thanks to the approximately $11 billion flowing through the Alberta Heritage Fund in 1980, Lougheed held IOUs from every Canadian province except B.C. and Saskatchewan (which had resource wealth of their own) and Ontario (which still preferred to borrow on the New York money market) — a total of nearly $2 billion at quite favourable rates (11.75% to 13.75%) negotiated during 1979 and 1980.

Yet it was not the revenues but what they betokened that appealed to others in the group, particularly Lévesque. It was exactly the kind of system he wanted to set up for language rights — reciprocal agreements (rather than entrenchment) that bypassed Ottawa. That way, if another province reneged on its treatment of its francophone minority, Quebec would decide on its own whether it wished to remain bound to the agreement; it would not be a matter for judges to ponder and administer. The only problem with reciprocal treaties, as Richard Hatfield had found out, is that they are determined by self-interest and can be ignored by subsequent governments. A Quebec–New Brunswick agreement on minority language rights was overriden by Robert Bourassa when he wanted to pass a more stringent language law (Bill 22) in the early 1970s. Similarly, when the constitutional battle was over, and tough economic times had set in, Lougheed cut back the amount of money in the Heritage Fund that would be available for provincial loans at preferential rates.

———————— ✦ ————————

The fall of 1980 was also when Ottawa opened a third front in the federal-provincial conflict, one that appeared wilfully aimed at bankrupting the PQ government. In the October budget, finance minister Allan MacEachen announced his intention to cut back (by $1.5 billion over two years) fiscal transfers to the provinces for established programs in health care and post-secondary education. This would take place when the Fiscal Arrangements Act came up for renewal in March 1982, and was the first time in the history of these five-year programs that Ottawa had sought to reduce the monies given to the provinces. The 1977 agreement had been a paean to co-operative federalism; this time the negotiations were a sham and MacEachen finally imposed cutbacks that would save the federal treasury about $6 billion over the life of the arrangement.*

The fiscal transfer dispute was part of Ottawa's attempt to save itself some money so it would have more cash on hand for its own favourite causes. Jean Chrétien often mused about the dichotomous nature of Quebec voters, who would support him, a strong federalist, in one election and then vote for a staunch Parti Québecois member provincially. He would tell the story about a sod-turning ceremony in his riding when, after the local PQ member had lifted the sod once, Chrétien, uninvited, grabbed the shovel and turned over nine more clumps to symbolize the federal government's contribution to the project. It was that style of competitive politicking, almost habitual in the prolonged struggle for the hearts and minds of Quebecers, that the Liberals were in the process of extending to the whole country.

———————— ✦ ————————

The English provinces had not given much thought to what eventu-

———————

*Under the new fiscal agreements, passed in the spring of 1982, the provinces were to get $105.4 billion in cash and tax points over the next five years, up from the $104.26 billion predicted in the October 1980 budget. This is still an increase of about 11 per cent in actual dollars but the rate has been significantly reduced; it will save Ottawa $5.7 billion over five years. MacEachen argued that reductions were needed to correct the "fiscal imbalance," by which Ottawa was saddled with huge deficits while many provinces basked in the glory of balanced budgets. But the cutbacks meant that many provinces would have to borrow or dip into resource funds in order to maintain health and educational standards; this would be especially difficult for Quebec, with its large population, its heavy commitments and already high tax rate — about 13 per cent greater than that of Ontario.

ally became known as their "London strategy," until Gilles Loiselle, Quebec's cosmopolitan agent general in London, flew to Manitoba in mid-November to brief the six dissenting provinces on the untapped rebelliousness at Westminster.

Loiselle, a dapper ex-journalist and adroit political operator, whose English has taken on the slightly clipped tones of the carriage set, had been inviting British MPs and various luminaries to his Kensington residence for fashionable lunches, seeking allies for the Quebec cause. He reported to the provincial ministers and officials meeting that day in the cabinet room at the Manitoba legislature that the average British MP was feeling put upon by Ottawa's demands and wished to be thought of as an independent thinker on all matters constitutional. Ottawa's presumption that Westminster was merely a rubber stamp was not sitting well with many backbenchers on either side of the British House.

At this point, Quebec was the only province actively lobbying in London but the notion of making a concerted effort greatly appealed to the heterodox provinces. Soon Alberta, B.C., and (a little later) Saskatchewan cranked up their London operations and added staff who had special responsibilities for the constitution. (Ontario and Nova Scotia also had government offices in London that were pressed into the constitution imbroglio, but their lobbying efforts remained modest throughout, although Ontario gave its building a $1.3 million facelift.)

The 'London strategy' was really quite brazen: to stir up discontent on the backbenches at Westminster, particularly Margaret Thatcher's Conservatives, emboldening them to reprimand their own government if the constitutional resolution were transferred to the British Parliament. It is hard to imagine the reverse situation being condoned in Ottawa; indeed, the Liberal government would later rebuke British high commissioner, Sir John Ford, for allegedly meddling in Canadian constitutional affairs.

However, the British are apparently accustomed to such lobbying, and Loiselle had hit upon a marvellous idea. In Quebec House in London, there was a list of British public figures known as "friends of Quebec," and it was to these people that he first turned for advice. One academic on the list suggested that Quebec might want to push for a parliamentary committee to study the issue, so Loiselle approached Sir Anthony Kershaw, the chairman of a select committee on foreign affairs at Westminster. Sir Anthony's committee had a free slate at the time and he was only too happy to oblige.

The Kershaw committee, which reported in January 1981, gave an enormous lift to the disaffected provinces. The committee recommended that the British Parliament reject Ottawa's request if the *proper* degree of provincial consensus was not forthcoming. The timing of the Kershaw committee's report was important too: it was published just days before the first of the provincial court challenges, in the Manitoba court of appeal, produced a legal victory for Ottawa. The unexpected juxtaposition of the two opinions allowed the dissenting premiers to refer to what Lougheed called "the constitutional tie-game" and to persist with their lobby.

Lost in the provincial euphoria over the report was the fact that the Kershaw committee effectively had taken it upon itself to dictate an amending formula for Canada. Ironically, the degree of provincial consent it thought would be necessary to make the constitutional resolution more palatable at Westminster was not the unanimity rule wanted by the provinces, but the regional concept of the 1971 Victoria charter (two provinces in the West, two in Atlantic Canada, Ontario and Quebec) — the formula in Trudeau's resolution, which was by now extremely disagreeable to most of those fighting Ottawa.

As part of the London gambit, the provinces had acquired a computerized list of British MPs, setting out where they stood on the constitutional issue and how often they had been importuned. Each province hired local solicitors, and inundated the offices of parliamentarians and influential figures with polemical literature.

However, the pièce de résistance was a scheme to have the premiers present individual petitions to prime minister Thatcher if the resolution went forward without their concurrence. Formal entreaties were drawn up on two-foot scrolls of Manitoba parchment; boldly, hand-lettered, they followed the traditional right of a British subject to petition Westminster. If Thatcher would not grant the premiers an audience, as they suspected she wouldn't, the contingency plan was to have the formal requests laid before Parliament and the Lords by sympathetic members.*

At times, in their private discussions about the British lobby, some of the eight sounded like ward captains at a political convention. ("How many MPs have you got? We've got forty. . . .") And despite the Conservative credo of most of them, they were not overly concerned with the political problems they were causing sister Tory Margaret Thatcher in this endeavour. (Neither, of course, was Pierre Trudeau.) Perhaps the most perplexing aspect of the London strategy was that, while all six premiers were committed to it, few — perhaps only Quebec — actually felt that a contested resolution would be defeated at Westminster if it ever came to a vote. At best it would be a delaying tactic, part of a continued guerrilla war to undermine Trudeau's public support. "I am sure we would have won in London," Claude Morin said in retrospect. "I was told *that* by very important people, not only MPs, but advisers to

---

*One of the provisional manoeuvres was to bring legal action before the judicial committee of the House of Lords, and appeal any adverse ruling to the World Court at the Hague. This stalling tactic was advanced by a group of B.C. advisers, led by retired justice J. V. Clyne, but was rejected by the various attorneys general, who were dubious about its chances of success.

Mrs. Thatcher. We were very well informed . . . Of course, one can't be technically sure. But let me say that we at least would have won in the sense that the British government would have postponed the thing so long that Trudeau would have had an election in the meantime and been defeated."

But in balmy Victoria, where the crocuses were sprouting in December, Bill Bennett was having second thoughts about the war with Ottawa and the impending battle of Britain ("I was prepared to do what I had to do, but I really didn't want to go to London."). His best political intelligence informed him the electorate was fed up with the constitution issue and wanted it resolved; his instincts told him another campaign in London would be messy and expensive. And, as one of the premier's political advisers observed: "In B.C., the first question everyone asks is 'How much will this cost?' "*

Bennett was also looking ahead to the following summer when he would become chairman of the annual premiers' conference and their main spokesman for the next year — an opportunity to assume Ontario's (now forfeited) role as honest broker, for which there has always been a certain amount of west coast envy. In many ways still the shy, hardware store keeper from Kelowna (his family actually owns a moderately large chain of stores), Bennett was an odd figure to be thrust into national prominence by these circumstances.

Regarded by many of his fellow premiers as a bit foggy, Bennett is someone who likes to think in large, simple concepts. He ignored many of the subtleties of the constitutional dossier and also had the disconcerting habit of staring off into the distance when someone else was making a point, a little like Trudeau, but without the prime minister's often snappy uptake.

In any case, in the winter of 1980-81, he became one of the first premiers to press for a more positive image to counteract the largely defensive attitude of the protesting provinces. On 2 January, the first working day of the new year, B.C. inter-governmental affairs minister Garde Gardom was sent on a ten-day tour of provincial capitals (including Halifax and Regina, whose governments were not officially part of the group at this

---

*Concern about cost appears to be bred into the Bennett family. In the mid-1960s, after a particularly lavish reception during a visit to Quebec, Bennett's father, premier W. A. C. Bennett, returned home convinced that the poorer provinces such as Quebec were squandering their equalization money. From then on, he argued that equalization payments should be made directly to people and not governments, a position B.C., alone among the provincial governments, has maintained ever since.

point) to see if a counter-proposal to the Trudeau initiative might be developed.

This idea, even though it might be no more than a public relations manoeuvre, had an unexpected ally in Sterling Lyon, still the leader of the dissident premiers, who saw it as a way of stifling the criticism that the protesters were only squabbling naysayers. Joe Clark had first advanced the notion, writing to Lyon and some of the other premiers in December to urge them to adopt a more positive approach, including some gesture on a charter of rights.

***

In late January, ministers from the six opposing provinces met to consider an alternative proposal at Montreal's Ritz-Carlton Hotel, the elegant watering hole for Montreal's anglo elite. It was not Claude Morin's first choice but it suited Lyon's tastes and, out of deference to the group's chairman, the PQ swallowed its chauvinism.

Behind the scenes, Morin was assuming a greater role in shaping the common front and he became the group's acknowledged spokesman when they met the press at the end of the day. Inside the meetings, he constantly reaffirmed Quebec's commitment to renewed federalism, at the same time stressing that the Lyon-Bennett goal of simple patriation had never been a priority with his government; if Quebec was to give up its stance on a new division of powers before patriation, it must have something in return. That something was a commitment not to overburden the package beyond simple patriation with an amending formula. "Our purpose was to drop the Trudeau plan, start with the one we had signed, and have three years of discussions," Morin said later. "Maybe Trudeau would go away by then. *He* was one of the problems."

During this period, Morin was also extremely keen to expand the defensive alliance by including Saskatchewan and Nova Scotia, believing that the direct opposition of eight provinces would be enough to scupper Trudeau. There was not much direct soliciting of Blakeney during the fall and winter months because the others were aware that he was negotiating with Ottawa for greater resource guarantees; and because the prospect of an NDP alliance with Trudeau served short-term Conservative interests on the prairies.

Buchanan was a different story, though, and both Lyon and MacLean lobbied him regularly for his support. Torn by conflicting advice, Buchanan wanted to enjoy the best of both worlds: opposition to Trudeau, without having actually to join the fight. His main constitutional adviser, Jeremy Akerman, the British-born former leader of the Nova Scotia NDP, was pushing him into the common front, and it was also because of him that Buchanan's support was so crucial to the group. Akerman was an old school chum of British Labour Party leader Michael Foot — they would have a long dinner together in London in the spring of 1981 — and this connection would help the provinces open up a new front on the opposition benches at Westminster.

On 6 and 7 February, the six premiers met again at the Ritz-Carlton to discuss the Alberta amending formula. Although Bennett emerged optimistic that an alternative scheme would hatch, Lyon was much more circumspect and told reporters from a prepared statement merely that officials had been asked to study the problem.

In mid-February, Blakeney and Buchanan succumbed and joined the common front. Both were in the final year of their term of office and soon would have to face the electorate. The constitution issue was playing havoc with provincial politics, particularly on the Prairies where the NDP was being squeezed by the old-line parties. But for Blakeney it was also a case of having nowhere else to go. His private negotiations with the Trudeau government — the Hawaii fiasco — had resulted in failure and bitter feelings on both sides. Blakeney had come around to believing that the Ottawa Liberals could not be trusted and that they had lost control of the process on which they had embarked. His party's polls in Saskatchewan showed them consistently favoured by a majority of the electorate there; but a number of disturbing signs were beginning to appear — such as the unrest among the bedrock supporters that was rearing up at the constituency meetings of their federal cousins who were allied with Trudeau. Blakeney had run out of options, the court challenges would be peaking soon, and it was time to get off the fence.

On 26 February, back once more at the Ritz-Carlton, the tableau was completed: the angry eight met as a group for the first time, something an exultant Claude Morin pointed out to the press. A week later, nestled in the cosy embrace of seven anglophone provinces, and with the opinion polls showing a majority of Quebecers favouring their provincial government's position, Lévesque called the election for 13 April. (The Davis government was already in the middle of an election campaign.) The major plank of the PQ campaign was Trudeau's unilateral action — that it offended the federal system, betrayed the promises to Quebec during the referendum and was being carried out without a mandate from the people. It was the election issue Lévesque had once dismissed back in September when the first ministers' conference ended in disarray.

------------------------- ✤ -------------------------

The eight weeks from mid-February to mid-April were hectic for the common front: they met seven times (three in Montreal, three in Winnipeg and once in Halifax) to hammer out the details of the forthcoming accord. A central mystery of these gatherings was the degree of encouragement Quebec was giving to the work the others were undertaking.

Having Blakeney and Buchanan as part of the group added new momentum but also disrupted the understandings that had been formed, since they, along with Bennett, represented a kind of soft centre, more willing to compromise than the others. As the only NDP government present, Saskatchewan was at pains to march to its own tune, so the alliance became fraught with further strains and jealousies. Blakeney's pan-Canadianism and Romanow's media star status were irksome to some in the eight's entourage; since the Regina bureaucracy was one of the best in the country, Blakeney and his staff generally came to meetings with their homework done and a batch of new proposals up their sleeves (the latter was a particular irritant to Quebec). In the hotel corridors throughout the summer following their re-election, Quebec's Morin and Claude Charron were quietly denouncing Saskatchewan. "Last on, first off," they told reporters privately.

There was also tension over Blakeney's standing in the West. While he had some cachet with Lougheed, who admired the Saskatchewan premier's tough stewardship* and his negotiating style on energy pricing, Blakeney was the one scuttling Lyon's planned election platform in Manitoba by refusing to agree to a joint western power grid based on the hydro-electricity potential of the Nelson River near Thompson. The regional politics of the West, in which the Tories and NDP are the main rivals for power, contributed to the mistrust within the gang of eight. Blakeney respected Lougheed, particularly his political stature in the West, and would never get into a public row with him. He had little regard for Lyon, however, once telling his staff that while he had heard lots of right wingers preaching their economic dogma when the occasion demanded, Lyon was the first one he had met who actually believed what he was spouting.

---◆---

Morin left after the first Winnipeg meeting in early March to campaign in the election, but his deputy and close friend, Robert Normand, stayed behind to safeguard Quebec's interests. It was Normand who insisted on full fiscal compensation for any province opting out of future amendments, a condition none of the others particularly cared about. Full fiscal compensation, which meant Quebec tax dollars would not be used to finance a constitutional agreement that had not been accepted by the province, effectively represented a veto for the wealthy provinces like

*Blakeney was not only an extremely able administrator but ran his province like a personal fief, to the point that even federal Saskatchewan New Democrats often checked with him first on many issues and practically made formal apologies afterwards if they did not always follow his advice.

B.C., Saskatchewan and Alberta. It meant that costly new social schemes would be impossible without their participation. It was also a potential veto for the central provinces, who could demand large per capita payments from the national treasury for a plan they would not be part of.

However, full fiscal compensation was the tradeoff for a qualifying clause which British Columbia wished to incorporate in the amending formula to make opting out a more difficult proposition: the requirement of a two-thirds vote in the legislature before a province could embrace that option. At that time, only four governments, Alberta, Nova Scotia, Saskatchewan and PEI, had majorities of more than two-thirds in their respective legislatures, an indication of how difficult it would be to bow out of future changes.

Ironically — an instance of history swallowing its own tail — fiscal compensation was the rock on which the Victoria conference foundered in 1971. There Quebec's Bourassa demanded a special constitutional guarantee for social and cultural affairs that would have included a financial indemnity. That meant that if the province transferred jurisdiction to Ottawa to run, say, a family allowance program, the money that would flow from the central government to Quebec householders would be administered by the Quebec treasury. At the time Trudeau said he was willing to discuss the transfer of funds on a case-by-case basis (the same answer he would give in November 1981) but he was not prepared to write a constitutional blank cheque by enshrining the principle.

On 27 March in Winnipeg, ministers and officials from the eight decided on an amending formula and booked the conference centre in Ottawa for 16 April, three days after the Quebec election. That weekend the final drafting was completed at the University of Saskatchewan law school in Saskatoon by Douglas Schmeiser, a professor there, and Mel Smith of British Columbia. Days later, on 31 March, the three judges of the Newfoundland Court of Appeal declared the Trudeau package illegal, thus setting the stage for the final showdown in the Supreme Court of Canada in a month's time. On 1 and 2 April, there were a hurried series of conference calls between the premiers of the eight provinces, for which Lévesque had to be tracked down on the campaign trail. On the third, Lyon telexed Trudeau that the eight premiers would be meeting in Ottawa on the sixteenth to sign an agreement, which they hoped could be the basis of a new accommodation.

On 10 April in Halifax, the intergovernmental affairs officials from the non-conformist provinces met to approve the Smith-Schmeiser draft and to write the press releases and background documentation for the signing ceremony. There followed another conference call between the eight premiers, just two days before the Quebec vote. Lévesque indicated that he had some minor problems with the draft but was essentially in agreement. No one pressed him to explain what exactly he was unhappy about and Bennett would later kick himself for not doing so. The B.C. premier was already feeling provincial pride of authorship in the April accord; the preamble, setting out the constitutional equality of each province, had been composed by Mel Smith in the den of his Victoria home.

The provision for the two-thirds vote in the legislature to justify opting out was what almost sank the provincial accord. Lévesque would not sign if that was retained, although some around the table felt he did not really wish to sign at all. On 16 April, following the signing ceremony, the strains within the eight were readily apparent. "What you see is what you get," Lyon stonily told reporters who had asked him why the negotiations had gone on until the wee hours that morning. An obviously tired and testy Lévesque snapped that he had just won an election mandate for his position and that reporters should be asking Trudeau why he didn't have one for his proposals, if the charter of rights was so important.

A week later, after the provincial ads touting the accord had appeared in newspapers across the country — the premiers' signatures beneath the red maple leaf — an incredulous senior Quebec official phoned one of his western counterparts: "Did you see that ad with the maple leaf? Did my premier actually sign that?"

The April accord did not capture the public's imagination. Although the gang of eight may have proved to themselves that they could agree, the press comment and public reaction was generally negative. Even Joe Clark felt betrayed. Publicly he lamented only that the premiers might have gone a little further with their counter-proposal. Privately he seethed that they had squandered the opportunity which he felt he had created for them.

In some respects, the accord highlighted the implicit tradeoff that had been on the table since September when Trudeau, in the dying moments of the constitutional conference — and more for the record than for those present — offered to accept the provincial amending formula if the premiers would adopt the charter of rights. Now, with the two camps digging themselves into fixed positions, and public opinion splayed on both sides but demanding a compromise, there were only two options: fight it out in a messy battle on foreign soil, or forge an accommodation on some middle ground.

But, during the summer of 1981, a deal had seemed an impossibility.

There were no channels of communication open between the two camps. Saskatchewan, the lynchpin throughout much of this final round, was mistrusted by both sides. British Columbia, which wanted to be the constitution's new broker, had to wait until the fall for its turn as provincial chairman and then for the Supreme Court's decision for there to be any change in the ground rules.

Roy McMurtry, trying to keep everyone talking, pushed Romanow to take part in a debate wth him at Cambridge University in England before an international law society. Chrétien was also one of the debaters and the three men, together with retired high commissioner Paul Martin, drank glasses of warm beer outside a pub. But there was no spark or interest. They exchanged pleasantries, kidded a bit about the past and then went their separate ways to lobby in London.

Within the gang of eight, the push for concessions and alternatives had withered. Slowly it had dawned on the others that Quebec was not just bluffing about no more negotiations. The Lévesque government's ultimatum was already there in the April accord and they were having difficulty maintaining even that; Claude Ryan's Liberals were chastising them in the assembly for giving away the veto. Only a premier with Lévesque's impeccable nationalist credentials could have signed the April agreement, forgoing as it did a new division of powers and an explicit veto; but it was becoming his albatross. No longer the feckless underdog, the gang of eight was becoming embroiled in its own deception and even self-delusion. Were Lévesque's intentions honourable? Was he capable of signing a pact with Trudeau for renewed federalism? Who was using who?

"We all knew Lévesque had a game to play," Sterling Lyon said afterwards. "It would have been naive to think otherwise. He would always use the caveat of sovereignty-association. . . ." But the others used him as well, and it was not entirely a devil's bargain. Certain premiers, Lyon among them, sincerely believed that Quebec's consent was necessary for constitutional reform and that, because of the personal relationships that were forming and the pressures of negotiation, Lévesque might be persuaded to sign a broader agreement. In that context, the April accord was a genuine achievement — at least in the minds of those who signed it. René Lévesque never backed away from the terms of the accord, once he gave his word, as several premiers have testified since. The difference was in what the pact signified. Months later, after the final constitutional deal had been signed without Quebec's signature, and Lévesque was claiming double-cross, Lougheed said: "I don't know how he [Lévesque] can feel it was betrayal, and I find that completely without foundation. How can it be betrayal? We all agreed that we were meeting together to stop Mr. Trudeau proceeding unilaterally. We were informed that morning that he [Trudeau] was prepared for real negotiation, that he was prepared to abandon his unilateral position. Now if that was so, and that proved to be so, then . . . that was clearly within the understanding from 14 October 1980 at the Harbour Castle Hotel. There's no way that's betrayal."

———————— ✤ ————————

In the stuffy cabinet room in Winnipeg at the end of July 1981, a little more than three months before the final arrangement, the constitutional ministers from the gang of eight are meeting yet another time to shore up their morale and to complete plans for the expected push in London. Claude Morin is expounding on the common front: how he never expected there to be such commonality of purpose, how the alliance is the proper vehicle to rid the country of this federal government, this Liberal Party steeped in patronage and grown corrupt from its long period in power. It is a protracted discourse, passionate, professorial and discursive, interrupted only briefly by Morin's excited efforts to keep his pipe alight.

At one point he says that whatever happens in the Supreme Court, "we win." The others think he is talking about the gang of eight. If the court stops Trudeau, we win that way, Morin says. If the court gives him a green light, we win again. Finally, the others realize that he is talking about the Parti Québecois. If the Supreme Court of Canada chooses the federal government over Quebec, it will advance the separatist cause in that province.

There is a slight pause in the recital. Roy Romanow and his deputy Howard Leeson mutter something to each other and then Romanow leans forward. "But Claude, how do *we* win; we, les anglais?" A long, awkard silence ensues. The question is never answered.

10
The British Connection: Lunchtime at Westminster

Would it be helpful at all if the British Parliament were to repeal the British North America Act?

A letter to *The Globe and Mail*
from S.B. Jackson, Simcoe, Ontario.

Thursday, 5 February 1981, is a day in the history of Anglo-Canadian relations that might better be forgotten.

In Toronto, Sir Anthony Kershaw, quintessential British Conservative MP (Balliol, barrister, service with the Hussars, pinstripes and known to wear a monocle), held an airport news conference before continuing on from London to Edmonton to deliver a speech. Sir Anthony, chairman of the British House of Commons foreign affairs committee, which one week earlier had recommended that Westminster not pass Trudeau's constitutional resolution in its present state, told reporters there would be "bad blood" in Britain's Parliament if Trudeau persisted in pushing it through.

Trudeau, too, was in Toronto that day. He told students at Osgoode Hall law school that he was going to do just that, push through the resolution. As he spoke, editors at several newspapers were preparing to publish the leaked minutes of a meeting between external affairs minister Mark MacGuigan and the British government's then-House leader, Norman St. John-Stevas. An irascible St. John-Stevas was revealed to have told MacGuigan the previous November that the British government did not like the charter of rights being included in the resolution and that it could not wait much longer, in any case, for the package to get across the Atlantic. (At that point the federal government had just used closure to move the constitution proposal out of the Commons and into committee.)

Meanwhile, in Ottawa during the Commons question period, Mac-

197

Guigan, replying to NDP leader Ed Broadbent, strongly implied that Sir John Ford, Britain's high commissioner to Canada, was meddling in Canadian affairs.

Two blocks away on Elgin Street, inside the British high commission, Sir John and members of his staff watched MacGuigan's performance on television and decided upon a blitzkrieg counterstrike — an immediate news conference in the National Press Building, where Sir John would say openly to journalists what he had been saying only slightly less openly to everyone he had talked to for the past several weeks: that it would be a "very grave mistake" to assume that Trudeau's constitution resolution would win easy approval from the British Parliament.

Elsewhere in the capital, attending an interparliamentary conference, former Australian prime minister Gough Whitlam, no stranger to constitutional crisis, told reporters that Canada should brook no interference from Britain in its internal affairs.

Finally, in London, A. Roy Megarry, Northern Irish emigré and publisher of *The Globe and Mail*, wound up a week of constitution speechmaking with an address to an all-party parliamentary committee of MPs and peers. He warned them about Trudeau's duplicity in using Westminster to make amendments to Canada's constitution which Canadians would not accept at home.

A furious day, 5 February. There were others like it.

———————— ❧ ————————

The political thunder and lightning unleashed between Britons and Canadians over the patriation of the constitution produced a great deal of deception, sleazy behaviour, silliness, xenophobia and expenditure of public money — mostly, but not exclusively, on the Canadian side. In an issue that seldom, at any time, displayed the best of political deportment, the so-called British connection served up the dregs. A lot of the thunder was classic behaviour that any psychologist would recognize: the unresolved ego conflicts between a grown offspring and its parent. Much of it was irrational and linked to an ignorance of each country's political institutions and national character. Quite a bit sprang from Westminster's passion for constitutional fictions — perhaps to be expected from a legislature that does not have a written constitution of its own but has produced them by the score for other states, its former colonies.

On 1 July 1867, Canada became the British Empire's first federal state — having been constituted by the British North America Act, an enactment of the British Parliament. One might think that this head start on federalism would have given Canadians more skills than other peoples at handling its tricky dilemmas. Alas . . .

There is a British connection to the Canadian constitution story because, until 5 November 1981 — nearly 115 years after Westminster wound up Canada and made it work — the provincial and federal governments could not agree on how to amend the British act that constituted the country; therefore, it had been left a British act, amendable only by the British Parliament.

The history is tangled and fatiguing. Only the essential part needs to be explained, and even this cannot be done briefly.* In 1926, the political leaders of the Empire gathered in Ottawa (ironically) for the Empire's penultimate imperial conference. They framed the historic definition of the relationship between Britain and its self-governing colonies, now called the Dominions: "They are autonomous communities within the British Empire, equal in status, in no way subordinate one to another in any aspect of their domestic and external affairs, though united by common allegiance to the Crown and freely associated as members of the British Commonwealth of Nations."

Lord Balfour was appointed chairman of a committee charged with the task of identifying what remnants of the old colonial machinery should be abolished so that a legal as well as political imprimatur could be placed upon the Dominions' independence. His committee's report was considered by the 1929 conference on the operation of Dominion legislation, which reported to the final imperial conference of 1930; this assembly in turn drew up a draft of what was to become the Statute of Westminster of 1931,† the act of the British Parliament ending all supremacy of Westminster over the Dominions.

The 1930 draft did not contain section 7, which stated that nothing elsewhere in the statute "shall be deemed to apply to the repeal, amendment or alteration" of the BNA Act. If the statute had been passed without this section, Canada may have become a chaotic country, or no country

---

*Moreover, some of the history has departed with the souls of the original players. In 1857, Westminster revised the New Zealand Constitution Act to give the colony's legislature the power to amend its constitution. In 1900, Westminster enacted the Australian Constitution Act, complete with an amending formula. In between, it enacted the BNA Act without an amending formula — purportedly taking only twelve minutes to push it through the House on third reading and then going on to debate dog licensing legislation. Why the difference? The BNA Act was written by the Canadian colonials, but that fact of offshore authorship need not have deterred British parliamentarians from poking into the substance of the bill. Consider their willingness to tinker with its revisions more than a century later, with Canada a fully independent country. If British MPs had added an amending formula in 1867, many people would have been spared migraines from 1927 to 1981.

†Parliamentary devotees know that this was the fourth Statute of Westminster. The first was passed in 1275; it prohibited the marriage of girls under seven and provided for free and undisturbed elections. The others were passed in 1285 and 1290 and dealt with the appointment of justices and the transfer of land ownership.

at all, or at the least a different country from what it turned out to be. Section 7 was added at the last moment, at the request of Ottawa and upon the insistence of premiers Howard Ferguson of Ontario and Louis Taschereau of Quebec.

Ferguson and Taschereau had decided in 1927 that Lord Balfour and the imperial legal draftsmen probably were heading down a road that would lead to the Canadian federal Parliament receiving from Westminster the power to amend any part of the BNA Act by simple statute. In other words, Ottawa would acquire the authority not only to encroach upon what the BNA Act said was provincial jurisdiction, but to wipe out the provinces completely and transform the country into a unitary state. The Ontario and Quebec premiers demanded that Ottawa leave the amending authority with Westminster until federal-provincial agreement could be reached on how constitutionally to preserve Canada's federal nature. The statute, nonetheless, made Canada a sovereign nation. Therefore, Westminster continued the practice that had been already established, to amend the BNA Act automatically upon receiving a joint request from the two Houses of the Canadian Parliament.

It was to end this anachronism of Westminster's constitutional stewardship that the federal government's resolution of 1980 requested the British Parliament to repeal section 7 — and, of course, to amend the BNA Act so that it would include both the charter of rights and an amending formula. What was not clear until (and not entirely clear after) the Supreme Court of Canada ruled on the resolution's legality and constitutionality was whether Westminster should accede to the request without substantial consent from the provinces.

This, then, was the playing field for transatlantic sport.

———————— ✤ ————————

Four scenes. In the beginning, Nicholas Ridley came to Ottawa. Ridley was Britain's minister of state for foreign affairs with responsibility for North America and the Caribbean. When he arrived in Ottawa during the week of 15 June 1980 — just after the one-day first ministers' meeting at 24 Sussex Drive — he met Chrétien and MacGuigan to talk about the constitution and later chatted with Canadian reporters. There was nothing clandestine about his visit or its purpose; indeed the British high commission invited journalists to meet him. And what Ridley had to say was important — because it was the position that the British government, harried, snapped at and used by Canadian politicians over the ensuing year-and-a-half, had tried at least publicly to maintain.

Ridley said there was only one sovereign authority in Canada and that was the federal Parliament. "The constitutional position [of the British government] is that if you send anything over, we would seek to enact it as requested." When he was asked if the British government would introduce the resolution at Westminster in the face of strong provincial opposition, Ridley began to walk on eggs. He said the question was hypothetical; it would depend upon the nature of the objection and the constitutional grounds on which it was based, adding: "But you must be aware of the risk of any opposition in Canada being transferred to the floor of the [British] House of Commons."

Scene two — one week later. Pierre Trudeau had lunch with Margaret Thatcher at Number 10 Downing Street on his way home from Venice, site of that year's Big Seven economic summit. The lunch lasted two hours. When he emerged from Number 10, Trudeau told Canadian reporters that Mrs. Thatcher had pledged her government's support — promising the imposition of maximum party discipline, a 'three-line whip' — for whatever resolution the Canadian Parliament would transmit. He also said that the possibility of provincial opposition was "a hypothesis" that "I didn't ask her to examine and I don't believe she did examine." The construction of the prime minister's sentence was curious: he did not *ask* her to examine the hypothesis, and he *didn't believe* she did examine it.

Two days later in Bardufoss, Norway* — scene three — where Trudeau had gone on a visit after leaving London — he slightly enlarged his account of his luncheon conversation. Asked in a television interview what he would do if the government or Parliament of Britain balked at acting on his resolution because of provincial opposition, he replied: "I hope we wouldn't come to that type of problem, and that's what I told Mrs. Thatcher." He also said: "It's my view as a constitutional lawyer that Britain would have no choice but to accommodate us."

Finally, two weeks later on 12 July — scene four — Trudeau told a Liberal Party convention in Winnipeg: "You probably heard the news that a group of backbenchers in Great Britain at the Westminster Parliament were saying that if the Canadian government didn't settle such and so, they would form a lobby in Westminster and prevent us from getting patriation when we asked for it. Well, all I can say is they better not try." The prime minister received vigorous applause.

The sum of these four scenes is that, within two months of the Quebec referendum and Trudeau's pledge to give Canada renewed federalism, he had misled the public about his meeting with the leader of the government which would have to manage the final legal sanction of his constitutional reforms, and he had insulted the legislators who would be required to vote on it.

---

*One of the more bizarre aspects of the constitution epic is the number of odd world corners where it was talked about and reported on: Venice, Amsterdam, Geneva, Bonn, Baden-Baden, Seoul, New York, Paris, Melbourne, Canberra, Fiji, Lisbon, London and Bardufoss (which may not be a complete list).

No record has ever surfaced of Margaret Thatcher promising to impose a three-line whip to drive the resolution through Parliament. Moreover, the subject of provincial opposition *was* raised at the meeting (as Trudeau later acknowledged, conceding he had spoken to the press with a "lack of candour"), with either Mrs. Thatcher or some British official who was present, indicating a British preference for substantial or unanimous provincial support.

Trudeau's verbal assault on British backbenchers, the first of many, was spurred by remarks made by two or three of them about using the issue of the constitution — once it arrived at Westminster — to press for better treatment of Canada's native people. By suggesting that Westminster's role was merely to rubberstamp a resolution, no questions asked (a constitutional argument that was respectable, even if the belligerent public utterance of it was not), the prime minister demonstrated either a deliberate or an unknowing ignorance of the dynamics of the British Parliament. As Canadians came to discover, there is no nosier, more brother's-keeperish, less controllable legislative body — particularly on constitutional matters — in the world.

Trudeau, as much as anyone, set in motion the acrimony that was to ebb and flow across the Atlantic. Why? He knew that the British government was reluctant to get embroiled in a Canadian domestic political dispute, and he wanted either to bludgeon it or publicly to embarrass it into acquiescence? Or else he knew that he could increase support at home for his resolution by raising the spectre of British interference in Canadian affairs? Or perhaps he was just being Trudeau and telling everyone he would punch them in the nose if they got in his way? Or maybe all three?

Trudeau's ministers took their lead from him. The September first ministers' conference failed. The unilateral resolution was announced on 2 October. Mark MacGuigan and environment minister John Roberts (who had worked with Jean Chrétien during the summer roadshow) flew to London on 5 October to brief first the Queen and then (on 6 October) Mrs. Thatcher. The two ministers chose Canada House, overlooking Trafalgar Square, to publicly press upon the British people the message their leader was delivering at home.

At a news conference, MacGuigan and Roberts were asked about a number of tart letters from British academics that had been appearing in *The Times*, saying that Westminster was not obliged — and, moreover, was obliged not to — pass a resolution from the Canadian Parliament that did not have majority provincial support and contained matter foreign to British constitutional practice, namely a written charter of rights.

The two ministers, both former professors, replied in that waspish manner which academics are prone to use when verbally dismembering each other. MacGuigan retorted: "That surely is a judgment for the Canadian Parliament to make, and not a [judgment] for the British Parliament — or British academics, for that matter," going on to say: "We could give [British MPs] the assurance that if they did not follow our recommendation, then that course of action would be extraordinarily unacceptable in Canada." Commenting on possible resistance from British backbenchers, Roberts added: "You can never discount mavericks seeking publicity." He then recalled how MPs hurried through their debate on the original BNA Act so that they could get on to talking about a dog tax. "I would recommend that they might usefully follow the 1867 example," Roberts said.

The two ministers told reporters that the only problem raised by Mrs. Thatcher and her officials concerned the timetable: when the resolution could be fitted into Westminster's legislative schedule in order for it to be passed in time for Trudeau's desired patriation date of 1 July. MacGuigan noted that British officials said they expected the debate to last four days — an extraordinarily long debate for Westminster, and an indication, at least for the initiated, that there was more to the British government's concern for 'timetable' than met the eye.

On the public stage, through the fall of 1980, the debate between Ottawa and the opposing provinces, and between the federal Liberals and Conservatives, was becoming rapidly hotter, the divisions more pronounced, the rhetoric louder and more inflamed. The first British politicians were responding to the taunts of Trudeau and his ministers. As early as 8 October, for example, Labour MP Bruce George, one of a half-dozen or so backbenchers with a consuming interest in the welfare of the world's aboriginal peoples, vowed he would "embarrass the hell" out of the Canadian government by working to delay passage of the resolution once it got to Westminster.

The British press was sniffing at the story with increasing interest. In an editorial on the day the September first ministers' conference ended in September, *The Times* had warned the Canadian government against unilateral action. *The Daily Telegraph* said in an editorial — a few days after MacGuigan and Roberts had met its editor, William Deedes, a golfing partner of Mrs. Thatcher's husband, Denis — that Westminster should resist Ottawa's threatened unilateralism. *The Guardian*, in a front-page article in late October, predicted "chaos at Westminster" if the Canadian government sent over a resolution that included a charter of rights.

The Guardian's story quoted a British government spokesman as saying: "Adding a bill of rights as a third major feature to the actual patriation bill and an amending formula makes the bill's passage more awkward and inevitably more complicated, since further time will be needed for

discussion and debate. . . . There is little doubt that constitutional experts in both Houses of Parliament would have major reservations about
giving swift endorsement to such a proposal which has constitutional
implications for Britain." This last was a somewhat arcane point probably
unappreciated outside the circles of British constitutional aficionados.
What it meant was that British MPs and lords might resist giving passage to something — a codified charter of rights beyond reach of simple
statutory amendment — that would be non-constitutional in Britain,
(where Parliament is supreme) yet at the same time would become an
enactment of the British Parliament (the Canadian resolution would be
introduced as a British government bill).

A very large number of Canadians, believing that Westminster operates much like their own Parliament, had difficulty attaching importance
to these British backbench mutterings. There were three assumptions
made: one, that party discipline on the floor of the House of Commons
was as tight in London as in Ottawa; two, that the parliamentary mechanisms of the guillotine and closure — used respectively to limit and to
end debate — were as readily available to the British government, should
the need arise, as they were to the Canadian government; three, that
something as devoid of consequence for British domestic politics as
Canada's constitution could not seriously cause a stir among British
parliamentarians. The suppositions were wrong on all counts.

The British MP is a much freer spirit than his Canadian counterpart.
British governments lose votes in Parliament all the time, deserted by
their own backbenchers. Use of the guillotine at Westminster is disliked
as much on the government side of the House as on the opposition side
— precisely because it falls just as hard on the debating time allowed to
backbenchers of the ruling party. Closure in Westminster is an instrument used at the discretion of the Speaker; he decides when to accept a
closure motion, something quite different from the Canadian practice
where the Speaker is obliged to accept a closure motion from a minister.
Finally, constitution matters are considered the pinnacle of parliamentary deliberation — with every MP both a party and a party leader unto
himself. Thus, for Britain's parliamentary parties to impose a three-line
whip on a constitution issue, even a foreign constitution issue, was
inherently unlikely.*

---

*The word 'whip,' used in Westminster-style Parliaments throughout the world,
is an abbreviation of 'whipper-in', borrowed in the eighteenth century from the
vocabulary of fox-hunting. A whipper-in kept the hounds from straying from
the pack. Hence, the whip is the sergeant-major of the caucus or parliamentary
party.

In British parliamentary procedure, the government and opposition chief whips
each week send out to their members a document — itself known as the whip —
which sets down the business of the House for the following week. Every item

It is important to note these parliamentary distinctions. Canadian journalists and politicians focussed far too much attention on how many British MPs might vote No on the Canada Bill. That was not the British government's central concern (although it acquired more body as the resolution sank deeper into the litigious ooze of the courts). The worry in London was over how many MPs would want to take part in the debate.

Westminster is the legislature of a unitary state, passing judgment upon many, many more items of government business than appear before the Canadian federal Parliament. The British parliamentary timetable, therefore, is extremely tight. Ninety MPs* wishing to make speeches on the Canada Bill at all stages of its passage through the Commons could have done terrible things to the government's legislative schedule. *That* was the problem. The more backbench interest that developed in the Canada Bill, the more loath the British government became to introduce it.

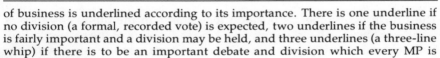

of business is underlined according to its importance. There is one underline if no division (a formal, recorded vote) is expected, two underlines if the business is fairly important and a division may be held, and three underlines (a three-line whip) if there is to be an important debate and division which every MP is expected to attend.

The practice is hoary. As long ago as 1621, notices of parliamentary business were sent out to the King's friends with as many as six underlines. Nowadays, there is some argument over whether a three-line whip is merely a summons to attend the House, or a summons to vote at the party leadership's direction. The latter view has greater currency.

The facts remain obscured on whether Mrs. Thatcher promised Trudeau at their June luncheon that she would impose a three-line whip on the constitution resolution. Logic suggests she would have been unlikely to make such a pledge so far in advance of the resolution arriving in London (unless the two leaders talked a lot more than either has ever let on about the political difficulties the issue was likely to cause).

A three-line whip would mean an expenditure of political capital. Promising it many months ahead of time would be a signal to restless government back-benchers — of which Mrs. Thatcher had many — that they could try to extract something from her in return. Despite the fact that no mention of a three-line whip appears in the British minutes of the June meeting, Trudeau continued to insist it had been pledged (30 October 1980: "If the federal Parliament presented the British Parliament with a resolution . . . [they] said they would consider it a government measure and put a three-line whip on it to make sure it passed.") A British official, who knew what took place at the meeting, said diplomatically but sarcastically: "Maybe she mentioned it at the door when they said goodbye."

*Ninety was about the number of Westminster's six-hundred and thirty-five MPs who paid any attention to the issue. It is awesome to contemplate one of them, Sir Bernard Braine, in full voice: he holds the known Westminster record for the longest speech on a point of order — in excess of three hours.

Trudeau and his ministers were absolutely correct on one point: Mrs. Thatcher had pledged her government's unqualified support for whatever resolution the Canadian Parliament transmitted. Much fuss was made in early 1981 over whether she had been misled by the Canadians into thinking the resolution would be a much simpler instrument — without a detailed charter of rights — if Trudeau decided to move unilaterally. (One account — made public four months after the event — of the October briefing session with MacGuigan and Roberts described Mrs. Thatcher picking up a copy of the resolution, examining it in amazement, and telling the two ministers that it was not what she had talked to Trudeau about in June.) This was a brouhaha manufactured in large part by the sly British, trying to throw rocks in the path of the Canadian government's juggernaut. Mrs. Thatcher and her advisers knew at all times what was likely to be in the resolution because her government's high commission was reporting every detail from Ottawa. The British simply didn't want to put a hot potato in their pocket.

———————— 🍁 ————————

The British government's position took shape in the dusty elegance of what was once the heart of empire — the India wing of the foreign office, built around a courtyard where Queen Victoria used to come with her friends to picnic and play bowls. The wing now houses the foreign office's Canada desk, which is where the resolution eventually came to rest (in December 1981), still in its brown envelope, lying on top of a cupboard. Sir John Ford had been sending back reports on Trudeau's constitutional intentions from the moment of the prime minister's election victory speech in the Chateau Laurier in February. Through the spring and early summer, foreign office officials looked back into the historical papers on BNA Act amendments and prepared a report — they were amused to find precisely the same debate on provincial opposition on past occasions as was being raised now.

It was a political as well as a legal report, outlining every imaginable eventuality, including the likelihood of a knock-down federal-provincial brawl. It speculated on Canadian public feeling, and on the probable reactions of Canadian and British MPs. The advice to the government from the foreign office was as follows: the legal precedents were clear — the British government had no choice but to act on a request from the Canadian Parliament; at the same time, the British government should not get involved in a dispute between the federal and provincial governments (to that end, British-Canadian ministerial meetings would best be avoided, for fear they might be seen as meddling); therefore, the recommended action was for the Thatcher government to make an initial commitment to introduce and support any resolution and thereafter to try to say nothing on the subject until the resolution had arrived.

What collapsed this careful diplomatic strategy was the entanglement of the resolution in the courts, the increasing anti-British rhetoric from Ottawa and the nagging from the Canadian government over when the resolution would be introduced in Westminster and how long it would take to get through. What was described by one senior British official as "the jumpiness and fidgityness in Canada over our pace of movement" irritated the British government far more than the rhetoric, which was more or less shrugged off at 10 Downing Street: Trudeau and his ministers were, after all, politicians playing to their constituents.

The nagging was a different matter. By late 1980, the British had come to the conclusion — strongly reinforced by reports from Sir John Ford — that the Canadians simply did not appreciate the difficulties of managing parliamentary business in Westminster. More to the point, they realized that the Canadian government either did not understand, or was refusing to understand, that the federal-provincial fight was crossing over to the other side of the Atlantic — precisely what Nicholas Ridley had warned against in June.

The British government, first at the diplomatic level, began suggesting tactfully to the Canadian government that it simplify the resolution, or back off on it until the political dispute had been resolved in Canada. The Canadian government not only refused to consider that suggestion, but Trudeau repeatedly reminded those who were interested of Mrs. Thatcher's pledge to support the resolution, and Ottawa continued to press the Thatcher government for a firm date on when the resolution would be handled. The British grew increasingly reluctant to provide a date as the temperature of debate rose in Canada. What they feared most was happening: the issue was attracting more and more attention from Westminster's backbenchers.

It had been widely noted in the British press that Trudeau had invoked closure to end debate on the resolution in the House and move it into committee. The announcement by six provincial governments that they would challenge the resolution in the courts also had been reported in Britain, and had led to a great deal of comment by British MPs that Trudeau was trying to ram the resolution through Westminster before the Canadian courts could get at it. The Quebec government, in the person of its suavely skilled London agent general, Gilles Loiselle, had begun lobbying British MPs within days of the 2 October announcement of unilateral action. Parliamentarians were being deluged by mail and propaganda from stop-Trudeau citizens' groups in Canada and from opposing provincial governments. Sir Anthony Kershaw's foreign affairs committee decided in October to examine Westminster's "responsibility" on Canada's constitution; it began hearings on 5 November. Conservative MP Jonathan Aitken wrote a letter about the constitution to *The Times* in late October; it was reprinted in a number of Canadian newspapers and brought him three thousand pieces of mail from Canada in a single week. In mid-November, he and Labour MP George Foulkes began planning the formation of an *ad hoc* committee of MPs and peers to study the Canadian constitution. Foulkes, a young Scottish social worker, had been campaigning for a parliamentary assembly for Scotland for more than twelve years and dreamed of a quasi-federal United Kingdom with two legislative tiers. Constitutions of federal states were Foulkes's passion. He and Aitken had been to Canada as members of a parliamentary delegation during the summer of 1980.

Throughout all this commotion, Canadian ministers still maintained that the only concern of the British government was timetabling. They were being either naive or crafty. Certainly the British were worried about their parliamentary schedule but it embodied so much more than the Canadian ministers were implying.

Trudeau's London tactics were based upon what one senior Canadian official liked to call "the strategic use of intransigence". They embraced the assumption that the British would have no choice but to comply, if pushed, with any Canadian request. They also were reinforced by Ottawa's feeling that it had the support of the major British political opinion-leaders and power-wielders. A case in point was Lord Diplock, considered the constitutional expert among the law lords (and who eventually closed the second reading debate on the Canada Bill in the House of Lords). Canadian high commissioner Jean Wadds met him at a reception late in the fall and asked him if he would like to talk to any Canadian specialists on constitution matters. Diplock said he was not interested, but he promised to read the resolution and perhaps call the high commissioner about it. Mrs. Wadds cabled home that he "doesn't lobby easily". A week later, Lord Diplock gave her a five-page double-spaced opinion on the resolution, which promptly was transmitted to Ottawa with comments from Mrs. Wadds and the admonition: "Private and personal. Don't make public."

Lord Diplock said that the British could not concern themselves with Canadian constitutional practice, only British constitutional practice respecting the BNA Act. His opinion was the same as the foreign office's: the British could not "look behind" a request from Canada for an amendment. At the same time, he questioned the need to put the charter of rights in the resolution and suggested that it be removed. Lord Diplock went on to say, however, that although Westminster constitutionally could pass controversial amendments (such as the charter) "our only responsibility is to protect the federal character of the country". In conclusion, he said that the resolution did protect the federal character by giving the provinces a role through the amending formula and the entrenching of equalization payments.

The Diplock memo was examined by Canadian justice department officials, who were amazed at its existence (it would have been astonishing for a Canadian judge to do the same thing). Their feeling, though, was that the judge had researched the subject superficially and was behaving more like a Westminster peer than a judge — giving a political, rather than a legal, opinion.

---------------- ✤ ----------------

Like an infuriating gnat, the Canadian constitution now had buzzed its way into domestic British politics. It surfaced several times at meetings of the full cabinet, where some ministers muttered grumpily about getting the thing out of the way. It sparked a testy exchange between Ridley and St. John-Stevas. Behind his public warning to the Canadian government, Ridley — an aggressive, strong-minded individual — was an advocate in cabinet for the Canadian brief, badgering St. John-Stevas to commit himself to a timetable. St. John-Stevas, equally wilful (and about to be sacked from the cabinet because of policy differences with the prime minister), at one point told Ridley haughtily that it would be "impossible" to provide the required House time to meet Trudeau's 1 July target. Ridley, using the same tone, replied that the House leader had no right to respond in such a fashion to a foreign office request. Yet the real testiness was reserved for the Canadians, even though it was seldom displayed. Sir Ian Gilmour, the lord privy seal, said privately to a group of MPs, in reference to Trudeau's repeated public statements about Mrs. Thatcher's support for the resolution; "He's played a dirty trick on us." An MP in the group murmured: "Really, only a cad could do this."

For Mrs. Thatcher, the issue was getting out of hand. Despite the foreign office's cautious admonitions, the time had come for British and Canadian ministers to meet. On 10 November in London, MacGuigan sat down with St. John-Stevas. As was revealed in a leaked Canadian high commission cable to Ottawa, it was not an amiable encounter.

St. John-Stevas suggested that the charter of rights be taken out of the resolution. He said that it would be extremely difficult to get the resolution passed in Parliament's current session unless it was received in London by the beginning of January. The House leader was exceptionally concerned about the court challenges, and told MacGuigan that the British Parliament would not proceed if the matter was before the courts (hearings on the first challenge — Manitoba's — were to begin before the provincial court of appeal in the first week of December). St. John-Stevas also said his government would pay close attention to the recommendations of the Kershaw committee, although it would not be bound by them.

MacGuigan responded forcefully. The charter had to stay; its guarantees of language and economic mobility rights were the heart of the matter. MacGuigan said the Canadian government would drop patriation before it would drop the charter, adding that if the federal government had not been seeking patriation, it would still have been asking for an amendment to the BNA Act to entrench the charter. On deadlines, MacGuigan said the earliest the resolution could clear the Canadian Parliament was mid-January, a date which St. John-Stevas appeared reluctantly to accept. MacGuigan dismissed the provincial court challenges as mere delaying tactics; by going to court one after the other, the provincial governments could tie up the resolution for years.

MacGuigan reminded St. John-Stevas again of Mrs. Thatcher's promise of support and referred to her pledge of a three-line whip. St. John-Stevas said nothing about whether this pledge was ever made, but he did tell MacGuigan that a three-line whip would be useless in the committee of the whole House — where the resolution would be dealt with because it was a constitutional matter, and where Westminster's procedures allowed for long debate and unrestricted amendments.* He also said: "Thatcher is not leader of the House. The government proposes but the House disposes" — the implication being that it did not matter what, if anything, Mrs. Thatcher may have promised.

MacGuigan was tough with St. John Stevas, telling him that no British interference with the resolution would be tolerated once it had been sent to London. The high commission's report concluded: "Summing up, it is clear that Stevas, while he will act correctly, will not of his own notion go very far out of his way to help us. . . . Although there is little give in his position, number of misconceptions have been cleared up and he has much better understanding of our position and now realizes that we will be relentless in pursuit of our objectives, and that measure will no way be tailored to suit his ideas what should or should not be done."

Four weeks later, on 6 December, MacGuigan and St. John-Stevas met again, this time in Lisbon for the funeral of Portuguese premier Francisco Sa Carneiro, who had been killed in a plane crash. St. John-Stevas took MacGuigan aside to say he had some unpleasant news: the British government now had advice from Parliament's legal officers that Westminster could not proceed if the resolution was before the "courts" — whatever courts these were — and this advice was "unfortunately binding".

The Canadians busily began looking for counter-precedents and found a far-fetched one: Newfoundland had joined Canada in 1949 requiring a Westminster amendment to the BNA Act while a legal challenge to the union — dismissed by two courts in Newfoundland as vexatious — was still before the judicial committee of the British privy council. It was sent off to St. John-Stevas.

---

*The committee consists of all members of the House of Commons; basically, it is a forum where matters of national importance may be discussed according to more informal procedures: for example, an MP may speak on a subject more than once.

Although the main worry of Mrs. Thatcher's government was the enormous mischief the constitution resolution could do to Westminster's business schedule, the fascinating question has always been whether the British government thought it could get the resolution passed. British officials have maintained, on and off the record, that passage was never in doubt. But in their most private communications? We jump ahead a little in our chronology to 1 February 1981, when MacGuigan and Trudeau, fielding questions in the House of Commons, mentioned a letter received from Mrs. Thatcher, affirming once again her government's commitment to introducing and supporting the resolution. MacGuigan said the letter had been written late the previous year, after he and John Roberts had met her in October to explain what was in the constitution package.

There was nothing accidental about MacGuigan's statement. Three days earlier, on 29 January, the Kershaw committee had announced its findings — recommending that Westminster not pass the resolution until there was substantial agreement from the provinces. Moreover, by this time, Trudeau had acknowledged publicly that the British government had been worried about the resolution for at least the past two months.

The reference to the letter and to its date had a clear purpose: to underline the fact that Mrs. Thatcher was still pledging her support *after* having been fully briefed by MacGuigan and Roberts on the resolution's contents. This was a vital piece of propaganda for the federal government, because Trudeau and his ministers stood accused of misleading Mrs. Thatcher — first, by not telling her that the government intended to proceed alone if it did not have the support of the provinces; second, by not telling her that it intended to proceed alone with a detailed package that included a charter of rights.

When journalists asked to see the text of the letter, they were told by Trudeau's aides that protocol dictated that a letter from a foreign head of government could be released only with the author's concurrence. Canadian journalists called 10 Downing Street. Would Mrs. Thatcher agree to release the letter? What letter? said the British. A "source close to Mrs. Thatcher" was quoted in the press as saying: "We have no collective recollection of written assurances."

Neither the British nor Canadian governments had any desire to publicize the full text, and the British were upset that its existence had even been mentioned. The text was leaked six days after MacGuigan and Trudeau first talked about it. Indeed, Mrs. Thatcher had been supportive: "I should say at once," she wrote, "that there has been no change in our policy since I saw you in June." But that wasn't the interesting part (except to the Canadian government).

Mrs. Thatcher had written to Trudeau early in December to suggest a visit to Ottawa by British defence minister Francis Pym, soon to succeed

St. John-Stevas as House leader. She said she hoped publicity around his visit could be minimized. Trudeau agreed immediately to the visit, telling Mrs. Thatcher in his written reply that he was "particularly pleased" that there had been no change in the British position. An official "press line" was developed to leave the fourth estate at slumber. Pym arrived in Ottawa on 19 December.

He did meet the Canadian defence minister, Gilles Lamontagne, although whatever it was they talked about is in danger of escaping the historical record. Not so Pym's discussions with MacGuigan and Trudeau, the minutes of which were leaked. Pym told the prime minister that unless the charter was dropped from the resolution, it would not be approved by the British Parliament. Then he went back to London. The Canadian government publicly described his visit as "reassuring".

Privately in London, as it listened to comments from Canadian politicians over the next few weeks,* the British government decided that its message still was not getting through to the Canadians. In late January, Pym again met Canadian officials. Canadian high commissioner Jean Wadds paid a courtesy call on him in his capacity as Mrs. Thatcher's new House leader.† She cabled a long message home to Ottawa after the meeting, quoting Pym as asking once more for the charter to be severed from the resolution. Pym had said there was no doubt that a resolution

---

*New Brunswick premier Richard Hatfield in London on 13 January: "I want to tell you that if this resolution is unduly delayed — or if it is not accepted in the terms in which it is presented by the Parliament of Canada — then the constitutional monarchy in Canada will be severely threatened. In fact, I think it will have a short life."

Hatfield again on 14 January: "If an appeal to the Queen of England [the resolution would be formally addressed to the Queen] is rejected by the Queen of England, or her answer is, 'I'm sorry', there will be people who will understand that we have to get rid of the Queen of England."

(One story told about Hatfield in London concerns a lunch he had with some British politicians. Trying to put the provincial premiers in a British political context, he said they were no more important than the lord mayor of Birmingham. Later on, Hatfield disputed a point with one of the luncheoners by saying: "Don't tell me that — I'm the premier of New Brunswick." The reply was: "No you're not, you're only the lord mayor of Birmingham.")

Trudeau on 22 January (after saying he expected that Mrs. Thatcher would keep her dissidents in line): "It's never been easy for the British. The abolition of slavery in the United States wasn't easy, but it had to be done. This is peanuts [the British government's job of getting the resolution through Westminster] compared to what had to be done there, and the methods we're using are much more democratic and peaceful."

†St. John-Stevas was not missed. A high commission cable said that Ottawa "should welcome [his] removal. It does away with a House leader who was opposed certainly to the timing of any patriation proposals and probably also in part to its [sic] substance."

requesting patriation with a reasonable amending formula would sail through Westminster. But he was blunt on the charter: it was "not our business". According to Mrs. Wadds, he asked the Canadian government to "contrive a situation" that would let the British government off the hook on its commitment to supporting the resolution, pointing out that it would be relatively easy for opposing MPs to block it in Westminster. He had spoken bluntly: if the resolution were to arrive at Westminster then, "it would not go through". In any case, he said, it was no longer possible to handle the resolution in Parliament's current session — the deadline of 15 January had passed — and the British cabinet would hesitate to put forward a measure it knew would not go through.

That cable was the British connection's bombshell — devastating news for the Canadian government. Certainly, it could explain why Ottawa developed such a sudden interest, after months of silence, in reopening negotiations with the Saskatchewan government. The march to London had bogged down.

———————— ✦ ————————

In early February, an exercised Canadian government would have been well disposed towards taking out its pique on someone British. Sir John Ford was the nearest British scapegoat.

The high commissioner first appeared publicly in the constitution story on 6 November 1980 in Lunenburg, Nova Scotia, telling reporters that the dispute had become a bother. "The sooner you have your constitution out of our hair, the happier we'll be in England," he said. Ford was within months of retirement in early 1981. His service in Canada had marked him with a well-deserved reputation for outspokenness. He had embraced the vogue notion of supply-side economics and did not mind giving Canadian government officials advice on a number of economic subjects from whatever platform was at hand. He had criticized publicly the National Energy Program and the Foreign Investment Review Agency. Obviously, the constitution wasn't going to get by him quietly.

Sir John had decided — without specific instructions from London — on his own way of serving his government's interests. Like his Whitehall masters, he was distressed to observe that Canadian bureaucrats and politicians were either not appreciating, or not choosing to appreciate, the minefields the constitution was running into in London. His own talks with Canadian ministers and mandarins he felt had been fruitless. The alternative course he decided upon was to start talking to a wider swath of politically influential Canadians at the next level down: opposition MPs, provincial leaders, journalists, community opinion-moulders of whatever stripe. He did not make speeches — that would have caused a diplomatic row. He had conversations.

For example, Richard Hatfield recalled a conversation he had with Ford in February — he had phoned the high commissioner about the news leaks — in which he (Hatfield) was urged to abandon his support for the federal resolution and convince Bill Davis to do the same, he also was urged to lobby federal MPs in his region to defeat the government, not only because of the constitution, but because it was making other mistakes as well, on such matters as FIRA and energy policy. "It was an incredible experience, well beyond the bounds of propriety," Hatfield said later. The premier called Mark MacGuigan and reported the conversation; he also had one of his officials call Michael Kirby and tell him.

The British themselves had a curious reaction to the call, which lasted nearly an hour. Sir John, after putting down the phone, said to one of his staff members: "What an extraordinary conversation." Hatfield had asked Ford to repeat certain comments several times, which led the British to suspect that he was writing things down. The British had a notion that Hatfield was trying to set up Ford on a meddling charge.

Sir John's conversation with New Democratic Party MPs Ian Waddell and Jim Manly at the governor general's skating party in early January gave MacGuigan the opportunity to go after the high commissioner publicly. If the reports of Ford's activities were true, MacGuigan said on 5 February, it would be "conduct completely unacceptable" to the Canadian government. He promised an investigation into Sir John's lobbying, and said he would complain to London if the criticisms were sustained. It is doubtful if anyone in external affairs or the prime minister's office anticipated Sir John's response.

Within two hours of MacGuigan's comments, Sir John was on the dais of the news conference theatre in the National Press Building, conducting an unprecedented seminar — in both official languages — with journalists on the subject of how difficult it would be to get the resolution passed at Westminster.

Five days later, Sir John unexpectedly cancelled a lunch appointment he had made with Broadbent and returned to London "for briefing". That same day, 10 February, his successor was announced. A foreign office spokesman in London said that Sir John's return and the announcement of his replacement were "completely coincidental" and had nothing to do with events in Ottawa. The statement strained credibility.

Sir John was the very model of a British high commissioner — forceful, erudite and one of the most experienced and professional British diplomats assigned to Canada in years — except for one flaw: he was too noticeable. Above all, the foreign office had wanted to keep the British government aloof from the fray, wishing to avoid any accusation that it was interfering in Canadian affairs. Sir John invited that accusation. He believed, like a number of other British officials and politicians, that for the long-term run of Anglo-Canadian relations it was better to have an initial spot of trouble on the Canadian side of the Atlantic, rather than a whole mess of trouble on the British side later. Nonetheless, he stuck his head up too high. The foreign office wished he had not.

———————— ✦ ————————

Of the many hands which helped carry the constitution conflict across the Atlantic to Britain, none were more skilled than those of Gilles Loiselle, Quebec's agent general in London. From his elegant office on Upper Grosvenor Street and his official residence in Kensington, Loiselle (with the culinary assistance of his wife and their Portuguese cook, Arturo) served his government and frustrated Ottawa with unparalleled distinction.

There was a symmetry and clean Gallic logic to Loiselle's strategy that earned him applause, and later emulation, from the enemy three blocks away and across Grosvenor Square at Macdonald House, the Canadian high commission chancery. Loiselle, a former Radio-Canada journalist who had reported on politics in Ottawa and Europe (he had been appointed to London by the Parti Québecois government in 1977), had mapped out his campaign and was into the field before the federalist side even thought seriously about there being a British problem.

Loiselle read Trudeau's resolution and assumed the ordinary British parliamentarian would not understand what it meant; he further assumed that the overwhelming majority of them would see no reason not to accede to a Canadian request to enact it. Therefore, the strategy he decided upon — with the advice of British politicians and academics who were known around Quebec House as 'friends' — was delay. It was one of these friends, political scholar Peter Lyon, who spoke to Labour MP Kevin McNamara, deputy chairman of Westminster's select committee on foreign affairs; and it was McNamara and committee chairman Sir Anthony Kershaw who decided that Britain's responsibilities for the Canadian constitution would be a useful subject for their group to examine.

With the Kershaw committee pot bubbling at October's end, Loiselle set out to identify those MPs and peers whom he and his staff thought would be delighted to poke into a tricky Commonwealth constitution issue. The list the Quebecers drew up included all the Scottish and Welsh devolutionists, Ulster loyalists, everyone with an interest in native peoples and the Commonwealth, everyone with a Canadian background, everyone with a strong legal bent, and all backbenchers who were influential. There were about 250 names — the number of parliamentarians Loiselle contacted personally between October 1980 and November 1981.

The vehicle for many of the contacts was lunch at the Kensington residence, superb meals planned by Madame Loiselle and executed by Arturo. A Quebec lunch came to be spoken of lovingly around Westminster. For posterity, one of them — with Labour MP George Foulkes as guest — was recorded somewhat mischievously by a National Film Board crew preparing a documentary on the constitution story (the director sped up the eating sequence and scored it to lively music). The message was always the same: polite, low-key ("Anything big, and we would have looked like South Africa," Loiselle said later), never a hint of *indépendantiste* rhetoric. Section 7 was in the Statute of Westminster for a reason, Loiselle told his guests, and the charter of rights was a matter for domestic political debate.

The last component of the agent general's strategy was to draw Ottawa into a London fight; in his view, the federalists were more dangerous keeping quiet — which, with the exception of the odd intemperate statement from a visiting minister, was exactly what they were doing (the people at Macdonald House were not enthusiastic about Ottawa visitors). The Quebecers reasoned that once Ottawa started lobbying in London, Westminster would pay much more attention to the issue. Their objective was to cause so much trouble in London that Ottawa would feel compelled to react. The cables sent home from the Canadian high commission at the end of 1980 suggest the gambit was successful. Many of the communiqués described the effectiveness of Quebec's lobbying, and on one occasion Ottawa was asked plaintively: "Should we be doing same?"

---- ♦ ----

The woman in command at Macdonald House was Jean Wadds, a former Conservative MP for Grenville-Dundas and the daughter of an Ontario lieutenant governor. Appointed high commissioner by Joe Clark in October 1979, she had social grace (an acquaintance once described her as being superb at hacking weekends), a great deal of enthusiasm for the constitution scrap and — as it soon became plain — more than a dash of political innocence. Cabinet ministers and justice department officials who came to London in October to brief the British and the Canadian high commission staff were soon persuaded that Mrs. Wadds was going to need help on the constitution. She got it in November — in the person of a rumply bear of a man with a shrewd, many-layered mind and a voice that sounded like Marlon Brando's in *The Godfather*.

Belfast-born Reeves Haggan had graduated from Trinity College, Dublin, read law in London's Inns of Court and then drifted over to Canada at the end of World War II with a group of Canadians he had met in London. He went to work for the Canadian Broadcasting Corporation, rose to be in charge of political broadcasting in Ottawa but was forced out of CBC in the mid-1960s in the titanic internal battle over a feisty public affairs television program called "This Hour Has Seven Days". Haggan was going to leave Canada but a friend, prime minister Lester Pearson, wanted him to stay and found him jobs, first with the commission planning Canada's centenary celebrations, later with external affairs. Later still, Haggan went to work with the solicitor general's department, was subsequently seconded to the federal-provincial relations office, and it was from there he was sent to London at the end of 1980 as the high commission's constitutional adviser.

Considerable information is available about the high commission's activities in the winter of 1980-81, largely because of a Canadian government sieve through which the high commission's confidential cable traffic leaked in buckets. Cables were sent daily, most of them signed by either Mrs. Wadds or Haggan. They contained a mammoth amount of information, in large part unfocussed, on what was going on in London vis-à-vis the constitution. Their tone was generally optimistic — somewhat surprising, because Haggan, a close student of Westminster from his London law student days, would have been aware of the problems that were taking shape.

Wadds and Haggan took a vacuum cleaner approach, sucking up every piece of information remotely connected to the constitution and blowing it back to Ottawa. Anyone who said anything about the subject was mentioned; all the minutiae of the Kershaw committee's deliberations were reported home. Foreign office officials were quoted at length. Speeches given in London by Brian Peckford, Roy McMurtry, Roy Romanow and Richard Hatfield were assessed; their movements and what access they had to British officials also were transmitted in detail. Many of their reports contained friend-and-foe messages: who was on Ottawa's side and who wasn't.

Mrs. Wadds reported often on her social contacts; Haggan dealt with procedure at Westminster. They passed along a lot of political gossip — for example, one wide-eyed message from Mrs. Wadds described an encounter with Labour Party leader Michael Foot at a cocktail party: "He's not up to date on issue. No firm opinion, but not sure he'll be bound by Callaghan view. He did say he went to school with David Lewis.* If

---

*James Callaghan, former Labour prime minister, strongly backed the federal position. Trudeau, a good friend, had spoken to him personally in late 1980 (Callaghan was later invited as a guest to the proclamation ceremony). The late David Lewis, former national NDP leader, had worked through the summer of 1980 to help shape his federal party's policy on the charter. Both the federal and Saskatchewan NDP lobbied Labour frantically, with Broadbent sending over a study paper prepared with the help of the federal-provincial relations office. Labour's leadership eventually supported the federal position; the party's international policy office did not.

Lewis is supportive, it might be suggested that he contact Foot." There is little indication that the commission was lobbying very strenuously during this period, and in fact, most of its activities until the spring of 1981 were responsive — replies to requests from parliamentarians for information, rather than the armgrabbing that came later.

One leaked cable caused a delicious furore in the British press and provoked wry comments to the high commission's staff from British foreign office officials. The cable contained the veiled warning that the high commission's telephones were being bugged. "We must take it for granted that phone conversations of this sort are all monitored and taped by suitably equipped countries including certainly Britain, France, the USA and the Soviet Union. Why give British notice of our strategy, concerns or judgments of some of its key players? Why give others . . . opportunity for mischief?" It was a case of clumsy wording; what the cable writer intended to imply — according to a high commission source — was that transatlantic telephone communications were insecure. Which, in general, they are; they can be monitored by spy satellites. What prompted the mention of this fact, however, has remained a guarded secret. (A British newspaper cartoon, depicting the high commissioner's office with bugged stuffed polar bears and mooseheads, was hung in Mrs. Wadds's office.)

Then there was the case of the rather dashing Jonathan Aitken — son of a Canadian-born British MP and the nephew of a former Canadian MP, Margaret Aitken, who had been a close friend of Mrs. Wadds. Socially and politically he came into contact with Mrs. Wadds, with some embarrassing results.

Aitken had been in Canada that summer as part of a British parliamentary delegation. He not only caught the flavour of the developing battle, but was given a thorough seminar by Quebec officials, met members of the Ontario legislature committee studying the constitution, and had a long chat — in Sault Ste. Marie, of all places — with one of Canada's experts on parliamentary procedure, John Holtby, then clerk assistant at Queen's Park, later a director of the Parliamentary Centre in Ottawa. Holtby tutored Aitken on the constitution issue, enlivening his interest and convincing him that the constitution should be brought home in a "sensible way".

After his letter was published in *The Times*, he came to be treated by his fellow MPs as something of an expert on the subject. They were being inundated by mail from Canada, most of which was going unread into the wastebasket. Here was Aitken, one of their own, who appeared to know what the thing was all about.

Mrs. Wadds's report home was not kind to the nephew of her close friend. "He's opposed," she said, "but he's anxious not to be made to look foolish in the end. He readily admitted being worked over by

Quebec. He sees the headline potential but on the other hand expresses admiration for the charter of rights." The cable suggested that "we shall need to do a snow job on him" when he next came to Canada (Aitken was planning a trip in 1981).*

By the beginning of 1981, Westminster was fully engaged with Canada's affairs. The Kershaw committee was poring over written briefs from dissident provincial governments and hearing evidence from foreign office officials and some of Britain's leading constitutional academics (most of those who appeared before the committee had at one time accepted retainers as consultants for provincial governments opposed to the Ottawa resolution). The Aitken committee, which met weekly from January to July, heard from provincial ministers and agents general, Indians, Inuit, the publisher of *The Globe and Mail*, and Sir Ian Gilmour, 'the deputy foreign secretary' — who attracted the largest audience, about sixty MPs and peers. Aitken himself publicly referred to the "growing hysterical mood" in Anglo-Canadian relations, and wrote to Mrs. Thatcher, urging her to stop off in Canada on a peacemaking visit — a suggestion decidedly not followed — on her way home from a meeting with the American president in late February. Aitken also was allowed to address the influential 1922 committee,† and Westminster's Commonwealth parliamentary association heard from many of the same people who had spoken to the Aitken committee, plus Mrs. Wadds. When she addressed association members in December, she committed what was later acknowledged — by the high commission staff among others — as an error in judgment: she characterized Quebec's lobbying on the resolution as the expected response from a separatist government. This was not well received by her audience; the clever Loiselle had not been talking about separatism, only about the constitutional responsibility of British parliamentarians.

---

*When that cable was leaked in February, Holtby was the first to call Aitken and tell him about it. Aitken then rang Mrs. Wadds and invited her to dinner at his house. They joked about the cable and drank a toast to "snow and sunshine". Attempts were made later by Canadian officials to deny Mrs. Wadds's authorship — "Mrs. Wadds is a lady; she wouldn't use an expression like snow job," said one — although her name did appear at the bottom of the cable. At dinner with Aitken, she did not deny authorship, merely thanked him for being understanding.

†The Conservative backbenchers' committee, a significant force in the party, takes its name from the famous meeting of Conservative MPs at the Carlton Club in October 1922 that led to the end of Britain's then-coalition government and the fall of Austen Chamberlain as Conservative leader. In opposition, all Conservative MPs have membership except the leader. When the Conservatives are in government, all ministers are excluded. The committee chairman is a senior backbencher who enjoys direct access to the party leader.

The rage of the Canadian free lunch came to London with the new year. Loiselle had established it. The agents general of Alberta, Saskatchewan, British Columbia and Nova Scotia picked up on it. The people at Macdonald House turned it into a gastronomic horserace. Ottawa at last had entered the London lists.

No one now could fail to comprehend the mood in Westminster. The resolution was going to run into deep trouble if it got to London in its present form. Pym had delivered his blunt warning. McMurtry had been to London in January and had returned home convinced — and saying so publicly — that a reference to the Supreme Court of Canada was going to be necessary. (Ross DeGeer, Ontario's agent general, had been cabling storm signals to Queen's Park for weeks. Unlike his government's allies in Macdonald House, DeGeer wanted Ontario's people — particularly Hugh Segal — to come to London to see for themselves what was going on.)

Roy McMurtry had two reasons for publicly urging the federal government to refer the resolution to the Supreme Court. One had to do with pique but was not a very large influence on his thoughts. Only a few hours after McMurtry had made a spirited defence of the federal resolution at a lunch given by Mrs. Wadds, Jean Chrétien unveiled a substantially rewritten charter of rights before the special parliamentary committee, without first having consulted the Ontario government.

By far McMurtry's greatest concern stemmed from a meeting he had with Britain's attorney general, Sir Michael Havers, and encounters with various MPs and peers. The parliamentarians told him the resolution would not go through Westminster so long as it was tied up in the Canadian courts. Havers did not go that far, but said it would be terribly embarrassing if Westminster passed it, only to have the Supreme Court subsequently rule it to be illegal. McMurtry assured Havers that the Supreme Court would be most unlikely even to look at the resolution once Westminster had passed it. But he was surprised to hear from the attorney general that the federal government had been telling the British that the reason they wanted Westminster to pass the resolution now was because the provinces could stall a Supreme Court case for two to three years. McMurtry told Havers that was absolute nonsense, that Ottawa could have the case heard within two months if it wanted.

When he returned to Ottawa, he asked Chrétien to make a reference to the court, but only on the legality of unilateral action, not on the convention requirements, because, as he told the justice minister, one doesn't have to be a legal genius to predict that the court might be all over the map on convention (which McMurtry continued to believe was a political science question, not a legal issue).

The Kershaw committee reported on 29 January. "I'm afraid it will upset Mr. Trudeau," Sir Anthony said. Indeed. Trudeau delivered the prize phrase of the British connection: If Westminster's MPs didn't like his resolution, he said, they would just have to "hold their noses" and pass it.

The Canadians in London did their homework on Westminster and came up with the same numbers — those two hundred and fifty MPs and peers identified by Loiselle as the prime lobbying targets. Day by day, week by week, month after month, the political Canadians in London enticed these British politicians — and British journalists and influential British businessmen who knew MPs — to their tables. They were wined, dined and feted beyond satiation.

The provincial agents general pursued them so aggressively that their activities were in danger of becoming counter-productive; they were tripping over each other, duplicating each other's work. After their governments had signed the April accord, the agents general got together in London and agreed to exchange notes on which politicians they were feeding or dispatching propaganda to in any given week. A joint task force on the constitution, known as the commando group (with Alberta's agent general James McKibbon as chairman), was established on the top floor of Alberta House with charts, stenographer, photocopier and shredder.

Throughout the spring, provincial ministers and officials were ferried in and out of London almost daily, formulating what would be known as the London strategy. Roy Romanow came in late March, just before Saskatchewan joined the gang of eight. Using subterfuge, he managed to see Nicholas Ridley and brought up the subject of the constitution (Mrs. Thatcher and the foreign office did not want members of her cabinet dilating on the subject with provincial ministers.) Romanow emerged from Ridley's office (according to a *Globe and Mail* report) "shaken by the force and frankness of the meeting". Romanow called a press conference in London to describe the *Globe* story as "subjective comment, apparently by some officials in attendance at the meeting. I could make observations on the state of agitation I observed on the part of [foreign office] officials, but I won't." Romanow was dissembling. He had been shaken. Ridley basically — and bluntly — had told him to get out.

The momentum of lobbying in London became a self-propelling force. It should have stopped after prime minister Trudeau agreed in April to refer the resolution to the Supreme Court. There was nothing more, really, for the lobbyists to do. Edward du Cann, chairman of the 1922 Committee, had already told Mrs. Thatcher that the Conservative backbench would not even look at the resolution until the Supreme Court of Canada had approved of its legality. That warning was a formidable political threat. Yet the lobbying only slowed down; it did not stop. It continued through the spring and summer of 1981, exploding into a final burst of frenzied activity after the Supreme Court's ruling in September.

Relationships between the federal and provincial camps in London became strained, as they did between some of the provincial officials. During a Canada Week function in Birmingham, Ontario's DeGeer reportedly rebuked Alberta's James McKibbon for speaking brusquely to Mrs. Wadds. McKibbon, for his part, was irritated by what he considered to be social snubs from the Canadian high commission staff. Loiselle was annoyed with McKibbon on another occasion for hiring a public relations firm to stage-manage a joint press conference given by the anti-Ottawa agents general. Nova Scotia's agent general, Donald Smith, was chided by his colleagues for sending a list of Westminster politicians supposedly favourable to the gang of eight's cause back to John Buchanan, who showed it to fellow premiers (if it had been leaked to the press, it would have been greatly embarrassing to the London operations, the agents general felt). British Columbia's agent general, Alex Hart, was accused of not pulling his weight. Hart, however, had a difficult brief as did most of Bill Bennett's foot-soldiers; he had instructions from his government in Victoria to be both a full fledged member of the provincial commando group in London but at the same time to be less aggressive than the others in his lobbying.

In the fall, with the Supreme Court's decision handed down, the London dissident agents general staged the most orgiastic of their lobbying efforts: a week-long assault on the Conservatives at their annual party conference in Blackpool. They held a lunch every day and a reception every night at a seedy hotel called the Savoy. Twelve to fifteen parliamentarians were invited to each lunch and fifty to sixty to each reception.

Meanwhile in commando headquarters, preparations for the London strategy — the gang of eight's formal assault on Westminster — were in top gear. Special gang-of-eight letterhead had been printed, the promotional brochure was ready, a parchment petition to the two Houses of Westminster was being drawn up, a gang-of-eight letter to Mrs. Thatcher was being drafted.

The provincial alliance's next planned event — for late November — was to have been a constitutional conference, sponsored by a Canadian-British political studies group and held at Leeds Castle. The dissident agents general were going to try to arrange it without federal participation. They would invite a select list of academics and politicians to the castle for the weekend, feed them, wine them and push their message home. Only late in their planning did they realize that the high commission funded the political study group and was going to make sure it had a federal representative at the conference. In the end, it was never held.

At six o'clock on the evening of 5 November, James McKibbon was about to go to Westminster for an informal meeting with a group of Conservative MPs. Just before leaving his office, he called Jim Seymour, the Alberta government's representative in Ottawa, to ask what was going on at the first ministers' conference. "I don't know," Seymour said, "but they've just come out and they have an agreement of some kind. The only thing I know is that Lougheed's smiling and Lévesque's frowning. So you can draw your own conclusions."

McKibbon went to Westminster, joined the Tory MPs in one of the members' bars, got himself a drink and said: "You don't have to worry any more. It looks like the whole thing has been solved." An MP replied: "Isn't that a bloody shame. I was looking forward to the fight."

11
The Frenzied Umpire

We are the umpire of the Canadian constitutional system, the only umpire; and in enforcing the rules under which the system operates, rules which we did not formulate but which we are sworn to apply, we are getting an occasional sting from some of the players and even from some of those on the sidelines, much like the soccer referee sometimes from the frenzy that in some places seizes both players and spectators at a soccer final.

Chief Justice Bora Laskin, 1978, in a rare public speech.

April 1981. Less than a week after the eight dissident premiers sign their alternative accord in the Ottawa conference centre, the federal government gathers together all its legal talent for the ultimate court challenge. They meet in the boardroom of the justice department building on Wellington Street, where Louis St. Laurent once agonized over the order to intern Japanese Canadians during World War II, where justice minister Davie Fulton and (later) Guy Favreau struggled to break the patriation impasse in the early 1960s, and where in 1967 Pierre Trudeau presided over a moral revolution to remove the state from the bedrooms of the nation.

It is only days before the Supreme Court of Canada is to begin hearing the constitutional case, and justice minister Jean Chrétien wishes to leave nothing to chance. He has called in Ottawa's allies — Ontario attorney general Roy McMurtry and his advisers, and the team representing New Brunswick — for a final consultation. The scene in the boardroom resembles a Breughel canvas: federal bureaucrats from a variety of departments cover every available patch of broadloom. By one count, there are more than fifty people in the room. Chrétien, edgy and preoccupied, sits at one end of the huge walnut table; across from him is the formal and formidable John Josiah Robinette, at seventy-four the preeminent legal counsel of his generation and Ottawa's favourite constitutional advocate.

When the line by line dissection of the federal case is over, the courtroom lawyers in the group put up their feet to gossip about senior judges and the law. An appearance before the highest court in the land is nothing new or exceptional for most of them, and many know intimately the personalities of the judges and their particular constitutional biases.

Robinette, a contemporary of most of the nine Supreme Court justices, had been appearing before that body for many years. McMurtry was a prominent Toronto criminal lawyer before his election to the Ontario legislature in 1975, and he appeared often before the Supreme Court. He plans to personally argue Ontario's case in the constitution fight, carrying out what he calls the "traditional role of an attorney general," although that from a time in Britain when the Crown's chief law officer sat outside cabinet and was a courtroom advocate rather than a policy-maker. Justice officials such as Roger Tassé and Barry Strayer have seen the court function at close range on a host of issues and meet regularly with chief justice Bora Laskin and his officials on administrative matters. Ottawa's other main counsel, Michel Robert, a jaunty Montreal advocate who represented the federal cabinet before the McDonald Commission inquiry into the RCMP, was for a time the *bâtonnier* of the Quebec bar.

So, at the end of their day's work, they sit around, as lawyers tend to do, chewing the fat, speculating amiably on how the court will decide, how each judge will come down, when McMurtry notices that, at the end of the table, Chrétien is working himself into a lather. "I guess to him we must have sounded a little bit detached from the whole thing,"McMurtry recalled later. For Chrétien, the constitutional battle is no abstract legal issue; it is a blood and guts struggle in which the federal Liberals, particularly those from Quebec, have invested considerable political capital. McMurtry said: "I remember Jean looking at me, sort of leaning forward, and finally in a pause he says: 'I tell you this, goddamn it, Jesus Christ, Roy, if we don't win that goddamn case, it's going to be Jonestown revisited around here!' "

"The paradox of Canadian sovereignty," as it came to be called — the spectacle of a fully mature and independent nation unable to amend its own constitution— baffled and divided the nation's judiciary as no other issue had done this century. Never before had a political crisis of this magnitude possessed the judicial system so entirely and made such great demands on the nine justices of the Supreme Court of Canada. It was "very nearly overwhelming," one of them confided afterwards, "by far the most important case in the history of the court."

Until then, only the 1976 anti-inflation board decision had had constitutional impact that came close to that of the patriation resolution, extending as it did the "peace, order and good government" responsibilities of the federal Parliament in an extraordinary peace-time situation. But even it paled beside the patriation challenge. The anti-inflation board case was referred directly to the Supreme Court of Canada by the federal cabinet. The constitution battle was fought arduously in three provincial courts before it reached the final arbiter, with the Trudeau government maintaining at every step of the way that the issue was not an appropriate one for the courts to be adjudicating upon.

In an odd way, it might be said that Canadian history was put on trial. The non-elected judiciary grappled not just with arcane and aged legal precedents, but with the fundamental nature of Canadian federalism. They sought to discover what had been in the minds of the original fathers of Confederation when they formed a country in 1867 — What was the nature of *their* compromise? — with "a Constitution similar in Principle to that of the United Kingdom," a unitary island state.

In December 1980, the legal debate began in the Manitoba court of appeal; in February and March 1981 it was continued before the Newfoundland and Quebec courts of appeal. By the end of April 1981, the competing visions of the country were gowned in legal cloth and brought before the highest court in the land, the nine Supreme Court of Canada justices, who formally, by custom, call themselves brothers, although they detest the term.

By a quirk of fate, the constitution case arrived at the Supreme Court of Canada with central Canada under-represented on the top bench. There were three (French Canadian) judges from Quebec, as the law provides, but only two from Ontario (rather than the traditional three). Of these two, chief justice Bora Laskin was the son of Lithuanian immigrants, and had been raised in Thunder Bay, far from the Upper Canadian establishment; and Willard Estey, born in Saskatoon (where his brother sat on that province's appeal court), has referred to his reasonings as "prairie dusters."

The Quebec judges were a diverse trio — from the youngest, forty-eight-year-old Antonio Lamer, with his bushy handlebar moustache, to the most senior, fifty-four-year-old Jean Beetz, dapper and goateed, and the court's only bachelor. In the middle, both in age and by appointment was Julien Chouinard, a man who was called "le colonel" when he ran the Quebec civil service, because of his clipped hairstyle, ramrod stiff posture and keen interest in the militia.

The Quebec judges were a generation younger than the rest of their colleagues, particularly the two Diefenbaker-appointed judges who were the hard centre of the court's conservative wing: Ronald Martland from Edmonton and Roland Ritchie from Halifax. Martland, the bluff, former corporate lawyer, would recline in his high-backed chair, taking in every movement in the courtroom and barking out questions with barely a tilt of his head. In contrast, Ritchie, the brother of former ambassador and belletrist Charles Ritchie, would sit stooped forward, head in hands, his eyes poring over documents inches away, only his bald pate visible to anyone facing the bench.

Rounding out the brethren were Brian Dickson, a Manitoba judge with a fatherly visage, who was reputed to be one of the court's more graceful writers; and William McIntyre, a quiet, open-faced former courtroom lawyer from Victoria.

It was left to these nine men to decide what the bickering politicans could not. Was Canada eleven partners; or was it two levels of government, one subordinate to the other? Were the two orders of government each sovereign in their respective fields, each equally representative of the Crown? Or were the provinces creatures of a central authority, which controlled the fundamental powers of nationhood?

Essentially, the argument of the eight dissenting provinces was that at some point in this century, particularly in the fifty years since the Statute of Westminster, Canada had come of age. They were asking the court to decree that Canada was a fully sovereign nation with divided federal and provincial legislative jurisdictions; and that the British role was purely pro forma, a notary's stamp on a decision agreed to on the Canadian side of the Atlantic.

The federal position was less charitable. In its view, Canada had not changed substantially since 1867, when many of the essentials of nationhood were "deliberately left to the circumstance and finally to the arbitration of the Imperial authority," in the phrase of scholar Paul Gérin-Lajoie. Britain had full legal authority over the Canadian constitution but had been constrained by past practices and could act only on requests from the federal Parliament. In Trudeau's opinion, articulated before the court, Canada had not reached legal adulthood; incessant squabbling had stunted its full growth and now it required the smack of a strong hand to shock it into accepting its responsibilities.

To assist in its deliberations, the court had two streams of judicial interpretation to draw upon. The conservative view, dating back to a judicial committee of the privy council decision of 1937, saw the ship of state sailing on "larger ventures and into foreign waters," while still retaining "the water-tight compartments which are an essential part of her original structure." The more liberal view, stemming from a slightly earlier ruling, saw the constitution as "a living tree capable of growth and expansion within its natural limits." As history has proven, much depends on whether the Supreme Court of Canada chooses to regard the constitution act as a ship or a tree.

———————— ❧ ————————

Of the four courts that heard the case, only Newfoundland was unanimous in its verdict. But its decision was eventually overturned in all important respects by the Supreme Court of Canada in its historic ruling on 28 September. For its part, the high court had tried over the past decade to pronounce unanimously on important constitutional matters (as the US Supreme Court does on race issues) in order to call to the nation's attention the fact that, although politicians might be divided, the court is of one mind. However, in the constitution judgment there was not just division but double division on the two fundamental issues of legality and "convention." All nine judges ruled that the federal resolution affected the rights and powers of provincial governments but they split in different ways over the resolution's importance. Seven said the process was legal; two disagreed. Six said a convention or practice exists whereby provincial consent was necessary, while the three others, led by chief justice Laskin, were in vigorous dissent. Four judges — Dickson and the three from Quebec — anchored both majority decisions. At first blush it seemed as if the court was galloping off in all directions. It was "a most peculiar judgment," Pierre Trudeau said later in an interview, shaking his head in bewilderment.

The constitution case, at root a political matter, appeared to torment the Canadian judiciary, both for the complexities of the arguments and because of its own role in the process. In effect, the courts were being asked to rule on a plan that purported to give considerably more power (by an entrenched charter of rights) to non-elected judges, and to decide an issue which quarrelling politicians could not resolve: Did Canada already have a *de facto* amending formula requiring provincial consent? As well, there was for the court a hidden agenda heightened by more than fifty years of attempts to break the last colonial tie. Would the chance ever come again to affect history so dramatically?

In this context it should be noted that for at least three of the Supreme Court judges, the constitution case embodied some personal history. Bora Laskin was one of the country's most distinguished constitutional scholars, with an international reputation in this field. As a law professor at the University of Toronto from 1949 to 1965, he championed a school of thought that was quite centralist in its outlook, in many ways providing the intellectual underpinning for what Pierre Trudeau was trying to accomplish. His two senior Quebec judges, Jean Beetz and Julien Chouinard, were political advisers at Victoria in 1971. Beetz, the courtly, soft-spoken professor from the Université de Montréal, was one of Trudeau's constitutional counsellors in the three years leading up to Victoria.* Chouinard, appointed in 1979 by Joe Clark, was Quebec premier Robert Bourassa's secretary to the cabinet in the early 1970s, the man who nego-

---

*Beetz disqualified himself from hearing the Senate reference case in 1979 because he had once given legal advice on this subject to the Trudeau government before his appointment to the bench. In 1979 Ottawa was contemplating changing the Upper Chamber into a more representative House of the Provinces, but without provincial approval. The eight sitting judges turned down the proposal unanimously.

tiated with Ottawa over the implementation of the War Measures Act in 1970 and over many of the principles of the Victoria Charter a year later.

❀

On 22 October 1980, twenty days after prime minister Trudeau went on national television to outline his daring new initiative, the legality of the measures he was proposing went before the Manitoba Court of Appeal on a reference from the provincial cabinet.* Meanwhile, Ottawa obstinately refused to submit a reference of its own, maintaining that its actions were legal, if unprecedented, and that it was prepared to pay the price at the polls later if the voters thought it had done wrong.

By refusing to frame a reference of its own, however, Ottawa forfeited the momentum to the provinces, who designed their questions (and their arguments) to build on judicial sympathy.† The three questions were:

> 1. *If the amendments to the Constitution of Canada sought in the "proposed resolution for a joint address to her Majesty the Queen respecting the Constitution of Canada," or any of them, were enacted, would federal-provincial relationships or the powers, rights or privileges granted or secured by the Constitution of Canada to the provinces, their legislatures or governments be affected and, if so, in what respect or respects?*

---

*Oral arguments began on 4 December in Manitoba, on 10 February in the Supreme Court of Newfoundland, and on 9 March in the Quebec court. The reference system allows the provinces to put matters directly only before the provincial courts, but there is an automatic right of appeal to the Supreme Court. Only Ottawa is allowed to make a direct reference to the Supreme Court to test the legality of proposed legislation. Chrétien said in October 1980 that to delay by referring the matter directly to the Supreme Court "would set a dangerous precedent, whereby any citizen or group could challenge the legality of government action before it was taken and thus suspend the ability of Parliament to pass legislation." This was more flim flam than logic because it ignored the fact that only governments can initiate — a procedure often used to obtain advisory opinions — whereas citizens have been able to challenge legislation only after it has been passed. The argument also was made at a time when Ottawa was following its "quick strike" strategy, hoping to have Westminster pass the measure early in the New Year.

†In each case three main questions were referred to the court by cabinet order. The questions differed slightly in each court. Quebec placed a different emphasis on the one dealing with constitutional convention, and the Newfoundland court was asked an additional question to do with the Terms of Union, the understanding on which Newfoundland entered Confederation in 1949. But the three questions put to the Manitoba Court of Appeal were the basis on which the Supreme Court of Canada made its eventual decision in September 1981.

*2. Is it a constitutional convention that the House of
Commons and Senate of Canada will not request Her Majesty
the Queen to lay before the Parliament of the United
Kingdom of Great Britain and Northern Ireland a measure to
amend the Constitution of Canada affecting federal-provincial
relationships or the powers, rights or privileges granted or
secured by the Constitution of Canada to the provinces, their
legislatures or governments without first obtaining the
agreement of the provinces?*

*3. Is the agreement of the provinces of Canada
constitutionally required for amendment to the Constitution
of Canada where such amendment affects federal-provincial
relationships or alters the powers, rights or privileges
granted or secured by the Constitution of Canada to the
provinces, their legislatures or governments?*

The nub of the issue was whether provincial agreement to a BNA Act amendment was "constitutionally required." To make their case, both sides listed a mass of historical political statements and precedents, some quaint, others overblown.

The basis of the provincial argument before the Manitoba court was that past practice or convention had become "crystallized into law," and that the court should now declare this to be the case. The main proponent of this viewpoint was Queen's University professor William Lederman, a respected constitutional authority, who, by his own subsequent admission, was bucking the main trend of political-constitutional thought, at least in English Canada.*

The provinces endeavoured to show that all previous federal governments believed in the precedents — the only maverick being Trudeau, who must be restrained. Since 1868, the year after Confederation, when the British Parliament shifted control of Rupert's Land from the Hudson's Bay Company to Canada, there have been twenty-two amendments to the British North America Act, only some of which affected the rights and powers of the provinces. Which ones touched upon provincial jurisdiction, however, was debatable. The provinces said there were five — all of them requiring provincial consent. The Supreme Court of Canada eventually agreed on the number, but they were a different five: the 1930 amendment giving the three prairie provinces control of their natural resources and B.C. its railway lands; the 1931 Statute of Westminster, whereby Canada waived *de jure* independence because it could

---

*Lederman, in turn, was basing his ideas largely on three general rules set down in 1959 by Sir Ivor Jennings, the noted British authority: what are the precedents? did the actors believe in them? and, is there a reason for the rule?

not decide on an amending formula; and the amendments of 1940, 1951 and 1964 that gave Ottawa jurisdiction respectively in the fields of unemployment insurance, old-age pensions and supplementary benefits.*

Ottawa said that only the federal Parliament has had the ear of the United Kingdom in the past; it was ridiculous to talk about provincial consent when the federal authority carved new provinces out of territories (Manitoba, Saskatchewan and Alberta) and invited an independent dominion (Newfoundland) to join the country without consulting the other partners in Confederation.† The transcending principle, Ottawa held, was responsible government. Only the Canadian Parliament ultimately speaks for the nation because only the Canadian Parliament is responsible to all voters; federal-provincial consultation was welcome but it was not necessary.

On 3 February 1981, in a split decision, the Manitoba Court of Appeal ruled that Ottawa had the right unilaterally to amend the constitution. Three of the five judges who heard the case said constitutional changes do not require provincial consent, even when they affect the balance of powers and alter provincial rights. But the court's decision was immensely complex — indeed it was five separate judgments, one from each justice, totalling 151 pages — and did not dispel the controversy. Chief justice Samuel Freedman, one of Canada's most respected jurists, rejected the provincial arguments that their consent was required either in law or practice: "That we may be moving toward such a convention is certainly a tenable view. But we have not arrived there yet. . . . A convention should be certain and consistent; what we have is uncertain and variable." Musing on what he termed "the paradox of Canadian sovereignty," Freedman also spurned the eight provinces' ancillary argument that Canada is a "compact" between the two orders of government, a theory that gained prominence during the Depression years. But at the same time the chief justice kept the provincial brief afloat by stating that conventions, while not an issue of law, are still "constitutional in character" and therefore appropriate ones for a court to consider.

The two minority judgments, by justices J. P. O'Sullivan and Charles Huband (a former leader of the Manitoba Liberals), were of only small comfort to the eight provinces. Huband based his decision largely on O'Sullivan's, who struck out in a somewhat different direction, rejecting the provinces' main argument that convention had crystallized into law.‡

---

*Lawyers for the federal government told the courts that there were fourteen amendments that significantly affected provincial rights, only four of which were fully consented to by the provinces. Moreover, they argued, six were requested and enacted in the face of opposition by one or more provinces.

†Newfoundland joined Confederation in 1949, despite the objections of Quebec, where the dispute over the Quebec-Labrador border remains alive.

‡All five Manitoba judges rejected the convention argument.

Instead, he said the Trudeau initiative was unconstitutional because each
level of government is supreme or sovereign in its own field, and it is
wrong for Her Majesty's federal ministers, to tender advice to the
sovereign on provincial matters, and vice versa.

The Manitoba judgment tended to influence the way both sides later
presented their cases before the other courts, particularly around the
O'Sullivan position. It was not the smashing legal victory for Ottawa
that it had appeared at first. Not only did the split decision inflame the
partisans in both camps, but it was handed down in a period of intense
political controversy. The judgment followed by only a few days the
report of the select foreign affairs committee of the British Parliament,
chaired by the bumptious Sir Anthony Kershaw, which advised rejection
of the Trudeau plan if there were to be no greater degree of provincial
consent. Moreover, it was handed down in the midst of a prolonged
political dispute over the leaking of Canadian diplomatic cables, indicating British parliamentary support for the Trudeau plan was considerably
less than fullhearted.*

What little federal euphoria there was over the Manitoba ruling evaporated a week later before the Supreme Court of Newfoundland. As a
federal lawyer embarked on the routine argument that the federal Parliament was clearly designed to be the senior authority, because of its
significant residual powers, including the disallowance of provincial legislation, he was peremptorily cut off. One of the justices leaned forward
and said: "You may have that power, but we wouldn't let you use it."

On 31 March, after more than six weeks of deliberations, the three-
member court pronounced unanimously in favour of the dissident
provinces on all four questions. The sixty-five page judgment, stark and
unyielding, referred to the ten provinces as "autonomous communities"
and said unilateral action by Ottawa would "defeat the whole scheme of
the Canadian federal constitution."

Further, the Newfoundland court asserted that Britain's role as "trustee"
of federalism applied equally to the federal and provincial legislatures in
matters of their respective jurisdictions — in effect, an extension across
the Atlantic of O'Sullivan's sovereignty decision. While the Newfoundland judges observed that, over the years, prominent public men have

*Also, at this juncture, there were signs that Ontario might be wavering in its
legal support of the resolution. In London to test the Westminster waters, Roy
McMurtry felt sufficiently unsettled to suggest publicly that Ottawa should refer
the question directly to the Supreme Court of Canada and so bypass the other
looming provincial decisions from Newfoundland and Quebec. His remarks
caught not only Chrétien but also William Davis by surprise. Up until then, the
federal side's main line had been that the dispute was political and not legal, a
position the Manitoba Court seemed generally to uphold by downplaying the
importance of constitutional convention.

delivered contrary views on the need for provincial consent, the court concluded that there has been a steady movement towards such a convention.

The Newfoundland judgment prompted a volte-face in federal strategy. Since the court cases began, there had been a series of memoranda prepared in the privy council office on what to do if a court ruled that the government's initiative was illegal. In the upper reaches of the justice department, there was still a great deal of doubt about whether judges properly should be answering these questions of convention, but the more political mandarins had decided that, if a court ruled against the federal government, the matter would have to be referred immediately to the Supreme Court of Canada. Prime minister Trudeau was attending the regular Tuesday morning meeting of the cabinet's priorities and planning committee when the Newfoundland judgment came down. An aide handed him a note on a government of Canada scratch pad relaying the judgment and reminding him of the bureaucracy's political advice. Within twenty minutes the decision had been made, and without opposition. The "inner cabinet" discussed how best to announce the new direction.

At the moment Trudeau and his ministers were assembling their new strategy, the Conservatives had the Commons hogtied by procedural snares. They had brought all House business to a halt in protest against the government's determination to move unilaterally on the constitution, and they had just about emptied their bag of tricks — not to mention overstraining their ever-fragile unity — when the Newfoundland decision came down.

Over the next two days, Trudeau, Clark and Broadbent carried out extraordinary negotiations on the floor of the Commons on whether there would be a final vote on the resolution before or after it was referred to the Supreme Court and a decision handed down. When Commons speaker Jeanne Sauvé dared to suggest that this was a topic which might be more appropriately discussed privately among House leaders, the prime minister's steely glare produced a moment of shocked silence in the normally rambunctious chamber. Trudeau argued that the resolution should be voted on before the reference, both to maintain the supremacy of Parliament over the courts, and to permit the Supreme Court to assess the resolution's effect upon the provinces in real rather than hypothetical terms. He didn't win his way.

Two weeks later, on 15 April, the Quebec Superior Court of Appeal ruled four to one in favour of Ottawa. Its judgment was an anti-climax. Parliament already had agreed on a plan to make final amendments before the opening of the Supreme Court hearing — set for 28 April — and to pass the resolution in two sittings after that ruling, assuming it was found to be legal.

The Quebec decision was substantially different from Manitoba's and Newfoundland's. All five Quebec judges found that the resolution infringed upon provincial rights, but four of them concluded that Ottawa was proceeding legally. Chief justice Marcel Crête observed that the court's response to the convention issue "constitutes an opinion and not a judgment," and that, in any case, the precedents did not support the provincial arguments: "The majority of these modifications to the constitution since 1867 were done without the approval of all the provinces and, in certain cases, over their opposition." He went on to stress that the majority view was set out "on the legal plane" only, and that the Quebec court was steering clear of the unchartered waters of constitutional convention.*

———————— ❧ ————————

"A quiet court in an unquiet land," is the way professor Ronald Cheffins, a close friend of Bora Laskin, described the Supreme Court of Canada in an article in 1966. It is an apt summation of the court, none of whose nine members, with the possible exception of Laskin, is a household name. Unlike the American Supreme Court, some of whose more momentous decisions can be chronicled by schoolchildren, Canada's top court labours silently in the shadows of Parliament Hill.

Bora Laskin, whose sharply chiselled features and vigorous intellect belie a frail body, is one of a long line of chief justices who have tried to propel the court more fully into the mainstream of Canadian life, generally to little avail. Both the cautious statecraft of the Canadian judiciary and the traditions of parliamentary supremacy have kept it from becoming an equal 'estate' in the political system.

Unlike the federal and provincial legislatures, the Supreme Court of Canada is not a constitutionally entrenched institution but is rather the product of a federal statute, which can be amended or withdrawn at Parliament's will. Indeed, the Court had rather uncertain beginnings. Bills for its creation were introduced and withdrawn on two occasions in 1869 and 1870 before the act establishing it was finally passed in 1875. For most of its history, until 1933 in criminal cases and 1949 in others (including constitutional cases), the Supreme Court also operated under the aegis of the judicial committee of the British privy council, which

———————

*The only dissenting opinion, from Mr. Justice Claude Bisson, was based on his reading of the conferences of the original fathers of Confederation, in Quebec City and London, which led up to 1867. It appeared to him to embody a more philosophical viewpoint: "Overall, if Canada is to be accepted as a federation, then a voice cannot be denied to one partner or another whenever one acts to intervene in the legislative competence exclusively held by the other."

was the final court of appeal. When he was teaching law at the University of Toronto, Laskin often railed against this lack of independence of the Canadian judiciary as well as against the pro-provincial stands the privy council took on a number of important issues. The Supreme Court of Canada did not even have its own separate building until 1946, and even now it shares that with the Federal Court of Canada.

In recent years, about a score of the approximately 125 cases the court hears annually require constitutional umpiring, although by 1981 only four of the nine justices had much experience in this realm: Laskin and Beetz were constitutional scholars before joining the bench; Martland (who retired in February 1982) and Ritchie, the only surviving members of the Diefenbaker-appointed court, had been around long enough to acquire expertise by osmosis.

Beetz, charmingly old-fashioned, has impressive scholarly credentials as a forceful defender of provincial rights (like Trudeau in his early days). He was considered by many to be the intellectual leader of the court's Quebec wing and the spark for its eventual decision on the convention question.

Two other influential justices in the constitution case were Dickson and Estey, who took opposite positions on the main convention issue. Dickson, regarded by many academics as one of the court's leading intellectuals, joined the three Quebec judges to anchor both majority decisions (on legality and convention). Estey, the outgoing, fidgety former chief justice of Ontario and scion of a judicial family, joined Laskin and William McIntyre, a relative newcomer, in a vigorous dissent on the importance of convention.

Since he was appointed chief justice by prime minister Trudeau in 1973, over more senior judges, Laskin has consistently tried to hold the court together on constitutional cases, but with mixed success. In 1979 in the *Senate reference* case, the court ruled unanimously that the federal Parliament could not by legislation change the nature of the Upper House; in 1980 it reaffirmed with one voice official bilingualism in Quebec and Manitoba (the *Blaikie* and *Forest* cases), striking down parts of Quebec's controversial Bill 101 in the process; and in 1979 it ruled that Saskatchewan's attempt to control potash production was beyond provincial powers.

However, in a variety of other important cases, the court has divided, often with serious political repercussions. In two related decisions in 1978 on which level of government controls the cable communications industry, the court ruled in favour of Ottawa with (for the first time in recent history) all three judges from Quebec dissenting from the verdict. In the 1976 decision on wage and price controls, the court split seven to two, with Beetz writing a forceful dissent. Osgoode Hall law professor

Peter Hogg has observed that because four other judges supported a key point in Beetz's minority ruling, there was an effective majority of five to four on a decisive constitutional issue.

During the mid-1970s allegations were rife that the Laskin court was biased towards the federal government on constitutional issues. But two independent studies, including one by a Quebec government official, have indicated otherwise. These suggested that since it took over from Britain's privy council as final constitutional arbiter in 1949, the Supreme Court has generally supported the central government in its decisions but without any apparent bias. Moreover, in the eighteen months leading up to the constitution case there were five disputes over the distribution of powers in which the court came down on the side of the provinces.

In order to ensure that the general public would better understand the court's role, the chief justice gave a rare public speech in March 1981, only six weeks before hearings began into the constitution case. "Constitutional issues are always sensitive ones, and if there is over-reaching by either Parliament or a provincial legislature, it is the court's duty to pull them back," he said. "Governments are better advised to draft their legislation with less bravado than to run the risk of overstepping the limits of their powers." To make sure no one missed the point, Laskin laid great stress on the independence of the judiciary. "Let me say, as forcibly as I can, that the Supreme Court of Canada is not a federal institution; it is a national institution and its members are under no federal allegiance merely because they are federally appointed. Just as there is no federal allegiance, there is no regional allegiance and no political allegiance."

———————— ✤ ————————

The line-ups formed at seven-thirty in the morning on the day the constitution case opened. It was a contest billed in some circles as Robinette versus Twaddle — two remarkable lawyers with remarkably different legal styles.

Kerr Twaddle has an unfortunate name for an advocate. Nevertheless, the short, plump Manitoba lawyer, with the stiff Glaswegian brogue and a taste for opera, easily took the national spotlight in the spring of 1981 when he carried Manitoba's brief before the Supreme Court of Canada. His opponent, the tall J.J. Robinette, was already a legend in his time: a consummate Torontonian, who left academia in the 1930s to win acquittal after acquittal for his clients in a series of spectacular murder cases, and then went on to bestride all facets of his profession, in criminal, corporate and constitutional law. Modest and hard-working, he would write his own notes in pencil during a case rather than leave it to an assistant. He had acted for the Trudeau government defending, among other things, the official languages act in the mid-1970s, wage and price controls in 1976, and Ottawa's attempt to change the Senate in 1979.

Twaddle and Robinette had never before tangled in the top court but they had championed opposite sides of similar issues in other courts. For the legal aficionados — and there were many who crowded into the sun-drenched courtroom for the five days of hearings — there was something of the air of a grudge match. Twaddle, the plodding constructionist who detailed carefully every step of his case contrasted sharply with the bold, summarizing style of Robinette, who with his fluid gestures sometimes seemed to hold The Law at the tips of his fingers.

In addition to these two barristers, the constitution case was argued by some of the best civil law minds in the country: Douglas Schmeiser, a former dean of law at the University of Saskatchewan, assisted Twaddle with Manitoba's brief, the main line of attack for the dissident provinces; Kenneth Lysyk, a dean of law at the University of British Columbia, represented Saskatchewan; Michael Goldie, a distinguished Vancouver lawyer, was the B.C. counsel; and Michel Robert, a vigorous, forty-three-year-old Montreal lawyer with the physique of a middleweight boxer and solid Liberal connections, assisted Robinette with the federal case (and, in fact, did most of the talking). In all there were nearly forty black-gowned lawyers in the high-ceilinged courtroom. About an equal number of press with special entry cards were sitting on plastic folding chairs in the aisles and some sixty spectators had been lucky enough to get in.

The Supreme Court of Canada was expected to decide, and decide clearly, between the two opposing views. An ambiguous or narrow legal victory for Ottawa would provoke furious provincial lobbying in London; a similar finding for the eight provincial governments would probably lead Ottawa to put the matter before the people, most likely through a referendum.* In nearly five days of intense hearings, constitutional lawyers argued passionately on behalf of their clients' respective visions of Canadian federalism. The debate was conducted in English and French with a seasoning of Latin, and both sides adduced a wide number of Commonwealth precedents.

For the most part, the cases had been finely honed through arguments in the lower courts.† But this time they were being made before a well-informed and sharply critical judiciary, who were not adverse to taking

---

*In April, in an off-the-record interview with the editorial board of the *New York Times*, Trudeau was asked what he would do if he lost before the Supreme Court. "There will be a hell of a fight," he replied, assuming the remarks would not leak out, which they did.

†Manitoba still managed to mis-spell the names of two Canadian prime ministers, Sir Wilfrid Laurier and Sir John A. Macdonald, in its written factum.

these high-priced counsels down a peg. Twaddle's initial line of reasoning on convention was met with a brusque rejoinder from the chief justice that conventions are political rules and so fall outside the court's purview. Similarly, Robinette's contention that the constitutional resolution has the same legal weight as a parliamentary birthday greeting to the Queen, and so was not subject to judicial scrutiny, appeared to exasperate the bench. "He's wrong on that one," Estey whispered to his seatmate Chouinard, unaware that their microphones were on. "He won't face this head on," Chouinard replied, "he's twisting it." Later, as both counsels' points became more and more arcane, a frustrated judge Dickson asked sarcastically: "Is the federal status of Canada irrelevant in all this?"

Building on the lower courts' judgments, especially Newfoundland's, Twaddle argued for what he called "the modified compact theory" to embrace both the orders of federalism and the notion that provinces are sancrosanct in their own jurisdictions. He suggested that anything touching these jurisdictions, such as patriation and an entrenched charter of rights, required unanimous consent of all eleven governments.

"You mean like a telegraph?" Estey said. "Yes," said Twaddle. "Eleven buttons are pushed in Canada which give effect to the machine in the UK." (Of the eight dissident provinces, only Saskatchewan did not fully support the unanimity position, pleading instead for *substantial* consent. Lysyk likened his proposal to a Mackenzie King dictum, "Sort of unanimity if necessary but not necessarily unanimity.") The convention argument, which ironically is what the court eventually accepted and embellished, was a "fall-back position," Twaddle maintained. His main brief was on the O'Sullivan notion that the provinces are sovereign in their own fields. Twaddle argued that the federal Parliament may speak for Canada, but only that part of Canada it legally represents: the federal jurisdiction under the BNA Act. Ottawa was trying to do by the back door what it did not have the express authority to do otherwise.

The federal lawyers argued that, on the one hand, there is no enforceable requirement for provincial consent in Canada, and, on the other hand, there is a "strong and unbending convention" on the part of the British Parliament to act on constitutional requests from its Canadian counterpart. No other federation in the world requires the unanimous consent of its component parts for constitutional amendment, they declared, and the Trudeau initiative better represented the spirit of federalism than the provincial desire to maintain a constitutional stalemate. The federal government conceded at the outset (something it had not acknowledged in the lower courts) that the resolution would affect provincial rights and powers in the same way it would touch those same rights and powers in the federal sphere. But it maintained that the power to amend the constitution, which sets out the two orders of government, was a different level of authority, held by the federal government. Taken to the extreme, this power would allow the establishment of a unitary state. But the "very fact that we have such power and could abuse such power is not a good reason not to justify it," Michel Robert told the court. Ottawa was resorting to an extraordinary measure to break an impasse but its proposals would at least maintain the equilibrium between the two levels and formally enshrine for all time a provincial role in further constitutional change.

Both New Brunswick and Ontario backed Ottawa's case to the hilt, even when Judge Martland tartly reminded McMurtry that Ottawa's untrammelled powers could allow it to impose official bilingualism on Ontario. Chagrined, the Ontario attorney general allowed, chuckling, that that would be the logical result of his government's submission. "It is simply the historical product that remains from evolution from colony to independent nation," he said. "It is clearly not a happy or desirable circumstance for the provinces. But it is our submission that it is clear law."

———————— ❦ ————————

On the afternoon of 4 May 1981, after the closing arguments, the nine judges adjourned to their small, book-lined conference room behind the main court, for the first of more than twenty formal discussions on the constitution case. The politicians who were expecting a decision in about a month, based on the time it took to rule on the wage and price controls case five years previously, were disappointed. For the next five months, the nine men studied and debated, cloaking their work in an unprecedented measure of secrecy.

The security measures adopted at that first deliberation were so tight that for the first four months anything written down was passed by hand from judge to judge. The law clerks and senior researchers, on whom the judges normally rely for background information and writing assistance, were not informed of the overall shape of the judgments until late August, and even then the names of which judge supported what positions were kept off the early versions that circulated, in case of a leak.

The week before judgment was delivered, the final drafts were given only to the most trusted secretaries and translators to be put in their final form. Up until then, even the senior court officials had no idea how many judgments there would be; they were only brought in when the magnitude of the task of printing was realized. Usually the court hands out about two hundred copies of its decisions on the day of judgment, depending on the demand. Over that weekend an offset printer and extra staff, borrowed from the department of supply and services and scrupulously vetted for security, were brought in to the Supreme Court building to print the copies for Monday's release. On 28 September, nearly two thousand copies of the constitution judgment were distributed, mostly to a mob of journalists, lawyers and spectators, struggling ten deep in a courthouse corridor.

—————————— ❦ ——————————

The decision-making process in the Supreme Court of Canada is quite collegial. If there are such things as compromises and canvassing for votes, the process is much more subtle than in the US Supreme Court; indeed, the Canadian participants deny that such things take place. By tradition, Laskin, unlike his American cousin, does not assign judgments to particular judges to write; all are welcome to participate. Judges with strong views are invited to write their opinions and circulate them within a few weeks, so that others can "join" or suggest refinements. "It's a building job," retired justice Wishart Spence once observed. "We're really quite informal." On the Supreme Court of Canada, judges tend to wander freely in and out of each other's chambers without fearing they may be suspected of creating a cabal against their fellow brethren.

In the first conference after the oral arguments had been heard in the patriation case, each justice was canvassed for his initial reactions — beginning, as custom had it, with the most junior judge, Lamer, through Chouinard, McIntyre, Estey, Beetz, Dickson, Ritchie and Martland, and ending with the chief justice, Laskin.

From the very first, it was evident that there would be no unanimity on this case, no anonymous *per curiam* from the court acting as one. The two "Diefenbaker" judges, Martland in particular, were unshakeably convinced that the resolution was illegal. While their colleagues focussed on the question of what law limited the federal Parliament's power to act in this way, these two asked what authorized it? The schism was real and fundamental, the issue for Martland and Ritchie being the character of the federal state. Other judges did not see the legality of the initiative in such black and white terms, but they were concerned about past practice or convention, an equally important part of constitutional law. Laskin rejected the convention proposition. For him that was part of the political sphere, what he once called "abstract constitutionalism," beyond the powers of the judiciary to curtail.

The judges' first responses, all put forward as tentative, did not change substantially throughout the long summer. They adjourned the first meeting after nearly two hours, agreeing to convene again in two weeks' time, so each would have a chance to research certain matters, including the Commonwealth precedents and the British authorities. Some even reread the original debates that gave rise to Confederation and the minutes of the imperial and dominion-provincial conferences preceding the

Statute of Westminster in 1931. When they reconvened, it appeared that all of them had some aspect they wanted to write on, and four major judgments began to circulate: two on the legality of the measure and two on convention. Laskin and those who agreed with him on the political nature of convention (Estey and McIntyre) did not initially wish to write on the issue but did so in response to the majority judgment.

The patriation case came at a turning point in the history of the Supreme Court of Canada. Martland was preparing to retire; the new judges (Chouinard and Lamer) appointed by Clark and Trudeau in 1979 and 1980 were considerably younger — a different generation from most of the others. And Laskin's recurring health problems were prompting speculation about how long he would continue as chief justice.

Until that point, the relationships had been friendly but somewhat formal. Although it appeared to regular observers that the brethren, for reasons of age, interests and background, were not a close-knit unit, the constitution case appeared to change that. Where it tore apart other groups in society, it seemed to create a new awareness on the bench despite, or perhaps because of, their fundamentally different views. "If anything, our relationships were warmer at the end than at the beginning because of all we went through," one justice said many months later.

———————— ❦ ————————

The first-ever Supreme Court of Canada decision to be brought down on national television was a technical disaster. Unaccustomed to having so many wires underfoot, one of the judges accidentally kicked a connecting cable, cutting off the sound in the middle of a crucial point and sending the officials in justice minister Chrétien's office lunging for the television set to adjust the volume. It was perhaps a fitting start to the complex judgment, which really took several days for the public to grasp fully.

In one stroke, the court fashioned both a smashing legal victory and a stern rebuke on the propriety of the federal plan. Legally, it supported Pierre Trudeau's vision of the country, the "anomaly" or paradox of Canadian sovereignty left a kind of power vacuum that the federal Parliament could fill if it dared. Morally, the court said the process "offended the federal spirit." A provincial lawyer, reaching into the mob outside the courtroom for his copy of the judgment, observed somewhat sadly that it was a "messy win for the provinces." Peter Russell, political scientist at the University of Toronto, who sat through the full hearings, wrote later that there was "a lack of intellectual coherence" to major elements of the court decision. But he confessed that one has to look beyond the internal logic of their arguments to the court's sense of "the necessities of judicial statecraft." If it had refused to answer the non-legal questions, a greater crisis of confidence in national institutions may have developed.*

Indeed, the Supreme Court judgment — or judgments; there were four: two majority rulings on convention and legality and two dissents — was not only remarkable for what it said but for the fact that it reached for the historical nettle:

> We are involved here with a finishing operation, with fitting
> a piece into the constitutional edifice; it is idle to expect to
> find anything in the British North America Act that
> regulates the process that has been initiated in this case. Were
> it otherwise, there would be no need to resort to the
> resolution procedure invoked here, a procedure which takes
> account of the intergovernmental and international link
> between Canada and Great Britain. There is no comparable
> link that engages the provinces with Great Britain.

The "old colonial machinery" had not changed substantially since 1867, seven of the nine judges ruled, and if the federal Parliament were to crank it up to remove "this remaining badge of subservience," it would be acting within its legal authority. There was nothing in the theories of federalism or the (conflicting) statements of public figures to "engage the law," the majority said, adding that there was "little profit in parading them."

Only Martland and Ritchie found the Trudeau plan illegal. While the others dealt with the form of the initiative and the process itself, they went beyond it to the substance of the action and concluded that, in a federation, one level of government cannot, on its own, alter the powers of the other. "The Parliament of Canada has no power to trespass on the area of legislative powers given to the provincial legislatures," the two wrote. It was the duty of the court, "in its role of protecting and preserving the Canadian constitution," to declare that no such power exists.

In any case, the majority ruling on the legality of the plan was relentless in its rejection of the provincial case. It was "misconceived" to say that a convention of provincial consent has crystallized into law, and the courts can play "no parental role" in determining this proposition. (Indeed, while the court disagreed on the precise nature of any convention

---

*Most of the initial academic comment has, so far at least, viewed the majority judgments as somewhat contradictory. For example, Queen's University law professor Noel Lyon has argued that the Martland-Ritchie dissent has a certain foundation that the majority view lacks: a *truly* federal system cannot accommodate one partner who is legally empowered to change the nature of the system.

requiring provincial consent, all nine judges declared that it was not legally enforceable.) The position of the dissenting provinces — that Canada came of age legally in the last fifty years, particularly as a result of the Statute of Westminster — "distorts history" and the principles of judicial interpretation. As Ottawa argued, the British Parliament continued to hold unfettered legal authority over the Canadian constitution. As for the fact that provinces are sovereign in their own respective fields, the court noted that the "watertight compartment" theory has generally stood the test of time. But the provinces have no official standing with Westminster, and there is nothing in law "to say the internal distribution of legislative power must be projected externally. . . . The law knows nothing of any requirement of provincial consent, either to a resolution of the federal House or as a condition of the exercise of United Kingdom legislative power."

Having crushed the provincial arguments on the one hand, the court then proceeded to make amends by challenging the propriety of the constitutional scheme. Recognizing that a convention exists requiring a "substantial measure of provincial consent," six of the justices ruled that "by no conceivable standard" could the present situation be thought "to pass muster." The convention ruling, an opinion without any legal standing, was easily the most complex of the court's views and will likely bedevil scholars for generations. The dissenters — Laskin, Estey and McIntyre — seemed to take a particularly sharp view of their colleagues' beliefs. "It is unrealistic in the extreme", these three wrote, to say a convention has emerged, even assuming that it is not legally binding. Moreover, they said, the court "should not conjure up questions of its own" to answer, but should stick to the formal references before it.

This barb was aimed at the majority's endorsement of substantial consent, a concept that was put forward only by one government, Saskatchewan, during oral argument. Laskin and his two colleagues obviously found it difficult to understand how some of their brothers could state in the legality judgment that it is not up to the courts to say an amending formula exists and then prescribe one, albeit somewhat vaguely, in the concurrent judgment on convention.

The six to three ruling on the nature of constitutional conventions was, in many ways, a diluted version of the Martland-Ritchie position on the legality of the federal action. Conventions are the unwritten part of a country's constitution and in Canada's case are designed to preserve the federal character. As Lord Dicey said in 1885 when he first defined constitutional conventions: they are "a body of constitutional or political ethics." Building on this definition, the six noted that "while they are not laws, some conventions may be more important than some laws. Their importance depends on that of the value or principle which they are meant to safeguard." They prescribed as important conventions the practice that a government resigns on losing an election or the confidence of Parliament. To do otherwise would amount to a *coup d'état*, the judges wrote, but it would be up to the political institutions in society — the legislatures, the electorate, the governor general — to amend the situation.

While it seems intellectually inconsistent for the court to pronounce on an issue which they agreed they could not enforce — they did so because they said it was "constitutional in character" and a major part of the submissions before them — it might be seen as a kind of warning shot across the nation's prow, perhaps even a constitutional brief for Edward Schreyer. In no uncertain terms, the six judges said that the purpose of the constitutional rule was "to protect the federal character of the Canadian constitution and prevent the anomaly that the House of Commons and Senate could obtain by simple resolutions what they could not validly accomplish by statute." Canada would still be a federation, but "a different federation, made different at the instance of a majority in the House of the federal Parliament acting alone." Entrenching a charter of rights "would thus abridge provincial legislative authority on a scale exceeding the effect of any previous constitutional amendment for which provincial consent was sought and obtained." As a court, they could do nothing legally to rectify the situation — assuming that they wanted to. The "sanctions of convention" rest with other institutions of government; otherwise, there is "the risk of creating a state of legal discontinuity, that is a form of revolution." However, as judges they could point the way. The Trudeau plan, they concluded in an otherwise bland phrase packed with new meaning, was "unconstitutional in the conventional sense."

12

The Boy Scouts from B.C. and the Bottle of Scotch

Most sorts of diversion in men, children and other animals are in imitation of fighting.

Jonathan Swift,
Thoughts on Various Subjects, 1711.

At nine o'clock on the morning of 29 September 1981, the voice and face of Pierre Elliott Trudeau are converted into millions of electronic impulses in the studios of the Korean Broadcasting Corporation and flung into space over Seoul. There, somewhere in the void, they find a communications satellite and are bounced earthwards again, touching down in Ottawa at seven o'clock on the evening of the previous day, Judgment Day. Canadians who entered the age of television in 1953 by watching the coronation of the Queen may feel reverberations of memory: the satellite picture received by the downlink dishes was of an uncertain quality. The only uncertainty in the voice, however, can be attributed to the man himself; the prime minister is not a morning person, and he has been roused at six-fifteen to begin preparations for this event.

"While I have not read the entire judgment of the Supreme Court of Canada," he begins, "it seems that it confirms what we have held all along — namely that the federal Parliament has the legal authority to ask Westminster to enact the constitutional measure now before the Senate and the House of Commons — though there is in Canada a political convention or practice that such a request not be made without the agreement of the provincial governments. I understand that the Supreme Court ducked the question of how many provincial governments should agree. We are, therefore, in the same situation we were in before the matter went to the Supreme Court. . . ."

At that very moment, a small group of British Columbians — premier William Richards Bennett and his closest constitutional advisers — break

245

into cheers in the National Press Building offices of the parliamentary bureau of CBC television. The cheers are repeated minutes later when Trudeau says, in response to a question from a Canadian reporter in Seoul: "I have not ruled out absolutely the possibility of listening to what the provinces have to say."

In the minds of the British Columbians, the prime minister is saying the court decision is unclear. And that is the signal that Bennett, the chairman of the gang of eight premiers, believes he and Trudeau had agreed upon at their private meeting four days earlier at 24 Sussex Drive. If either the federal side or the opposing provincial governments imply in a public statement that the decision is not clear-cut, it will indicate a willingness to return to the first ministers' negotiating table.

In the face both of strong federal government opposition and of pressures from CBC's news managers, Bennett had earlier insisted on waiting until Trudeau spoke before sitting down in front of the television cameras to give his own reaction to the judgment. The CBC had agreed, but only on condition that he leave his provincial government offices two blocks away in the Royal Bank of Canada building at Sparks and Metcalfe Streets and come to the CBC's parliamentary studios. Bill Bennett has five minutes to prepare after Trudeau finishes speaking; he does not need a great deal of time. His aides have written a statement for him in advance that takes a soft line; it implies a victory for the provinces, of course, but it is without the teeth-kicking rhetoric that has become the common feature of the slanging exchanges between the two constitutional camps. Bennett also says he will be embarking upon a tour of the ten provincial capitals to consult with his colleagues on the next steps to be taken. He leaves Ottawa the following day. The boy scouts from B.C. are going to go and do good national works.

✦

The thirty-three days of Canadian history that followed the Supreme Court's judgment possessed a special lyrical quality. They were much more a testament to man's endearing fallibility than to his vaunted claims to plan and execute the most complex acts. They spawned the stuff of legend, of stories — the anecdote of Jean and the two Roys and the bottle of scotch, of a splendidly romantic night in Fiji when leaden discourse on the federal government's fallback position on the charter of rights sank through the perfumed layers of South Pacific air, of curious brown paper envelopes being passed in a Montreal hotel corridor and sped by taxi through Toronto streets, of a quixotic premier playing a strange political gambit. It was also a time of frenzied backroom plotting, juxtaposed with long — almost leisurely — philosophical discussions about the nature of Canada and its laws.

This period — a *scherzo* interlude — had its main antecedents in Victoria in the late spring and summer. Bennett was to become the premiers' official spokesman for the twelve-month period following their annual conference in August. He asked his senior advisers to give him their thoughts on the major nationwide provincial issues with which he would be required to deal. There were two: the constitution, and the possibility that the federal government might act on a problem even hoarier than the constitution — the revision of the railway tariffs on grain shipments to export harbours. Bennett was advised to concentrate all his attention on the constitution.

This suited him. He felt that the current spokesman, Sterling Lyon, had done himself and the other gang of eight premiers political harm by the rigidity of his antagonism to Trudeau. British Columbians are inclined to put limits on the amount of fed-bashing they like their government in Victoria to engage in. Bennett did not share the intensity of Lyon's opposition to a charter of rights (such things as French-language education, for example, had some popularity in the province and Bennett's government was not particularly opposed to it). Neither did he share Lévesque's and Lougheed's furious hostility towards the central government and all its works. Bennett's passion was the amending formula: he could not tolerate the Victoria formula, which carried his capital's name and which his father as premier had accepted ten years earlier; it lumped in B.C. with the three prairie provinces, instead of designating it as a region of its own.

Bennett consistently had felt that if the constitution package could be altered to embrace an amending formula that could be acceptable to both his government and Ottawa — something along the lines of the Vancouver consensus but with tighter strictures against opting-out — there was every possibility for an accommodation. He had begun 1981 by sending his intergovernmental relations minister, the affable, florid-spoken Vancouver lawyer Garde Gardom, on a winter's mush across the country to see if there were glimmerings anywhere of a new constitutional initiative; in particular, Gardom's instructions were to urge the provincial governments in harshest opposition to Trudeau to develop their own resolution, preferably one which Ottawa could accept.

In the full skein of events, it is doubtful if Gardom's mission had any value (other than to trigger the suspicions of Claude Morin and Alberta's Dick Johnston, among others, that Bennett was likely to play an appeaser's game). But it was an indication that the B.C. premier genuinely did wish to find a constitutional solution. Gardom's errand was also one of the beginnings of the road to the April accord — which, of course, was not what Bennett wanted (even though he turned out, curiously, to be one of its chief architects). The accord, without a tighter formula and without a charter of rights, stood no chance of being accepted by Ottawa, and therefore no chance of ever reaching Westminster.

Thus having swung out one way, into the gang of eight, Bennett then began to swing back, towards Ottawa. In June, six weeks after the signing of the April accord, Allan Gotlieb, the undersecretary of state for external affairs, came to Vancouver on business. James Matkin, B.C.'s deputy minister of intergovernmental relations, rang him up and hopped across the Strait of Georgia from Victoria for a meeting. Matkin and Gotlieb knew each other from their former jobs — when Matkin was B.C.'s deputy minister of labour and Gotlieb was deputy minister of the old federal department of manpower and immigration. Matkin, knowing full well that Gotlieb was one of Ottawa's most influential mandarins, with full access to the innermost circles, told him that he wasn't happy with the April accord and asked if there was still room for a compromise. Gotlieb said yes. Matkin, an intelligent and highly principled public servant — he had once been a Mormon missionary in the South Pacific — would not have spoken without being aware of what was on his premier's mind.

The next feeler from British Columbia came in August, during the Canadian Bar Association's annual convention, held in Vancouver. Roger Tassé, the federal deputy justice minister, was in town, and Richard Vogel, B.C.'s deputy attorney general, arranged for him to meet Matkin over lunch. This time, with Gardom's knowledge and in front of Vogel — who was philosophically opposed to an entrenched charter — Matkin told Tassé that the April accord was a mistake, that the gang of eight should have gone for at least some entrenched rights, and that he, Matkin, was personally in favour of the charter of rights. Matkin also hinted that Bennett could be moved on the charter. Tassé, in turn, indicated that his political masters might compromise on the amending formula.

Such talk could only kindle the flames of ardour in Ottawa. Tassé had hardly left town when Michael Kirby arrived, purportedly on some federal-provincial matter to do with pensions. He met Matkin and went over the same ground that Tassé had, returning to Ottawa — briefly. In early September, he was back in Victoria, this time to arrange a private meeting between Trudeau and Bennett, who by now had become official spokesman for the premiers.

———————————— ✦ ————————————

The 24 September meeting in the sunroom of the prime minister's residence was an intricate dance through gossamer veils. Ostensibly, it was about a first ministers' conference on the economy, something the premiers had called for at their annual meeting. Trudeau began with a screed against first ministers' conferences, saying he had held more than any prime minister in Canadian history and was through with them; they didn't work. He did not want to have one on the economy, and asked rhetorically where had all these first ministers' meetings of the past got him. The country was now more decentralized than when he had started, he said, and still everyone thought he was a bastard.

Bennett, who had never particularly liked the prime minister, replied with rather touching sensitivity. He said: "You know, I remember my dad saying to me, 'No matter what people are saying about you, the country still has progressed and you shouldn't look back on what you've done as a failure. We've grown, we've developed, the country's better than it was.'" Bennett, twelve years Trudeau's junior, almost was speaking to the prime minister in a fatherly way himself.

It had been agreed in advance in Victoria by Kirby, Matkin and Norman Spector (who was working in the premier's office as a constitutional adviser) that Bennett should bring up the subject of the constitution. This he did, as the conversation drifted into a broader discussion of federal-provincial relations. In effect, Bennett said to Trudeau: "Look, you're about to go out of the country*, the Supreme Court decision will soon be handed down, we're going to have to talk about the constitution again at some point. Why don't we look at some scenarios now — federal win, provincial win, decision unclear — and see where they lead us."

The constitution portion of their discussion did not last long — twenty to thirty minutes. Trudeau — his mind on both the Quebec government and the possibility of strong *obiter dicta* from the Supreme Court on constitutional convention — asked Bennett if the premiers would still be insisting on unanimous agreement to reform should he agree to sit down with them again; he wanted to know whether the more flexible members of the gang of eight would be ungagged. And, for the first time, the prime minister hinted at the possibility of submitting the whole package — charter as well as amending formula — to a referendum in two years' time.† Bennett did not reject that notion.

As for their speculations on the court ruling, Trudeau at one point commented that the federal government would have to live with whatever the verdict said. Bennett came away with the impression that Trudeau could accommodate himself to a smaller charter of rights, something federal officials afterwards denied. The two men then agreed that if either side were to indicate publicly that the decision was unclear, it would be interpreted as a sign that that party was interested in returning to the bargaining table. The meeting ended with Bennett saying he would canvass his fellow premiers about loosening the bonds of the gang of eight.

———————————— ❧ ————————————

---

*Trudeau was about to leave for Melbourne and the biennial Commonwealth heads of government meeting, with a stop en route in Seoul.

†As it stood, the package provided for putting competing amending formulas to a referendum decision within two years if the federal and provincial governments could not reach a negotiated agreement.

Judgment Day was as furious in all its activity as the biting, vectoring gusts of wind that snapped at the capital's flags. Jean Chrétien, his back wrenched from a weekend golf game, had his usual breakfast of orange juice, toast and coffee. Aline kissed her husband goodbye and promised to join him later in his office.

Chrétien, for form's sake — the separation of executive and judiciary — and also for protection from the press, did not want to be in the courtroom. He intended to see it all take place on television in his office on the third floor of the justice department building, just across the lawn from the Supreme Court. Political and departmental aides were waiting for him when he arrived. They were joined by Kirby and two of Trudeau's senior staff members, principal secretary Tom Axworthy and legislative assistant Joyce Fairbairn. Serge Joyal and Chrétien's newly appointed parliamentary secretary, Toronto MP James Peterson, were also there. So was the indispensable Eddie Goldenberg, Roger Tassé, external affairs' George Anderson (who was dealing with the British on the case), Hershell Ezrin, who directed the Canadian Unity Information Office, Torrance Wylie, chairman of the Liberal Party's fund-raising agency, and Gérard Veilleux, head of federal-provincial affairs in the finance department.

Four blocks away, Bill Bennett and many of the constitution ministers and attorneys general of the gang of eight governments were in the boardroom of the B.C. offices. One floor above them, Dick Johnston was in the Alberta government's Ottawa office.

Some of the other major players were in curious places. Lougheed was in Baden-Baden, Germany, making a pitch to the International Olympics Committee to have the 1988 winter games held in Calgary. Bill Davis was in Fiji, on his way home from an Ontario trade mission in Australia. Ed Broadbent was on a plane returning from Paris.

Trudeau, in Seoul, was given the highlights of the ruling and then went to bed — it was midnight there. He left Michael Pitfield to work through the night, spending most of the time on the telephone to Ottawa, digesting the verdict and preparing a briefing paper for the prime minister.

———————— ✦ ————————

At ten-thirty, the big double doors behind the courtroom bench swung open and the most exalted judges in the land paraded into the chamber, dressed in their workaday black robes, rather than their ceremonial scarlet and ermine. Chief justice Bora Laskin glared at the broadcasting paraphernalia and six dazzling banks of lights cluttering his usually tranquil chamber, took his seat and began to read, alternating between English and strongly accented French. Laskin was a casting director's dream, stern, grave, his snow-white hair reflecting the irradiation from the television lights; the other eight justices flanked him, four and four, in their high-backed, red leather chairs, looking pensively into space. Three CBC cameras and a live radio unit fed the performance across Canada.

As electronic theatre, however, it was bad. As former Newfoundland premier Joey Smallwood commented, what Laskin had to say was "as clear as mud". Although not to Chrétien. When the verdict was read out, seven-to-two, that the federal government's resolution was legal, the justice minister turned to Tassé and said: "We won." Tassé replied: "Yes."

The question now was: What next? For a few hours, there was a manifest hesitation. Claude Morin arrived at the door of the B.C. government offices for a scheduled meeting and was asked by hovering journalists if he had a comment. "No," he said curtly, and ordered a television crew to get out of his way. Dick Johnston came down from the Alberta government office. They joined Bennett and other provincial ministers and their officials to watch Joe Clark and Jean Chrétien give televised press conferences — Clark warning the prime minister against any "legal trickery"; Chrétien calling the decision a firm victory for the federal side. Then the gang of eight representatives began their own long, and frequently heated, discussion on how to respond.

Bennett and his officials — Matkin, Spector and assistant deputy attorney general Mark Krasnick — wanted to take a conciliatory approach, to follow the 'unclear' game-plan that had been discussed at Bennett's meeting with Trudeau (although Bennett had some dissension within his own camp: the two members of his cabinet accompanying him, Gardom and education minister Brian Smith, favoured a harder line). The Quebec and Alberta people predictably wanted to be tough and to call the verdict a victory for the gang of eight. The other provincial delegations fell along the intervening spectrum.

During the afternoon, Bennett spent nearly two-and-a-half hours on the telephone, talking to fellow premiers, trying to work out a common position for him to take as spokesman. René Lévesque did not wait for him. In Quebec City, he made a pre-emptive strike, reducing Bennett's manoeuvring room; Lévesque called his own press conference to declare the Supreme Court's ruling a clear win for the anti-Ottawa side. At four-thirty, Bennett, somewhat reluctantly came down to the lobby of the Royal Bank building for a brief meeting with the press. He said he was pleased with the ruling; it vindicated the stand of the dissident provincial governments. But there was little heat in his words. He then went back up in the elevator to work on his formal statement for the television cameras.

❦

By ten o'clock that night, the frantic pace of Judgment Day had waned. Millions of words had been spoken into microphones, millions more set in print in newspapers. Trudeau had spoken; Bennett had reacted. In the hotels and offices around Parliament Hill, the lights were going out. In his justice department office, a weary Jean Chrétien asked his press secretary, Carole Pressault, to find out where Roy Romanow was staying in town and get him on the telephone. She got the name of his hotel from the staff at CTV's *Canada AM* and called him; he was with Roy McMurtry. She put her boss on the line. "We won," said Chrétien. "You owe me a bottle of scotch."

The bet had been made early in the summer, the last time Chrétien and Romanow had spoken to each other. Chrétien had not even bothered to consult Romanow (contrary to normal practice) before the prime minister appointed a new chief justice of Saskatchewan's court of appeal. Now, as they talked, something perhaps tugged at Chrétien's insides. Tired as he was, he invited the two Roys over to his house.

Romanow did not bring a bottle of scotch; it was too late; the liquor stores were closed; and he didn't altogether feel Chrétien had won. Instead, the three men sipped beer, with Aline Chrétien anxiously cautioning her husband against staying up too late. The discussion was not long, about an hour. McMurtry said that, eventually, they all had to get together and make a deal; the other two agreed, speaking in rough generalities, but neither gave any ground. They all went over a list of items of what might form an agreement. Then the two attorneys general went back to their hotel rooms. The next morning, a bottle of scotch arrived at the Chrétien house, signed by Romanow and McMurtry.

* * *

The morning after Judgment Day, as Bennett was preparing to leave Ottawa for his tour of the provincial capitals, Kirby asked for a meeting of clarification with Matkin and Spector. Tassé was also there. The British Columbians — although they had been a little puzzled by Chrétien's firm line on a federal victory — were convinced that a great drama was now in progress, triggered by Trudeau's 'unclear' signal. To them, the prime minister's message had been unmistakeable. Now, on the morning after, they found themselves in the office of Trudeau's chief constitutional strategist being told they were wrong.

Kirby said he wanted to make sure that there was no misreading of what Trudeau had said vis-à-vis the 'unclear' signal and 'living with' the court decision. He implied strongly that what Bennett had already begun telling other provincial governments was a misinterpretation of events: 'living with' the court ruling did not mean being stopped by it. As for the decision itself, it was by no means clear that it was 'unclear'; if anything, it was a federal win. Ottawa had been saying this all along, Kirby told them: winning meant being adjudged legal.

Spector and Matkin were convinced that there had been no misreading; they felt that Kirby was trying to unsay what Trudeau had said. Kirby, for his part, was alarmed at the intelligence he was receiving from his sources in various provincial capitals about what Bennett was saying — that Trudeau was not wedded to all of the charter, *and* that Trudeau had given the signal that he would come back to the bargaining table; the juxtaposition of the two statements made Trudeau look ready for the kill.

The meeting between the federal and British Columbia sides resolved nothing. Bennett left Ottawa on his cross-country mission, finding himself hailed by ordinary citizens in various airports, who patted him on the shoulder or shook his hand, wishing him good luck. But he was given a very different message by the provincial government representatives he met: they told him bluntly that they didn't believe what he was saying, that he had misread Trudeau. Where were they getting this information? From Kirby and other federal officials who were spreading the word through their private channels in advance of Bennett's path. Press stories — quoting no sources by name — were appearing with the same message.

It was frustrating and embarrassing for the B.C. premier, who never at the best of times was considered a powerhouse in federal-provincial diplomacy. It also was causing considerable confusion. The fact that Bennett turned out to be right in the end stuck in few people's minds outside his own capital. One senior official from another province (whose minister was among those convinced that Bennett had botched things) surmised at the end: "A man doesn't become premier of a province by misunderstanding all the signals that are given to him at various times. All that bobbing and weaving in Ottawa may have been due to the fact that Trudeau really hadn't quite decided in his own mind."

One explanation for the incident is that too many people let the wish become father to the thought. Bennett may have overstated the Trudeau signals when he had his initial telephone conversations with his nine fellow premiers; they in turn may have overstated what Bennett had said in their conversations with officials that were reported back to Kirby. Kirby, who would have been feverishly anxious to disabuse any of the provincial wolves of the notion that Trudeau had been weakened by the Court's decision, then sat down with Matkin and Spector and perhaps deliberately underplayed the signals. Federal-provincial relations, to say the least, can be an imprecise business.

———————— 🍁 ————————

Meanwhile in the South Pacific. For all that it mattered to the Canadian press contingent travelling with Trudeau — and it didn't seem to matter a great deal more to Trudeau and his advisers — the prime minister could have been attending a ten-pin bowling league convention in Kansas City. The only subject that truly interested the Canadians (except for the external affairs people in the party) was the constitution.

In the cavernous Commonwealth conference press centre in Melbourne's Royal Exhibition Building, the appearance of Pitfield or Trudeau's press secretary, Nicole Sénécal, would cause a furious clustering by Canadian reporters,* who would be joined promptly (until they caught on) by journalists from other Commonwealth nations, thinking some choice item of conference news had surfaced. Instead, the Canadians were talking about their constitution — would Trudeau have a private meeting with Mrs. Thatcher in Melbourne? Had he arranged a meeting with Bennett upon his return home? On the two occasions when Trudeau himself gave a full news conference in the centre, some foreign correspondents would ask him about the Commonwealth or the North-South dialogue; inevitably, however, the proceedings would be taken over by Canadian reporters, asking questions in French about the constitution. At that point, foreign reporters would leave.†

On 5 October, Pierre Trudeau met Margaret Thatcher in the suburban Melbourne residence of the British consul general. It was a most significant encounter, the first contact the two leaders had had since the Supreme Court ruling, and this time there was no possibility for independent interpretation of who said what to whom. Pitfield and his British counterpart, Sir Robert Armstrong, worked out an advance statement — sources in London later implied that it was done at Britain's request — that Trudeau and Mrs. Thatcher would make public.

The statement affirmed, once more, that Mrs. Thatcher would introduce and support whatever resolution the Canadian Parliament sent across the Atlantic. The only change Mrs. Thatcher requested in the text was the deletion of the words "as soon as possible" in reference to passage of the resolution through Westminster. Trudeau quoted her as telling him: "'For heaven's sake, let's not put the words in, because British members of Parliament have their dignity and they want to be consulted on this bill.' So I said," Trudeau went on, "'Take that out if it helps.' But I have her word that she will do it as soon as possible. Isn't it great news?"

---

*The shy and mannerly Pitfield, accustomed to the tranquil corridors of public service power, was startled and appeared discomforted by the press of bodies and microphones and the babble of questions at his first Melbourne scrum. As days passed, however, he seemed more and more to enjoy these occasions.

†Trudeau, at his final press conference of the Commonwealth meeting, conceded he had not even read the leaders' communiqué; he then went on to talk about the constitution.

British officials, who met Canadian reporters that night in a Melbourne hotel room, were not as ebullient. In rather strong terms, they pointed out the difference between British and Canadian backbenchers and the amount of difficulty that Westminster's "barracks room lawyers" might cause on the constitution bill if it were to be introduced without substantial provincial consent. Thatcher did not give a Commonwealth press conference; the foreign secretary, Lord Carrington, who did, refused to comment on the constitution affair beyond reading aloud the joint Thatcher-Trudeau statement. As he began to read, non-Canadian reporters quickly left the press theatre.

Five days later, the Canadians were in Fiji for a night's stopover on their way home. There is a scene by a hotel poolside in Suva not likely to be forgotten by those who were there.

Early in the evening, the Fijian government had put on a ceremonial feast for Trudeau and the Canadian contingent of officials and press. The prime minister was presented with a ceremonial whale's tooth and the ritual important visitor's drink made from squeezed (and hallucinogenic) yaqona roots. The dining tables had been laden with platters of lovo lili, vuaka kovu, palusami and uvi natu. Young men and women students at the university in Suva had executed a Tongan war dance, a Fijian spear dance, a Samoan knife dance done with burning torches, a Samoan slap dance, the *sasa*, performed by both sexes. Two women students from the Cook Islands did movements with their hips and midriffs never seen in Ottawa. Everyone drank a lot of beer.

Michael Pitfield was not at the party. He had spent the time in his hotel room with a portable typewriter, tapping out a 405-word statement on the constitution. When the Canadian reporters returned from the feast near to midnight, he gathered them around the hotel pool for a press briefing. On the other side of the pool a party was in full swing, with laughter, giggles, the tinkling of ice cubes in tall, chilled glasses. Pitfield and the journalists were talking in stupefying detail about Trudeau's planned meeting with Bennett and whether the federal government had a fallback position on the charter of rights. At one moment, *en passant*, Pitfield mentioned quietly that his track record on the entire trip was unbroken: he had not been to one social function.

The prime minister's armed forces Boeing 727 touched down at Ottawa's Uplands air force base on the morning of 9 October. Trudeau travelled downtown and found his constitutional advisers in philosophical disarray over what the court ruling meant.

One group, basically Kirby's federal-provincial relations office, argued that the federal government was obliged now either to get substantial provincial consent or to jettison those parts of the resolution which impinged on provincial jurisdiction. A second group of advisers, led by Tassé and Fred Gibson, believed the court had raised no new important principles in its decision and they urged full steam ahead to Westminster.

The officials were also divided on any strategy vis-à-vis meeting the premiers for another first ministers' conference. Kirby wanted to make a new offer to try to meet the court's constitutionality test, and, if that failed, to consider end-running the opposing provincial governments and 'conventionalizing' the constitution (every new event in the constitution epic produced its own jargon) by taking it to the people in a referendum. Tom Axworthy and Gibson were not convinced that was desirable; they reasoned that if a new offer were to be rejected, it would be almost impossible to return to the original proposal. Moreover, once Ottawa made a new offer, it would permit Joe Clark to reopen debate in the House; the Conservatives would be able to say that the resolution on which they had agreed to limit debate and submit to a vote was no longer the resolution the government was talking about. The Kirby side disagreed; if an offer were made and rejected, it would demonstrate provincial intransigence; reverting to the original proposal would be difficult, but it could still be done.

A third debate concerned alternatives to the application of the charter — opting in, opting out, delaying application and putting the whole thing to a referendum.

———————————— ✤ ————————————

On other fronts. In Edmonton and Quebec City, the politicians and their aides were getting uneasy; they began to feel that some of the more pliable members of the gang of eight might be in danger of peeling off. Lougheed* had met Bennett on his cross-country tour. He didn't like any of this soft-peddling, 'unclear' business; to the men in Edmonton, the court verdict was a clear win for the provinces.

In Regina, Romanow walked into Blakeney's office and told him that Saskatchewan had two choices: it could either stick with the gang of eight or try again to make a deal, perhaps grouping together another alliance of provinces. Romanow suggested that the Saskatchewan government was uniquely free to move: it was mistrusted by both sides. Blakeney accepted the second course. He called Davis, Buchanan and Bennett to ask them to mandate a minister and some officials to discuss reopening negotiations.

In Victoria and Ottawa, aides to Bennett and Trudeau agreed on a date

---

*The Alberta premier had caught up with the Supreme Court judgment in London, on his way home from Germany. He read it in his hotel room, and was delighted by it.

for a second meeting, and, on the afternoon of 13 October, the two men and their notetakers — Kirby and Spector, the same two for the earlier meeting — met first in the garden behind the prime minister's quarried stone residence and, then, as a light chill breeze came off the river, they moved into the glassed-in sunroom with the ceremonial spears on the wall. They talked for three hours. A full moon rose. A bat swooped around the trunk of an ornamental fruit tree. A grey cat slid hurriedly along the wall.

Trudeau first wanted Bennett to report on his ambiguous trip around the provincial capitals. The premiers had not at this point publicly agreed to hold another first ministers' conference, but Bennett told Trudeau that many wanted to get back to the bargaining table. He said that most premiers were in a reasonable mood. In Bennett's view, they wanted to get the issue off the table so as to concentrate on other matters, such as the economy.

Trudeau was suspicious; what proof was there that the premiers simply did not want to tie him up in a stall? Bennett agreed that certain of his colleagues wanted to wreak political havoc on the prime minister, and he recounted his visit to Quebec City, where Lévesque had brought out some private polling results, showing Trudeau to have the lowest popularity of any prime minister since Canadian polling had begun in the 1940s. Trudeau greatly resented this, asking what sort of message Lévesque was trying to convey. Bennett still insisted that everyone wanted to talk.

He started pressing Trudeau to name somewhere negotiation could take place, something he could take back to the other premiers so that they would know he was not setting them up to be manipulated into a publicly perceived position of obstinacy. Trudeau allowed that that was a reasonable request, but he said to Bennett: "You don't have a mandate. You're asking me to expose my position but you don't have a mandate [to commit the other premiers]. If we put something on the table, can we clinch it quickly? I don't want to be set up and led to believe that there is room for agreement." Bennett replied: "My assessment is that they are agreeable if there is something that is reasonable." He tried to get Trudeau to talk about what they had discussed at their first meeting: flexibility on the charter of rights. At one point Kirby broke in, and told Bennett that the prime minister was being pressed to commit himself; what about the gang of eight — where were they prepared to move? Bennett replied that he did not — as Trudeau had said — have a mandate to speak for the premiers.

It was a painfully frustrating meeting, drenched in caution and mistrust. They fenced, they tried to draw each other out. For fear of weakening their bargaining positions, neither man was willing to indicate where, specifically, he would be flexible. The sum of their meeting, however, was that Bennett and (much more important) Trudeau agreed that both sides had to compromise on what was most popular of all about the constitution package: the charter of rights. That was where the negotiating would take place. Trudeau agreed to another first ministers' conference.

The two leaders stepped out of the front door of the residence to meet the press. Trudeau said that he had "substantially compromised," but gave no details. Two days later, Hugh Segal reported to the constitution team in Queen's Park that he had heard from his Ottawa sources that Trudeau had thought Bennett was naive in reporting that Lougheed and Lévesque seriously wanted to reach an agreement. Still, the 2 November date for the first ministers' meeting was announced — the 'one last time'.

———————— ❧ ————————

After his meeting with Trudeau, Bennett directed Matkin and Spector to go to Regina and start writing down some alternative proposals with Saskatchewan officials. It was a portentous moment. For the first time since the April accord, there was actually to be an authorized attempt to put something on paper. Ontario officials had received the same instructions.

A couple of days later, on 18 October, in Montreal's Ritz Carlton Hotel, there was a gathering of all ten premiers, their constitution ministers and senior officials. The Quebec government made the arrangements. It was pure Agatha Christie: the Ontario and New Brunswick delegations were placed on one floor together where they couldn't see what the others were doing; the Quebec and British Columbia delegations were placed on another floor together, where Quebec *could* see what British Columbia was doing.

Saskatchewan and Ontario officials came to Montreal with the understanding that they and the B.C. people would exchange their so-called no-author draft proposals (the label comes from the jargon of collective bargaining: proposals are put down on paper without the author being committed to them). Matkin received instructions to leave a cocktail party, go up to the Saskatchewan delegation's floor and knock at the door of a certain room. The door opened. A junior official invited him into the room, opened a drawer, handed him a plain brown envelope and ushered him back into the corridor. At that moment, Blakeney came out of a room across the hall. Both men walked together to the elevator, got in, and descended, saying not a word. The Saskatchewan draft paper showed an amending formula that did not include opting-out provisions; it also contained a reduced charter of rights, plus options on each of its major theses. Matkin and the Saskatchewan people tried to arrange a meeting, but were too worried about being seen together.

Spector met Ontario's Don Stevenson, the province's deputy inter-governmental minister, who passed over a chart shaped like a teeter-totter: the bigger the number of components in the charter that were accepted, the more generous the terms of the amending formula; the fewer components in the charter, the more restrictive the amending formula.

British Columbia's delegation passed no paper. Bennett had very carefully told his officials only to *ask* for paper, not to give paper. As chairman of the premiers, he was reluctant to become involved in any clandestine dealings. On the other hand, he now knew what no one else knew: where two key provincial governments were prepared to go to arrive at a settlement.

Meanwhile, the gang of eight premiers, meeting in Bennett's eighth-floor hotel room, asked the two 'federalist' premiers, Hatfield and Davis, to leave. Davis was amiable enough about his ejection; Hatfield, after staying up late into the night, brooding about what had happened, gave an emotional press conference the following day in which he accused dark forces (the dissident premiers) of trying to take over the country. One provincial minister got the feeling that Claude Morin was taking over the gang of eight — "casting a web around them" — and that Bennett was being pushed aside. With Hatfield and Davis gone, the eight spent the rest of the meeting plotting, considering, among other things, a detailed report from Alberta's deputy intergovernmental relations minister, Peter Meekison, on the progress of the London strategy.

On their way home, Bennett and Matkin chatted privately on the plane. Matkin proposed taking the Ontario and Saskatchewan drafts and working them into a single text with some British Columbia proposals mixed in; then the single-text draft would be circulated among the three delegations. Bennett did not give an answer one way or the other; Matkin decided to do it on his own. In the process, he had a long discussion — one of a number — with his friend Paul Weiler, former chairman of the B.C. labour relations board, at the time teaching law at Harvard. At Weiler's suggestion Matkin attached a *non obstante* clause to some of the provisions of the charter of rights. And with his draft in his briefcase, he flew east to the grim gathering in the Toronto Hilton Harbour Castle Hotel of the gang of eight constitutional ministers.

Every history has its grey areas. There is one here. How much authority did Bennett grant his officials to — in the trade jargon — 'pass paper'? When he sent Spector and Matkin to the meeting in Regina, had Bennett "mandated" them to look at alternatives, as Blakeney had asked him to do on the telephone? Or had he merely assigned them to "explore" matters, which is Bennett's version of what he told Blakeney. Certainly Bennett received paper in Montreal without passing paper. The instructions from the premier's office to Matkin about what to do with his single-text draft in Toronto are obscured by conflicting versions. Gardom, for his part, did not know anything about the passing of paper, which led senior officials in Victoria and other capitals to conjecture that Bennett kept his minister going at one pace and his officials at another. It is unlikely that Matkin, being the sort of person he is, would have done so much on his own.

At any rate, by 27 October, when the gang of eight constitution ministers convened in Toronto, the story of the three-province draft proposals had seeped into the press (and had been carefully dismissed by Bill Davis). The anecdote of the bottle of scotch also had appeared in print. Romanow was increasingly of a mind that he and Blakeney had been tricked by Bennett, while Morin and Johnston held firm suspicions that they harboured, if not traitors at their bosoms, at least some weak sisters.

The one-day meeting opened — with baskets of fruit for the attending ministers thoughtfully provided by Tom Wells, who wasn't invited — with a special caucus to deal with backsliders. In his courteous way, Morin laid the rasp of his tongue on Spector and Matkin. "These gentlemen," he said, "were no doubt trying to be helpful, but they are weakening our position." Romanow also came in for black words from Morin — not only had he fooled around with the B.C. people, but he had met secretly with McMurtry and Chrétien. (When first confronted with this accusation in Montreal the previous week, Romanow had said he had met only to talk about judicial appointments. Morin subsequently decided that Romanow had lied to him.) Romanow felt he was being caught in an unkind crossfire: his gang of eight confrères were accusing him of double-dealing when, in fact, he had been double-dealt; Bennett had obtained negotiating proposals from Saskatchewan, but Romanow and Blakeney had received nothing out of B.C. Matkin and Spector, for their parts, felt that Morin and Johnston and the others did not understand what British Columbia was trying to do — they were not attempting to shift bargaining *positions*, but were striving to broaden some of the participants' bargaining *interests* so that a healthier negotiating environment could be created, one that admitted the possibility of compromise.

Pressured by Morin and Johnston, the other gang of eight ministers agreed that they would not change their bargaining position without first appearing before the whole alliance to declare their intentions. Romanow gave his pledge, but he warned his allies that his government would be looking around to see if a better package existed. Gardom said the same thing. To be true to their consciences, both had to say this because they were about to meet the enemy. Tom Wells had invited representatives of Ontario and the 'soft three' — Nova Scotia, B.C. and Saskatchewan — to the Park Plaza headquarters of the Ontario Tories' Big Blue Machine (a leased room with wall-plaque aphorisms praising diligence and perseverance in the face of adversity; Garde Gardom recalled being startled to discover that there actually was a clubroom for the Big Blue Machine).

Meanwhile, shortly after the gang-of-eight meeting drew to a close, Matkin unexpectedly received sharp instructions from Bennett to pass no paper (at the last minute Bennett had been pressed by some of his premier colleagues). It was too late. By secretarial error, Matkin's draft had been sent off by taxi (it had been typed in Toronto) to Don Stevenson at Queen's Park. Stevenson called Matkin just as the group in the Park Plaza were to sit down for lunch. He said he had shown the text to Wells and other Ontario officials and they thought it was superb. Matkin told him: "For God's sake, don't use it." It never got beyond the Ontario people, but Romanow found out about it and was enraged when Gardom refused to share it with him (Gardom had only just learned of its existence).*

The meeting in the Big Blue Machine room went on for more than two days, ending on a Friday, 30 October; it was neither pleasant nor particularly constructive. Romanow was in a sour mood. Nova Scotia's Harry Howe didn't stay long. Gardom felt uncomfortable. Only Wells was upbeat; he later reported to his Ontario colleagues that he felt he had learned useful information about the bargaining positions of Saskatchewan and British Columbia — which, of course, he had; he had seen Matkin's paper. In the end, the gathering had no greater significance than any half-remembered skirmish on the eve of a great battle.

The thirty-three days of *scherzo* that had followed the Supreme Court ruling were coming to a close; the final movement, *largo* (with much percussion), was to begin in Ottawa on Monday — forty-eight hours away. Bill Bennett's paper tricks, much like Michael Pitfield's strange poolside press conference in the South Pacific, was a passing oddity of the constitution story.

———————— ♦ ————————

There are two footnotes to the interlude. The first concerns Bennett; the thirty-three days did not end happily for him. He had had an exceptionally difficult triple role to play: leader of a provincial government, chairman of the gang of eight, official spokesman for all ten premiers. It created conflicts for him; he came to see himself both as mediator and as antagonist — an impossible role, Claude Morin said later. "He started to believe he had been given some kind of national mission. So, instead of sticking

---

*The paper had Saskatchewan's modified Vancouver amending formula, with no opt-out clause. It had fully entrenched fundamental and democratic rights. The rest of the package contained a slightly abbreviated charter, subject to the *non obstante* clause. Romanow was so angry with Gardom and Bennett that he went to Ottawa determined to have as little to do with them as possible.

with us [the hardline opponents to Trudeau] he tried to compromise us. . . ." And was swiftly bypassed by events.

Bennett certainly would assess things differently. He saw his task as serving the interests of his province, loosening the fixed positions of Ottawa, its allies and the gang of eight, and bringing the two sides back to the bargaining table. Those things happened — largely out of their own momentum, but nonetheless they happened. The point is that, once the premiers came into Ottawa for the 'one last time' first ministers' conference, a different dynamic took hold. The strongman premiers were back at centre stage: Lévesque, Lougheed, Blakeney, Davis. Bennett's pivotal role was over, and he reacted as most human beings would who suddenly find that the action has moved away from them to other players: he became noticeably depressed.

The second footnote is an anecdote completely characteristic of the man it is about — Claude Morin. In his sermon against backsliding at the Toronto Hilton Harbour Castle Hotel, Morin movingly told his gang-of-eight colleagues that his career hung on the maintenance of the common front. He implied that he personally had brought the separatist government of Quebec into the alliance. If it fell apart, he said, his position would be untenable, his political future bleak. It was classic Morin, Metternich-like to the end. In fact, he had decided to leave politics after the Quebec referendum and, only at Lévesque's request, had stayed on for the constitution struggle to fight Trudeau.

But *largo*. The curtain was going up in Ottawa. . . .

13
Four Days in November: A "Fascinating Madhouse"

Each man has his own reasons, I suppose, as driving forces, but mine were twofold. One was to make sure that Quebec wouldn't leave Canada through separatism, and the other was to make sure that Canada wouldn't shove Quebec out . . .

Pierre Trudeau, in a television interview, 1973.

Official Ottawa takes on a kind of siege mentality at the outset of every first ministers' conference. The locus of political attention shifts abruptly from the bear-pit of Parliament to the more formalized joustings at the government of Canada conference centre, two blocks to the east. The House of Commons becomes irrelevant to the press when the premiers are in town. The prime minister moves from his parliamentary office, one floor above the House of Commons, to the Langevin Block, across Confederation Square from the conference centre, while the premiers take up camp in various hotels around the perimeter of the downtown core. As is his custom, Peter Lougheed sets up in the penthouse suite at the Skyline Hotel, on the western fringe of the city centre, his entourage filling up the adjacent rooms. Premiers Davis, Hatfield, Bennett and Peckford are spread out on different floors in the more luxurious Four Seasons Hotel, directly south of Parliament Hill. The other four English premiers encase themselves in the Chateau Laurier, the command post for the gang of eight, connected by underground tunnel to the conference centre across Wellington Street.

René Lévesque also takes a room along the fourth-floor corridor of suites at the Chateau Laurier. But he and his delegation are actually staying across the river in Hull, preferring their home turf and the much less stolid ambiance of L'Auberge de la Chaudière (ironically built in the mid-1970s by a notorious Liberal supporter, Robert Campeau). Their suite in the Chateau Laurier goes largely unused.

At one time the building where the first ministers' conferences now take place had a different role in Canada's political life. A former railway terminal — Union Station — it was the symbolic hub of the electoral campaigns that stretched out into the hinterland, where former prime ministers, back to Laurier, began and ended their election travels for political power. For these four days in November, the second to the fifth — the "one last time" meeting — the conference centre also takes on the transitory role of nerve centre for the national media, where the nation's business is recorded and analyzed in all its fits and groans.

Throughout the weekend, while the politicians and backroom boys gather, television technicians unload the miles of cable and heavy equipment for the live opening session on Monday morning. Bulky cameras are hoisted onto third-floor lookouts to capture more panoramic views of the proceedings. Others are placed prominently near doorways, so they can be used for the scrums that begin as soon as the participants enter the hall. Cables are taped to the floor, television lights strapped to iron bars, and cubby-holes in the back corridors turned into make-up rooms and mini-studios, the Chroma-key blue crepe covering the concrete. It is a media event of the first order. Nearly eight-hundred journalists, technicians and researchers will pick up the plastic accreditation cards that allow them into most of the rooms on the first floor, including the main conference hall with its forty-foot ceilings and huge railway-station clock ticking quietly on each wall. With the authorized observers, intergovernmental officials and assembled pundits, there are more than a thousand people in the building. Respected deans of law and retired senators sit like commentators at a hockey match, in high, glassed-in booths overlooking the conference table, the ubiquitous ear plugs dangling like intravenous tubes. They will have the best view in the house — staring straight down at Pierre Trudeau's expressionless mask.

A first ministers' conference is like no other political event in this country, perhaps in the world. It is institutionalized dealmaking. And this time it is being done under such a deadline that everyone seems continually to be watching the hands of the clock. For the journalist, there is a numbing mixture of boredom and suspense: what is going on in the backrooms? Through the course of any particular day, when the first ministers are meeting in private, information trickles out second and third hand, federal and provincial officials circulate through the main hall and workrooms, chatting a bit here, imparting a few scraps of news there. It all has an air of unreality, the absence of context. Somewhere in this cavernous structure, amid the endless cups of coffee and plates of doughnuts that are snatched up in minutes, in the gait of an official scurrying down a hallway, or the preoccupied air of a minister or premier, history is being made and a handful of scribes are straining to discover it. When does it happen? At different times for different people? Who will ever know?

——————————— ✦ ———————————

Shortly after one o'clock on Sunday afternoon, the Ontario government's rented executive jet touches down at Ottawa's Uplands airport. Bill Davis is one of the last of the provincial premiers to arrive, timing his landing so he can catch most of the afternoon's football game on the hotel's television. Other provincial delegations have been drifting into the capital since Friday night. Bill Bennett was the first to come; he tucked himself away in his hotel room with his staff for most of the weekend. Richard Hatfield also arrived early and spent Saturday in the justice building with senior federal officials, discussing the proposal he will be tabling on the first day of the conference.

Leaving their premier to watch the tube, the Ontario people head off straightaway to a series of strategy meetings with their federal counterparts. Intergovernmental affairs minister Tom Wells and his deputy, Don Stevenson, meet Michael Kirby and Roger Tassé at the Four Seasons, where the Ontarians push Ottawa to consider a legislative override on the charter as a bargaining counter with the gang of eight. The federal officials are receptive but insist it would have to be limited by a five-year "sunset" provision. However, unknown to Wells and indeed everyone in the Ontario delegation, except for Davis and his personal emissary, Hugh Segal, Ottawa has a last ditch fallback position — a national referendum to legitimize the charter of rights. Over a quiet lunch in a rear alcove at the Chateau Grill the previous Friday, Kirby had spelled out the referendum plan for Segal. Neither Segal nor his boss were impressed; in their view Trudeau is crazy even to contemplate it. No one can predict how people will vote in a referendum, Segal argued, "It will be like a free shot in a by-election." Even the support of Ontario voters cannot be assured. Davis feels the same way and schedules a late afternoon meeting for Sunday at 24 Sussex Drive to try to talk Trudeau out of it.

As constitutional allies, Trudeau and Davis have developed a close working relationship and even some admiration for each other's styles, close associates say. But it is hard to imagine more diverse personalities. Promptly at five o'clock on Sunday, Davis, the small-town Ontario Protestant, calls on Trudeau, the rebellious Jesuitical Montrealer. The Ontario premier shows up in his hound's-tooth jacket, pressed pants and loafers. Trudeau welcomes him at the door wearing jeans, a designer sweatshirt and clogs. The two leaders and their aides, Kirby and Segal, retire to Trudeau's favourite room, the sunporch at the rear, which looks north across the Ottawa River.

In his low-key style, Davis presses Trudeau to keep his options open for a deal, not to foreclose too soon, to let the conference play itself out. Trudeau is dubious that an accommodation can be salvaged, and will not be swayed from the referendum option. Kirby is very eager to get the fallback position out on the table soon into the private meetings of the first ministers. They talk for nearly two hours until the fading sunlight forces the note-takers to plead for mercy. Ottawa has a very simple strategy at this point: on day one you show flexibility; on day two you offer the basic trade — the amending formula in exchange for the charter; and on day three, if there is no counter-offer, out comes the referendum solution. Davis is the only confidant to be aware of the full plan; Hatfield is told on Wednesday morning, a few hours before the other premiers.* But even Davis has difficulty gauging Trudeau's commitment to it.

------------- ✢ -------------

From his penthouse in the Skyline Hotel, Peter Lougheed also has a spectacular view of the sunsets over the Ottawa River. The gang of eight premiers is meeting Sunday night at eight for a strategy session before the conference starts and the Alberta premier is being briefed by his minister Dick Johnston and Johnston's deputy, Peter Meekison.

British Columbia and Saskatchewan are eager to make a deal, and Johnston relates how he and Quebec's Claude Morin had to whip them back in line at private meetings in Toronto the previous week. On the evening's agenda is a review of the London strategy, Bennett's role as chairman, and the notification that must be given if any members are going to break with the common front. Johnston stresses the latter point and for the first time raises an issue that has been in the back of many people's minds for some time: if there is going to be a deal here, Quebec might not go along, for a variety of historical and political reasons, and the premier should consider how he will proceed in that eventuality. Other Quebec premiers, such as Lesage and Bourassa, have backed away from constitutional deals at the last minute, Johnston reminds his chief. There is no guarantee that Quebec will even agree to simple patriation. Lougheed nods his understanding, and Johnston and Meekison leave for a dinner meeting of the group of eight.

------------- ✢ -------------

*The prime minister was prepared to tell Hatfield of his plan a week before when the two met privately in Ottawa, but the New Brunswick premier said he did not want to be burdened with that knowledge, in case it impaired his, and Trudeau's, flexibility.

Monday, 2 November 1981

Flanked by two senior ministers, Jean Chrétien and Allan MacEachen, Pierre Trudeau brings down the gavel at ten-fifteen to begin the first public session of the conference. The participants have agreed to limit their set speeches to fifteen minutes. For the past half-hour, the premiers have been milling about the conference hall being interviewed in small batches by the radio and television networks that are carrying the proceedings live. The networks estimate that as many as two million Canadians might tune in that morning.

The eleven first ministers are ranged around the large, ring-shaped conference table in a precedence established by the date on which their province entered Confederation. The prime minister is at the centre, flanked by the premiers of Ontario and Quebec. (Unable to banish the smokers to the other end of the table, as he does with his own cabinet, Trudeau must suffer countless hours breathing in the fumes from Bill Davis's pipe and René Lévesque's constant supply of Players filter.) Next come the leaders of Nova Scotia and New Brunswick, Manitoba and British Columbia, PEI and Saskatchewan, Alberta and Newfoundland — the last three, the eventual dealmakers, sitting on the outer perimeter.

Beginning in French, Trudeau goes right to the heart of the matter in his opening remarks: "We are here to find an accord and it will only be possible if everyone is prepared to compromise." He then sets out the three elements on the agenda: patriation, the amending formula, and "should" there be a charter of rights for all Canadians? But having struck a conciliatory tone, the prime minister closes dogmatically. "We would be prepared to be flexible on timing and on substance. But we cannot be flexible on the principle of the charter itself."

In his opening statement, William Davis concentrates on the amending formula, stating that Ontario is not wedded to the provincial veto it receives in the federal resolution. It is a tactic meant to assuage the western provinces, particularly Alberta, who have railed against the special status afforded Ontario and Quebec under the Victoria formula. But Davis's offer is also largely designed to cut some ground out from under Lévesque. If there is to be a compromise on the provincial formula, Lévesque cannot back out over its lost veto if the largest province, Ontario, is prepared to live with a revised arrangement.*

---

*Adding to the pressure, Claude Ryan, watching on television in Montreal, seizes on the Davis offer to send a telegram to Lévesque: Don't give up the veto. He follows up with a telephone call to the Quebec delegation to emphasize his point. Ryan, rapidly losing the confidence of his own party, is carving out his own nationalist position, distancing himself from the Quebec premier and the gang of eight, and limiting the bargaining room Lévesque has if he wants to maintain a common front in Quebec against the Trudeau plan.

When it is his turn, René Lévesque ignores the particular issues under discussion and challenges the legitimacy of the federal resolution, daring Trudeau to call an election if he wants a mandate to patriate and modify the constitution. This topic was not debated during the last federal election campaign, he reminds Trudeau; and during the 1979 election when the prime minister referred to his constitutional dream, his government was defeated. An imposed charter of rights weakening the jurisdiction of the Quebec National Assembly would be a legal and political absurdity, Lévesque protests, especially since it would be enacted "through the use of a foreign power." It is a bitter, accusatory speech, aimed as much at his provincial allies as the audience in Quebec.

When it is time for Nova Scotia's John Buchanan, many observers lean forward in their chairs, anticipating that this might be the first sign of a break in the dissident group, since he is said to feel uncomfortable with the strident 'fed-bashing' of some of the others. Buchanan's arrival in Ottawa had been preceded by high-level rumours that he was anxious for a compromise. But he surprises many that morning with a blunt speech urging Trudeau to adopt the provincial amending formula and leave the rest, the charter of rights, to the next stage.

New Brunswick's Richard Hatfield is the only premier that morning to place a detailed proposal on the table. His plan is to enact parts of the charter of rights immediately but postpone some of the more controversial sections — legal rights, equality rights, and enforcement by the courts — for three years of further talks. At the end of that period, six provinces could prevent the enactment of these sections by passing resolutions in their legislatures which they would then deposit in Ottawa. Hatfield's proposal causes some flurries within the press corps. But it is soon clear that he is preaching to a deaf audience. None of the eight are much interested, and even Trudeau is lukewarm.

Both 'federal' offers are now on the table but they crash into the stone wall of Manitoba's Sterling Lyon. The premier most ideologically opposed to an entrenched charter of rights, Lyon is also the one most obviously playing to the television cameras: he has about two weeks to go in a provincial election campaign. "We already have an agreement," Lyon tells Trudeau; sign *our* provincial package. The Manitoban then dashes off a series of quotes from the Supreme Court decision and lists the economic woes facing his constituents. "The process which you have initiated has made us less unified and less able to deal with other problems." Trudeau's constitutional obsession is at the root of all ills, in Lyon's view, and he is squarely opposed to it.

The first small sign of a break in the group of eight occurs next, when B.C.'s Bill Bennett urges compromise and accommodation on all sides. "This country does not need a new Battle of Britain to solve its constitutional problems." He too flourishes the Supreme Court decision, but suggests that it provides an escape from the "straight jacket of unanimity."

And while Bennett supports the April accord he signed with the seven other premiers, he observes that it is not the only solution.

Premier Angus MacLean tells the conference that he is not keen to make wholesale changes to the present constitution. For him, the commemorative plaque in the wood-heated legislative chamber in his provincial capital of Charlottetown, the "birthplace of Confederation," says it all: "They builded better than they knew."

Allan Blakeney of Saskatchewan takes much the same tack as Bennett. The Supreme Court opened the way to a different kind of compromise, in his opinion. "The tyranny of unanimity is but a ghost of conferences past. We come to this table with a whole new set of rules." Blakeney is prepared to compromise on a variety of items if others are interested; his shopping list is well-known, he says. Not enamoured with the notion of an entrenched charter of rights, the Saskatchewan premier neatly quadruples Trudeau's three agenda items, seeing the various elements of the charter — fundamental rights, democratic rights, language rights, and so on — as separate issues to be bargained over.

But in the see-saw world of federal-provincial diplomacy, Blakeney's placatory remarks are immediately followed by the most hawkish statement of all. Alberta's Peter Lougheed, his voice seldom concealing his contempt, says Ottawa's actions "violate the spirit and intent of Confederation." Tradition is the basis of the federal spirit, Lougheed contends; the Trudeau government is proceeding in a way that is "instinctively wrong" and it could have "tragic consequences." There is no bargaining position hidden in Lougheed's rhetoric. He makes no mention of the charter of rights, or tradeoffs or compromise. Predictably, he speaks in favour of his amending formula.

As premier of the last province to enter Confederation, Brian Peckford concludes the open session by reminding the participants of the referendum "battles" — he points out he is using the word deliberately — to join Canada in the late 1940s. Many of his constituents still recall those times, he says. Confederation is a living force in Newfoundland, the terms of union are a political reality that must be safeguarded. Like Lougheed, Peckford does not reveal his bargaining goals. But his perspective is a little different from some of his fellow premiers. "We cannot afford the luxury of a 'winner-take-all' attitude." Peckford says he has come prepared to compromise this time and he expects that all the others have, too.

The morning session ends a little before noon. Trudeau briefly sums up, appearing to clutch at every slender thread that might lead to compromise. His face is still as solemn as it had been all morning, when occasionally he would lean back in his chair while the others spoke, the dark suit jacket open and flopping to one side, his eyes staring off into space. His voice is almost a monotone.

The premiers are canvassed quietly to see if all eleven would like to lunch together. Most decline. They agreed to return at half-past-two for a private session in the fifth-floor conference room, a miniature of the main hall, with corridors zigging away to a coven of offices. The open skirmishing is over, the hard bargaining is set to begin. As everyone mills about on the conference floor, reporters sidle up to their favourite sources, seeking their reading of the morning's events. No one is sanguine. Federal officials see no sign of a break in the eight. The two peacemakers, Bennett and Blakeney, appear to have been beaten back by the hardliners. The Hatfield and Davis proposals are being treated with overly polite scepticism by the other premiers.

* * *

After lunch, while the premiers lock themselves away in their fifth-floor room to discuss the procedure for this last extraordinary conference, their ministers gather four floors down, still in the restricted area of the building, to trade "scenarios" (a favourite constitutional word) and smoke up a cache of smelly cigars Garde Gardom has brought from Victoria. At three, they are summoned into the bargaining room, the ground rules having been set: there will be a limit of three people per delegation allowed into the main room (some of the larger contingents later stretch this to four). If there is going to be a deal, it will be concocted by about thirty people — only one woman (New Brunswick health minister Brenda Robertson) — who agree to lock themselves away in that airless eyrie.

Trudeau, taking off his suit jacket and rolling up his sleeves, sets the tone. He is charming and witty, according to some; cool and calculating, according to others. "If we break up, you guys are never coming back here," he remarks at one point. But it is said with an engaging grin and no one is certain if he is serious or not. A little later, while discussing whether provinces really need to protect themselves so carefully with opting-out provisions and vetoes, Trudeau quips laconically: "You know, there is a limit to how much the rest of Canada can gang up on one."

The afternoon is taken up discussing amending formulas. When Trudeau ventures a debate on the charter of rights, there is a pregnant silence. "I don't think I've ever seen a group of politicians so quiet," Davis observes, trying to pry forth a response. Lougheed, Lyon, Peckford and Lévesque say they want to continue thrashing around the various amending procedures. Lévesque notes it is the first time all eleven governments are finally getting into the meat of the issue. Lyon is adamant that the Supreme Court ruled the charter unconstitutional and that Trudeau must change it to make it more acceptable. They break for coffee a little before four.

* * *

Allan Blakeney bursts into the Saskatchewan delegation's office in the conference centre and demands they turn up a pair of scissors. One is procured and he spins on his heels and returns to the closed-door conference. Saskatchewan officials are astonished. Has the bargaining proceeded so quickly that the first ministers are now into the cutting and pasting of a new deal?

When they reconvene, both Trudeau and Davis attack the opting-out amending formula in the common-front position. Trudeau says that enabling one province to pick up its marbles and go home is a denial of the national will. Davis describes the fiscal compensation clause as "silly." Ontario could opt out of major new programs, he claims, and "be laughing all the way to the bank." Lougheed replies that Trudeau and Davis are exaggerating the defects in the formula but that he himself might not be so attached to it if there were to be a jointly appointed Senate as the provinces' "second line of defence" in constitutional matters. This gambit leads to some talk about alternative formulas. Trudeau suggests one that would contain a veto only for Quebec but muses that he would have difficulty selling it in Alberta; Lougheed agrees — even he couldn't sell such a proposal in his home province — and the matter is dropped.

The bargaining begins with the discussion of Davis's offer to give up the provincial veto. Blakeney presses him, asking if he will accept an altogether different amending formula from the two on the table, without a veto and without the opting out proviso, changes to be made by a set number of provinces — say seven or eight — and the federal government. Davis answers vaguely but is prepared to consider it. Lougheed appears perturbed. It is clear Blakeney is trying to open up a third option, perhaps too eagerly for some in the room.

The conversation drifts around to Hatfield's morning proposal to delay the implementation of the charter. There is an embarrassing silence when he becomes confused in explaining the blocking mechanism. Trudeau helps him out, to knowing smiles around the table.

Meanwhile, downstairs, a buzz goes through the room set aside for reporters. The scissors story is being passed about. Small groups gather near the doorways. The television networks, with walkie-talkies covering all exits, set off a series of false alarms by testing the lights on top of the cameras. There is another false alarm: Trudeau's empty car pulls closer to the door. Finally, close to six o'clock, the first ministers emerge. They are tight-lipped and report little progress. Trudeau steps out the back way and for the first time in years finds himself in the middle of a press scrum. A Toronto camera crew, unaware or uncaring of the unwritten rule that no one jostles the PM, bashes its way into his path. Others, not to be out-scooped, immediately join the fray. For an instant, Trudeau's eyes flash steel. Then they soften and he answers the not particularly probing questions with an apparent candour. It may be coming together, he says, but don't bet your last dollar on it. At the other end of the hall, Lougheed says there has been no progress at all.

Trudeau's bodyguards force their way through and free a path. His aides discover that there is no way to leave the conference centre without meeting the press. So the next day they set up a microphone stand behind a roped barrier for a more dignified affair — *un scrum organisé*, as the Quebecers like to call it.

The scissors story was a red herring. The fastidious Blakeney wanted only to clip his nails. There does not appear to be any deal in progress that first night. A handful of federal and Ontario officials meet for a few hours in the Langevin Block to draft alternative amending formulas. The death watch of hotel lobbies and bars turns up little of interest. For reporters who cover these events regularly, there is an almost eerie calm in Ottawa. The phone lines are not ringing; little is going on.

Later that night, in the bar of the Four Seasons, a handful of senior officials from B.C. are chatting with some reporters, analyzing the day's events and talking about the strategies and 'what ifs' that sustain and fascinate the political elite through seemingly endless rounds of constitutional discussions. As the long day and booze take their toll, the conversation becomes more pointed. One official is patiently explaining how he sees the various bits and pieces dovetailing when another cuts him off. "What he wants to know," he says gesturing at the reporter, "is whether we'll have the guts or not to abandon Quebec, assuming Trudeau and Lévesque won't sign the same paper. That's a good question. I just don't know . . ."

———————— ❦ ————————

Tuesday, 3 November 1981

It is a few minutes to eight in the morning and Peter Lougheed is strolling down the Sparks Street mall in his blue trench coat, savouring the early morning sunshine and feeling good. He has come to Ottawa for a political battle over the constitution and is looking forward to the scrap. Lougheed has just finished taping an interview on CTV's "Canada AM" in which he echoed Lévesque's words that if Trudeau intends to bash ahead without provincial consent, he should first go to the people in an election. Lougheed's crinkling blue eyes appear to sparkle even more than usual as he stops to chat to a reporter. "It would be fun to campaign against the prime minister" in that kind of an election, he says with a broad grin and then spins off for his Chateau Laurier breakfast meeting with the group of eight.

With a discreet waiter in a red vest hovering nearby to serve the bacon and eggs, the eight dissident premiers gather shortly after eight o'clock for the first of their three breakfast meetings. In a room next door, a clutch of officials and ministers wait in case they are summoned, grumbling about the Chateau's breakfast fare. But it is a quiet, uneventful meeting, mainly turning on an analysis of the previous day's events. Although the eight men have met dozens of times and profess that as a group they have a certain chemistry, these breakfast meetings are quite formal events in which one's displeasure is generally conveyed in low-key terms; no one lets down his guard.

This morning some of the moderates are concerned that the federal side appears to be winning the propaganda war by seeming more flexible and willing to compromise. They suggest getting together again over lunch and perhaps formulating a counter-offer if the next few hours show more of the same. Bennett says he has a proposal of his own which he might advance on behalf of the eight later, if the others agree. But the hardliners, Lyon and Lougheed in particular, are not keen to open up provincial bargaining positions at this point. Trudeau is on the ropes, they say; let him come to us. They joke about his apparent weaknesses and grumble that he has not so far made any direct offers himself.

When the full first ministers' conference convenes in private that morning, there is a change in attitude. The rancour has returned. The discussion revolves around the various amending formula proposals, the premiers prodding Trudeau to make his own views known. He hesitates. He repeats that he does not like the provincial formula: "it opts out of Canada." Almost casually, the prime minister suggests that if the first ministers cannot agree, "then I suppose the people will have to decide" through a referendum. His message does not immediately sink in with those around the table. There are, after all, two referenda already in the present resolution: one to decide between Ottawa's preferred amending formula and any provincial counter-offer in two years' time; the other a part of the Ottawa formula that Trudeau likes to call a tie-breaking mechanism. But it is the first of several references that day to a referendum and sparks a bitter morning row between Trudeau and Lévesque over the Quebec referendum eighteen months earlier.

Lévesque accuses the prime minister of manipulating the Quebec referendum with cash, scare tactics and slick advertising campaigns. "At least we won't manipulate the question," Trudeau shoots back, sarcastically observing that the PQ would, "of course," be too pure to use advertising techniques of its own. At one point, Chrétien and Lévesque also square off over the referendum and language rights. And Richard Hatfield weighs in, accusing Lévesque of being so isolationist, he is turning Quebec into a Warsaw ghetto. Predictably, the Quebec premier explodes. Bennett and Lyon try to bring the conference back on track but end up lecturing Trudeau on the Supreme Court decision.

Backing off a bit, Trudeau indicates that he is prepared to defer some of the issues, such as native rights, equalization payments and resources, until a next stage; or accept the Hatfield proposal in which six provinces, in two years' time, could scuttle large parts of the charter by passing resolutions in their own legislatures. "Both of us are gambling that we are either going to win all or lose all," Trudeau observes. "The question is, how do we decide?"

At this point, Lougheed, Bennett and Blakeney try to focus the discussion on a deal now rather than a showdown at some future point. But Lévesque is angry at all the talk about shortlists and new formulas. Why are you in such a hurry to take away our powers? he asks the prime minister, objecting to "this circus." Goaded by a remark of Davis's, Lévesque embarks on a long harangue in which he rails against the centralizing federal perspective which is trying to turn Canada into a unitary state along the lines of the United States. "We're going to all end up like U.S. governors with no practical powers at all," he says, growling that the Quebec assembly would give up its control of crucial areas like education, "over my dead body."

It is about eleven in the morning, and the conference is going nowhere. At the coffee break Trudeau walks stiffly off into the back room reserved for the federal delegation. Bill Davis follows to spread some Brampton balm. When they return twenty minutes later, Davis makes a forceful, occasionally emotional speech, appealing to the sense of integrity and public trust of his fellow premiers. "Say what you think. Don't play games," he scolds them. This problem has been around too long and we have to resolve it; our publics are expecting it from us. Davis then spells out the implicit tradeoff that has been part of everyone's hidden agenda for some time. He will accept the eight's amending formula if they will agree to a charter of rights. In his usual fashion, Davis is not overly specific about the charter, and many of the participants draw different conclusions from his offer. First he talks about *the* charter, later it is *a* charter, suggesting a scaled-down version in exchange for changes in the amending formula.

Predictably, Lyon is not interested in any kind of charter, preferring simple patriation with an amending formula. Lougheed has much the same response, although he leaves the door open a crack, saying he might accept a rights code if it were not fully entrenched. You were in favour of an entrenched bill of rights in 1979, Trudeau reminds Lougheed. We shouldn't tie the hands of future legislatures, the Alberta premier shoots back. Blakeney says he would accept a charter only if it were part of a larger package; Buchanan is not opposed to "the concept" of a charter; Bennett says he would like some aspects of one.

The surprise is that Trudeau is not at first particularly interested in the Davis proposal and sneers at it in such a way that some think he is turning on his principal ally. There is confusion even within most of the

Ontario delegation. Is it feigned anger on the part of Trudeau, as Davis believes, merely to keep his options open? Or is he really uninterested in that sort of deal? The byplay also confuses the gang of eight. All along they thought Davis was speaking for Trudeau; now they aren't sure. Some even wonder if there is a crack in the federal side? Can Davis be brought over to the provincial position?

The conference adjourns for lunch. In the main hall downstairs, Quebec ministers tout the Davis offer as a victory for the eight provinces, crowing that Ontario is coming around to their side. Ontario now finds itself in a crossfire, with both federal and provincial officials interpreting the Davis proposal in different ways. Bennett quietly draws Davis aside and outlines the main points of the plan he wants to put forward that afternoon, telling him it is similar to one their officials discussed the previous week in secret meetings in Toronto. Davis nods, recalling those meetings somewhat differently from the British Columbian. Bennett leaves for a lunch with his officials and a two o'clock huddle with the eight, believing that he has secured Davis's sympathy for his proposal.

The Davis offer and Bill Bennett's counter-offer effectively break up the first ministers' conference for the day. While Trudeau and his strategists wait at the conference centre along with Hatfield and the pragmatic pols from Ontario, the eight hole up in their Chateau Laurier suite, hotly debating the Bennett proposal. Some, Lyon and Lévesque in particular, don't think it's the appropriate time to be proposing alternatives, and are not enamoured with the offer anyway. Bennett has already told reporters over the lunch break that "the initial skirmishing has been completed. This is the moment of truth." But most of the others feel it is tactically better to wait out Trudeau and force him to shift ground. Besides, they resent Bennett pushing himself into the leadership role, particularly with a proposal most of them are only seeing for the first time. Many don't trust his judgment, regarding him as someone who wants to settle, irrespective of the costs.

Across the street, consternation develops in the impromptu federal strategy session when there is no word that the eight are prepared to return. Ontario's Roy McMurtry and Tom Wells keep suggesting that the *non obstante* override is the key to any tradeoff on the charter. McMurtry argues persuasively that the override is merely a safety valve that would be used only in extraordinary circumstances but Trudeau is still noncommittal. He has heard all this before, mainly from Chrétien, who only half believes it. The Ontarians are desperately trying to convince Trudeau of the necessity of forging a deal, not being at all sure he grasps the urgency of it.

In their Chateau Laurier war room, the eight somewhat reluctantly agree to put the Bennett proposal forward for Trudeau's reaction. Lévesque and Lyon, however, are withholding their approval until they see what the prime minister has to say. So the proposal is presented without the imprimatur of the eight as a group. Davis is called over to test Bennett's assumption that the plan might fly.*

Davis leaves and Bennett asks for "a hawk and a dove" to accompany him back to the conference centre. Lougheed and Buchanan are designated but they don't set off right away. Buchanan misunderstands what is expected and slips off for a swim in the Chateau Laurier's pool, while the others search frantically for him in the various suites there. At about five o'clock they leave to meet Trudeau and Davis in the conference hall, and are gone for about forty-five minutes.

The B.C. proposal is not particularly complicated or detailed. Given the context, it is even a bit goofy. It is mostly ideas, typewritten on a single sheet of paper, copies of which Bennett collects before he heads off across the street.†

While the three emissaries are across the street, some of the eight's intergovernmental affairs ministers gather in a Chateau Laurier corridor. They wonder whether Trudeau might accept the proposal. Claude Morin replies, sphinx-like, that he doubts it, but Quebec might.

When the proposal is explained to him, Trudeau explodes in rage. "You must be joking," he says to Bennett, not even trying to conceal his scorn. Contemptuously shuffling the papers on his desk, he seems to study each premier independently. His voice nearly hissing, he accuses them of being dupes of Lévesque, of being led around by the nose by a separatist premier. History, he says, will judge them harshly. It is a rare performance, raw prime ministerial anger. Whether it is real or feigned may never be known. But it seems to emanate from every pore. The message is clear: the premiers will have to choose between him and Lévesque. There is no middle ground. They must do what is right for

---

*Most of those present later recall that Davis listens attentively to the proposal, indicates he can live with it, but does not promise to advocate it as a final solution. "He certainly didn't nix it," one premier says later. "Or else it would never have gone across the street in the first place."

†The basis of the deal would be acceptance of the eight's amending formula and a drastically scaled-down charter of rights. Only democratic rights, dealing with the length of sittings of a legislature and the right to vote, would be entrenched now. Fundamental rights, like freedom of speech and assembly, and the minority language education provisions, would be subject to opting-in. The rest would be turned over to a commission for two years study; the commission's report would not be binding on the first ministers. B.C. was also adding a new and somewhat intricate codicil to the resources section to include water power, which had not been on the table for some time, since 1979. (It gained little support then.) And they throw in their favourite wording on the equalization clauses, which no other province likes.

Canada, he says. He is prepared to make concessions, to save face. But if they think he is mortally wounded by their attacks, they are wrong.

Only Lougheed stands up to the prime minister, challenging him to say how his federal resolution meets the promises to Quebec. Trudeau does not reply with words, just a withering glance.

When the three report back, some of the eight look at John Buchanan's beet-red face and deduce that he was shell-shocked by the experience. Lougheed downplays Trudeau's anger, telling his cohorts he thought it was all a performance and he had seen worse during the energy negotiations. Back at the conference centre, Trudeau stalks out, saying nothing to his ministers or officials about the meeting. He is curt to the press. There is an offer of a tradeoff but it is not his offer; he is not interested in any mini-charter. He leaves for home, to prepare for a cabinet meeting in less than two hours' time.

At the Chateau, the premiers are developing a quiet rage of their own over Trudeau's reaction. It saddens some, hardens others. The fight in London looms closer. For Bennett and Blakeney, Trudeau's response pushes forward a major decision: they prepare to break with the group of eight. Of the two, Blakeney is the more resolved: he informs his fellow premiers then and presses his lawyers back in the Saskatchewan suite to prepare a new draft proposal (it will take them until six the next morning to complete). For Bennett it is a night of anguish as he struggles with his loyalties and his own peculiar sense of history.

❀

While Pierre Trudeau is cooling off in the familiar luxury of the swimming pool at 24 Sussex Drive, the B.C. delegation is having their final confrontation with the Quebec fact. Over the dinner hour, in the immediate aftermath of Trudeau's blowout with the three musketeers, Bill Bennett's senior officials meet Quebec's top-ranked civil servant, Louis Bernard, Lévesque's cool and competent clerk of the cabinet. They have one question: can the gang of eight make any compromise on language rights? There is one answer: No. For about ninety minutes the group explores every conceivable possibility, even that of making the minority language guarantees totally salutatory, without meaning. The answer is the same. We've gone too far already, Bernard says. We shouldn't even have gone as far as you did in your proposal. Quebec cannot further compromise its provincial powers. Back at their hotel, almost the entire B.C. delegation gets together for a brainstorming session. Education minister Brian Smith, in Ottawa for the conference, says the minority language guarantees pose no practical problems for the province. The problem is how Bennett can satisfy Trudeau without compromising Quebec? The group hits on what one later calls the "juridical solution" — accepting these rights for B.C. and leaving it to Ottawa to decide how they will apply in the rest of the country. A kind of "I'm all right, Jack" approach that Bennett is to take to the breakfast meeting the next morning.

———————— ❧ ————————

In the newly renovated cabinet room, with its soft earth tones and oak-panelled walls, one floor above the House of Commons, the Liberal ministers gather, shortly after eight, for a special session. Federal aides play down the cabinet meeting, telling reporters that it is to be a short one simply to report on the state of negotiations. It drags on until after midnight. It is the first time that most of those present are made aware of the "ultimate fallback" strategy: to go to the people in a referendum in two years' time (immediately before the next federal election, in all probability) on the constitutional package. For reasons of security — some might say paranoia — federal officials have been drafting memos on this strategy, then destroying them after they have been circulated among the chosen few. The full cabinet is not aware of the soul-searching that went on in the privy council office following the Supreme Court decision, the belief at the senior mandarin level that somehow the package has to be legitimized in the eyes of the public.

Trudeau begins with a brief review of the negotiations, spicing his summary with some views on the premiers' negotiating styles. He believes the conference will end the next day. Chrétien also reports on the bargaining so far. Two broad questions are laid out for the cabinet to ponder. If there is no agreement at the bargaining table, does the federal government still have to meet the conventionality test set out by the Supreme Court? If so, how? A range of options is set forth: allowing the provinces to opt-in or opt-out of provisions of the charter, working in a *non obstante* override so legislatures can have the last word on court decisions, and an eventual referendum on the charter of rights to ease its passage at Westminster. Trudeau asks his ministers for their views. A tired-looking Chrétien emerges from the cabinet room shortly before eleven to tell assembled journalists in the corridor that the government is strongly committed to the charter of rights and is not intending to water it down for any provincial concessions. It is bargaining talk and is treated as such.

But inside the cabinet meeting, the mood is surprisingly combative. A majority of ministers around the table appear to favour the referendum option. It maintains the purity of the package, it speaks to 'Liberal principles,' and it might be the vehicle for revitalizing some provincial Liberal parties — a notion Allan MacEachen, for one, finds attractive.*

———————————————————————————

*There has even been some talk in the prime minister's office of having the referendum timed to coincide with the next federal election so voters would mark their ballots twice, once for their choice of candidate and once for the charter of rights.

But, *au fond*, the referendum option is discussed more as a strategic ploy to shake up the provinces than as the agent for legitimizing the charter of rights. It is not clear whether many in the cabinet who are advocating it actually believe they will see it implemented.

The fourth floor at the Chateau Laurier is nearly deserted at eight in the evening, and Allan Blakeney is going over some last-minute instructions with his staff. They have resolved to bring out a detailed alternative package the next day in order finally to "put some paper on the table," and Blakeney is telling his people where he wants changes made to a draft they brought from Regina. He calls Bill Davis to inform him of his plans. Then he, Romanow and Howard Leeson, the deputy minister, head off for dinner at Mamma Teresa's, a crowded Italian restaurant popular with the government set.

Blakeney's group is given the table that had been set aside for Bill Bennett and his entourage, who passed up their reservation to continue their soul-searching at the Four Seasons. Next to that table just happens to be the Ontario premier, his two ministers, Wells and McMurtry, and a handful of senior officials. After some joking, the two groups pull their tables together, mindful that this is the first time members of the opposite camps have broken bread together during these delicate negotiations. However, Mamma Teresa's is a boisterous spot with black-suited waiters rushing about with great trays of wine and pasta. It is not, like the alcoves in the Chateau Grill, suited to quiet negotiations. Besides, the configuration around the table doesn't encourage much interchange of views. Davis and Blakeney are at opposite ends, buffered by their own people, unable to talk directly to one another unless they yell. Romanow and McMurtry are across from each other and engage Blakeney in a discussion about *non obstante*. Romanow offers to drop by later to brief McMurtry about the new Saskatchewan proposal.

The groups break up and Romanow, Leeson and McMurtry stroll over to the Ontario suite at the Four Seasons. When they arrive, Romanow and Leeson are left cooling their heels for nearly half-an-hour, like unwanted salesmen. It is an exasperating wait for the prairie boys. They are readying themselves to break with the common front and put forward the only detailed proposal of the conference, and here no one on the other side seems particularly anxious to hear about it. Finally, about half-past eleven, they leave, their message undelivered, the extra link in the chain unforged.

The last of the Liberal ministers leaves the cabinet room shortly after midnight. Trudeau has already gone. If there is a consensus, it is possibly in his mind alone. Strong differences of view were apparent as the prime minister went around the room. Trudeau was tired and did not take a vigorous part in the discussion. Some of his cabinet were for plunging ahead regardless. The courts should not proscribe political conventions, they argued, and the Liberal Party has invested too much political capital in the charter of rights to circumscribe it now. Others were more cautious, fearing the political repercussions of flying in the face of the courts. Canadians are great believers in authority, they remind their colleagues, citing opinion polls and other examples. But there was no agreement on how best to "conventionalize" the package. Some prefer opting-in or allowing for a legislative override. The so-called hardliners (such as Mark MacGuigan, Gerald Regan and John Roberts) see the referendum as the most workable option. If nothing else, it will keep Trudeau around for two more years and probably into the following election. It is not necessarily the most popular choice. But it is neither vetoed nor curtailed. Trudeau leaves the cabinet without arriving at a final decision. He has been given a blank cheque and can pick his option as the situation demands. A team of senior officials is told to start drafting his final statement for the next day, explaining why he has to push ahead.

———————— ✦ ————————

Wednesday, 4 November 1981

The soft *brrr* of the hotel room telephone jars Romanow awake shortly before seven. For the first time since the Supreme Court decision in September, Chrétien is at the other end of the line, suggesting they get together for a chat. Romanow agrees, says he'll call McMurtry to complete the old boys' network, and suggests they meet in an hour's time at the conference centre before anyone else will be there to see them.

Down the hall, Allan Blakeney passes the razor across his face and reviews one last time the paper he will be putting forward that morning as a possible compromise. Although he told the other seven premiers the previous afternoon about his plan, he is not expecting an easy time of it today. Nor does he have too many illusions that the Saskatchewan paper will catch fire around the table. At best it might be the basis for discussion around which other options might gel.

Blakeney is aware that his proposal will break the tactical front of the gang of eight, but he is still trying to tailor his package to the members of the group, including Lévesque. Blakeney's scheme essentially would sacrifice the entrenchment of language rights for a compromise on the amending formula.*

———————— ❦ ————————

Wednesday, cool and overcast, appears to be the last day for most of the participants. On the four short blocks from his hotel to the eight o'clock breakfast meeting at the Chateau Laurier, Bill Bennett tugs at his collar and agonizes over his next course of action. Buffeted by conflicting advice from his cabinet ministers pulling him one way and senior aides pushing him another, even as they wend their way that morning, Bennett later describes it as the hardest decision he's ever made in his political career. By the time he arrives at the side door of the Chateau Laurier, his mind is apparently made up. He will tell the group that he is prepared to move towards what he perceives is Trudeau's ultimate position and accept the entrenchment of minority language education rights, not an easy political decision for the leader of a province that occasionally still rebels against bilingual corn flakes boxes. Bennett understands he will be choosing Trudeau over Lévesque, but he doubts that the Quebec premier will sign any constitutional accord. He remembers the showcase his father, W.A.C. Bennett, put on in sunny Victoria in 1971, and how Quebec's Robert Bourassa first promised to sign and then went home and caved in to the nationalists; and he recalls in the same Chateau Laurier suite, the agonizing struggle until the early hours of the morning before Lévesque would sign the provincial accord in April.

———————— ❦ ————————

The uneasy comradeship of the gang of eight disintegrates even further over the scrambled eggs and soggy croissants that morning, when Blakeney announces his own proposal. Lévesque is furious. Bolstered by Sterling Lyon, who is preparing to leave shortly to campaign in his provincial election on 17 November, they attack Blakeney for compromising the group's tactical advantage. Trudeau is in a corner they argue.

———

*The Saskatchewan proposal calls for a greatly scaled-down charter of rights, in which only fundamental freedoms, democratic and mobility rights are to be entrenched immediately. Legal and equality rights would apply only at the federal level but provinces could opt-in. A stronger resource section is added and there is a hortatory commitment, without enforcement, for provinces to provide minority language education services — not enough to meet Trudeau halfway. On the amending formula, the Blakeney proposal ignores the Lougheed principle of provincial equality and goes for a different arrangement altogether, whereby no one province has a veto, but any seven and the federal government can bring about future change.

If we hang together, he'll have to come to us. Blakeney retorts that he is trying to smoke Trudeau out, to see if he has any intention of negotiating, and, in any case, it is good public relations to show some flexibility. Lougheed is in the middle of this debate and appears to come down on both sides. He would prefer to wait a little longer, but if Blakeney wants to try and flush out Trudeau, that's his decision. Lougheed says he won't agree with the substance of the Blakeney proposal, but he should feel free to put it out in any case. Lougheed's words are an important sign around the table, a portent that the group-front approach might be bent. Bill Bennett tries to make known his own proposal but it gets lost in the din. Most of the participants don't even recall it being made.

Meanwhile in the federal offices at the conference centre, Romanow and Chrétien are sitting around with their feet up, trying to appear casual, discussing their views of the bargaining to date. Romanow tells Chrétien about the Saskatchewan proposal that will be put that morning, and then they slide into a conversation about what elements might make up a possible deal. Four choices are put forward, and on the back of a four-by-four inch yellow memo slip from a government of Canada telephone pad, Romanow writes them out in a kind of constitutional shorthand.*

Romanow folds the paper in half and puts it in his shirt pocket, forgetting about it for the rest of the day. McMurtry shows up about 8:40 and they spend the next half-hour urging Chrétien to work on Trudeau so the conference will go on for at least one more day. Chrétien is acting on his own at this point and does not appear overly optimistic that he can influence "the boss."

It is only that morning, at the regular strategy session of the group of three, that Trudeau tells Hatfield of the referendum plan on the charter of rights. The New Brunswick premier is angry. It goes against all his instincts and principles. "I'm going to have to swallow myself a second time," he tells no one in particular. Yet he agrees to it eventually, on the clear understanding that it is only a ploy; if Trudeau decides to carry through with it, Hatfield will oppose it strongly and come to Ottawa to fight it in Parliament. "Don't worry," Trudeau tells him. "Lévesque will never accept."

---

*Option one is the Vancouver amending formula preferred by the provinces and the charter as is — a straight-up swap.

Two is the Vancouver formula minus fiscal compensation (important to Quebec) plus the Hatfield solution to the charter that was set out on opening day.

Three is the Vancouver formula minus fiscal compensation plus some phasing-in of the charter à la Hatfield, and the *non obstante* override on other sections.

Four would see the *non obstante* clause apply to everything except mobility rights, democratic rights and language of education rights, and would use the Saskatchewan amending formula of seven provinces representing sixty per cent of the population.

———————— ❀ ————————

Pierre Trudeau is in a dour but not yet dark mood when the full meeting of first ministers begins at quarter to ten that morning. The immediate tone, however, is set by Lévesque, who announces bluntly that he is leaving at noon. The Quebec premier has already set back the opening of the National Assembly once because of the constitutional conference and he does not intend to do it a second time. Sterling Lyon is also leaving shortly for the campaign trail, and John Buchanan plans to depart at the end of the day to attend the funeral of his father-in-law, who has died suddenly in Halifax. The conference appears to be dissolving.

Acknowledging the time difficulty, Trudeau reviews how things stand. He proceeds to enumerate the proposals already on the table. At Peckford's insistence, he returns to the B.C. proposal of the day before and, more calmly this time, sets out why he cannot accept it. The prime minister lists the Davis proposal on the veto, the Hatfield proposal on the phasing-in of the charter, and the Saskatchewan proposal that is about to be tabled. He then repeats what he said he told the three emissaries the day before: that he would go for a straight-up trade of the charter for their amending formula, or a variation of it, if some of the more offensive elements could be removed. There are raised eyebrows around the table. No one recalls him making quite that offer; it is the first time Trudeau has expressed any significant interest in the Alberta amending formula, the one he says "opts out of Canada," and its compensation clause.

Blakeney then takes the floor to outline his proposal, methodically ticking off each item with a pen as he runs through it. Trudeau indicates that *he* could live with the offer but adroitly turns it over to Lévesque to derail. The Quebec premier is still angry with Blakeney from the breakfast session and peremptorily thumbs through the written proposal, his eyes lolling in derision. "It's a non-starter with us." Quebec could never accept the loss of its historic veto in this fashion, Lévesque says, insinuating broadly that the Saskatchewan plan is the work of federal officials. Blakeney is hopping mad; Trudeau amused.

They break for coffee and the players mill about in small groups. Romanow strides up to Morin, angry at the suggestion that the Saskatchewan proposal is a stalking horse for Ottawa. "You guys are such great tactitioners, [sic] you're overreacting to this," he tells his Quebec counterpart. Morin is unperturbed. In his view, Saskatchewan had broken faith with the eight that morning and Quebec was not about to allow any middle ground to form. "There is no other way out for us," he replies.

When the private session resumes, Trudeau goes around the table, finding little support for Blakeney's efforts. Prince Edward Island and

Nova Scotia indicate some movement, however, saying they would prefer the Davis swap proposal over Blakeney's. But the other premiers are tight-lipped. For himself, Trudeau says he can accept the Saskatchewan plan on two conditions: language rights must be entrenched and a Quebec veto restored. But, he adds, he is not prepared to go out on a limb unless Lévesque does so as well; and the Quebec premier is clearly not buying it.

It is now about eleven-forty and Lévesque is still talking about breaking off that afternoon. How do we resolve this, asks Trudeau. "Maybe we should agree to keep talking and hold a referendum in two years' time? There, that's a new offer."

"Don't assume you'd win," retorts Lévesque, rising to the bait. Maybe that's the only way, Trudeau muses. "Surely a great democrat like yourself won't be against a referendum?" he adds, goading Lévesque further. "That would be a definite starter with us," Lévesque replies, "In spite of our recent experience with referenda . . . . it's an honourable way out." The exchange is solely between the two leaders; Lévesque takes the challenge on his own. Morin, in his shirtsleeves, sits ramrod stiff between the two men, staring blankly ahead, poker-faced.

And so the trap, if it is a trap, is sprung. When Lévesque opts for the referendum, there is muttering in the back rows of some delegations that he is deserting the eight, taking a course that is anathema to most of them. Some, like Blakeney and Lougheed, don't react immediately, seeing it as just another episode of Lévesque-Trudeau bravado. There are a few protestations, but the two French-Canadians appear unmoved, caught up in a kind of macho rivalry. Strange bedfellows, the prime minister jokes, as the private session adjourns for lunch. Lévesque agrees. Exhilarated at the new turn of events, he declares he'll stay around for the afternoon.

🍁

Moments later in the downstairs lobby, on his way home for lunch, Trudeau passes Jim Manly, one of the federal NDP official delegates to the conference, in conversation with a B.C. official. "Ça va?" asks Manly casually. "Ça va bien," beams Trudeau, raising his fists to his chest vigorously, clearly pleased with himself. He strides to the microphone in the outer corridor for an impromptu announcement. He has some "great news." There is a new Quebec-Canada alliance. The charter of rights will go to the people in two years if there is no agreement among governments. "And the cat is among the pigeons," he adds mischievously, walking off.

In another corner of the conference hall, René Lévesque is also embracing the referendum proposal for the television cameras. "It seems an honourable way out," he says, shrugging. "We've been saying all along Trudeau has no mandate from the people for this *coup de force."*

What appeared to start out almost as a schoolboy taunt is fast becoming the new demarcation line. When they return after lunch, clutching the Canadian Press wire copy in their hands, the other premiers realize there is a new dynamic to the meeting, and they are now the ones on the defensive.

Brian Peckford does not like being known as Confederation's bad boy and in recent weeks he has been giving considerable thought to how he might ease tensions between the two levels of government. Not philosophically opposed to a charter of rights — in fact he feels it to be a good thing — Peckford might have agreed to one fourteen months earlier had not Trudeau needled him so mercilessly about trading fish for rights. Now, with this second constitutional conference falling into disarray and the only prospect a referendum fight over an issue difficult to oppose, Peckford decides it is now time to be bridge-builder. In his sixteenth-floor suite at the Four Seasons, he sits down over the lunch break to construct his own compromise. Operating on gut instincts — his hit-and-miss trademark — the Newfoundland premier fashions a proposal that has a little something for everyone. He takes the Lougheed amending formula and knocks off the fiscal compensation clause that so angers Ottawa; he adds the full charter of rights, but makes legal and equality rights subject to the *non obstante* override, as Lougheed had suggested that morning; for himself, he changes the mobility section (later known as "the Peckford wiggle") so that governments with high unemployment in their province can discriminate in favour of their own workers; and for Lévesque, Peckford reasons that if the Quebec premier wants a fight, he can have one, and throws in a referendum in two years' time on language rights for any province that does not accept them immediately. Feeling pleased with himself, Peckford hands it over to a typist and returns to the conference centre after lunch, determined to scout out allies.

Descending the stairs from the fifth-floor meeting room at lunch, Peter Lougheed is psyching himself up for a referendum fight. Officials nearby notice there is something in his gait that demonstrates a turning-point has been reached in the morning session. Both fists are clenched and there is an intensity in his voice: "We'll fight 'em and we'll win!" It is half-time at a Grey Cup match and the team needs to be rallied.

Over the lunch hour Lougheed maps out a strategy. It is very simple: get it in writing. Trudeau has been talking about various referenda for days now; let's pin him down. At half-past-two, as the first ministers start to reconvene, Lougheed's senior constitutional official, Peter Meekison, approaches his federal counterpart, Michael Kirby, with a piece of paper which sets out Alberta's understanding of the referendum principles that were discussed that morning. The paper deals mostly with a referendum on the amending formula in which a double majority is needed to decide between two competing plans; failing that, unanimity is restored. Kirby nods; that is his understanding, too, but he won't sign the Alberta paper.

When the *in camera* meeting begins, Lougheed springs to the attack. He doesn't like the referendum idea — it is stupid and divisive — but don't think that means Alberta won't fight one. He challenges the assumptions in Trudeau's plan that the referendum votes will be counted on a regional basis. "Canada is a nation of provinces." Lougheed wants something in writing from the prime minister.

It is at this point that a new wrinkle is introduced. For the first time, Trudeau explains that he would have the British Parliament pass the resolution first, and that its proclamation would be decided by a referendum in Canada. He is not talking about putting everything on hold for two years and then going to the people if there is no agreement, as many thought. He envisages the plan being pushed through to its final stage, a *fait accompli*, awaiting only the people's verdict.

There is another mood change in the room. Blakeney and Lougheed are the first to react. Trudeau's plan is not the honourable way out that had seemed to be proposed at first, but a vehicle to go to London without provincial consent and ease his resolution's passage there. Trudeau shrugs obliquely. Some feel they detect a certain slyness in his manner. Yes, he can always ask Joe Clark to agree to amend the resolution before Parliament to include the referendum provision, he says. Or all the governments here can agree to it. Even Lévesque appears unamused by this gambit. He launches into a long fiery speech, his second that afternoon, about the need to protect the fragile French-Canadian spirit in the crushing weight of anglo North America. Some of his fellow premiers are very moved by it, and it sparks a series of similar personal statements from the alienated — the "goodbye speeches," as one premier dubbed them later.

Once again, language forms the crux of the issue. Lougheed, Lyon and Blakeney are expressing some reluctance to entrench language rights. Blakeney says he will entrench if others will, but emphasizes how divisive this issue is in the West. Bennett, to his credit, says he is willing to bind B.C. to minority education guarantees but he wants other changes in the charter, particularly on native and non-discrimination rights, repeatedly stressing the need to show people the danger of an entrenched charter, particularly one with such "glib" statements.

Trudeau's case is that language will only cause division if the political leaders allow that to happen. "If we fight for it as a noble cause, then we will win together." He acknowledges in the private session what he doesn't publicly: that Quebec has treated its minority better than any other provincial government, and that Quebecers elected a PQ government largely because they wanted to warn the rest of the country to behave more tolerantly. Lévesque agrees with this analysis: outside Quebec, the French are treated as just another group of immigrants, he says. That is why he believes it is better for Quebec and Canada to split up. "I hope we can sell this idea again in the future." Returning to Lévesque's point a short while later, Trudeau tells Lougheed that is why he objects to his opting-out amending formula: "It allows someone like Lévesque to go his own way and still seem like a good guy."

Peckford circles the table, telling Bennett and Lougheed that he has a proposal of his own to put forward, but they urge him to wait. The timing is not right and everyone is preoccupied with the discussion on the referendum and language rights. Various interpretations of the Supreme Court decision are kicked around. Trudeau says he is interested in the referendum regardless of provincial consent. The notion appears to be taking greater hold with him even as it is waning with Lévesque. The prime minister is asked how he will implement it. Lougheed again insists on something in writing. The pent-up frustration surfaces and Trudeau is getting testy: "This is going nowhere. Let's wrap it up tonight." Two-and-a-half hours in a room together is wearing on everyone's nerves. Roy McMurtry leans forward to his premier and whispers, "We've been had. That son of a bitch doesn't want a compromise." Davis has become tense, chewing a little more vigorously on his pipe stem. It is five o'clock and someone suggests a coffee break. They adjourn for nearly an hour, while federal officials start drafting a paper on how to implement a referendum on the charter of rights.

In a small meeting room on the fifth floor, Peter Lougheed gathers the rest of the group of eight around a coffee urn for a quick caucus, lasting maybe fifteen minutes. It is one of the few sour moments of the conference. The differences in the eight have been exposed for all to see, and they feel a little uneasy in each other's company. Lougheed argues strenuously that the referendum notion is politically foolish; the provinces would be giving up the moral and judicial authority of the Supreme Court judgment if they agree to one. The others all nod. It is a trap by Trudeau, Lougheed says; if we hang tough, he'll have to give in. The others nod again. The crisis within the common front seems to be averted. They disperse to their various delegations.

By late afternoon, the fifth-floor eyrie — a somewhat drab meeting room with freshly painted, earth-tone walls — has become a kind of cauldron in which the provincial common front is slowly dissolving. Ontario's Tom Wells, Alberta's Dick Johnston and B.C.'s Garde Gardom move from group to group sampling the mood, picking up intelligence, testing each other's rock-bottom demands.

Davis and Trudeau invite Allan Blakeney into the federal government's back room and put to him a new proposal. If they make the charter of rights subject to legislative override, would he buy the federal (Victoria) amending formula? Blakeney says he'll think about it but when he wanders back into the main conference room he gets involved in other discussions and the offer slips his mind. It is one of several missed signals that afternoon.

In the general milling about, there is only one member of the federal team still in the main room. Jean Chrétien has been watching the development of the referendum gambit with growing apprehension. He is standing there, sipping his coffee and feeling dejected, when Roy Romanow walks up in the same frame of mind. "It looks like it's all over, Jean. It's all coming apart." Chrétien grunts his agreement, but warns Romanow that if there are no more concessions, the provinces will be stuck with a referendum. "We shot our bolt this morning," Romanow says. "It's your turn." They think back to their morning chat and Romanow reaches into his pocket and pulls out the memo slip with the four options.

They decide the only one with a chance is the proposal to marry the provincial amending formula, less the provision for fiscal compensation, with the charter, its effect minimized by the legislative override and perhaps even by Hatfield's suggestion to set parts aside for the time being. Chrétien asks if any of the eight are interested and Romanow makes a quick tour of the room, heading instinctively for the soft centre — Nova Scotia and British Columbia. After talking with their ministers (Harry How and Edmund Morris from Nova Scotia and Garde Gardom from B.C.) but not the premiers, Romanow thinks there might be the nucleus of a deal. He speaks to Blakeney, who promises to talk to Lougheed, asking Romanow to get a written offer from Chrétien. Romanow and Blakeney decide that whatever happens, they will host a meeting in their hotel suite that night at nine-thirty.

Grabbing a yellow notepad, Romanow and Chrétien slip off down the corridor, searching for a quiet place to talk. In an out-of-the-way corner, they come upon a little used kitchen pantry that connects the federal offices to the delegates' lounge. The two men set about determining which parts of the charter should be subject to legislative override and which should be fully entrenched. They list some of the other categories, such as resources and equalization rights, that should be in but make no mention of native rights. Romanow includes part of Peckford's proposal for a referendum on language rights for Quebec, which he has gleaned from Gerry Ottenheimer, Newfoundland's attorney general, in one of the many bilateral talks that afternoon. Chrétien grabs a pencil and in bold letters writes NEVER beside the referendum suggestion. The two men decide to get McMurtry and bring him in on the project, believing it might take every last bit of persuasion to bring Trudeau around. When McMurtry arrives, Romanow writes out a copy of the outline for each of them. A deal of sorts has been struck, reflecting at this point only a tired gleam in the eyes of three men who have a little influence but no power to exploit it to the full.

While Chrétien and Romanow are seeking out McMurtry, the burly Ontarian has been looking for them. In the Ontario delegation's room during the coffee break, McMurtry was seething with anger at Trudeau's bargaining tactics and gave something like a locker room pep talk: "It's time we bared our teeth at these guys." Like ward captains at a leadership convention, or a hockey team between periods, they decided each to take a man on the federal side and press their case for more time. Davis was to work on Trudeau, Segal on Kirby, and McMurtry on Chrétien. There was no one solution being pushed, just keep talking. Tom Wells was given probably the most difficult assignment of all and one that only he had the credibility to carry off. He was to talk to Dick Johnston of Alberta and let him know that if Alberta wanted to take a lead role at this point, Ontario would stand aside and be supportive. There would be no scrap for political credit.

The Chrétien-Romanow manoeuvre is not discussed openly but it does cause a slight stir in the few delegations that are aware of it. Picking up some talk of this, Wells joins Davis and Trudeau in the back room to report that there is considerable optimism for a meeting the next day and that he has heard (mistakenly) that Blakeney has another proposal to put forward. Trudeau shrugs. He is not convinced that there is a good reason to continue. It is shortly before six. The referendum paper is ready and Trudeau walks back into the main room. On the way he passes Blakeney and asks him if he has another plan to present. Blakeney says no, not me. Trudeau, looking confused and angry, walks on.

In another hallway, Michael Pitfield is half-jokingly berating Michael Kirby for screwing up. "When I left a little while ago it was all together and now it's all falling apart," Pitfield says. "Are we ever going to get a settlement on this thing?" Kirby replies that the referendum plan is on.

A B.C. official, joining them, asks what about the kitchen deal that Chrétien made just twenty minutes ago? Pitfield and Kirby say, without knowing anything about it, that they don't think it will fly. The B.C. official reports back to his delegation later that the feds are apparently keeping both options alive.

———————— ✦ ————————

It is a few minutes after six when the conference reconvenes. Trudeau reads out the implementation proposal, which is then passed around like an exam paper. His eyes fixed on the ceiling, Trudeau says he would like to get their reaction, and goes around the table to each delegation. It appears that everyone is against it. Why are you afraid of the people? Trudeau asks. Because a referendum is not the Canadian way, PEI's Angus MacLean shoots back, and is foreign to the parliamentary system. Politicians have to make these difficult choices; Confederation is a bargain among governments. The argument infuriates Trudeau, and there is a brief contretemps that embarrasses even some of the prime minister's allies around the table.

It is Lévesque's turn. "I can go along for obvious reasons," the Quebec premier says. "It's not repugnant to the parliamentary system; it would take a great weight off our minds." Now it's Lougheed's turn to stare at the ceiling.

It is half-past six and everyone is tired. The Ontario premier tries to soothe Trudeau's impatience, urging his colleagues to keep working towards an agreement: "I'm here to sit, Mr. Chairman, as long as I need to sit. Through the weekend if necessary . . ." Trudeau finally gives in to the concerted demands of Blakeney, Lougheed, Peckford and Davis to meet again the next morning at nine o'clock. "But let's go before the television cameras at ten o'clock," he adds. If there is no agreement, he intends to give notice in the House of Commons that he will proceed with the present resolution, and that will have to be done by the afternoon. It is the one-last-time deadline. But it is said quietly, more in sorrow than in anger.

Blakeney sidles up to Lougheed and Peckford as they gather their papers at the end of the meeting, suggesting they both send their top officials to his suite at the Chateau Laurier at half-past nine for a final drafting session. Both agree, although later Lougheed does not recall speaking to Blakeney. In his mind, it was just the Peckford proposal that had to be worked upon that night.

Downstairs, Lévesque is telling an improvised press conference that his alliance with Mr. Trudeau is becoming "terribly uncertain." He describes the day's negotiations as "one of the most fascinating madhouses I've ever seen." Because the federal government is locked into a two-day final debate in Parliament on its proposed resolution, requiring the consent of each MP to change, it has produced a complex implementation process to get around the deal which, ultimately, requires unanimous consent of the provinces. "It is not far from being Chinese," a sardonic Lévesque observes, beginning to slink slowly away from the federal embrace. His remarks are beamed out immediately by radio and television to the Quebec audience but, since they have been said to the cameras and not to his counterparts, they have no effect on the coming night's events.

———————— ❦ ————————

Lévesque's acceptance of a referendum fight is the one event the federal strategists did not anticipate, but they are chortling with glee at the end of the day at the rupture they have provoked within the gang of eight. Richard Hatfield, though, is not amused and catches up to Trudeau as he prepares to leave the conference centre. "I thought you said Lévesque would never go for a referendum?" Hatfield asks. "I said he'd never accept one," Trudeau reminds him with a roguish smile. Don't worry, the prime minister says obliquely, there will never be a referendum. Hatfield leaves, believing it was all a ploy.

———————— ❦ ————————

Blakeney and Romanow are among the last to leave the centre, sitting around the bargaining table on the fifth floor discussing Chrétien's plan. Eddie Goldenberg sidles over and looks over their shoulders. "What about native rights?" he asks, noticing it's not in the outline. Romanow shrugs; it had been overlooked. "The native groups are not united on it,"he observes. "Maybe we should just have a conference with native leaders to discuss it further." Goldenberg nods and wanders off. The little exchange apparently fuels Blakeney's conviction that the feds are not overly eager to entrench native rights at this point and that a deal would be easier to achieve if these were left out.

Eventually the Saskatchewan premier heads downstairs to meet reporters. He is very frank: "What we do not need in western Canada is a referendum on language rights for franco-Canadians."

Back at his hotel, B.C.'s Garde Gardom is analyzing the two streams of information his officials have gathered about Ottawa's intentions. He calls Chrétien to hear it from the horse's mouth. Satisfied, he calls Romanow about half-past seven to ensure that one of the B.C. delegation can attend the working session that night.

Shortly after eight, a B.C. functionary calls René Lévesque's hotel suite in Hull to remind the premier about the breakfast meeting the next morning. Morin takes the call. He and the rest of the Quebec delegation are unaware that anything else is happening. Before leaving the conference centre, Morin asked Dick Johnston whether there was anything planned for the evening and Johnston said no — nothing he was aware of. For a time, Morin contemplates dropping in on the Chateau later on, but decides there is no need to recross the Ottawa River. ("It was inconceivable that after eighteen months I would have suddenly said to myself that evening 'Maybe these guys are going to trick us, perhaps I should check,' " he says later.)

Between seven and half-past eight, in Lévesque's room at L'Auberge de la Chaudière, the premier and Morin apprise the rest of their delegation of what had transpired that day. It is a fairly large group and the nuances are important for the preparation of the forthcoming Throne Speech to open the National Assembly. After that, Lévesque, Morin and the other senior officials enjoy a leisurely dinner in the hotel's dining room, believing the conference is about to end in disarray. Morin is in bed after the eleven o'clock news; Lévesque, as is his custom, stays up until after midnight chatting in the bar end of his hotel suite with some of his delegation.

───────────── ❦ ─────────────

Silently, in the cool November night, the ministerial limousines glide down the tree-lined driveway at 24 Sussex Drive. It is about half-past eight and this is the meeting of the inner sanctum, to produce the decision the cabinet never gave. There are eight ministers present: Jean Chrétien, Marc Lalonde, Mark MacGuigan, André Ouellet, Donald Johnston, Allan MacEachen, Lloyd Axworthy and John Roberts; and five officials: Michael Pitfield, Michael Kirby, Roger Tassé, Fred Gibson and Tom Axworthy, Trudeau's principal secretary.

They agree at the outset that there are two alternatives. The constitutional package, the cause of so much toil and strife, must be made legitimate, either through a referendum or a deal with the premiers. That night, Chrétien is the chief proponent of a compromise with the provinces. For a variety of reasons, political and personal (because some of the individual careers in that room are indelibly linked to Trudeau's), others favour the referendum. The discussion hinges on what many would see as an obscure point: the so-called tie-breaking referendum that is part of the federal government's proposed amending formula. A device that gives Ottawa the whip hand in future negotiations, it has become the *sine qua non* for Pitfield, Kirby and Trudeau — the right of the people to decide between two warring levels of government. They cannot envisage a deal which will not contain this mechanism. Chrétien points out how this is a red flag to the provinces, but that only seems to

encourage its adherents. Chrétien urges Trudeau to abandon his fascination with a referendum, where the people will vote with an eye on the
government's financial record, and compromise with the premiers the
Canadian way. He recounts his conversations with certain provincial
ministers. But while Chrétien is optimistic that something can be salvaged, Trudeau is not. "Romanow can't deliver," the prime minister
snaps at one point. "The premiers will never buy it. They'll never desert
Lévesque."

✦

In suite 481 at the Chateau Laurier all is going swimmingly. The countless months of tedious arguments and muttering retreats fade away. There
is now only the quick, exhilarating, chop-chop-chop of compromise. One
senior constitutional official from each of four provincial governments is
present. Practiced domestic diplomats, most of whom have specific
instructions about what to accept, they are able to put together a package in remarkably short order. Two of them, Alberta's Peter Meekison
and B.C.'s Mel Smith, have been constitutional advisers to their respective
governments since Victoria in 1971. They know their own and everyone
else's positions by heart. Saskatchewan's Howard Leeson, a former
university professor and president of the Alberta NDP, has been around
since 1977, when it was that province's turn to be the provincial chairman going into a new round of constitutional talks. Newfoundland's
Cyril Abery also has been part of his province's senior intergovernmental
bureaucracy since the early 1970s. Abery arrives with his premier's lunch-
hour proposal and Leeson quickly informs the group of the details of the
Chrétien-Romanow talks. Blakeney is there for the beginning of the meeting but soon leaves for dinner.

The officials start in on the charter of rights. What is to be made subject
to the legislative override? Saskatchewan and Newfoundland want to
entrench democratic and fundamental rights fully, to make the package
more palatable to Ottawa. But Alberta resists the entrenchment of fundamental rights and in the end only democratic rights escape the override.
What to do about language rights? Chrétien's objections to Peckford's
referendum solution are made known. The four men decide to make it
subject to opting-in. Lougheed will not be part of any indirect legislation
in another province, Meekison tells the group.

The only "sticky part" of the meeting, one of the quartet recalls later,
was the debate over native rights. The two native rights clauses in the
resolution — the affirmation of rights and the promise to hold a conference with native leaders to define these further — are in both the Blakeney
and Peckford proposals. But B.C. has historically never recognized aboriginal title to vast tracts of land in that province and insists that the

clauses be deleted.* They discuss this point for about fifteen minutes, during which time some of the officials speak by phone with their respective delegations. In the end, the two native rights sections fall to the floor. When Blakeney returns, he notices the omission but understands the politics. He also feels that it will make it easier to sell to Ottawa, and decides that he had better phone around and determine how much support this new effort has.

———————— ✦ ————————

In the drawing room of the prime minister's official residence, a frustrated Chrétien is exhausting all his arguments. He tries to phone Romanow to find out how the proposal is taking shape but Romanow won't return his calls — afraid, almost superstitiously, of breaking the momentum that is forming. Chrétien urges Trudeau to call Davis as the Ontario premier had requested earlier in the day. Then, while the prime minister is in the other room, he pleads with the others to help him change Trudeau's mind. It's this or nothing, he argues. There won't be anything else. "I won't put on my running shoes for another referendum!" But the officials cannot be swayed to give up the tie-breaking referendum mechanism, and some of the ministers present are suspicious of Chrétien's own ambitions in this particular drama.

Bill Davis is the pivotal man in these final hours of negotiation — the only premier who can talk with both Trudeau and the gang of eight, through Blakeney or Blakeney's people. He is the gate through which all communications between the two camps must pass. But when Trudeau's call comes shortly after ten — interrupting an informal dinner of take-out Chinese food on paper plates in his hotel suite — Davis has not yet heard to what extent a compromise proposal has gelled. Nevertheless, after a private forty-minute chat, Davis returns to the outer room and tells his group: "If it all works out tomorrow, mark down that one of the most crucial elements was put in place at 10:40 tonight." His ministers, who have been urging him to adopt a tougher line with Trudeau by threatening to withhold Ontario's future support, are confident that that card has been played. But at the other end of the line, Davis's points had been met with silence. Ontario's support is important for the project to proceed but Trudeau will not be bullied and Davis, ever cautious, knows this best of all.

When Trudeau returns to the living room, he argues strongly in support of the referendum solution because the "integrity" of the reforms are important and he wants to leave the tie-breaking mechanism for his

---

*Bill Bennett said in an interview later that he might not have signed the accord if the native rights sections were still in with the original wording.

successors. Besides, if Ottawa wins the referendum, it would set an historic precedent that would right the pendulum once and for all. Some think Trudeau has already made up his mind what to do. Others believe he is only playing the Socratic doubter and is really leaning the other way. Once again the majority view appears to be for a referendum. There is no clear counter-offer on the table, and the prospect of merely some vague consensus of provinces that may or may not satisfy the Supreme Court's dicta is not enough on which to make a final decision.

———————— ✦ ————————

Back at the Chateau Laurier, the compromise is starting to find favour. Angus MacLean, who had gone to bed early that night feeling poorly, is roused about eleven and asked his views. John Buchanan is tracked to the airport, waiting for a late plane to Halifax. At Blakeney's urging, he takes a cab back downtown to look into the proposal first-hand. What started with four senior officials and two Saskatchewan drafters swells into a crowd of about sixteen as the night wears on. Horace Carver, PEI's attorney general, informs his Manitoba counterpart, Gerry Mercier, of the proposal, about midnight, but Mercier decides it's too late to call Lyon back in Winnipeg. No one calls Quebec. There is no conscious decision not to call them, several participants recall later. It is more a tacit understanding. ("It was one of those times when geography made a difference," one said afterwards. "They [the Quebecers] just weren't around.")

Bennett and Lougheed go to bed early that night, both resolved not to take part directly in the negotiations, in order to leave themselves free to make a final decision in the morning. Lougheed feels that even if the proposal doesn't fly, it is at least good public relations; the provinces will have been seen to be flexible.

At about eleven-thirty, Brian Peckford heads over to the Chateau Laurier. On his way out, he runs into Roy McMurtry in the lobby of the Four Seasons and urges him to go upstairs and see Gerry Ottenheimer. Over a tall, slow glass of Screech, McMurtry and Ottenheimer discuss the proposal that has been put together. McMurtry, for a variety of reasons, leaves the Newfoundland rooms an hour later, feeling pretty good.

In the Saskatchewan suite, Peckford is very bullish. He makes a strong pitch to the rest to accept a deal. "It's time to move," he says, urging the others to get behind it. Pride of authorship is pushing him into a new camp.

———————— ✦ ————————

Driving home along the Rideau Canal, where the water has been drained only a few days before in anticipation of an early freeze, Chrétien still does not know what Trudeau intends to do. He calls Romanow again from his home. No response. He calls Eddie Goldenberg about midnight. Has he heard anything? No, but how did it go with Trudeau? It was rough, Chrétien says. He doesn't know whether he convinced the prime minister or not.

It is rare when Jean Chrétien does not enjoy a good night's sleep. But that night he doesn't catch a wink. There is too much excitement in the air, and he feels like a kid at Christmas. He makes some calls, tries to sleep, gets up and reads for a bit, finally taking a shower, before starting another series of calls around half-past five in the morning. It is all starting to look like a dealmaker's dream.

━━━━━━ 🍁 ━━━━━━

The final drafting is finished and copies are made a little before one in the morning. It is suggested that Lougheed should call Lyon and Lévesque in the morning, but it is too late to wake him at this point. Romanow's executive assistant, Aidon Charlton, is sent over to the Four Seasons to give a copy of the proposal to Ontario, but he finds no one around on their floor. Charlton spots a Quebec official in the downstairs bar and, feeling conspicuous, darts off down a hotel corridor. This leads to a kind of Keystone Cops escapade when hotel security guards track him down to question what he is doing skulking around the corridors at this hour of the morning.

Charlton tries Hatfield's suite, where there are sounds on the other side of the door but no Ontario officials. His curiosity piqued, Hatfield rings Romanow to find out what is going on and is read the main elements of the proposal over the phone. It is nearly two by the time the final two-page draft is slipped under Tom Wells's door. Since shortly after midnight, Ontario officials have been passing along elements of the deal to their federal counterparts. But they have not seen the final draft or gauged its acceptability among the eight. At about half-past two, Wells's deputy, Don Stevenson, rouses Leeson to clarify a few points. The final deal is nearly complete. It is now a question of who will buy it in the cool light of day.

━━━━━━ 🍁 ━━━━━━

Thursday, 5 November 1981

In his bathrobe and slippers, Bill Davis is awaiting the arrival of his breakfast from room service when Michael Kirby knocks on his door. It is half-past six and Kirby is there to go over the provincial proposal. There may still be problems, Kirby confesses. Trudeau wants the tie-breaking referendum in the amending formula; he doesn't know if the prime minister can buy this the way it is. Davis is perplexed. After only three hours sleep, it is not what he wants to hear. Across town, Tom Axworthy happens by Eddie Goldenberg, waiting for the bus. Is there a deal? Goldenberg asks. Axworthy says he doubts it.

In their respective hotels, Lougheed and Bennett are going through the proposal with their advisers. Both agree, independently, that it is acceptable. Or, at the very least, a good tactical move. Lougheed heads off early for the breakfast meeting of the eight.

Roy McMurtry wakes up early, shakes the cobwebs away, and decides on a little political mischief. He and Hugh Segal call Senator Nathan Nurgitz in Winnipeg, Sterling Lyon's campaign manager, at a little before six Manitoba time. The gang of eight has now become the gang of two, McMurtry informs him. "I wouldn't presume to advise you on Manitoba politics," McMurtry says. But the prospect of being isolated with a separatist premier of Quebec in the final days of an election campaign is more than a little worrying for Nurgitz and his leader.

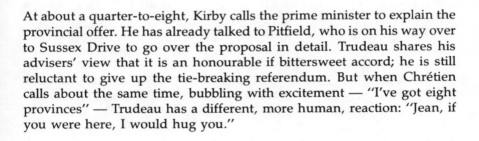

At about a quarter-to-eight, Kirby calls the prime minister to explain the provincial offer. He has already talked to Pitfield, who is on his way over to Sussex Drive to go over the proposal in detail. Trudeau shares his advisers' view that it is an honourable if bittersweet accord; he is still reluctant to give up the tie-breaking referendum. But when Chrétien calls about the same time, bubbling with excitement — "I've got eight provinces" — Trudeau has a different, more human, reaction: "Jean, if you were here, I would hug you."

Entering that last breakfast meeting on the final morning of the "one last time," Lévesque is, characteristically, twenty-five minutes late, apologizing abstractedly to anyone who cares to listen, the ever-present cigarette dangling from his lips. Bennett had arrived on the stroke of eight to find most of the others already there, engaged in a heated discussion around Lougheed at the head of the table. ("I was the chairman in name only," Bennett confides to a reporter later that day.) When Lévesque turns up, the others have been arguing about whether the legislative override should apply to fundamental rights, as Lougheed wants and Blakeney doesn't, fearing it would not sit well with Trudeau. Their meeting is almost over. "We have a new proposal, René," Peckford says laconically, as the others collect their papers for the full morning session across the street. "It's there by your plate."

There is a brief silence in the room. Visibly tensing, Lévesque moves stiffly to his place at the table. "What's this?" he asks angrily, reaching for the two-page document near the chafing dish, which is keeping the remaining eggs and bacon warm. There are no histrionics, but Lévesque is clearly furious, accusing the others of forming a cabal behind his back. "We were just building blocks through the night," Peckford replies. "One block at a time. Now it's your turn."

The other premiers head off to the tunnel that will take them across to the conference centre. Only Lougheed and Lévesque remain behind. For another twenty minutes they stand at the doorway of their breakfast room at the Chateau Laurier, arguing, pleading, accusing.

In the next half-hour Lévesque's mood veers from rage to a kind of falsely casual aplomb. ("You could see the withdrawal setting in," a senior official observes later.) The final private session of the eleven first ministers begins about twenty-five past nine. Downstairs, where the journalists wait, there has been no inkling of any breakthrough; the cautious optimism of some of the participants is weighed against the long faces of others.

Before Peckford proceeds with his proposal, Lévesque cuts in: "I won't have much to say this morning. Let me make this point." He is still interested in the referendum. Will Trudeau consider it? The people should be canvassed. One observer recalls there being a kind of quiet desperation in Lévesque's voice, an element of one French-Canadian pleading with another. Claude Morin strolls casually around the table to the B.C. delegation. He leans over to Bennett and asks him to support the referendum idea. Trudeau does not tip his hand. He turns to Peckford. Davis interjects. The proposal this morning comes from the last province to enter Confederation, the Ontario premier observes good-naturedly. For him, it completes the circle.

Peckford reads out the two-page, five-clause document, a proposal by the government of Newfoundland that eventually comes to be known by the more grand title of "the November accord." When he finishes, there is a silence in the room. "We are all in a tactical difficulty here," Trudeau says. "I don't want to be the first to say something." There is another silence. Bill Bennett breaks in. He is prepared to accept the proposal. It is a good deal for Canada, a good deal for British Columbians, he says. Peter Lougheed follows with a similar view. He will accept language rights if a substantial number of the others do, too. Then Allan Blakeney, Angus MacLean, Gerald Mercier (sitting in for Sterling Lyon),

Harry How (sitting in for John Buchanan) and Bill Davis. All support it. (Lougheed and Mercier have already called Lyon that morning and explained the facts to him.)

Trudeau then turns to New Brunswick's Richard Hatfield for his approval, making it nine of ten provinces before it is Lévesque's turn to speak again. Quietly, and with an air of resignation, Lévesque says he could not possibly accept the deal. The new mobility rights section would affect the job-tendering process in Quebec's construction industry in a way that was unacceptable, he argues lamely. And he could not give up Quebec's traditional veto if there is no fiscal compensation for opting-out. Language rights are not an issue just then because the Peckford draft allows provinces to opt-in.

All eyes turn to Trudeau, and his masked visage appears to shimmer and change just for the instant. ("I knew then we had a deal," one premier recalled. "You could tell by his body language." It was as if a light went on somewhere, another said.) Trudeau looks down at the proposal before him. "Well, you worked all night. I just saw this myself. Mr. Chrétien tells me it has some merits. What about this?" And quickly he moves to the main principles. The new *non obstante* clause that allows legislatures to expressly override most of the rights provisions: would the provinces agree to a five-year sunset provision to limit its use? "Sure," says Lougheed immediately, trying to clinch the deal. "That's a great idea. I'd like that in my Alberta bill."

Trudeau is not happy with the new amending formula. He still feels the opting-out provision might lead to incremental separatism. Would the premiers consider a stiffer legislative vote to activate it? No, take it or leave it, Lougheed replies.

Trudeau moves on to language rights. Would Lévesque accept entrenched minority language obligations? "No," the Quebec premier replies, "there would be riots in the streets of Montreal" if he were to entrench constitutionally more rights for the English minority.

The negotiations freeze at this point. "Look, I appreciate what you're trying to do," Trudeau tells the English premiers. But the prime minister cannot accept a checkerboard on language rights. He has a suggestion. Let the nine English provinces agree, but it will not be proclaimed anywhere until Quebec comes on side. His chair already pushed back from the table, Lévesque throws up his arms in exasperation at the idea. He won't discuss it. How about a referendum? Trudeau asks. The same reaction. Lévesque contemptuously dismisses it as a joke. Lougheed speaks up. He does not want to be part of any coercion, any scheme that indirectly legislates in Quebec.

For Peter Lougheed, the political satisfaction in bringing Pierre Trudeau to his knees is about to be tainted by prior loyalties. Earlier in the year, by turning down the oil taps, he beat back the Trudeau government's unilateral attempt to set energy prices, and won agreement more or less on his terms. "Hang tough and he'll collapse," was his assessment of Trudeau's bargaining ability. Now, in the final throes of constitutional battle, he senses a major victory as well, but it means sacrificing certain principles and perhaps even some allies for another political win. The stakes are huge, and also enormously personal. After all, it is his amending formula — with the opting-out provision designed to protect *existing* provincial powers against any federal encroachment — that is at the heart of the deal. When Lougheed first put forward the formula only three years before, there were no takers. Now it is on the verge of becoming the fundamental law of the land, the defining point of Confederation, even if the innovation (fiscal compensation — essential for Lévesque's support) has to be dropped.

Now, in these last climactic hours, Trudeau is demanding that Lougheed implicitly abandon Quebec a second time on the even more crucial issue (from Quebec's point of view) of language rights. All along, Lougheed had fought for the principle, embodied in his amending formula, that the provinces are sovereign in their own fields and that no powers may be taken away without their consent. It is the principle that forged the group of eight and brought Lévesque into the alliance, where he signed away his province's historic veto for an amending formula with a more modest safeguard.

In a corner of the fifth-floor conference room, during a morning break, Lougheed, Dick Johnston and Chrétien stand for nearly twenty minutes debating the language issue. Lougheed says he does not want to be part of any constitutional blackmail. It is *entre nous*, Chrétien argues back; let us from Quebec decide. This is historic, the opportunity may never come again, of a French-Canadian prime minister with such a powerful mandate in Quebec. In the end, Lougheed (and the others) acquiesce. If Ottawa is to impose these conditions on any province, it would not be with Lougheed's approval. But he would not stand in the way. Trudeau does not specifically state that he will impose the language obligations on his home province. That comes later. But no one doubts his intentions. "I cannot sacrifice my minorities," he says.

———————— 🍁 ————————

It is nearly eleven o'clock and Trudeau and Lévesque are having a last confrontation in the fifth-floor chamber. It is curiously tranquil, both men leaning back in their chairs, side by side, talking quietly in French, in voices that can barely be heard at the other end of the table. Lévesque is explaining why he feels the fiscal compensation clause is important in lieu of the veto, why the collective rights of the Québecois should not be held ransom to financial constraints, the levers of which could be controlled by an anglophone government in Ottawa. Trudeau says he is prepared to negotiate on compensation and search out some wording that might meet Lévesque halfway, but he cannot make it a constitutional guarantee. It is what he had to deny Bourassa in 1971, although it was partly granted later through an administrative arrangement.

But Lévesque wants no part of well-intentioned promises at this point. You don't realize what you are doing, he tells Trudeau; the consequences may be incalculable. He challenges the prime minister to call a referendum, at least in Quebec, to show that he has a mandate for his views. Trudeau returns the challenge. You hold the referendum, Trudeau says, on those items you disagree with — mobility rights, compensation and education; if you win, then we will ask the others to reopen the accord. Without compensation, the accord is "an empty shell," Lévesque argues back. Will you return us our veto? Each case must be judged on its merits, Trudeau replies. Ottawa cannot ignore Quebec on a whim without paying a political price; there is still a veto in opting-out.

Coming into the conference room that morning, a provincial official of long standing says he has never seen Claude Morin so angry. "This will hasten Quebec's separation," Morin tells him. At the end of the session, after the exchange between Lévesque and Trudeau, others see tears in Morin's eyes at the sense of personal betrayal. Lévesque, too, appears shaken.

The Quebecers gather their papers and leave for their delegation's office to prepare a public statement. While the others relax in their chairs, joshing about whether they should sign the final agreement there or before the television cameras downstairs in the main hall ("We'll sign it here," Trudeau says, only half-joking, "I'm not taking any chances."), Lévesque goes off by himself to the delegates' lounge and sits alone for nearly twenty minutes, sipping a coffee and reading an English newspaper.

Almost as an afterthought, as the draft is being readied for retyping by the conference secretariat, Trudeau mentions the natives for the second time that morning. "Why don't we just agree to have the conference?" He does not mention the hard-fought-for affirmation clause that had fallen to the floor the previous night, a victim of the cut-and-paste job. He is simply asking, as he did at the outset that morning, that the section inviting native leaders to a conference to discuss these rights be reinstated. None can disagree at this point. The document goes off to the secretariat and returns with a drafting error which only Trudeau catches. The wrong wording would have prohibited fiscal compensation from ever being granted, and it is the intention only not to grant it automatically, a nice but important distinction.

At a little after noon, the prime minister, seven premiers and two ministers representing their absent bosses add their names to two official versions, plus a number of souvenirs, and then go downstairs to repeat the performance once for the viewing public.*

Word of the accord and the isolation of Quebec spreads quickly to the assembled journalists downstairs about half-an-hour before the first ministers descend to the main hall. Small groups cluster around provincial officials, scribbling down details of the day's events from the several perspectives. (A film crew makes plans to shoot Chrétien, Romanow and McMurtry in the upstairs pantry, chronicling for all time the so-called "kitchen deal.") As the political leaders convene in the main hall, Trudeau says he has two regrets. That the amending formula does not contain any reference to the ultimate sovereignty of the people through a referendum, and that Quebec would not be party to what is otherwise "a noble day" for Canada with the entrenchment of minority language rights.

While the others sing various hymns to unity and compromise, a bitter René Lévesque, his lips curling in scorn, predicts the new accord will have "incalculable consequences" for Canada. Never would his government capitulate. Once again, he says, drawing on the memories of Riel and conscription, the supposed duality of Canada has been shown to be a sham. "The Canadian way" — he nearly spits the words out — means leaving Quebec by itself, in a corner, when the crunch comes.

---

*Manitoba's Gerry Mercier signs, with the caveat that the language right guarantees are subject to approval by the Manitoba legislature. But this never happens. The Lyon government is defeated and its NDP successor agrees to have these conditions 'imposed,' as they are on Quebec, when the revised resolution is put before Parliament two weeks later.

14
Rebirth of a Nation

Well, as between the British parliamentarians holding their noses and me hold-
ing mine, I chose the latter.

Pierre Trudeau, 18 November 1981, explaining
at a press conference why he compromised so generously to make a deal
with the provinces.

I guess it's back to Spam and buying our own lunches now.

A British MP,
8 March 1982, commenting on the final passage through Westminster of
the Canada Bill.

The last day of colonial dependence — 17 April, 1982, — began sunny
and warm. Only the ground had not yet awakened; nothing was green
except the weathered copper roofs of the capital buildings. On the streets
leading up to Parliament Hill, the proprietors of the fried-chip wagons
jostled for position with the vendors of T-shirts and lapel buttons (*La
séparation — NON merci* sold for two dollars). The middle-class monarchist
crowd — they picked up their litter afterwards, one observer noted —
treated the occasion more like a country fair than the solemn, culminating event of nation-building. They had come to see the Queen, and, as
she alighted from her open landau with an RCMP escort, they pressed
forward, cheered, offered her flowers, and welcomed her with shouts of
"Way to go, Bess" and "Yea, Queenie."

About thirty thousand people came to the Hill, only a third of the
number that had turned up a few weeks before for a rally sponsored by
the Canadian Labour Congress to protest against high interest rates. The
lawns still bore the charred circles where the union brothers and sisters
had burned their placards to keep themselves warm while their leaders
speechified from Parliament's steps.

Future historians may borrow a piece of slang from the period and
write that on this Saturday morning, it rained on Trudeau's parade. As
the prime minister walked to the microphone on the scarlet stage that
workmen had hammered together, storm clouds blew across the Ottawa
River from the Quebec side. The prime minister's speech was too long,
too political, too small in spirit, and, as he spoke, the first lace of rain
swept over the crowd. Trudeau had nothing really of moment to say, no
great words for history's record. He had little more than his triumph to

303

declare. In French, Trudeau said: "By definition, the silent majority does not make a lot of noise; it is content to make history." It was the back of his hand to Lévesque and Quebec's nationalists. Much of his speech — too much — was an attack on the Parti Québécois. The sky was dark when he finished, "Après lui, le déluge," some wag remarked.

The prime minister sat beside the Queen at what looked like a small card-table for the simple, formal ceremony. Michael Pitfield and Michael Kirby, behaving like true clerks, held chairs, proffered a pen (Pitfield had sent an aide out to buy it, for seventy-five dollars, from nearby Birks Jewellers) and presented the formal proclamation document to the signatories. The Queen signed Elizabeth R with a flourish and handed the pen with a smile to the prime minister. Fat raindrops fell on the document, smudging the first calligraphed word and the signature of André Ouellet, Trudeau's trouble-prone minister of consumer and corporate affairs, who signed in his capacity as registrar-general. The only two signatures on the document — apart from that of the Queen — were French-Canadian names: Trudeau and Ouellet. Then the Queen came to the podium to speak, and the heavens opened.

Her brief speech called the refurbished constitution "a defiant challenge to history". She faltered only once in her delivery: while praising the country's leaders "for the good sense and tolerance which they have displayed in bringing about a successful conclusion." Around her the rain crashed down. Parliament Hill became a field of umbrellas and green plastic garbage-bag ponchos. People squealed at the drenching they were taking. In the unsheltered VIP section, many of the premiers, diplomats, MPs, senators and provincial opposition leaders with their spouses stoically withstood the torrent. Dozens fled. Bill Davis put his top hat on his wife's head. A gust of wind nearly tore the script from the Queen's hand and, with a desperate look, she turned to the prime minister. Who knows what passed between them? After a moment, she soldiered on as a queen would be expected to do, her words lost in the hammering downpour. When she finished, five hundred pigeons, masquerading as doves, were let loose in the air, and a sopping Bryce Mackasey climbed onto the stage with an instamatic camera to record the event.

No matter; it rained on René Lévesque's parade, too. Later that same day, he led a sombre, soggy march through Montreal's streets to Jeanne Mance Park with its huge statue of Father of Confederation Georges-Etienne Cartier. The contrast between the two political events could not have been more sharply etched. In Ottawa, Trudeau, his ministers and many of the premiers dressed for the day's pomp and ceremony in top hat and morning coats (Peter Lougheed wore a business suit. "They don't understand that sort of thing in the West," an aide explained). In Montreal, Lévesque wore a striped-grey suit and open shirt as he stood before his audience — most of them young, many wearing jeans, about the same size in numbers as the crowd on Parliament Hill. They chanted (in English) "Elizabeth go home!" and (in French) "Trudeau au poteau" and "Le Québec aux québecois". To each his own proclamation, Lévesque told them.

He repeated what he had said on television two nights earlier on the eve of the Queen's arrival in Canada, when he called for Quebecers to opt for political independence and "a real country where we'll really be at home", and had hissed the English words: "le Canada Bill" and "le BNA Act". In his television speech he suggested that maybe the Queen was holding *her* nose in proclaiming the new constitution. ("We are being royally screwed," said his deputy premier, Jacques-Yvan Morin.) As for Trudeau's new charter of rights, Lévesque dismissed it as "the most soporific lawyerishness you could find anywhere in the world." If nothing else, he was a man who could turn a phrase.

In Ottawa, Liberal politicians and hangers-on partied in the Parliament buildings and garnered the best seats at receptions. The press told of an Ottawa elementary school principal who handed out government-supplied flags and decals and had his pupils sing "O Canada" in French and English and munch chunks of a huge cake with a frosted maple leaf on top. "Wow," a grade six student said, "We're free!"

But at Ecole Pierre Laporte in Trudeau's Montreal riding of Mount Royal, the other solitude went quietly about its week. "There's nothing happening," a vice-principal told a reporter. "It's not St.-Jean Baptiste Day."

———————— ❦ ————————

Those who expected the railway station accord of 5 November to quell at last the nation's constitutional fuss were disappointed. It marked only the end of one chapter and the beginning of another. There were immediate yelps of anguish not only from Quebec nationalists, but from those Canadians who felt their birthright had been plundered in the compromise charter of rights. Paramount among them were native peoples — whose aboriginal and treaty rights clause fell to the floor in the late-night cut-and-paste session on 4 November — and women's organizations which were outraged at the gutting of the clause guaranteeing equality of the sexes.

Both clauses were extraordinarily complex and highly symbolic (they had been added during the heat of parliamentary battle over the winter and early spring of 1981). Their removal scored a jagged tear in the national conscience. More important, the extraordinary campaign for their restoration demonstrated that the constitution, for the first time, belonged to the people of Canada; it was no longer the exclusive property of the politicians and their bureaucratic Wolseys and Richelieus.

On 18 November — thirteen days after the deal had been struck — Trudeau unveiled the final resolution that was to be approved by Parliament and sent to Westminster. It contained special language and cultural considerations for Quebec, but nothing for women and native peoples.* In an unadmirable display of delayed outrage (he had had nearly two weeks to react), NDP leader Ed Broadbent formally withdrew his party's support for the package, saying: "National unity without national integrity is not possible." The NDP, of course, had known since 5 November that the aboriginal rights and sexual equality clauses had been cut out. The party's leadership had stayed quiet, partly in the hopes of doing some behind-the-scenes repair work, partly because it was irritated with the native groups for having undercut support for the aboriginal rights clause that the NDP had worked so hard to have included in the charter in the first place.

There was no such jellied response from one of the country's high court judges with at least historic ties to the party. Thomas Berger of the British Columbia Supreme Court, a former leader of the B.C. NDP, was outraged. In radio and newspaper interviews, one speech at Guelph University and an op-ed article he wrote for *The Globe and Mail*, Berger decried the fate of the native rights clause and the disappearance of Quebec's traditional veto (the latter issue had attracted only lackadaisical interest from the federal NDP). This eyebrow-raising judicial incursion into the country's major political debate earned him public rebukes from the prime minister — in Ottawa and Vancouver — and a formal complaint from a brother judge, George Addy of the Federal Court. Addy's complaint triggered an inquiry by the Canadian Judicial Council into whether he should be removed from the bench. An investigating committee of three judges (the lawyer retained to conduct the investigation was J. J. Robinette, the federal government's chief counsel for the Supreme Court of Canada's constitution case) sharply criticised him. But in May 1982, the full judicial council let the matter slip by with rather an oblique slap on Berger's wrist; the council merely reaffirmed the principle that judges should stay out of politics, and Berger, for his part, was utterly unrepentant.

------------------------- ❦ -------------------------

*Trudeau told the Commons on 18 November that he considered binding just the federal government to the native rights clause — that is, making it applicable to federal lands in the North — but he had received a mixed reaction from the groups concerned. "And that is the nature of the problem; I honestly don't know what the aboriginal people of Canada, the native people, want," he said. He was being a little clever. The Indians and Métis wanted more, not less, than what the original clause guaranteed them; and the Inuit had stuck firmly with Trudeau's charter from the beginning.

The seven days following the unveiling of the "final" resolution produced a textbook illustration of grassroots political action. Native groups swarmed into Ottawa; they could be seen everywhere on Parliament Hill — in the corridors, the Commons' visitors gallery, in MPs' and senators' offices. There were mass rallies in provincial capitals. At one of them four thousand Indians and Métis and their supporters (the number of white faces in the crowd was notable) confronted Peter Lougheed on the steps of the Alberta legislature. Lawyers who dealt with native briefs, and others who were close students of native politics, reported a never-before-seen phenomenon — the normally deeply divided factions of Canada's aboriginal peoples were overcoming their differences and working together for the re-instatement of their constitutional guarantees.

Canadians also saw, for the first time, a dazzling demonstration of the organizing skills and political clout of women's groups. The Canadian Advisory Council on the Status of Women (a federal government-established organization) met in Vancouver and mobilized their provincial associates to lobby provincial governments, the press and just about every Canadian of importance in the country including cabinet ministers and their spouses (although some were themselves lobbyists; lawyer Sharon Gray, wife of federal industry minister Herb Gray, called one Ottawa columnist to urge him to support the sexual equality clause). Judy Erola, federal minister responsible for the status of women, quietly lent official space, staff and telephones to pressure groups. Federal politicians, who until this moment had been alone on the receiving end of public criticism of the constitution, were delighted to see their provincial counterparts taking heat.

Provincial leaders were stunned — and distraught at being portrayed in the national press as callously insensitive to the rights of women and natives. It was a phenomenon most of them had not encountered before. One prairie minister recalled feeling powerless in the face of the national news media onslaught; he spoke of how the usual techniques of dealing with protest groups had had to be cast aside. "Normally you meet with the leadership of these groups and bring them into your cabinet office and argue your point of view," he said. "Or you go to your own groups, the ones that are sympathetic, and start some counter-pressure. But that didn't work this time." No one was sympathetic.

Under these kinds of pressures, the provincial governments folded like omelettes. A compromise wording from Lougheed on the aboriginal rights clause — which guaranteed to protect *existing* rights — was agreed to by the provincial and federal governments. The sexual equality clause was restored. The provinces then urged Trudeau to hurry up and get the resolution through Parliament before other protest forces could gather strength (a coalition of women's groups and handicapped organizations, supported by the formidable former senator, Eugene Forsey, already was petitioning MPs to remove the *non obstante* clause; an anti-abortion group, claiming half a million supporters, was swinging into action, demanding stronger constitutional protections for the unborn; the Indians were stepping up the pressure for more unequivocal rights). Ottawa, by this time, was happy to oblige. With the lobbying activity acquiring frenetic intensity, the federal cabinet began to worry about how to turn it off.

There remains the questions of why the clauses had been scrapped. The aboriginal and treaty rights protection was objected to largely — but not exclusively — by the B.C. government, which faced the strongest land claims from its native residents because only two treaties had been signed in the province.* The speed with which the clause was excised remains surprising. None of the dealmakers so much as murmured a protest; were Canadian political leaders really that insensitive? The only half-respectable explanation for what happened comes from a western provincial official who was present for the negotiations. He said it was not an act of commission but one of omission. Aboriginal rights were on no delegation's 'must' list; no one insisted on them being in and therefore no one — in the intensity of eleventh-hour bargaining — thought anything about them coming out.

The excision of the sexual equality clause was the product of (male) logic.† When officials met after the signing of the accord to clean up loose ends, some of the provincial people saw that the equality clause contributed to a legal inconsistency — two so-called paramountcy clauses were in conflict with one another. The equality clause said that "notwithstanding" anything else in the charter of rights, the equality of male and female persons was guaranteed. But the other general *non obstante* clause gave legislatures the power to override anti-discrimination provisions, including sexual equality. Therefore the officials, with the tacit approval of the politicians, created what became known in the jargon as the "modified women's clause" (resulting in demonstrators carrying placards saying that their bearers resented being "modified women").

The governments of the four western provinces and Nova Scotia initially said no to all suggestions that the equality clauses be restored.

---

*Other western provinces also had problems with the clause, particularly as it affected Métis who were being given legal recognition for the first time. Moreover, Ontario's Roy McMurtry privately wrote Chrétien to say that recognizing and entrenching aboriginal rights could entail the recognition of property rights "with very serious consequences for the people of Canada."

†It initially was inserted to counter what women's groups felt might be the negative impact on the equality of women resulting from constitutional entrenchment of aboriginal rights and "the enhancement of the multicultural heritage". In other words, it was an attempt to assert the blossoming North American value of sexual equality against the customs of other cultures.

Three premiers quickly capitulated, leaving only Blakeney and Buchanan. Buchanan struck his colours after a long telephone conversation with Conservative MP Flora MacDonald. Blakeney lasted through the weekend (his neatly ordered mind had rebelled against the legal messiness), and then he, too, buckled.*

———————— ❦ ————————

In a broader context, the theatrics over the restoration of native and equality rights had been a display — as so many matters are in Canada — of the country's central dichotomy. The two solitudes, as usual, were immersed in their separate preoccupations: the charter of rights debate was being held in English Canada; Quebec's veto was the concern of French Canada.

On the weekend following the signing of the accord, Jean Chrétien and Roger Tassé met to look for ways to get around René Lévesque's self-imposed isolation. The exclusion of their native province marred the enthusiasm that the federal justice minister and his deputy otherwise would have felt for the agreement. Tassé developed a series of proposals which Chrétien cleared through the federal cabinet and then tried to influence Claude Ryan to accept and proffer as his own (a scheme which caused Chrétien some difficulty; Ryan hung up on him the first time he called). Tassé also made use of his own lines into the Quebec Liberal Party, via René Dussault, a former provincial deputy attorney general who had been an unsuccessful Liberal candidate in the recent Quebec election.

In their proposals, Chrétien and Tassé tried to steer a careful course that would meet some of Lévesque's demands without granting Quebec special status — anathema to Trudeau. They broached a plan to Ryan that would allow any province to receive "reasonable compensation" should it opt out of any future constitutional change dealing with education or culture, the two key areas of jurisdictional concern for Quebec governments. Quebec also would not be bound by quite the same constitutional strictures as the other provinces to provide education services to their official minorities.

Ryan accepted the federal proposals, added some of his own, and placed them before Quebec's National Assembly. Trudeau gave the appearance of accepting them under pressure from his own Quebec caucus — most of whom were aware that the midwives for the Ryan package were Tassé and Chrétien — and included them in the resolution. Lévesque, however, rejected them as only half a loaf. He promised renewed court action over the constitutionality of the accord and passed

———————————

*He had argued that if the charter was going to be re-opened, native rights should go back in too.

a formal order-in-council exercising what he called his province's historic veto to block the constitutional reforms. The order-in-council was laughed off by Ottawa as a meaningless gesture. "He can pass a decree saying there will be no snow over Quebec this winter and it will have about the same effect," Chrétien said. Trudeau was only a little more polite. In a stuffy exchange of letters — "prime minister," "my dear premier" — Trudeau said he found it "aberrant and, indeed, irresponsible" that a premier of Quebec would give up his province's traditional veto. But, said Trudeau, that was Lévesque's decision when he threw in his lot with the seven other provinces and signed the April agreement; at that point Quebec had conceded it was a province just like the others, and an agreement of ten of eleven governments satisfied the Supreme Court's dictum for a reasonable consensus.

Joe Clark tried to win over Lévesque with a brief flurried wooing of Quebec nationalists, but there was little response. In the end, only a handful of Tories, mostly in the Senate, voted against the measure because of Quebec's exclusion (and some Conservative MPs voted against the measure because too much special attention had been paid to the province to bring it into the fold). "Lévesque will never sign," Chrétien told reporters. "We've done all we had to do." Indeed, the premiers seemed to feel much the same way and, having been buffeted rudely by relentless lobbyists on the charter of rights, were only too happy to get the matter over with. A survey of provincial premiers found only two, Lougheed and Blakeney, who at this point were willing to negotiate further with Lévesque; Davis and Hatfield were concerned that the Quebec demand for fiscal compensation for provinces exercising their veto would endanger future national programs, and the others were content to let things rest.

On 2 December 1981, with the scars of division still deep in the nation, the Commons moved Canada one step closer to formal independence by passing the controversial constitutional resolution. Twenty-four MPs — seventeen Conservatives, five Liberals and two New Democrats — defied party discipline and voted against it.*

---

*The Tories who rejected the resolution were: Roch LaSalle, Clark's only Quebec lieutenant; former ministers, Elmer MacKay and Ronald Huntington, who objected in principle to an entrenched charter of rights; and backbenchers Alex Patterson, Len Gustafson, Gordon Gilchrist, John Gamble, William Domm, Ronald Stewart, Gordon Towers, Douglas Roche, Frank Oberle, Douglas Neil, Gus Mitges, Daniel McKenzie, Otto Jelinek and Thomas Cossitt, for a variety of reasons ranging from opposition to a charter to the absence of property rights and guarantees against abortion. The Liberal dissidents were former cabinet minister Warren

The vote provoked agonizing crises of conscience among many MPs, of which there is no better illustration than Warren Allmand, almost alone among the Liberals not wearing a red carnation in his lapel, sitting ramrod stiff in his seat on the front benches awaiting the moment when he would stand and vote against his party and against the government of which he was once an executive member.* Pierre Trudeau — when his supporters stood to cheer him — blew his cheeks out in the manner that men do when deep emotion stirs within them. When the final tally was counted — 246 yeas, 24 nays — government house leader Yvon Pinard gestured to Liberal MP Carlo Rossi, whose rich tenor voice led MPs in the singing of the national anthem, the English and French versions criss-crossing in unintended counterpoint; onlookers in the packed public galleries joined in. Only a few hours earlier, René Lévesque began his formal challenge to the initiative in court, and ordered the flags on all Quebec government buildings to be flown at half-staff. Montreal's *Le Devoir* said in an editorial that the vote represented "a fatal day" for Canada.

——————— ❧ ———————

On 8 December, the resolution passed the Senate by a vote of 59-23. Five Liberal senators joined most of the Conservatives and two independents to oppose it, mainly because Quebec was not part of the accord.

That night, the two copies of the resolution, leatherbound in red (for the Senate) and green (for the Commons) were taken to Government House. There, amidst forced pomp, Senate speaker Jean Marchand and Commons speaker Jeanne Sauvé handed them over to governor general Schreyer, who in turned passed them over to his Buckingham palace-trained secretary Esmond Butler for delivery to London. Michael Kirby had been promoted to deputy clerk of the privy council for the occasion, so that he could have a ceremonial role. On hand were most of the fed-

---

Allmand, who objected to the "second class" status afforded the English in Quebec; Louis Duclos, because of the imposition on Quebec; Jean-Robert Gauthier, because it lacked important rights for the Ontario francophones; and Garnet Bloomfield and Stanley Hudecki, because of the abortion issue. B.C. New Democrat Svend Robinson voted against the resolution because of the override provision on the charter; his colleague James Manly, because native peoples were not given veto power over amendments affecting them; a third New Democrat, Robert Ogle, a Roman Catholic priest, was the sole abstainer; he had misgivings about the charter's ambiguity on the abortion issue.

*In his speech in the Commons, Allmand, a former solicitor general and minister of consumer and corporate affairs, made a blistering attack on the prime minister, using more than a score of his past statements and actions to argue that Trudeau was abandoning his and the party's principles in accepting uneven language guarantees across the country.

eral Fathers of Re-Confederation: Joe Clark and about thirty members of
his caucus; Ed Broadbent and some of his MPs; senior staff members
from the federal-provincial relations office and the department of justice, and, of course, prime minister Trudeau, his cabinet and many Liberal MPs. Backstage, Marchand had temporarily balked at having to take
part in a tawdry *mise en scène* which he felt was a coarse gesture to Quebec,
but he eventually played the role assigned to him. As it happened,
provincial attorneys general — including McMurtry and Romanow —
were in Ottawa that day for a conference. They asked if they could attend
the constitution ceremony. The answer was no; this was a federal party.
When it was over, Butler and Jean Chrétien left immediately for London.

On 25 March 1982 the British House of Lords passed the Canada Bill in
third reading, formally ending the United Kingdom's responsibility for
Canadian affairs. It was the fifth (and final) constitution that Westminster
had legislated for Canada since the eighteenth century. A columnist for
the *Times* called it "the most boring bill in history." His history, perhaps.
Nonetheless, the Canada Bill produced considerable busyness for British
MPs. They proposed fifty-seven amendments (twenty-three of which
were allowed for debate) and went to great lengths to "ventilate" their
concerns (in the barbarous phrase of Labour's shadow foreign secretary,
Denis Healey) about Canadian constitution-making. Canadian observers
in Westminster's visitors' galleries were unpleasantly aware that these
foreign politicians were enjoying themselves dabbling in Canadian affairs and were in no hurry to move on to other business. Many of them,
in fact, wanted to do more than ventilate. A mélange of about fifty MPs
(some of whom had been wined, dined and whisked around Canada by
provincial governments and native groups, expenses paid) — actively
opposed the package. They dragged out the famous Kirby memorandum,
and Trudeau's remarks about British MPs holding their noses and passing
whatever they were told to pass, and they compared Canada's policies
towards its native peoples to the South African government's policy of
apartheid. Arrested in mid-oratory by another MP and asked whether
he would not describe his speech as "gross interference in the internal
affairs of another country?" Clinton Davis, Labour's junior critic on foreign affairs, was unabashed. "No I would not," he replied. "Is it wrong
to criticize the situation in El Salvador or South Africa?"

The debate in the Commons went on for nineteen hours over four
separate days. From the gallery, Jean Chrétien watched it as long as he
could, often slumping forward, his head buried in his hands, as yet
another British MP flogged Canada for its treatment of natives. Chrétien,
who spent more than six years as minister of Indian affairs, who presided

over the Trudeau government's momentous change of policy in 1973 when it recognized native land claims, and who is the father of an adopted Indian son, was frustrated, hurt and more than a little angry. Less than thirty feet away sat Chief Sol Sanderson, a 40-year-old Saskatchewan Cree, following the debate with considerable satisfaction.

The lord justices of Britain's court of appeal had already turned down the Indian groups' legal challenge, ruling that sometime between 1900 and 1950 the Crown became divisible, and that native treaties with the sovereign were held in right of the Canadian — not the imperial — Crown. But the ruling was also a moral and political victory. "No Parliament should do anything to [threaten] Indian rights," Lord Denning, Master of the Rolls, wrote. "They should be honoured as long as the sun rises and the river flows." The judgment was ammunition for every extravagant speech in the Commons. In the twelve months leading up to this debate Sanderson had met more than two hundred British MPs, attended various party conventions and posed with his ceremonial war-bonnet to grab the attention of Fleet Street. He had even lobbied the Archbishop of Canterbury. The native groups were in the forefront of the various parties trying to win over the hearts, minds and digestive tracts of British opinion makers. "There certainly has been a gastronomic explosion since the Canadians hit town," Labour MP Bruce George observed.

The constitution debate in the Mother of Parliaments brought out the windbags and the Cassandras of British politics. For example, Sir Bernard Braine, who embraced the native cause with total abandon. Jeffrey Simpson, the *Globe*'s London correspondent, described Braine's debate:

> *Every day at the appointed hour, he bursts through the main doors of the House of Commons like a cowboy entering a saloon. Under his arm, he carries an awesome file of documents, the very sight of which sends other members fleeing from the chamber. He always sits on the front bench reserved, incongruously, for Tory backbenchers of long service, whose pain at forever missing the cabinet has been assuaged by the receipt of a title. From there, he fairly pops up, strikes a Churchillian pose with hand on hip, glowers, and begins rumbling like a long-extinct volcano come to life. The fumbling is occasionally interrupted by a full-blown eruption, during which the voice roars, the body shakes, the hands gesticulate and the head turns toward the yawning emptiness of the Tory benches.*

The smoke and belchings of British backbenchers in themselves might not have been so difficult to accept, if it were not for the rather perfunctory way the British government fostered the bill. Even the first official government spokesman, lord privy seal Humphrey Atkins, made a point of saying the bill was not perfect but that it was time the British had done with the Canadian constitution — that is, held their noses. In the Lords, foreign secretary Lord Carrington urged much the same course, although in a more refined way. He told peers "to be realistic and not be overly concerned with the residual controversy surrounding this bill."

The British House of Commons gave final approval to the Canada Bill on 8 March, voting 177 to 33, which meant that slightly fewer than a third of the 635 British MPs bothered to turn up, despite mild pressure to do so from their parliamentary parties. It was certainly no three-line whip at work. Ten days later the Lords gave unanimous approval to the bill after a good-humoured five-and-a-half hour debate with two Canadian peers, Lord Shaughnessy, an oil company executive, and Lord Rodney (both making their maiden speeches) setting the jovial, non partisan tone for the debate. But it was Lord Diplock, then chairman of the law lords' judicial committee, Britain's equivalent to the Supreme Court of Canada, who set out the political facts of life, warning his colleagues that they did not have the constitutional right to amend the Canada Bill. "All we can do is accept it or reject it," Lord Diplock said, reiterating the advice he had given the Canadian government privately more than a year previously. "It would be constitutionally improper for this House to instruct Canada as to how it should conduct its internal affairs."*

Seven days later, on 25 March, the House of Lords formally ended Britain's constitutional responsibility for Canada by passing the controversial bill in third and final reading. In the public galleries an unemployed actor interrupted the proceedings by shouting something unintelligible about the international convention on human rights and hurling a sheaf of papers to the floor below. "That is the truth," he called out, mystically. A British peer, the Earl of Gosford, whose ancestor was governor-in-chief of British North America from 1835 to 1838, attempted to read a long speech on Indian rights but was muzzled by his colleagues in a rare vote challenging his prerogative to speak at length and from notes on final readings. ("That's only the third time I've seen that happen in my thirty years here," a Hansard reporter was overheard saying later.)

Both opposition party spokesmen had their say in less than thirty seconds, in keeping with the tradition that speeches on final reading in the genteel upper House be short and non-controversial. The final speaker

---

*During the debate, Lord Diplock also said that the Lévesque government was wasting its time by claiming an historic veto through further action in the courts. He said he had analysed Quebec's written arguments then before the Quebec court of appeal and found them wanting. In his opinion, there was no way the Supreme Court of Canada could hold the Constitution Act 1982 *ultra vires* or void once it had been passed by Westminster.

was Conservative Lord Morris, who was also nearly cut off by his impatient peers. But he sat down quickly after criticizing the Thatcher government for hurrying the bill through Parliament and observing that the attendant controversy may have educated some British parliamentarians about Canada: "Many now know not only where Saskatchewan is — they know how to spell it."

———————— ✤ ————————

Meanwhile, on Canada's side of the Atlantic, the constitution issue bumped along to patriation day, leaving a series of political convulsions in its wake. In January, in an interview with the *Canadian Press*, governor general Schreyer mused that if substantial provincial consent had not been forthcoming in November, he might have had to use his ultimate constitutional powers and cause an election to settle the dispute. In the flap that followed, Schreyer said he was only talking hypothetically and that his remarks had been misconstrued. Trudeau issued a rare press release on their otherwise privileged conversations to say that at no time had Schreyer ever intimated that line of thinking to him, "even as an hypothetical assessment of the powers of his office." In Montreal, Lévesque sarcastically observed that Schreyer should go back to his normal occupation — sleeping. "Now that English Canada's provinces are satisfied, Mr. Schreyer apparently feels nothing more is indicated. . . ."

In the West, in what was either a harbinger or a fluke, a separatist was elected to the Alberta legislature in a by-election in the southern Alberta riding of Olds-Didsbury, partly by alleging that Lougheed was too cosy with Trudeau, partly by claiming the new constitution was a socialist plot to take away the right to own property. "Talk about making political mistakes, that was a dandy," Lougheed told an interviewer later, discussing the Olds-Didsbury phenomenon. "I come home [from the constitutional deal] thinking, 'Hey, we really did great!' And what happens to us? Across this province, people think that we didn't. But I blame myself for that . . . We didn't do the communication job. . . We made the mistake of drinking champagne [on television] with Mr. Trudeau and made the mistake of not recognizing that property rights thing as being something."

But the premier who made the biggest miscalculation was Allan Blakeney. Thinking to nip the western separatist movement in the bud before it took hold in his province, Blakeney called an early April election and was handed a humiliating defeat. Since 1971 his democratic-socialist regime was lauded even by tough-minded Bay street investment houses as the best run in the country. In the week following the patriation ceremony, he was reduced to leading a seven-member opposition; Roy

Romanow, the heir apparent of Saskatchewan politics, lost by a handful of votes to twenty-two-year-old JoAnn Zazelenchuk who worked part-time in her father's Petro Canada service station.*

In Quebec, December 1981 until April 1982 was the winter and spring of René Lévesque's discontent. Seeking to quell any doubts about his performance at the November constitutional conference he cranked up the nationalist indignation rhetoric to new heights and then threatened to resign when the militants within the Parti Québecois took him at his word. Returning from the Ottawa summit, Lévesque talked of "betrayal" by the English premiers, said Quebec had been "screwed . . . the Canadian way," called the federal Liberals "whores" and ranted against "the economic terrorism" practised by some of the English premiers during the May 1980 referendum campaign. On the eve of his party's convention in early December, the rage reached its paroxysm and Lévesque accused "the anglophone mandarinate" in Ottawa of trying to stifle French-speaking Quebec with "slow genocide." At the convention, the delegates, in a groundswell of anger and nihilism, gave a standing ovation to Jacques Rose, a convicted member (as an accessory after the fact) of the FLQ cell that in October 1970 had kidnapped and murdered former Liberal minister Pierre Laporte, an old friend of Lévesque's from the Lesage years; and they passed as party policy a motion dropping all references to economic association with Canada and asserting that a victory in the next provincial election would be considered an automatic mandate to exercise sovereignty. Part of the motion read that the election win would be enough to declare independence, even without a majority of the popular vote, prompting Lévesque to observe that even he would hesitate to vote for that platform. There were scattered boos — perhaps for the first time — from within the party he had embodied since founding it in 1968.

Lévesque told the delegates that he was considering resigning, but a few weeks later, buttressed by the internal pledges of support, changed his mind and organized a party referendum — dubbed the Renérendum — to counteract the policy motion. (Meanwhile, the PQ cabinet had held an extraordinary meeting without Lévesque, resulting in a public plea for him to stay in office.) Before the internal referendum was completed in late January (overwhelmingly supporting Lévesque's position) and a policy convention held in February to undo the previous one, Claude Morin, the man they call "the sphinx" in PQ circles, quit politics. "They lied to us," he said of the other provincial premiers at the time. "I can't see myself sitting at the same negotiating table as them." But he

*October 1981, John Buchanan was re-elected in Nova Scotia, and in April 1982, Brian Peckford was returned to power in Newfoundland by creating a campaign issue over his fight with Ottawa for the offshore resources.

was also a hurt and beaten man. When the National Assembly opened in November and the opposition demanded explanations of the constitutional accord, Morin was nowhere to be found. He was in France, attending a minor political meeting of the International Francophone Cooperation Agency. A month later, at the PQ convention, there was also no sign of the father of *étapisme*: Morin was in Gabon, attending another meeting of the same agency. When he returned, it was to hand in a four-page letter of resignation, accepted a few weeks later by Lévesque, on 6 January.

Morin's resignation was treated as a political obituary in both the English and French press. He had been at the fulcrum of power for nearly two decades, had served five premiers and was a legitimate father of the Quiet Revolution. His place at the helm was taken by Jacques-Yvan Morin (no relation) the goateed deputy premier, an embracer of abstract ideas more than a tactician, the promoter of several formulas for special status, including one imposed during World War II by the Nazis on a neighbouring country. It was Jacques-Yvan Morin who convinced Lévesque to try one more time in the courts where Quebec argued it had a special constitutional veto because it was the basis of the French fact in North America, the cradle of the Canadian duality. The Quebec court of appeal rejected the argument in April, basing its judgment on the Supreme Court's previous ruling. By June, the matter was back before the top court and Lévesque was already preparing his excuses and laying the groundwork for another campaign. The nine justices listened patiently for two days to what has become known as the Quebec veto case; they barely asked any questions, almost as if aware that this case was more politically potent than the last.* If he lost, Levesque said, "it's a good lesson for Quebec and it's also sort of a pointer to the future."

———————— ❧ ————————

Reflections on the Canadian Way

"It bore upon its face all the marks of compromise," Sir John A. Macdonald said of Confederation. So did the revised constitution of 1981. But this latest "accord" was first and foremost a compromise mortgaged upon the ability of future generations of Canadians to bridge the chasm between a disillusioned Quebec and the rest of Canada. Few can ignore the dismay and cynicism that swept through Quebec at its isolation, and not be worried about the future.

"It would be optimistic in the extreme to think that we can avoid a

---

*Quebec was not asking that the November accord be declared invalid, only that the court find a provincial veto exists "as a matter of convention" or moral right.

new crisis on the question of separation in a very few years," former privy council clerk Gordon Robertson, the grandfather of federal-provincial diplomacy, wrote, almost before the ink on the 5 November agreement had fully dried. The compromise reached that day gave Canada the legal means to renew its federalism but it did not achieve any of the changes sought by successive governments in Quebec, or the West, over the previous twenty years. Pierre Trudeau may have fashioned the tools to win the hearts and minds of Quebecers — a "flexible" amending formula and the entrenched language and education guarantees so French Canadians might feel more at ease outside Quebec — but he sullied the prospects for greater reconciliation in the near future with the way these tools were forged.

Precisely because of the inevitability of the result that occurred — a constitutional compact that excludes Quebec — legal scholars warned Trudeau at the outset against using constitutional reform to fight separatists. The *indépendantiste* Parti Québecois could never back away from its stated goals, could never sign an agreement to renew federalism, except on its terms. But Trudeau had his own ideas. And these took on a momentum that he could not control.

His smashing re-election in February 1980, with all but one of the seventy-five seats from Quebec, allowed him, a French-Canadian prime minister, to act as the pre-eminent spokesman for that province. He, Trudeau, would speak for Quebec if its separatist premier did not 'do the right thing' on matters constitutional.

For Trudeau, the federalist victory in the May 1980 Quebec referendum also gave him a unique, once-in-a-lifetime opportunity to prove the constitutional professors wrong, to act decisively to effect history and create a sense of accomplishment that might be generous of spirit. But for his personality, a decade of festering ill will between the federal and provincial levels of government, and the ambitions of a born-again Liberal government, it all might have been accomplished with some neatness and élan. In the spring and summer of 1980, Trudeau's two main political opponents, Conservative leader Joe Clark and Quebec premier René Lévesque, were political eunuchs, their aspirations dashed by the voters, an election defeat for Clark, the referendum loss for Lévesque. The opportunity to finesse a noble act of nation-building was there; it was not taken.

Who would have thought that Clark could have rallied his disparate party as well as he did, and swing public opinion to a different view of the propriety of Trudeau's plan? Who could have predicted Lévesque nestled in the embrace of seven English premiers, a common bonding only a few short months after the bitter referendum campaign, because they all shared, in copious amounts, the same mistrust of Trudeau's Canada? It is not that the gang of eight abandoned Lévesque at the end, it is that they included him so fully in the first place, that is one of the great mysteries and human dramas of contemporary politics.

If Trudeau had not been Trudeau — stubborn, arrogant, perverse, tactless. If his cabinet had not been so flushed with victory after the referendum win — if it had not reached for more than it could grasp by seeking to entrench contentious language rights and other constitutional protections — the nation might have been spared some trauma. But if Trudeau had not been Trudeau — determined, forceful, visionary — the process of coming of age might not have sharpened Canadians' self-awareness as it did.

----------------- ❦ -----------------

What have our leaders wrought? Uncertainties, mostly. Trudeau achieved patriation and he wrung agreement from the English premiers to embed Canada's bilingual nature in the supreme law of the land. That can be no small victory, but what meaning will it have? Will francophone Canadians now truly feel at home throughout all the country, or will they retreat further behind the walls of Quebec?*

And what about the measures that Trudeau failed to achieve? He did not obtain for the central government the powers to control the economy which he had argued were essential for the maintenance of the Canadian common market and the country's economic growth. In addition, he was unable to create the instruments that might have helped future federal governments accomplish the 'nation-building' he had envisioned. He gave up the so-called tie-breaking referendum that would have allowed Ottawa to end-run the provincial governments and involve the people directly in constitutional reform; and he agreed to an amending formula which will allow some provinces to opt out of future constitutional change — a defensive shield to fend off future power grabs and perhaps a sword to create markedly different societies from their neighbouring provinces.

Canada is now the only country in the world that makes opting out a central feature of constitutional amendment. Peter Lougheed won the formula he had been championing, but the victory may be Pyrrhic, and the formula not as pliant as its architects claim. Moreover, it is really a mechanism for tinkering with the existing system, and does not address the need for fundamental change. An Alberta premier may now be able to protect the *existing* rights and wealth of his province against any avaricious ganging up by the rest of his Confederation partners. But it is

---

*It is an interesting question. The 1981 census data shows French Quebecers migrating west in search of jobs, in a period of tough economic times and strong nationalism at home.

difficult to see how he will be able to limit the federal government's ability to encroach in the field of natural resources, which has been the goal of the various producing provinces throughout most of the 1970s.

It strains credibility to imagine a federal government bargaining these powers away. Trudeau put Ottawa's case plainly at the 1982 first ministers' conference on the economy: "We refuse to transfer powers from the federal government to the provinces unless there [is] a corresponding transfer of provincial powers to the federal government, because we believe Canadians want a strong national government." What chance there might have been for the provinces to achieve a fair portion of what they wanted at the conference table was blown away by the gang of eight. By presenting only a minimal alternative to Trudeau's plan, they failed to capture the public's imagination, and left themselves with little leverage to exert on Ottawa.*

What likelihood of future negotiated changes? In July 1981, with the constitution debate in full clamour, one of the Trudeau administration's most senior officials mused to a journalist about the odds at stake. "If we don't win," he said, "no government will have the political will to try again for years." He then went on to talk about what he thought would be the really exciting constitutional challenges ahead — what he called "phase two," such things as reform of the Senate, the Supreme Court and a number of central agencies, revision of the electoral system and some redivision of powers between the two orders of government. He thought "phase two" could begin in early 1982 — if Trudeau won.

There was, of sorts, a Trudeau victory. The Supreme Court of Canada handed him a stinging rebuke on propriety, but by then the prime minister had succeeded in narrowing the final agenda to his preferred items and was able to winkle out a compromise he could live with. But phase two — what one might call the renewed federalism that underlay the shopping lists of most of the premiers — seems as dead as Laurier's reciprocity. November 1981 came at such high political cost that it is unlikely that any government will have the will to take up the rough issues again for years to come. The provinces emerged from this round with only minor adjustments to their powers but an important symbolic win — recognition of their formal role in the amending process; equal partners, almost, with the federal Parliament. The pendulum of centralization and decentralization will continue to swing as before, but there are now new checks and balances to prevent one level of government from forcing its constitutional views on another. There can be no more

---

*In terms of new powers for the provinces, the constitution now gives them authority to make laws in the field of interprovincial trade (subject to federal paramountcy) and to levy indirect — or volume-determined — taxes on natural resource products, a manoeuvre that is severely limited by existing federal tax regimes.

constitutional bullying. In the end, perhaps, it may all have been an elaborate exercise in affirming the status quo.

Except, there is one final wild card to be considered: the charter of rights, truncated, sneered at, puréed, but still extant. Almost certainly it will introduce a new legal era, even if it makes Canada unique in having "entrenched" rights that can be overridden by a simple legislative act. But in a perverse way, the override provision may even lead to more creative and daring civil rights judgments from the courts: judges may feel a new sense of freedom, secure in the knowledge that they will not be substituting themselves for elected politicians as the final arbiters of Canadians' moral and legal standards.

So . . . nation-builders at work: eleven men who took eighteen months to strike a deal in a converted railway station and were praised by their monarch for their "good sense and tolerance". What nonsense. They were petulant, intransigent and they put their countrymen through hell. But on that rainy day in April, the Queen also called their achievement "a defiant challenge to history". That it was — even if it was done the Canadian way!

Epilogue

On Wednesday, 18 November 1981, at four-thirty in the afternoon, it was raining in Ottawa and already dark. In the ground floor theatre of the National Press Building on Wellington Street, Pierre Trudeau was winding up the first full-scale news conference he had held since signing his constitutional accord thirteen days before. The prime minister wore a grey suit with a very handsome, mostly red, silk tie that nicely complimented the rose affixed to his lapel. For thirty minutes he had been answering questions on his achievement — polite questions, as always, but many of them insistent and occasionally accusatory.

Had the accord not cost him a slice of his own principles and integrity? Had he not bartered away people's rights to make a deal, something he had said he would never do? Had he not agreed to drop the section affirming treaty and aboriginal rights for native people? Agreed to let legislatures override fundamental legal and equality rights? Accepted the prospect of a checkerboard Canada, something else he had said he would never do? Consented to different language rights for Canada and the rest of the country?

"Well, yes," said the prime minister with some candour. The override clause in the charter of rights made him sad; so did the loss of the referendum provision "so that the people's will cannot be tested". Then, replying to the last question, an icy tone chilled his voice and a half-sneer, half-smile crossed his face. "You're asking me now," he said, "if I consider it a success? No, I consider it an abject failure." He abruptly stood up and walked hurriedly outside into the rain and his waiting black limousine — leaving the riddle behind him.

Success? Or failure? However sarcastic Trudeau may have been, the question will be debated so long as the rivers flow.

Appendix

CONSTITUTION ACT, 1982

PART I

CANADIAN CHARTER OF RIGHTS AND
FREEDOMS

Whereas Canada is founded upon principles that recognize the supremacy of God and the rule of law:

Guarantee of Rights and Freedoms

Rights and
freedoms in
Canada

1. The *Canadian Charter of Rights and Freedoms* guarantees the rights and freedoms set out in it subject only to such reasonable limits prescribed by law as can be demonstrably justified in a free and democratic society.

Fundamental Freedoms

Fundamental
freedoms

2. Everyone has the following fundamental freedoms:
(*a*) freedom of conscience and religion;
(*b*) freedom of thought, belief, opinion and expression, including freedom of the press and other media of communication;
(*c*) freedom of peaceful assembly; and
(*d*) freedom of association.

Democratic Rights

Democratic
rights of
citizens

3. Every citizen of Canada has the right to vote in an election of members of the House of Commons or of a legislative assembly and to be qualified for membership therein.

Maximum
duration of
legislative
bodies

4. (1) No House of Commons and no legislative assembly shall continue for longer than five years from the date fixed for the return of the writs at a general election of its members.

Continuation in
special
circumstances

(2) In time of real or apprehended war, invasion or insurrection, a House of Commons may be continued by Parliament and a legislative assembly may be continued by the legislature beyond five years if such continuation is not opposed by the votes of more than one-third of the members of the House of Commons or the legislative assembly, as the case may be.

Annual sitting
of legislative
bodies

5. There shall be a sitting of Parliament and of each legislature at least once every twelve months.

Mobility Rights

Mobility of
citizens

6. (1) Every citizen of Canada has the right to enter, remain in and leave Canada.

Rights to move
and gain
livelihood

(2) Every citizen of Canada and every person who has the status of a permanent resident of Canada has the right
(a) to move to and take up residence in any province; and
(b) to pursue the gaining of a livelihood in any province.

Limitation

(3) The rights specified in subsection (2) are subject to
(a) any laws or practices of general application in force in a province other than those that discriminate among persons primarily on the basis of province of present or previous residence; and
(b) any laws providing for reasonable residency requirements as a qualification for the receipt of publicly provided social services.

Affirmative
action
programs

(4) Subsections (2) and (3) do not preclude any law, program or activity that has as its object the amelioration in a province of conditions of individuals in that province who are socially or economically disadvantaged if the rate of em-

ployment in that province is below the rate of employment in Canada.

Legal Rights

Life, liberty and security of person

7. Everyone has the right to life, liberty and security of the person and the right not to be deprived thereof except in accordance with the principles of fundamental justice.

Search or seizure

8. Everyone has the right to be secure against unreasonable search or seizure.

Detention or imprisonment

9. Everyone has the right not to be arbitrarily detained or imprisoned.

Arrest or detention

10. Everyone has the right on arrest or detention
(a) to be informed promptly of the reasons therefor;
(b) to retain and instruct counsel without delay and to be informed of that right; and
(c) to have the validity of the detention determined by way of *habeas corpus* and to be released if the detention is not lawful.

Proceedings in criminal and penal matters

11. Any person charged with an offence has the right
(a) to be informed without unreasonable delay of the specific offence;
(b) to be tried within a reasonable time;
(c) not to be compelled to be a witness in proceedings against that person in respect of the offence;
(d) to be presumed innocent until proven guilty according to law in a fair and public hearing by an independent and impartial tribunal;
(e) not to be denied reasonable bail without just cause;
(f) except in the case of an offence under military law tried before a military tribunal, to the benefit of trial by jury where the maximum punishment for the offence is imprisonment for five years or a more severe punishment;
(g) not to be found guilty on account of any act or omission unless, at the time of the act or omission, it constituted an offence under Canadian or international law or was criminal according to the general principles of law recognized by the community of nations;
(h) if finally acquitted of the offence, not to be tried for it again and, if finally found guilty and punished for the offence, not to be tried or punished for it again; and

(i) if found guilty of the offence and if the punishment for the offence has been varied between the time of commission and the time of sentencing, to the benefit of the lesser punishment.

Treatment or punishment

12. Everyone has the right not to be subjected to any cruel and unusual treatment or punishment.

Self-crimination

13. A witness who testifies in any proceedings has the right not to have any incriminating evidence so given used to incriminate that witness in any other proceedings, except in a prosecution for perjury or for the giving of contradictory evidence.

Interpreter

14. A party or witness in any proceedings who does not understand or speak the language in which the proceedings are conducted or who is deaf has the right to the assistance of an interpreter.

Equality Rights

Equality before and under law and equal protection and benefit of law

15. (1) Every individual is equal before and under the law and has the right to the equal protection and equal benefit of the law without discrimination and, in particular, without discrimination based on race, national or ethnic origin, colour, religion, sex, age or mental or physical disability.

Affirmative action programs

(2) Subsection (1) does not preclude any law, program or activity that has as its object the amelioration of conditions of disadvantaged individuals or groups including those that are disadvantaged because of race, national or ethnic origin, colour, religion, sex, age or mental or physical disability.

Official Languages of Canada

Official languages of Canada

16. (1) English and French are the official languages of Canada and have equality of status and equal rights and privileges as to their use in all institutions of the Parliament and government of Canada.

Official languages of New Brunswick

(2) English and French are the official languages of New Brunswick and have equality of status and equal rights and privileges as to their use in all institutions of the legislature and government of New Brunswick.

Advancement of status and use

(3) Nothing in this Charter limits the authority of Parliament or a legislature to advance the equality of status or use of English and French.

Proceedings of Parliament

17. (1) Everyone has the right to use English or French in any debates and other proceedings of Parliament.

Proceedings of New Brunswick legislature

(2) Everyone has the right to use English or French in any debates and other proceedings of the legislature of New Brunswick.

Parliamentary statutes and records

18. (1) The statutes, records and journals of Parliament shall be printed and published in English and French and both language versions are equally authoritative.

New Brunswick statutes and records

(2) The statutes, records and journals of the legislature of New Brunswick shall be printed and published in English and French and both language versions are equally authoritative.

Proceedings in courts established by Parliament

19. (1) Either English or French may be used by any person in, or in any pleading in or process issuing from, any court established by Parliament.

Proceedings in New Brunswick courts

(2) Either English or French may be used by any person in, or in any pleading in or process issuing from, any court of New Brunswick.

Communications by public with federal institutions

20. (1) Any member of the public in Canada has the right to communicate with, and to receive available services from, any head or central office of an institution of the Parliament or government of Canada in English or French, and has the same right with respect to any other office of any such institution where

(a) there is a significant demand for communications with and services from that office in such language; or
(b) due to the nature of the office, it is reasonable that communications with and services from that office be available in both English and French.

Communications by public with New Brunswick institutions

(2) Any member of the public in New Brunswick has the right to communicate with, and to receive available services from, any office of an institution of the legislature or government of New Brunswick in English or French.

Continuation of existing constitutional provisions

21. Nothing in sections 16 to 20 abrogates or derogates from any right, privilege or obligation with respect to the English and French languages, or either of them, that exists or is continued by virtue of any other provision of the Constitution of Canada.

Rights and privileges preserved

22. Nothing in sections 16 to 20 abrogates or derogates from any legal or customary right or privilege acquired or enjoyed either before or after the coming into force of this Charter with respect to any language that is not English or French.

Minority Language Educational Rights

Language of instruction

23. (1) Citizens of Canada
(a) whose first language learned and still understood is that of the English or French linguistic minority population of the province in which they reside, or
(b) who have received their primary school instruction in Canada in English or French and reside in a province where the language in which they received that instruction is the language of the English or French linguistic minority population of the province,
have the right to have their children receive primary and secondary school instruction in that language in that province.

Continuity of language instruction

(2) Citizens of Canada of whom any child has received or is receiving primary or secondary school instruction in English or French in Canada, have the right to have all their children receive primary and secondary school instruction in the same language.

Application where numbers warrant

(3) The right of citizens of Canada under subsections (1) and (2) to have their children receive primary and secondary school instruction in the language of the English or French linguistic minority population of a province
(a) applies wherever in the province the number of children of citizens who have such a right is sufficient to warrant the provision to them out of public funds of minority language instruction; and
(b) includes, where the number of those children so warrants, the right to have them receive that instruction in minority language educational facilities provided out of public funds.

Enforcement

Enforcement of guaranteed rights and freedoms

24. (1) Anyone whose rights or freedoms, as guaranteed by this Charter, have been infringed or denied may apply to a court of competent jurisdiction to obtain such remedy as the court considers appropriate and just in the circumstances.

Exclusion of evidence bringing administration of justice into disrepute

(2) Where, in proceedings under subsection (1), a court concludes that evidence was obtained in a manner that infringed or denied any rights or freedoms guaranteed by this Charter, the evidence shall be excluded if it is established that, having regard to all the circumstances, the admission of it in the proceedings would bring the administration of justice into disrepute.

General

Aboriginal rights and freedoms not affected by Charter

25. The guarantee in this Charter of certain rights and freedoms shall not be construed so as to abrogate or derogate from any aboriginal, treaty or other rights or freedoms that pertain to the aboriginal peoples of Canada including
   (a) any rights or freedoms that have been recognized by the Royal Proclamation of October 7, 1763; and
   (b) any rights or freedoms that may be acquired by the aboriginal peoples of Canada by way of land claims settlement.

Other rights and freedoms not affected by Charter

26. The guarantee in this Charter of certain rights and freedoms shall not be construed as denying the existence of any other rights or freedoms that exist in Canada.

Multicultural heritage

27. This Charter shall be interpreted in a manner consistent with the preservation and enhancement of the multicultural heritage of Canadians.

Rights guaranteed equally to both sexes

28. Notwithstanding anything in this Charter, the rights and freedoms referred to in it are guaranteed equally to male and female persons.

Rights respecting certain schools preserved

29. Nothing in this Charter abrogates or derogates from any rights or privileges guaranteed by or under the Constitution of Canada in respect of denominational, separate or dissentient schools.

Application to
territories and
territorial
authorities

30. A reference in this Charter to a province or to the legislative assembly or legislature of a province shall be deemed to include a reference to the Yukon Territory and the Northwest Territories, or to the appropriate legislative authority thereof, as the case may be.

Legislative
powers not
extended

31. Nothing in this Charter extends the legislative powers of any body or authority.

Application of Charter

Application of
Charter

32. (1) This Charter applies

(a) to the Parliament and government of Canada in respect of all matters within the authority of Parliament including all matters relating to the Yukon Territory and Northwest Territories; and

(b) to the legislature and government of each province in respect of all matters within the authority of the legislature of each province.

Exception

(2) Notwithstanding subsection (1), section 15 shall not have effect until three years after this section comes into force.

Exception
where express
declaration

33. (1) Parliament or the legislature of a province may expressly declare in an Act of Parliament or of the legislature, as the case may be, that the Act or a provision thereof shall operate notwithstanding a provision included in section 2 or sections 7 to 15 of this Charter.

Operation of
exception

(2) An Act or a provision of an Act in respect of which a declaration made under this section is in effect shall have such operation as it would have but for the provision of this Charter referred to in the declaration.

Five year
limitation

(3) A declaration made under subsection (1) shall cease to have effect five years after it comes into force or on such earlier date as may be specified in the declaration.

Re-enactment

(4) Parliament or a legislature of a province may re-enact a declaration made under subsection (1).

Five year
limitation

(5) Subsection (3) applies in respect of a re-enactment made under subsection (4).

Citation

Citation   **34.** This Part may be cited as the *Canadian Charter of Rights and Freedoms.*

PART II

RIGHTS OF THE ABORIGINAL PEOPLES OF CANADA

Recognition of existing aboriginal and treaty rights   **35.** (1) The existing aboriginal and treaty rights of the aboriginal peoples of Canada are hereby recognized and affirmed.

Definition of "aboriginal peoples of Canada"   (2) In this Act, "aboriginal peoples of Canada" includes the Indian, Inuit and Métis peoples of Canada.

PART III

EQUALIZATION AND REGIONAL DISPARITIES

Commitment to promote equal opportunities   **36.** (1) Without altering the legislative authority of Parliament or of the provincial legislatures, or the rights of any of them with respect to the exercise of their legislative authority, Parliament and the legislatures, together with the government of Canada and the provincial governments, are committed to

(a) promoting equal opportunities for the well-being of Canadians;

(b) furthering economic development to reduce disparity in opportunities; and

(c) providing essential public services of reasonable quality to all Canadians.

Commitment respecting public services   (2) Parliament and the government of Canada are committed to the principle of making equalization payments to ensure that provincial governments have sufficient revenues to provide reasonably comparable levels of public services at reasonably comparable levels of taxation.

PART IV

CONSTITUTIONAL CONFERENCE

Constitutional conference   **37.** (1) A constitutional conference composed of the Prime Minister of Canada and the first ministers of the provinces shall be convened by the Prime Minister of Canada within one year after this Part comes into force.

Participation of
aboriginal
peoples

(2) The conference convened under subsection (1) shall have included in its agenda an item respecting constitutional matters that directly affect the aboriginal peoples of Canada, including the identification and definition of the rights of those peoples to be included in the Constitution of Canada, and the Prime Minister of Canada shall invite representatives of those peoples to participate in the discussions on that item.

Participation of
territories

(3) The Prime Minister of Canada shall invite elected representatives of the governments of the Yukon Territory and the Northwest Territories to participate in the discussions on any item on the agenda of the conference convened under subsection (1) that, in the opinion of the Prime Minister, directly affects the Yukon Territory and the Northwest Territories.

PART V

PROCEDURE FOR AMENDING
CONSTITUTION OF CANADA

General
procedure for
amending
Constitution of
Canada

38. (1) An amendment to the Constitution of Canada may be made by proclamation issued by the Governor General under the Great Seal of Canada where so authorized by
(a) resolutions of the Senate and House of Commons; and
(b) resolutions of the legislative assemblies of at least two-thirds of the provinces that have, in the aggregate, according to the then latest general census, at least fifty per cent of the population of all the provinces.

Majority of
members

(2) An amendment made under subsection (1) that derogates from the legislative powers, the proprietary rights or any other rights or privileges of the legislature or government of a province shall require a resolution supported by a majority of the members of each of the Senate, the House of Commons and the legislative assemblies required under subsection (1).

Expression of
dissent

(3) An amendment referred to in subsection (2) shall not have effect in a province the legislative assembly of which has expressed its dissent thereto by resolution supported by a majority of its members prior to the issue of the

proclamation to which the amendment relates unless that legislative assembly, subsequently, by resolution supported by a majority of its members, revokes its dissent and authorizes the amendment.

Revocation of dissent

(4) A resolution of dissent made for the purposes of subsection (3) may be revoked at any time before or after the issue of the proclamation to which it relates.

Restriction on proclamation

39. (1) A proclamation shall not be issued under subsection 38(1) before the expiration of one year from the adoption of the resolution initiating the amendment procedure thereunder, unless the legislative assembly of each province has previously adopted a resolution of assent or dissent.

Idem

(2) A proclamation shall not be issued under subsection 38(1) after the expiration of three years from the adoption of the resolution initiating the amendment procedure thereunder.

Compensation

40. Where an amendment is made under subsection 38(1) that transfers provincial legislative powers relating to education or other cultural matters from provincial legislatures to Parliament, Canada shall provide reasonable compensation to any province to which the amendment does not apply.

Amendment by unanimous consent

41. An amendment to the Constitution of Canada in relation to the following matters may be made by proclamation issued by the Governor General under the Great Seal of Canada only where authorized by resolutions of the Senate and House of Commons and of the legislative assembly of each province:

(*a*) the office of the Queen, the Governor General and the Lieutenant Governor of a province;

(*b*) the right of a province to a number of members in the House of Commons not less than the number of Senators by which the province is entitled to be represented at the time this Part comes into force;

(*c*) subject to section 43, the use of the English or the French language;

(*d*) the composition of the Supreme Court of Canada; and

(*e*) an amendment to this Part.

42. (1) An amendment to the Constitution of Canada in relation to the following matters may be made only in accordance with subsection 38(1):

(*a*) the principle of proportionate representation of the provinces in the House of Commons prescribed by the Constitution of Canada;

(*b*) the powers of the Senate and the method of selecting Senators;

(*c*) the number of members by which a province is entitled to be represented in the Senate and the residence qualifications of Senators;

(*d*) subject to paragraph 41(*d*), the Supreme Court of Canada;

(*e*) the extension of existing provinces into the territories; and

(*f*) notwithstanding any other law or practice, the establishment of new provinces.

(2) Subsections 38(2) to (4) do not apply in respect of amendments in relation to matters referred to in subsection (1).

Amendment of
provisions
relating to some
but not all
provinces
43. An amendment to the Constitution of Canada in relation to any provision that applies to one or more, but not all, provinces, including

(*a*) any alteration to boundaries between provinces, and

(*b*) any amendment to any provision that relates to the use of the English or the French language within a province,

may be made by proclamation issued by the Governor General under the Great Seal of Canada only where so authorized by resolutions of the Senate and House of Commons and of the legislative assembly of each province to which the amendment applies.

44. Subject to sections 41 and 42, Parliament may exclusively make laws amending the Constitution of Canada in relation to the executive government of Canada or the Senate and House of Commons.

45. Subject to section 41, the legislature of each province may exclusively make laws amending the constitution of the province.

Initiation of amendment procedures

46. (1) The procedures for amendment under sections 38, 41, 42 and 43 may be initiated either by the Senate or the House of Commons or by the legislative assembly of a province.

Revocation of authorization

(2) A resolution of assent made for the purposes of this Part may be revoked at any time before the issue of a proclamation authorized by it.

Amendments without Senate resolution

47. (1) An amendment to the Constitution of Canada made by proclamation under section 38, 41, 42 or 43 may be made without a resolution of the Senate authorizing the issue of the proclamation if, within one hundred and eighty days after the adoption by the House of Commons of a resolution authorizing its issue, the Senate has not adopted such a resolution and if, at any time after the expiration of that period, the House of Commons again adopts the resolution.

Computation of period

(2) Any period when Parliament is prorogued or dissolved shall not be counted in computing the one hundred and eighty day period referred to in subsection (1).

Advice to issue proclamation

48. The Queen's Privy Council for Canada shall advise the Governor General to issue a proclamation under this Part forthwith on the adoption of the resolutions required for an amendment made by proclamation under this Part.

Constitutional conference

49. A constitutional conference composed of the Prime Minister of Canada and the first ministers of the provinces shall be convened by the Prime Minister of Canada within fifteen years after this Part comes into force to review the provisions of this Part.

PART VI

AMENDMENT TO THE CONSTITUTION ACT,
1867

Amendment to Constitution Act, 1867

50. The *Constitution Act, 1867* (formerly named the *British North America Act, 1867*) is amended by adding thereto, immediately after section 92 thereof, the following heading and section:

"Non-Renewable Natural Resources,
Forestry Resources and Electrical Energy

Laws respecting non-renewable natural resources, forestry resources and electrical energy

92A. (1) In each province, the legislature may exclusively make laws in relation to

(a) exploration for non-renewable natural resources in the province;

(b) development, conservation and management of non-renewable natural resources and forestry resources in the province, including laws in relation to the rate of primary production therefrom; and

(c) development, conservation and management of sites and facilities in the province for the generation and production of electrical energy.

Export from provinces of resources

(2) In each province, the legislature may make laws in relation to the export from the province to another part of Canada of the primary production from non-renewable natural resources and forestry resources in the province and the production from facilities in the province for the generation of electrical energy, but such laws may not authorize or provide for discrimination in prices or in supplies exported to another part of Canada.

Authority of Parliament

(3) Nothing in subsection (2) derogates from the authority of Parliament to enact laws in relation to the matters referred to in that subsection and, where such a law of Parliament and a law of a province conflict, the law of Parliament prevails to the extent of the conflict.

Taxation of resources

(4) In each province, the legislature may make laws in relation to the raising of money by any mode or system of taxation in respect of

(a) non-renewable natural resources and forestry resources in the province and the primary production therefrom, and

(b) sites and facilities in the province for the generation of electrical energy and the production therefrom,

whether or not such production is exported in whole or in part from the province, but such laws may not authorize or provide for taxation that differentiates between production exported to another part of Canada and production not exported from the province.

"Primary production"

(5) The expression "primary production" has the meaning assigned by the Sixth Schedule.

Existing powers
or rights

(6) Nothing in subsections (1) to (5) derogates from any powers or rights that a legislature or government of a province had immediately before the coming into force of this section."

Idem

51. The said Act is further amended by adding thereto the following Schedule:

"THE SIXTH SCHEDULE

Primary Production from Non-Renewable Natural Resources and Forestry Resources

1. For the purposes of section 92A of this Act,
(a) production from a non-renewable natural resource is primary production therefrom if
    (i) it is in the form in which it exists upon its recovery or severance from its natural state, or
    (ii) it is a product resulting from processing or refining the resource, and is not a manufactured product or a product resulting from refining crude oil, refining upgraded heavy crude oil, refining gases or liquids derived from coal or refining a synthetic equivalent of crude oil; and
(b) production from a forestry resource is primary production therefrom it if consists of sawlogs, poles, lumber, wood chips, sawdust or any other primary wood product, or wood pulp, and is not a product manufactured from wood."

PART VII

GENERAL

Primacy of
Constitution of
Canada

52. (1) The Constitution of Canada is the supreme law of Canada, and any law that is inconsistent with the provisions of the Constitution is, to the extent of the inconsistency, of no force or effect.

Constitution of
Canada

(2) The Constitution of Canada includes
(a) the *Canada Act*, including this Act;
(b) the Acts and orders referred to in Schedule I; and
(c) any amendment to any Act or order referred to in paragraph (a) or (b).

Amendments to
Constitution of
Canada

(3) Amendments to the Constitution of Canada shall be made only in accordance with the authority contained in the Constitution of Canada.

Repeals and
new names

53. (1) The enactments referred to in Column I of Schedule I are hereby repealed or amended to the extent indicated in Column II thereof and, unless repealed, shall continue as law in Canada under the names set out in Column III thereof.

Consequential
amendments

(2) Every enactment, except the *Canada Act*, that refers to an enactment referred to in Schedule I by the name in Column I thereof is hereby amended by substituting for that name the corresponding name in Column III thereof, and any British North America Act not referred to in Schedule I may be cited as the *Constitution Act* followed by the year and number, if any, of its enactment.

Repeal and
consequential
amendments

54. Part IV is repealed on the day that is one year after this Part comes into force and this section may be repealed and this Act renumbered, consequential upon the repeal of Part IV and this section, by proclamation issued by the Governor General under the Great Seal of Canada.

French version
of Constitution
of Canada

55. A French version of the portions of the Constitution of Canada referred to in Schedule I shall be prepared by the Minister of Justice of Canada as expeditiously as possible and, when any portion thereof sufficient to warrant action being taken has been so prepared, it shall be put forward for enactment by proclamation issued by the Governor General under the Great Seal of Canada pursuant to the procedure then applicable to an amendment of the same provisions of the Constitution of Canada.

English and
French versions
of certain
constitutional
texts

56. Where any portion of the Constitution of Canada has been or is enacted in English and French or where a French version of any portion of the Constitution is enacted pursuant to section 55, the English and French versions of that portion of the Constitution are equally authoritative.

English and
French versions
of this Act

57. The English and French versions of this Act are equally authoritative.

Commence-
ment

58. Subject to section 59, this Act shall come into force on a day to be fixed by proclamation issued by the Queen or the Governor General under the Great Seal of Canada.

Commence-
ment of
paragraph
23(1)(a) in
respect of
Quebec

59. (1) Paragraph 23(1)*(a)* shall come into force in respect of Quebec on a day to be fixed by proclamation issued by the Queen or the Governor General under the Great Seal of Canada.

Authorization
of Quebec

(2) A proclamation under subsection (1) shall be issued only where authorized by the legislative assembly or government of Quebec.

Repeal of this
section

(3) This section may be repealed on the day paragraph 23(1)*(a)* comes into force in respect of Quebec and this Act amended and renumbered, consequential upon the repeal of this section, by proclamation issued by the Queen or the Governor General under the Great Seal of Canada.

Short title and
citations

60. This Act may be cited as the *Constitution Act, 1982*, and the Constitution Acts 1867 to 1975 (No. 2), and this Act may be cited together as the *Constitution Acts, 1867 to 1982.*

Chronology

1980

18 February   A majority Liberal government is elected under prime minister Pierre Trudeau, with 74 of the 75 seats from Quebec, and none west of Manitoba. The Quebec National Assembly is in the midst of a three-week debate on the referendum question over sovereignty-association.

3 March   The new cabinet is sworn in; Jean Chrétien is made justice minister with responsibility for constitutional reform.

15 April   In response to the Speech from the Throne, Trudeau warns of "the enemy within" and argues convincingly that acceptance of the sovereignty-association position by Quebecers would only lead to a legal and political impasse. Later that day, Quebec premier René Lévesque announces the date of the long-awaited referendum, 20 May.

29 April   Trudeau addresses the national conference of Indian chiefs and elders and asks for their support in building a new country together.

2 May   The first of three speeches Trudeau gives in Quebec during the referendum campaign, to the Montreal chamber of commerce; others follow on 7 and 14 May, in Quebec City and at the Paul Sauvé arena in east-end Montreal.

11 May   Lévesque says Trudeau is "naturally" for the No side in the referendum because his middle name is Elliott and he is following the Anglo-Saxon side of his character.

20 May   Referendum day; Quebecers vote down the sovereignty-association mandate requested by the ruling Parti Québecois by a margin of approximately 60 to 40 per cent, a majority even among French-speaking residents.

21 May Trudeau, Chrétien and a handful of senior federal officials decide to test the waters for constitutional reform; Chrétien sets off on a whirlwind cross-country tour of all provincial capitals except Quebec, where the Lévesque government is still recovering from the referendum loss.

9 June The ten premiers meet all day with Trudeau at 24 Sussex Drive and agree on a twelve-point agenda, which their constitutional ministers will study all summer in a series of meetings, and report to a full-scale first ministers' conference in September.

25 June Trudeau meets British prime minister Margaret Thatcher at 10 Downing Street and briefs her somewhat on his constitutional plans, receiving in return a cautious endorsement.

7 July The constitutional "roadshow" of federal and provincial ministers begins in Montreal, where the federal government sets out a major new demand for more central powers over the economy if it is to devolve others to the provinces. The roadshow continues for twenty-eight days, spending a week each in Toronto, Vancouver and Ottawa.

20 August The provincial premiers gather for their annual meeting, this year in Winnipeg, on the same day that a leaked memorandum appears from Michael Pitfield, clerk of the privy council, to the prime minister, setting out a fall timetable for a unilateral resolution to patriate the constitution, assuming no provincial agreement.

30 August The federal cabinet committee on priorities and planning, effectively the inner cabinet, meets at Lake Louise, Alberta. On their three-day agenda is the so-called Kirby memorandum (named after Michael Kirby, secretary to the cabinet for federal-provincial relations), which sets out the government's conference strategy and other options.

7 September The first ministers meet Sunday evening for a disastrous pre-conference dinner under the auspices of governor general Edward Schreyer in the dining room of the Lester B. Pearson building of external affairs. Later that evening, Lévesque quietly distributes leaked copies of the Kirby memorandum to his fellow premiers.

8 September The formal public conference begins before the television cameras at the government of Canada conference centre on Wellington Street in Ottawa.

9 September The Kirby memorandum appears in the *Toronto Star*, leaked by New Brunswick premier Richard Hatfield; portions of it are also announced that morning on CBC radio and in *La Presse*.

12 September After four days in public, the conference adjourns to 24 Sussex Drive for a full day of closed-door bargaining that goes on to about nine-thirty that night — without success.

13 September The eleven first ministers reconvene before the television cameras to tell the country they have not been able to agree on any of the agenda items. Trudeau talks ominously about the two competing "visions" of the country and says he will have to consult with his cabinet about his next move.

17 September Liberal MPs are called to Ottawa for a special meeting. National Liberal caucus chairman Jacques Guilbault tells the press afterwards that the MPs are "very bullish . . . I think they're ready to go to war."

18 September The first full cabinet meeting agrees in principle to press forward unilaterally on patriation, an amending formula and a charter of rights but leaves open the question of whether the charter will be binding on the provinces. There are two more full meetings and a number of smaller committees over the next two weeks while the charter of rights and the amending formula procedures are developed.

2 October The final cabinet meeting decides to extend the full charter, including the so-called new rights of non-discrimination, to provincial jurisdictions. The resolution is sent back to the printer for revisions and the prime minister goes on national television that night to announce his government's plans. Conservative leader Joe Clark strongly denounces the scheme and commits his party to fighting it; NDP leader Edward Broadbent indicates his party's general support; and Ontario premier William Davis endorses it fulsomely, to the point that he encourages federal Conservatives to break with their party leader on the issue.

6 October Debate begins in Parliament on the resolution. External affairs minister Mark MacGuigan, back with environment minister John Roberts from London, where they explained the government's plans to the Queen, prime minister Thatcher and Labour leader James Callaghan, states the British government's only concern is to get the resolution as quickly as possible for approval by Westminster.

14 October The ten premiers meet at the Toronto Hilton Harbour Castle Hotel in Toronto for discussions. Five of them, British Columbia's William Bennett, Alberta's Peter Lougheed, Manitoba's Sterling Lyon, Quebec's René Lévesque and Newfoundland's Brian Peckford, announce they will fight the resolution in the courts. Davis, Hatfield and Allan Blakeney of Saskatchewan reject that plan; Angus MacLean of Prince Edward Island and John Buchanan of Nova Scotia say they will have to consult their cabinets.

15 October   Hatfield meets Trudeau in Ottawa and offers his support; the prime minister observes that he admires "the elegance" of the New Brunswick premier's decision. Two days later Hatfield announces his support publicly and questions the wisdom of the court challenges by the other provincial governments.

21 October   Trudeau writes to Broadbent, agreeing to make three resource-related additions to the resolution, thereby winning federal NDP support.

23 October   After a private meeting in Winnipeg, the dissident provinces announce their specific plans to challenge the resolution in the courts of Manitoba, Newfoundland and Quebec.

24 October   The Liberals apply closure in the Commons to cut off debate and move the constitution resolution into committee.

6 November   The special joint parliamentary committee on the constitution formally begins but is bogged down for days on a number of procedural wrangles.

13 November   Bowing to opposition pressure, the government agrees to televise the proceedings of the special committee, making it the first committee of the House to be broadcast in its entirety.

2 December   Giving in to opposition pressure again, the government extends the life of the committee by two months to 6 February.

4 December   Hatfield appears before the committee and requests that New Brunswick's official languages act be entrenched in the constitution. Oral arguments begin in the Supreme Court of Manitoba.

7 December   A crowd estimated at 14,000 gathers in Montreal to hear premier Lévesque denounce the Trudeau resolution as a *coup d'état*.

9 December   A Gallup poll indicates that 58 per cent of Canadians disapprove of the federal government's plans to patriate without substantial provincial consent. In London, Thatcher tells the British Commons that her government would deal with the request "expeditiously and in accordance with precedence."

1981

12 January   Responding to the concerns of a number of groups, Chrétien effectively rewrites large parts of the charter of rights, strengthening its provisions and increasing the powers being given the courts.

20 January   The Conservatives bring in their own amendments but say the charter should not be entrenched until the provinces approve it through a new amending formula.

23 January Energy minister Marc Lalonde and senior federal officials begin secret talks in Toronto with Saskatchewan minister Roy Romanow and top constitutional officials from that province, seeking to win their support with better resource arrangements.

25–27 January These talks continue in Hawaii where premier Blakeney is vacationing, but eventually break down in a long-distance telephone call between Blakeney and Trudeau; the federal government is represented by senior justice official Fred Gibson.

28 January Chrétien introduces more amendments to protect the rights of mentally and physically disabled people.

29 January The select committee of the British Parliament, chaired by Sir Anthony Kershaw, recommends that Westminster reject the Canadian request because it lacks sufficient provincial support.

30 January Faced with a revolt in the ranks of the federal NDP, the government's main parliamentary ally, Chrétien accedes to a further amendment affirming aboriginal rights and recognizing the Métis as an aboriginal people. The government also begins to come under fire for not telling the full story about the support offered by the Thatcher government, as a number of leaked memos and diplomatic cables surface.

3 February The Manitoba court rules three-two in favour of the federal government.

5 February MacGuigan says external affairs is investigating allegations that British high commissioner Sir John Ford acted improperly in trying to influence two New Democrats and others to oppose Ottawa's constitutional plans.

10 February Oral arguments begin in the Supreme Court of Newfoundland.

13 February The special joint committee reports back to Parliament, having made sixty-five amendments to the charter; final debate begins four days later.

18 February Four New Democrat MPs from Saskatchewan announce they will oppose the resolution because it lacks sufficient provincial consent.

19 February Blakeney announces that his government has no other choice but to oppose the measure.

9 March Oral arguments begin in the Quebec Superior Court of Appeal.

11 March The Conservatives still trail by five points, but a Gallup poll indicates that the Liberals' long honeymoon is ending as the Tories make gains at the expense of the NDP, which drops four points in voter esteem.

19 March   The Ontario Tories are re-elected with a majority government; in Ottawa, the federal government introduces a form of closure in Parliament to end the long constitutional debate.

23 March   Trudeau formally enters the constitutional debate for the first time, speaking for over two hours in a compelling performance in the House of Commons.

24 March   The Conservatives begin to stall business in the Commons in an attempt to derail the constitutional proposal, a 'filibuster' that lasts over two weeks.

31 March   In an unanimous decision, the Newfoundland court says the Trudeau resolution is illegal, setting off a *volte-face* in government policy and a series of extraordinary public negotiating sessions on the floor of the Commons.

8 April   The three federal parties strike a deal to end the Conservatives' delaying tactics and put off a final vote on the resolution until after the ruling of the Supreme Court of Canada.

13 April   The Parti Québecois is re-elected in Quebec with a sizeable majority.

15 April   The Quebec Supreme Court of Appeal rules four to one in favour of the federal government, even as the eight dissident premiers gather in Ottawa to sign an alternative accord for simple patriation with the so-called Alberta amending formula and no charter of rights.

16 April   Premiers of eight provinces — B.C., Alberta, Saskatchewan, Manitoba, Quebec, Nova Scotia, PEI and Newfoundland — sign their own "April accord" before the television cameras at the conference centre. It is promptly rejected by Trudeau and his two allies, Davis and Hatfield.

28 April   The Supreme Court of Canada begins hearing five days of oral arguments on the constitution case.

2–5 July   NDP national convention in Vancouver.

11–13 August   Annual premiers' conference in Victoria; Bill Bennett assumes chairmanship of premiers' group.

24 September   Trudeau and Bennett meet privately in the sunroom at 24 Sussex Drive.

28 September   Supreme Court renders judgment on constitution case, finding (seven to two) that Trudeau's plan is legal but (six to three) contrary to convention and offensive to the federal spirit.

5 October   Trudeau meets privately with British prime minister Thatcher in Melbourne at the Commonwealth heads of government conference.

13 October Trudeau and Bennett meet a second time at 24 Sussex Drive; then the B.C. premier sets out on a cross-country jaunt to sample the mood of his fellow premiers.

18 October All ten premiers gather at Montreal's Ritz-Carlton Hotel; after a few hours, the two federal government allies are asked to leave and the gang of eight continues meeting for that and part of the next day.

27 October The ministers of the gang of eight have their final strategy meeting at Toronto's Harbour Castle Hotel, one week before the "one last time" conference is to begin.

2 November The final constitutional conference begins before the television cameras with fifteen-minute opening statements; after lunch the eleven first ministers adjourn to a private meeting room on the fifth floor of the government of Canada conference centre.

4 November The so-called night of the long knives, when the officials of four provinces sit together, on their premiers' instructions, to hammer out a compromise, eventually communicating this to all provinces that night except Quebec.

5 November Trudeau and the premiers of the nine English provinces sign an agreement for renewed federalism and end nearly eighteen months of rancorous debate. "The Canadian way," Lévesque says, means leaving his province alone in the crunch.

2 December The resolution, with some extra clauses added as a result of national lobbying campaigns by women's organizations and native groups, passes the House of Commons; twenty-four MPs from all three parties oppose.

8 December The joint resolution passes the Senate by a vote of 59–23.

1982

14 January Thatcher turns down Lévesque's request to delay proceedings until the courts have ruled on a Quebec veto.

28 January British judges reject Indian claims against the patriation resolution.

8 March The bill is passed by the British House of Commons.

25 March The bill is passed by the House of Lords.

29 March Royal assent is given to Canada Act, the fifth and last time the British Parliament has legislated a constitution for what became Canada.

17 April   Queen Elizabeth II proclaims the new constitution in a rain-splattered ceremony before a crowd of about 30,000 on Parliament Hill in Ottawa; René Lévesque leads a protest crowd of about the same number through the streets of Montreal. Canada is now a fully sovereign nation in all respects.

Glossary of Terms

Amending formula   The elusive mechanism for changing the constitution which has bedeviled Canadian politicians since at least 1927. At that time Britain declared it was formally cutting loose its white colonies, finally doing so in 1931 with the Statute of Westminster. There are essentially three types of constitutional amendment: those that can be made by Parliament acting alone; those that can be made by provincial legislatures acting alone; and all others.

Amending formula ("accord")   Known also as the Vancouver consensus or the Alberta formula, it contains five amending mechanisms: changes to Parliament require only consent; similarly with changes affecting only provincial legislatures (such as whether to establish a provincial upper house); changes affecting some but not all provinces can be effected through bilateral arrangements with Ottawa; changes to the monarchy, central institutions such as the Supreme Court of Canada or the status of Canada's official languages require unanimous consent of all eleven governments; and all others.

   This last broad category is where the main formula takes effect. Changes require resolutions in Parliament and the legislatures of two-thirds of the provinces (seven), representing fifty per cent of the population. As many as three provinces can opt out of any change that derogates from existing powers or proprietary rights.

Bill 101   The charter of the French language, as the Lévesque government calls it, was passed in 1977, the Parti Québecois' first major act after taking office. It makes French the official language of the province and establishes a language board to ensure that business and other institutions comply with its edicts. In the field of education it guarantees the right to English schools only to children of parents who were themselves

348

educated in English in Quebec (the so-called Quebec clause) or who had a sibling already in the English system when the charter was passed.

British North America Act, 1867   The BNA Act is a statute of the British Parliament uniting the former colonies of Upper and Lower Canada, Nova Scotia and New Brunswick in a federal union. It has been amended twenty-three times.

Canada Act   Is the name the constitutional resolution (including the Constitution Act) was given before the British Parliament.

Constitution   The system of fundamental principles on which a nation (or club) is governed. In Canada's case this generally refers to the British North America Act of 1867 but also includes a number of other British statutes and orders-in-council (such as those admitting provinces and territories to the federation), chunks of British and Canadian common law, provincial acts of a fundamental nature and, now, royal proclamations and native treaties.

Constitution Act 1982   The result of two years of wrangling, consolidates the BNA Act and all the other statutes and incorporates some new changes, notably the charter of rights and freedoms and an amending formula.

Constitutional convention   A legalism that the Supreme Court of Canada has now made part of the political vernacular. Essentially the unwritten rules on which the constitution is based, the court presented them as something of a moral code — the flip side of constitutional law — but said that while it could discuss conventions, it could not enforce them.

Distribution of powers   Under the BNA Act, the two levels of government are given separate responsibilities, which often tend to overlap.

Section 91 outlines the broad areas of responsibility given the federal Parliament and also empowers it to legislate in areas not specifically given the provinces, which is known as the federal government's residual powers, the authority by which it claims to control the entire field of communications, for example.

Ottawa also has the power of disallowance (now considered largely vestigial), by which it can set aside provincial legislation within a year of passage, broad emergency powers for "peace, order and good government" as well as what is called the declaratory power to declare a work (usually a bridge) or resource (uranium during the war) in the national interest, what the western resource provinces in particular want to eliminate or reduce.

Section 92 lists the powers given the provinces such as education, health and civil rights, originally intended to encompass those areas that were considered local in nature.

Duality   An old concept that became popular in certain intellectual quarters in the 1960s — part of the deux nations notion that the federal Conservatives flirted with and then dropped — it would give a basic right of cultural and political self-expression to the two founding peoples, English and French, and imbed permanently guaranteed representation in central institutions. It is this concept the Lévesque government used to argue a second time before the Supreme Court for a special Quebec veto (albeit only in the conventional sense) as the representative homeland of French Canada.

Economic union   The PQ uses this term to define its economic association with Canada; the federal government introduced it during this latest round to mean breaking down interprovincial trade barriers (protectionism by provinces) and provide for a more rational common market (managed by Ottawa, of course).

Entrenchment   Means to incorporate in the constitution some new right or power that becomes part of the basic law of the land and is beyond the authority of one legislative tier to change unilaterally.

Equalization   The principle of transferring funds from rich to poorer provinces so a basic standard of living is enjoyed by all. In one way or another part of Canada since Confederation, the modern-day practice began in 1957 with unconditional transfers to poorer provinces.

Fiscal compensation   Quebec argues that a province that opts out of future changes should not be penalized by double taxation, that is having its taxpayers contribute to a national scheme that the province does not want to be part of. However, Ottawa rejected the proposal to pay a province not participating in any new national scheme because it felt this was an incentive to thwart a common will. In the end it relented somewhat and now will compensate any province that relinquishes some of its authority to the national government for common programs in the fields of education and culture.

Fulton-Favreau formula   Developed between 1960 and 1964 by Conservative justice minister E. Davie Fulton and his Liberal successor Guy Favreau, it was nearly agreed to in 1964 and then rejected at the last in early 1966 by Quebec premier Jean Lesage, who felt it was too rigid. It too created a number of categories but the basic formula was the predecessor of the accord formula — Parliament and two-thirds of the provinces representing fifty per cent of the population. There was no opting out.

Indirect taxation A new taxing power given the provinces this time around, it applies only to resources. Provinces have traditionally only been able to raise revenues through royalties or sales tax (which is considered a direct tax); they are now able to apply indirect or bulk taxes at the production or wholesale levels, a power that may only be useful in booming economies. In 1979, Ottawa was prepared to accept a broader application of this power to areas other than resources, subject to certain conditions.

Joint address While the history of constitutional amendment in Canada does not clearly state whether provincial consent (unanimous or otherwise) is required for change, the technical way of carrying this out has been a joint address, a formal request to the Queen from the Senate and House of Commons. This was the "old colonial machinery" that Trudeau was cranking up for the last time with or without provincial approval.

Minority language education rights Now entrenched, is the right to education in either official language "where numbers warrant," a phrase that may be ultimately interpreted by the courts if provincial governments do not live up to their obligations. These now apply to nine provinces on the basis of a resident (a) being able to demonstrate that his "mother tongue" is either English or French, or (b) that his parent, a Canadian citizen, was educated in either language somewhere in Canada, the so-called Canada clause. It is this latter that applies now to Quebec (although the Lévesque government is trying to limit its reach) and that province can adopt the broader mother tongue clause at some future date.

Official or institutional bilingualism Section 133 of the BNA Act says English and French are official languages and can be used in the courts and legislature of Quebec. Section 23 of the Manitoba Act of 1870 (its terms of union) provides for the same but historically has been ignored. When the Lévesque government tried to make French the official language of the legislature (part of Bill 101), it was found unconstitutional by the Supreme Court of Canada.

The Constitution Act 1982 extends official bilingualism to New Brunswick. And Ottawa has done the same for the federal government and its agencies, effectively entrenching the 1969 Official Language Act.

Offshore resources   Essentially the same ownership rights enjoyed by the land-locked provinces are desired by the coastal provinces (primarily Newfoundland and British Columbia). Ontario has traditionally enjoyed these powers for resource extraction in the international waters of the Great Lakes. The federal government regards these new resource finds as part of the national patrimony and is proposing shared administrative arrangements under which "have-not" provinces will enjoy 100 per cent of the new revenues until they become "have" provinces. Provincial demands for ownership are based on the premise that only the government most directly affected can adequately manage the development of the resource and cushion any adverse impact. This latter may take the form of a provincial heritage fund (separate from the revenues used to calculate "have" and "have-not" provinces) set aside for some future date when the resource runs out.

Opting out   Means that a province that does not want to be part of an across-the-board arrangement can pick up its marbles and go home, or set up its own equivalent, as Quebec did with its pension plan.

Paramountcy   The nub of much of the federal-provincial haggling is which level is paramount in the case of overlaps. An example from the 1980-81 round is the slight devolution to the provinces of the authority to make laws in the field of international trade (only as it applies to resources). However, should there ever be a conflict between a provincial law or regulation and a federal one, Ottawa's version would take precedence. The joint jurisdictional approach was also considered for communications and fisheries management, where the provinces wanted paramountcy.

Patriation   This uniquely Canadian political term refers to domiciling the legal authority to amend the constitution in Canada after more than two centuries as a British colony (since the conquest of Quebec in 1763).

Quebec referendum   20 May 1980. It was actually a plebiscite: referendums are binding, plebiscites are expressions of popular opinion. The question: "The government of Quebec has made public its proposal to negotiate a new agreement with the rest of Canada, based on the equality of nations; this agreement would enable Quebec to acquire the exclusive power to make its laws, administer its taxes and establish relations abroad — in other words, sovereignty — and at the same time, to maintain with Canada an economic association including a common currency; no change in political status resulting from these negotiations will be effected without approval by the people through another referendum;

on these terms do you agree to give the government of Quebec the mandate to negotiate the proposed agreement between Quebec and Canada?"

Renewed federalism A vague concept, meaning different things to different people, but essentially it is a revitalization of Canada's federal nature. It was popularized by the Pépin-Robarts royal commission on unity report in 1979, one of a number of major studies in that period anticipating the Parti Québecois' proposed referendum on secession.

Resource ownership The current test of federalism; provinces own natural resources and this gives them (almost) the rights of any other property owner. They can grant leases for exploitation, charge royalties, determine the rate of production and possibly also set the price of the resource, although this is where the constitutional law becomes unclear, and is circumvented by the jurisdiction of Parliament.

The federal power of trade and commerce can be used to set prices crossing provincial boundaries; its taxing power reaches out to include these resources as commodities as soon as they are taken out of the ground and put in trucks or pipelines; the declaratory power can be used to declare any work in the national interest and is the Damoclean sword hanging over the heads of producing provinces. The federal trade and commerce powers are also sweeping and were used (in the Petroleum Administration Act of 1975, finally proclaimed as part of the national energy program in October 1980) to "occupy the field" of interprovincial trade and grant Parliament the ability to set well-head prices on its own. It did in the fall of 1980 and was forced back to the bargaining table for a negotiated settlement when the Alberta premier turned down the oil taps to limit production.

Sovereignty-association The PQ's referendum plank in which it asked for a mandate to establish a sovereign Quebec state (with its own army, laws and external relations) that would still be part of an economic or customs union with the rest of Canada.

Spending power Usually refers to the way Ottawa invades areas of provincial jurisdiction (grants to hospitals and universities are prime examples) because of its larger purse. This is how Ottawa has initiated (sometimes shared-cost) programs in the fields of medicare, old-age security, crop insurance, the arts and amateur sport, and the whole area of regional economic expansion.

Veto The search for an amending formula has been to try to find a mechanism that does not give any one province a veto over future changes. Throughout this last two-year battle, the majority of provinces claimed that unanimous consent was required.

Victoria formula   Was the Trudeau government's preferred amending mechanism because of pride of authorship and because it had been agreed to by all eleven governments at the Victoria conference in 1971, which foundered on other issues.

It is based on a regional concept: Parliament and any province having or once having had twenty-five per cent of the national population (a perpetual veto for Ontario and Quebec), along with any two provinces in Atlantic Canada and any two in the West, with the latter two having at least fifty per cent of the population of that region. There would be no opting out; the agreement would be binding on all.

Index

Charter of Rights and Freedoms in. *See*
Charter of Rights and Freedoms
conferences on, 1–5, 10, 20, 40, 43, 58–64,
73, 96, 155, 193, 228, 281, 293
equalization formula in, 41, 179–80, 274,
288
imposition of on provinces, 66, 68, 76. *See
also* Unilateralism
joint committee on, 135–59
judicial consideration of, 97–98, 132, 172,
180, 183, 187–88, 207, 209–10, 220, 225,
245–46. *See also* Supreme Court of
Canada
Manitoba, 209, 226, 229, 230, 231, 232
Newfoundland, 226–29, 232–33
Quebec, 226, 229, 232–34
legal precedents on, 206
negotiating strategies on, 47–48, 266, 268,
276–77
veto in
for Quebec and Ontario, 51, 106, 175,
267, 270–71, 281, 283, 284, 300–1
for Senate, 134
Cooper, George, 89, 101
Corbin, Eymard, 136, 140
Cossitt, Tom, 92, 97, 138, 310
Council of Yukon Indians, 168
Coutts, James, 74, 115, 120
Crombie, David, 88, 107, 137, 155
Curley, Paul, 93, 108

Daniels, Harry, 164, 169
Davis, William, 3, 8–10, 26, 33, 38, 43, 63, 78,
84, 93, 99–109, 167, 178–82, 214, 232, 250,
259–60, 262–63, 265–66, 270–71, 274–76,
310
Decentralization, of federal powers, 11,69,
248–49
Denning, Lord, 169, 313
Dickson, Brian, 226–28, 235, 238, 240
Diplock, Lord, 208–9, 314
Division of powers, 3–4, 41, 50, 61, 63, 91,
148, 200, 230–31, 235, 277

Epp, Jake, 79, 85–90, 92, 94–96, 98, 100–5,
113, 137, 140, 162
strategy on constitution, 79, 81–82, 86–88
Equalization rights under constitution, 41,
179, 180, 274, 288
Estey, Willard, 226, 235, 238, 240–41, 243

Federalism, 225–27, 236–39
centralization of federal powers, 3, 11,
39–40, 68, 73, 106, 274
co-operative, 1–2
decentralization of federal powers, 11, 69,
248–49
provincial views on, 47–48
"airtight compartments," 14–15, 243

"renewed," 2, 34, 37, 85, 99, 160, 201
views of Progressive Conservative Party on,
79–80, 85, 107
Fiscal powers, 41, 51, 71, 96–97, 186, 192–93
compensation, 51, 96–97, 192–93
federal, 41, 186
transfers, 71, 186, 192–93
Foot, Michael, 123, 191, 217–18
Ford, Sir John, 123, 187, 198, 206–7, 213–14
Fraser, John, 88, 90–91, 107, 137

Gang of eight, 109, 132, 174–96, 222, 246–49,
256–67, 273–77, 280, 283-84, 291, 294
Gardom, Garde, 43–44, 189, 247–48, 251,
260–61, 270, 288, 291
Gauthier, Jean-Robert, 139–40, 158
Gibson, Fred, 72, 79, 127, 128–31, 256, 292
Goldenberg, Edward, 72–73, 105, 108, 250,
291, 296–97

Haggan, Reeves, 72, 216–17
Handicapped, lobbying by, 128–29, 144, 149,
154
Hatfield, Richard, 4, 8–10, 13, 43–44, 58–60,
84, 93, 105, 170–80, 212, 214, 217, 259,
263, 265, 268, 270, 282–83, 299, 310
Hays, Senator Harry, 136, 139
How, Harry, 43, 261, 288

Indians, representations by to constitutional
hearings, 122, 138, 160–70
Inuit, as bargaining group, 162, 166, 168, 170
Ittinuar, Peter, 119, 162, 168

Jewett, Pauline, 119, 120, 124
Johnston, Dick, 44–45, 182, 247, 251, 260, 266,
288–89, 292, 300
Joyal, Serge, 136, 139, 159, 250

Kaplan, Robert, 70–71, 127, 151
Kershaw, Sir Anthony, 187–88, 197, 207, 209,
211, 215, 217, 219, 232
Kirby, Michael, 7, 43–44, 55, 72, 74, 107, 115,
120–21, 127–29, 214, 248–57, 265–66,
286, 289, 290–92, 296–97, 311–12
memorandum, 4, 54–59, 96
Knowles, Stanley, 123, 133–34

Lalonde, Marc, 15, 20, 70–74, 126–27, 129,
139, 143, 151, 160, 292
Lamontagne, Senator Maurice, 136, 138–39
Language rights. *See* Bilingualism; Charter of
Rights and Freedoms
Laskin, Bora, 70, 122, 224–26, 228, 235–36,
240–41, 243, 250–51
Leeson, Howard, 7, 128–32, 279, 293, 296
Lévesque, René, 2, 4, 8, 24, 31, 41, 47–48, 54,
60–64, 85–86, 99, 156–58, 175–76, 180,
182–85, 193, 195, 223, 247, 251, 257,